OWNERSHIP AND JUSTICE

OWNERSHIP AND JUSTICE

Edited by

**Ellen Frankel Paul, Fred D. Miller, Jr.,
and Jeffrey Paul**

CAMBRIDGE
UNIVERSITY PRESS

PUBLISHED BY THE PRESS SYNDICATE OF THE UNIVERSITY OF CAMBRIDGE
The Pitt Building, Trumpington Street, Cambridge, United Kingdom

CAMBRIDGE UNIVERSITY PRESS
The Edinburgh Building, Cambridge CB2 8RU, UK
32 Avenue of the Americas, New York, NY 10013-2473, USA
477 Williamstown Road, Port Melbourne, VIC 3207, Australia
Ruiz de Alarcón 13, 28014 Madrid, Spain
Dock House, The Waterfront, Cape Town 8001, South Africa

http://www.cambridge.org

First published 2010

Printed in the United States of America

Typeface Palatino 10/12 pt.

A catalog record for this book is available from the British Library

Library of Congress Cataloging-in-Publication Data
Ownership and Justice
edited by Ellen Frankel Paul, Fred D. Miller, Jr., and Jeffrey Paul.   p.   cm.
"The essays . . . have also been published without introduction and index, in the
semiannual journal Social Philosophy & Policy, volume 27, number 1"-T.p. verso.
Includes bibliographical references and index.
ISBN 978-0-521-17543-2 (alk. paper)

1. Right of property.
I. Paul, Ellen Frankel. II. Miller, Fred Dycus, 1944- III. Paul, Jeffrey. IV. Title.

HB711.O96 2010
323.4'6--dc22

2009048081

The essays in this book have also been published,
without introduction and index, in the semiannual journal
Social Philosophy & Policy, Volume 27, Number 1,
which is available by subscription.

CONTENTS

INTRODUCTION

"The Reason why Men enter into Society," John Locke wrote, "is the preservation of their Property,"[1] and, indeed, the institution of private property lies at the heart of contemporary Western societies. But what are the limits of property ownership? Do principles of justice require some measure of governmental redistribution of property in order to relieve poverty or to promote greater equality among citizens? And what do principles of justice, whether egalitarian or libertarian, have to say about individuals' ownership of their own talents and the products of their labor, and about the initial acquisition of land and natural resources?

The essays in this volume—written by eleven prominent political and moral philosophers—address these questions and explore related issues. A number of essays consider the theoretical foundations of property ownership, asking how the rights of individuals to acquire and use property can be justified, and how extensive these rights are. Some essays focus on the concept of self-ownership, discussing how the individual's right to control his own mind, body, and actions relates to his right to gain control over extrapersonal objects and resources. Other essays look at connections between property ownership and various values, including democratic political participation and equality of wealth and opportunity. Still others examine issues of ownership and justice that relate to the justification of liberal political institutions, or the implementation of centralized social and economic planning.

The collection opens with five essays that explore various ways of justifying property ownership. In "The Right to Private Property: A Justification," John Kekes begins by setting out a trio of familiar theories of property. Interest-based theories justify property as an institution that serves human interests: in particular, our interest in using resources to satisfy our needs. Entitlement-based theories justify an individual's ownership of property based on how it was acquired: in the familiar Lockean version, individuals initially acquire property in a resource by mixing their labor with it, and property so acquired may then be sold, traded, or bequeathed to others. Utility-based theories justify property as a means to achieving some good that they take to be essential for human well-being—a good such as freedom or economic prosperity. Kekes examines each of these theories in turn and finds problems with each. If we justify property in terms of human interests, for example, then what do we do in cases where individuals use their property to pursue goals that aren't

---

[1] John Locke, *Two Treatises of Government* (1690), revised edition, ed. Peter Laslett (New York: New American Library, 1965), *Second Treatise*, section 222.

really in their interest, or when they neglect to pursue goals that are in their interest? If property is based on a history of transactions, as on the entitlement view, then what do we say about historical cases where land and other resources have changed hands not through voluntary trade but through violence? If we justify property as essential for the pursuit of goods like liberty and prosperity, as on the utility-based view, then how do we handle cases where the pursuit of these goods conflicts with the pursuit of other recognized goods, such as justice, order, peace, public health, or security? Kekes argues that each of these theories—interest, entitlement, and utility—is too simple to provide a satisfactory justification for property ownership. As an alternative, he describes a more complex justification that combines the strengths of all three theories. On this account, the possession of property is justified if it has been acquired according to prevailing conventions that are followed voluntarily and serve the well-being of those who conform to them. Kekes concludes his essay by filling in the details of his theory and discussing the limits that may legitimately be placed on individuals' use of their property.

Edward Feser offers a defense of property rights grounded in human nature in his essay, "Classical Natural Law Theory, Property Rights, and Taxation." As he notes, classical natural law theory derives moral conclusions from an essentialist and teleological understanding of nature, the understanding enshrined in the classical metaphysics of Plato, Aristotle, Augustine, and Aquinas. This theory has been revived by Philippa Foot and other contemporary philosophers, and Feser draws on their work to argue that living things (including human beings) have certain natural ends that they must realize in order to flourish: ends that relate to biological development, self-maintenance, reproduction, the raising of young, and so on. These ends entail a standard of goodness, in the sense that a living thing that achieves its ends can be viewed as a good example of its kind. In the course of his essay, Feser shows how this idea of natural goodness leads to a theory of natural law, which sets out the foundations and the content of our moral obligations to ourselves and to others, and which leads, in turn, to a doctrine of natural rights. The most basic natural right, on this view, is the right to pursue our natural ends, as we are obligated to do by natural law. The right to private property derives from the fact that the pursuit of these ends requires the possession, control, and use of external resources. Feser discusses the extent and limits of the right to property, arguing that individuals have a right to use their property in any way they wish so long as (1) they do not use it in a way that directly violates the obligations imposed by natural law, and (2) they allow others who lack sufficient resources to use or take ownership of some part of their property under certain limited circumstances. This latter limit on property would justify taxation by government to provide assistance to those in desperate circumstances, though it would not justify extensive governmental provision of health care, education, or other welfare ser-

vices. Ultimately, Feser concludes, the natural right to property is neither
so strong as to support laissez-faire libertarianism, nor so weak as to
allow for socialism; nonetheless, it tends to favor free enterprise over
social-democratic policies.

In "The Natural Right of Property," Eric Mack offers a classical liberal
account of property ownership, based on the idea that individuals have a
fundamental moral claim to be allowed to pursue their own good in their
own way. In order to pursue their own good, individuals must be able to
acquire and exercise discretionary control over extrapersonal objects or
resources, and this provides the foundation for what Mack calls a natural
right of property. In specifying this right, he argues for two main theses:
first, that persons possess an original, nonacquired right not to be precluded from making extrapersonal resources their own (or from exercising control over what they have made their own); and second, that this
right takes the form of a right that others abide by the rules of a justifiable
practice of property ownership, a practice that facilitates persons' acquisition and discretionary control of extrapersonal resources. Mack goes on
to discuss how property rights in specific objects or resources are generated, distinguishing between two prominent views on this subject. According to the *inherent-feature view,* all actions that generate property rights
have the same inherent feature. On a Lockean theory, for example, the
relevant feature is "labor-mixing": individuals acquire initial property
rights by mixing their labor with previously unowned resources. The
alternative to the inherent-feature view is the *practice view,* according to
which actions generate property rights in virtue of their being part of a
justified practice of private property. The practice view recognizes that
the actions through which people acquire property may, in fact, be highly
conventional: to acquire ownership of a piece of land, for example, an
individual may not actually be required to clear and cultivate the land; it
might be enough for him to mark off the boundary and register his claim
with the local land office. Mack concludes that the practice view is the
more plausible one, and that excluding individuals from participation in
a practice or institution of private property constitutes a violation of their
natural right of property.

In "Property and Justice," David Schmidtz looks at the relationship
between abstract theories of justice and real-world systems of property
rights. A common approach among contemporary philosophers is to begin
with intuitions about justice, formulate theories based on those intuitions,
and then argue that systems of property ought to conform to these theories. A better approach, Schmidtz argues, is to start with an understanding of (1) what our world is like and (2) which institutional arrangements
promote our thriving in communities and which do not. If we take the
latter approach, we find that ownership conventions and property law
have developed over many generations as ways of resolving conflict and
allowing people to achieve peace and prosperity. The right to property,

Schmidtz notes, is first and foremost the right to exclude other would-be users from one's property; it is the right to say no to a proposed transaction. This right to say no establishes a system of mutual expectations that allows production and trade to flourish; individuals are able to bring the fruits of their labor to market with the knowledge that those fruits will not be taken from them, but can instead be exchanged with others on mutually agreeable terms. This understanding of property gives us a basis for evaluating proposed principles of justice, by asking which principles are compatible with institutions, norms, and expectations that people need to live by if they are to live well together. In the course of his essay, Schmidtz touches on a range of topics, including the distinction between negative and positive rights, the limits of property, and the role of government in securing its citizens' rights. He concludes that while existing property institutions may be imperfect, they nonetheless provide a framework for respecting people as ends in themselves and enabling them to realize the potential benefits (and avoid some of the potential costs) of living in society.

Jan Narveson argues for a libertarian view of property ownership in his contribution to this collection, "Property and Rights." To own something, on this view, is to have normative authority over it: to be free to use it as one sees fit, to exclude others from using it, and to transfer one's ownership to others as one sees fit—assuming, of course, that one respects the similar rights of other agents. Narveson sketches this view and goes on to discuss the issue of how we may come to legitimately acquire property in external things. The initial acquisition of property is often thought to be problematic; indeed, some critics have viewed it as a kind of theft. When an individual closes off a tract of previously unowned land and makes it his own, he denies others the use of it: his own liberty is increased, while the liberty of others is diminished. But Narveson rejects the idea that initial acquisition reduces the liberty of others; they retain their liberty to seek to acquire property of their own, and to act in pursuit of their own goals. To assume that people are harmed when others acquire property in previously unowned resources is to deny that the resources were really unowned; it is to assume the existence of some sort of collective ownership of resources. Narveson argues, however, that collective ownership is not ownership at all: ownership essentially involves the right to exclude, but if everyone owns something, then no one can legitimately exercise any right to exclude. In the remainder of his essay, Narveson discusses a number of problems that arise when we seek to apply the idea of property rights in light of new cultural and technological developments. These include the problems posed by subsurface mining rights and rights to airspace; issues concerning intellectual property; and issues related to public ownership of parks and roads. He concludes that the specific rules of property may change over time as conditions change, but that the basic principles remain intact, and that these basic principles allow us to negotiate and resolve whatever problems arise.

The collection continues with a pair of essays that discuss the notion of self-ownership and how it relates to the ownership of property. In "Embodiment and Self-Ownership," Daniel C. Russell examines various forms of libertarianism that incorporate the idea of self-ownership while at the same time being committed to very different ideas of the self. Russell defines self-ownership in terms of a bundle of rights: the right to control oneself and one's actions; the right to exclude others from such control; the right to compensation for the infringement of these rights; and so on. A crucial question concerns how far the boundaries of the self extend, and Russell notes that many libertarians seem to believe that an individual's self extends no further than his physical body. Thus, libertarians on the left hold that self-ownership is compatible with placing significant restrictions on individuals' ownership and use of extrapersonal property (including taxation for the purpose of egalitarian redistribution, and limits on the private ownership of capital). In contrast, libertarians on the far right hold that the self-ownership rights of the very poor remain intact even when they are able to exercise little or no control over extrapersonal property. (Russell refers to such far-right libertarians as "no-proviso libertarians," since they deny the legitimacy of a Lockean proviso that would require those who appropriate resources to leave "enough and as good" for others.) He argues that both left-libertarians and no-proviso libertarians hold a mistaken conception of the self; the correct conception, he suggests, recognizes that the boundaries of the self extend outside the body and into the world beyond one's person. According to the view that Russell defends, the self is defined in terms of a person's psychological identity — that is, his sense of who he is, including his character, his options and abilities, and his engagement in ongoing activities, projects, and relationships. On this view, an individual's self-ownership can be violated not only by harms to his physical body, but also by certain noninvasive infringements of his ability to engage the extrapersonal world. Russell concludes that both left-libertarianism and no-proviso libertarianism should be set aside in favor of an intermediate version—a version that rejects egalitarianism but embraces a Lockean proviso forbidding property owners from acquiring or using property in ways that worsen the situation of others.

In "Self-Ownership and World Ownership: Against Left-Libertarianism," Richard J. Arneson challenges the view of self-ownership embraced by certain left-libertarian theorists. He focuses specifically on the work of Michael Otsuka, who attempts to combine the idea that each person is the full rightful owner of himself with the idea that each person should have the right to own a roughly equal amount of the world's resources. On Otsuka's view, each individual has a strict self-ownership right to control his own mind and body, as well as the income he gains from his own labor; however, each individual may appropriate previously unowned resources only if his appropriation is compatible with everyone's having an equal opportunity for welfare (understood as the satisfaction of fully informed and rational preferences). Arneson argues that there is more tension than Otsuka acknowledges between private ownership of the self and equal ownership of the world. The concept of self-ownership employed by Otsuka and other left-libertarians is, according to Arneson, both too weak and too strong. It is too weak because it defines the self in terms of one's body, mind, and labor, and ignores the fact that virtually everything human beings do requires the use of external resources; thus, self-ownership alone guarantees us no real or effective freedom to do anything. At the same time, the concept of self-ownership is too strong because it gives each individual a right to do whatever he chooses with himself, so long as he does not harm others in ways that violate their rights; but this means that individuals have no enforceable obligation to render aid to others, even in emergency situations (e.g., in "easy rescue" cases where one person is in a position to save another's life, without any risk or significant cost to himself). Arneson concludes his essay by contrasting the positions of left-libertarians with those of John Locke (from whom many left-libertarians claim to draw their inspiration), and by offering a number of suggestions for refining left-libertarian theory in order to make it more plausible.

The next two essays explore the relationship between property ownership and other liberal values. In "The Uneasy Relationship between Democracy and Capital," Thomas Christiano asks whether (and under what conditions) the exercise of private property rights might abridge fundamental norms of democratic decision-making. He begins by noting that private firms are capable of exercising their rights in ways that undermine democratically determined public aims. For example, government officials might be elected to office based on their promise to impose limits on carbon dioxide emissions, in order to combat a perceived threat of global warming. Complying with the new limits might prove costly to the affected industries, and they might choose instead to move their operations to another country with less-stringent regulations. When companies behave this way, they act within their rights as the owners of private capital, yet their actions undermine the government's goal of combating global warming, a goal that, by hypothesis, has been chosen by the people through a democratic process. In cases of this kind, Christiano argues, a proper commitment to democratic norms implies that private capitalist firms must cooperate with the government in the pursuit of the aims of a democratic assembly, even when this cooperation leads to a reduction in the profits of the firms. Private firms that fail to cooperate are, in effect, violating a principle of political equality which holds that all citizens should have an equal voice in choosing what aims their society is to realize, at least within certain limits. Christiano goes on to discuss these limits, which include cases where the proposed policies are so costly that they would drive companies out of business, as well as cases where the policies impose other sorts of undue burdens on individuals or companies (e.g., where they abridge fundamental rights of life, expression, association, or privacy). Nonetheless, he argues that these limits do not undermine his central conclusion: namely, that when private firms fail to cooperate with democratically chosen aims, they act in a way that is incompatible with fundamental norms of democratic governance.

George Sher explores questions relating to the justice of inequalities in wealth and property holdings in his essay, "Real-World Luck Egalitarianism." Luck egalitarians maintain that inequalities are always unjust when they are due to luck, but are not always unjust when they are due to choices for which the parties are responsible. Sher argues that the two halves of this formula do not fit neatly together, and that we can arrive at two different versions of luck egalitarianism depending on how we interpret the idea of luck. On the first interpretation, luck is defined as that which is not within the agent's control—that which did not come about as an expected consequence of his choices. According to this interpretation, no inequality between two people counts as just unless the less-advantaged person was aware at some point of having an option which, if he had taken it, would have made him as well off as his more-advantaged counterpart. On the second interpretation of luck, however, we begin with a very broad notion of responsibility, which holds that agents can be responsible for outcomes that they did not directly choose or even foresee. According to this second interpretation, we hold people responsible for outcomes that result from their negligence, their lack of attention to the options available to them, and their lapses of memory or judgment. Consequently, inequalities that result from these failings are not considered to be matters of luck and are not deemed to be unjust. These two versions of luck egalitarianism, Sher contends, lead us to very different judgments in cases where inequality results from the failure of agents to foresee the effects of their actions. He goes on to argue that many real-world cases of inequality fall into this category, and that when we attempt to make judgments in such cases, we are forced to ask hard questions about the relation between equality and responsibility. Sher concludes with a discussion of how we might resolve the tension between the two interpretations of luck egalitarianism, and suggests that the best version of the theory may be one that does not allow equality to trump other values such as responsibility and desert.

The collection's final two essays discuss property ownership as it relates to political and economic institutions. Gerald Gaus explores the justification of liberal political institutions in his essay, "Coercion, Ownership, and the Redistributive State: Justificatory Liberalism's Classical Tilt." The broad theory he defends is justificatory liberalism, which respects each individual as free and equal, and insists that coercive laws must be justified to all members of the public. Within this broad framework, it is possible to defend a range of substantive liberalisms, from the classical liberal's vision of limited government, to contemporary welfare-state capitalism, and on to more egalitarian versions of liberalism. Among contemporary liberal theorists, as Gaus observes, it is widely believed that the liberal principle of respect for persons requires that the state must regulate the distribution of resources to conform to principles of fairness, that all citizens must be assured of employment and health care, and that citizens' economic activities must be regulated to insure that they do not endanger the "fair value" of rights to political participation. The central aim of Gaus's essay is to consider which substantive version of liberalism is most favored by the justificatory liberal approach. He sets out justificatory liberalism's core features, including its presumption in favor of individual liberty and against coercion by the state, its commitment to the public justification of laws, and its assumption that reasonable people may disagree about whether particular laws are justified. He goes on to argue that, rather than calling for extensive redistribution, justificatory liberalism actually favors classical liberal political institutions, including a robust system of private property rights. He concludes that while modestly redistributive policies are justified—including, for example, the provision of public goods and assistance to the poor—more extensive forms of redistribution are likely to require levels of coercion that are inconsistent with liberalism's respect for persons.

Finally, in "Adam Smith and the Great Mind Fallacy," James R. Otteson examines the limits of state action and seeks to explain why attempts to institute centralized social and economic planning are bound to fail. Drawing on the work of Adam Smith and Friedrich Hayek, Otteson identifies two problems faced by legislators who wish to implement some form of central planning. First, human beings have plans and purposes of their own, which will necessarily come into conflict with the aims of legislators (call this the Herding Cats Problem); and second, the information that a central planner would need in order to be successful is not (and cannot be) possessed by any single individual or legislative body, but is instead dispersed among all the members of society (the Gathering Information Problem). The belief that some person or persons could overcome these two problems and institute effective central planning is what Otteson calls the Great Mind Fallacy. The Herding Cats Problem and the Gathering Information Problem together imply that the state's authority over individuals' decisions about how to use their property should be strictly limited, and that individuals should be given wide scope to pursue their own ends. Yet, as Otteson argues, contemporary political theorists persist in recommending policies that presume that legislators or regulators can overcome these two problems. As examples, he discusses the work of Cass Sunstein, Richard Thaler, and others, who propose various governmental interventions that curtail freedom in order to redirect individuals' actions toward supposedly beneficial ends. Otteson contends that such theorists attempt to overcome the Herding Cats Problem and the Gathering Information Problem by using one of two methods: by arguing that their own recommendations are equivalent to the ones that would result from proper democratic deliberation; or by relying on the opinions of experts concerning which policies would improve human well-being. Otteson discusses each of these methods in detail and concludes that theorists who employ them are simply committing another version of the Great Mind Fallacy.

Questions about the nature and limits of property ownership are central to ongoing debates about the justice of social and political institutions. The wide-ranging discussions of ownership contained in these eleven essays offer important contributions to those debates.

ACKNOWLEDGMENTS

The editors wish to acknowledge several individuals at the Social Philosophy and Policy Center, Bowling Green State University, who provided invaluable assistance in the preparation of this volume. They include Program Manager John Milliken, Mary Dilsaver, and Terrie Weaver.

The editors also extend special thanks to Administrative Editor Tamara Sharp, for her patient attention to detail, and to Managing Editor Harry Dolan, for providing editorial assistance above and beyond the call of duty.

CONTRIBUTORS

John Kekes, Professor Emeritus of Philosophy and Research Professor, State University of New York at Albany, has retired in order to devote himself to writing full-time as an independent author. His books include *Against Liberalism* (1997), *A Case for Conservatism* (1998), *The Illusions of Egalitarianism* (2003), and most recently, *Enjoyment* (2008). He is currently at work on his next book, *The Human Condition: A Secular View*. He may be reached at jonkekes@nycap.rr.com.

Edward Feser is Assistant Professor of Philosophy at Pasadena City College in Pasadena, California. He has been a Visiting Assistant Professor at Loyola Marymount University and a Visiting Scholar at the Social Philosophy and Policy Center at Bowling Green State University. He is the author of *On Nozick* (2003), *Philosophy of Mind* (2005), *Locke* (2007), *The Last Superstition: A Refutation of the New Atheism* (2008), and *Aquinas* (2009), and he is the editor of *The Cambridge Companion to Hayek* (2006).

Eric Mack is Professor of Philosophy and a faculty member of the Murphy Institute of Political Economy at Tulane University. He specializes in moral, political, and legal philosophy. He has been a Visiting Fellow in Political Philosophy at Harvard University, a Visiting Scholar at the Social Philosophy and Policy Center at Bowling Green State University, and a Resident Scholar at Liberty Fund, Inc. He has published many articles in scholarly journals and anthologies, primarily on such topics as the agent relativity of value, the nature and foundation of moral rights, property rights, Lockean provisos, rights and public goods, liberalism and pluralism, and economic justice. He is the author of *John Locke* (2009).

David Schmidtz is Kendrick Professor of Philosophy, joint Professor of Economics, and Director of the Center for Philosophy of Freedom at the University of Arizona. He is the author of *Person, Polis, Planet* (2008) and the coauthor with Jason Brennan of *A Brief History of Liberty* (2010).

Jan Narveson is Distinguished Professor Emeritus of the University of Waterloo in Canada. He is the author of several books, including *The Libertarian Idea* (2001), *Respecting Persons in Theory and Practice* (2002), and more recently, *You and the State* (2008). His next book is tentatively titled *This Is Ethical Theory*. He is also active as the director of the Kitchener-Waterloo Chamber Music Society. In recognition of his achievements in both musical and academic respects, he was made an Officer of the Order of Canada in 2003.

Daniel C. Russell is Associate Professor of Philosophy at Wichita State University. He received his Ph.D. from the University of Arizona, and his areas of specialization are ancient philosophy and contemporary virtue theory. He is the author of *Plato on Pleasure and the Good Life* (2005), *Practical Intelligence and the Virtues* (2009), and numerous papers on ancient and modern moral philosophy. His most recent book project, tentatively titled *Virtue, Happiness, and the Self*, focuses on the role of conceptions of the self in our understanding of the relation of virtuous activity to happiness.

Richard J. Arneson is Professor, Above Scale (Distinguished Professor) of Philosophy at the University of California, San Diego. In the fall of 2008, he was Adjunct Professor at the School of Law, University of San Diego, where he is also affiliated with the Institute for Law and Philosophy. His recent writings are in political philosophy (on theories of justice) and in moral philosophy (on act consequentialism versus deontology).

Thomas Christiano is Professor of Philosophy and Law at the University of Arizona and co-director of the Rogers Program in Law and Society. He has been a Visiting Fellow at All Souls College, a Visiting Fellow at the Research School of the Social Sciences of the Australian National University, and a Fellow of the National Humanities Center. He is the author of *The Rule of the Many* (1996) and *The Constitution of Equality: Democratic Authority and Its Limits* (2008), and the coeditor of the journal *Politics, Philosophy, and Economics*. He has edited *Modern Moral and Political Philosophy* (with Robert Cummins, 1998), *Philosophy and Democracy* (2003), and *Contemporary Debates in Political Philosophy* (with John Christman, 2009). He has written widely in the areas of democratic theory, distributive justice, and moral and political philosophy. His current projects are a book on the foundations of egalitarian distributive justice and research on issues in global justice.

George Sher is Herbert S. Autrey Professor of Philosophy at Rice University. His essays on topics in ethics and social and political philosophy have appeared in *Philosophy and Public Affairs, Ethics, Noûs, The Journal of Philosophy*, and numerous other journals. His books include *Desert* (1987), *Beyond Neutrality: Perfectionism and Politics* (1997), *Approximate Justice: Studies in Non-Ideal Theory* (1997), *In Praise of Blame* (2006), and most recently, *Who Knew? Responsibility without Awareness* (2009). His current project, of which the essay in this volume is a part, is a book tentatively titled *Egalitarianism for Inegalitarians*.

Gerald Gaus is James E. Rogers Professor of Philosophy at the University of Arizona. His essay "On Justifying the Moral Rights of the Moderns," published in *Social Philosophy and Policy*, won the 2009 Gregory Kavka

Prize. Among his books are *On Philosophy, Politics, and Economics* (2008), *Contemporary Theories of Liberalism* (2003), *Justificatory Liberalism* (1996), and *Value and Justification* (1990). With Christi Favor and Julian Lamont he edited *Essays on Philosophy, Politics, and Economics* (forthcoming from Stanford University Press); and with Chandran Kukathas he edited the *Handbook of Political Theory* (2004). Along with Jonathan Riley, he was a founding editor of the journal *Politics, Philosophy, and Economics*. He is currently at work on two books: *The Order of Public Reason*, and *Economic Justice* (with Julian Lamont).

James R. Otteson is Professor of Philosophy and Economics at Yeshiva University in New York. He earned a B.A. from the Program of Liberal Studies at the University of Notre Dame, an M.A. in philosophy from the University of Wisconsin–Milwaukee, and an A.M. and Ph.D. in philosophy from the University of Chicago. He is the author of *Adam Smith's Marketplace of Life* (2002) and *Actual Ethics* (2006), the latter of which won the 2007 Templeton Enterprise Award. He is also the editor of *The Levellers: Overton, Walwyn, and Lilburne* (5 vols., 2003) and *Adam Smith: Selected Philosophical Writings* (2004). He is currently working on a book titled *Adam Smith*, which will be part of Continuum Press's series *Major Conservative and Libertarian Thinkers*.

THE RIGHT TO PRIVATE PROPERTY:
A JUSTIFICATION

By John Kekes

I. Introduction

The aim of this essay is to propose a new way of thinking about the justification of the right to private property. The proposal builds on old and familiar ways, but goes beyond them.[1]

I begin with some assumptions. The first is that the starting-point of the justification is where we presently are. The "we" are those living in contemporary Western democracies. There is a not very long list of political goods we agree about valuing: among them are education, justice, liberty, order, peace, prosperity, public health, security, and stability. Private property is also one of them. I am assuming that a justification of the right to private property must explain why it is reasonable to value it both in itself and in relation to the other political goods. This starting-point may seem too obvious to require mention, but it is routinely denied by political thinkers situated all along the left-right spectrum.

Some of those who deny it start with a semihistorical account of the origin of private property in the mist of prehistory.[2] One reason against this approach is that there is no credible evidence that the account is true to anything resembling what has really occurred. Moreover, even if the account were true, it would have no more bearing on the justification of the right to private property here and now than an account of the origin of magic would have on its justification here and now.

Another alternative is to start with a theory about what an ideal society would be like and then justify or criticize the right to private property from its point of view. The problem with this approach is that ideal theorists are led by their political predilections—I do not say prejudices—to choose one (or perhaps a small number) of the many goods we value, and then ascribe overriding importance to it (or to them). Then they make the justification of the right to private property depend on the supposedly

---

[1] For surveys and bibliographies, see Lawrence C. Becker, "Property," in *Encyclopedia of Ethics*, 2nd ed., ed. Lawrence C. Becker and Charlotte B. Becker (New York: Routledge, 2001); Stephen R. Munser, "Property," in *Routledge Encyclopedia of Philosophy*, ed. E. Craig (London: Routledge, 1998); J. Roland Pennock and John W. Chapman, eds., *Property: Nomos XXII* (New York: New York University Press, 1980); and Jeremy Waldron, "Property," in *Stanford Encyclopedia of Philosophy*, http://plato.stanford.edu/entries/property/.

[2] This is the approach of Thomas Hobbes, *Leviathan*; John Locke, *Second Treatise of Government*; Jean-Jacques Rousseau, *The Social Contract*; and their many contemporary followers.

doi:10.1017/S026505250999001X

1

overriding good(s). Ronald Dworkin does this with equality, John Rawls with justice, Robert Nozick with rights, Friedrich Hayek with liberty, and there are, of course, others as well. I will return to both the semihistorical and the ideal-theorizing approaches later, but only to claim that both are vitiated by arbitrariness.

Yet another possibility is to start with the idea of self-ownership and then gradually extend it to include property as it is usually understood. The reason against this strategy is that the sense in which we have a self is very different from the sense in which we may have a house. We and the property we own are contingently connected: we can sell, loan, bequeath, give away, or forfeit our property, but we cannot do this with our self. We are connected to the self we have necessarily, not contingently. This is radically different from what is normally meant by owning something. The self we have cannot be nationalized or expropriated, and there is no law needed to guarantee that no one will steal the self we have. We have many things we do not own, such as a good marriage, a bad temper, or a passion for Bach, and our self is another. Of course, political thinkers are free to stipulate any meaning they like, but it is highly misleading to claim that having a self is like owning a material object, or vice versa.

A further approach is to begin with the claim that we have a natural right to own property. I find the idea of a natural right to anything as problematic as the idea of self-ownership. What seems to be meant by "natural right" is that we have some basic needs, for food and rest for instance, and their satisfaction is a minimum condition of our well-being. Natural rights, then, are the rights of individuals to pursue such satisfactions, and the rights impose a corresponding obligation on others not to interfere with individuals as they try to satisfy their basic needs.

I agree that the satisfaction of some needs is a minimum condition of individual well-being, that it is good to satisfy these needs, and that it is bad to prevent others from satisfying their basic needs. I also agree that basic needs derive from the nature we share with other members of our species. If this were all that is meant by natural rights, I would not find the idea problematic. But defenders of the idea mean more. They mean that we are entitled at least to noninterference with our natural rights. I can make sense of this only on the assumption that we live in a society whose laws, conventions, or customs create our entitlement. I fail to see how anyone would be entitled to anything outside of one society or another. Nothing entitles a chimpanzee to be free of interference with his food or rest by other chimpanzees. There are rights, of course, but they are conventional, not natural in the sense that defenders of natural rights intend.

It makes matters worse that even if there were natural rights, the right to private property would not be one of them. For the individual ownership of private property is not a basic need whose satisfaction is a minimum condition of well-being. Basic needs could be satisfied even if all property were owned by the state, or by benevolent people, or jointly by a community. Beggars, spongers, mendicant friars, ascetic hermits, monks, and nuns who took an oath of poverty have been enabled by the kindness of others to satisfy their basic needs even though they forswore the ownership of private property.

Moreover, the right of individuals to own property is conditional, because there are legal and moral limits on what individuals may do to obtain the satisfaction of their needs, and because there are legally and morally justifiable interferences with the pursuit of such satisfaction. These limits and justified interferences depend on prevailing conventions, which are historically conditioned and changeable. And that is part of the reason why all rights are conventional and conditional.[3]

I will start, then, with where we are, with the plurality of political goods we value. The right to private property is one among them. I am assuming that this right is conventional, conditional, and defeasible: conventional, because it is defined by conventions; conditional, because it depends on changing conditions; and defeasible, because it may conflict with other political goods we value and such conflicts may be reasonably resolved in a particular context in favor of a political good other than the right to private property. I am assuming further that just as there is a plurality of political goods, there is a plurality of reasonable political principles, theories, and ideals. This plurality is quite extensive. It is also nonhierarchical, because the political goods, principles, theories, and ideals can be and often are ranked in a plurality of reasonable ways.

The core idea of property is the ownership of some material object, such as a car or a violin. But the idea is often extended to include money, patents, undeveloped resources, shares, future payments, abilities, options, ideas, reputation, and so forth. I will restrict the discussion of property to a relatively narrow sense, to include only material objects and money. The issue of justification is difficult enough, and I want to avoid complications that follow from a consideration of intangible possessions. If the justification works, it may be extended beyond the narrow sense.

It is also necessary to distinguish between possessions and property. I may possess a car, because I stole it or bought it from someone who stole it. It is in my possession, but it is not my property, because I came to possess it illegally. Property is legal possession. Furthermore, property need not be owned by an individual. It may be owned jointly by several people; or by some collectivity, such as a cooperative, a church, or a labor union; or by a state, as are roads or parks. The justification of the right to

---

[3] I follow H. L. A. Hart, "Are There Any Natural Rights?" *Philosophical Review* 64 (1955): 175–91; and H. L. A. Hart, "Utilitarianism and Natural Rights," in Hart, *Essays in Jurisprudence and Philosophy* (Oxford: Clarendon Press, 1983).

private property, the property of an individual, must do more, therefore, than justify the right to property. It may be that a collectivity or a state has a right to property, but individuals do not. My concern, then, is with the justification of the right to the legal possession of private property.[4]

But what precisely is the right to private property a right to? I think it is the right to possess and use material resources within legally defined limits. Each constituent of this right—possession, use, and limits—is in turn constituted by several more specific rights. The right to private property, therefore, is a bundle of rights, not a single one.[5] The more specific rights that constitute the constituents of the bundle typically vary with societies, legal systems, and changes in specific laws. Reference to the right to private property, then, is nothing more than a convenient short-hand. Two societies may each be committed to the right of private property and yet interpret the right quite differently.

The right to possess private property includes having exclusive physical control of it; deriving income from it; holding it without any time limit; having legal protection against its expropriation, theft, or un-wanted destruction; and so forth. The right to use it includes deciding whether, how, or when to use it; permitting others to use it; consuming, modifying, or destroying it; selling, exchanging, bequeathing, or giving it away as a gift; and so forth. And the limits include not having acquired it in a legally impermissible way, and using it in ways that do not harm others.

Given this understanding of the right to private property, I turn to the question of why we regard it as important. Countless ascetic people throughout history have renounced property as a means to their well-being. And even if owning some property were necessary for an accept-able life, it may be owned by a state or a collectivity, not by individuals privately. Yet we think of the right to private property as being more like the rights to liberty or the pursuit of happiness—rights that really matter—than like unimportant rights such as solving crossword puzzles or show-ering in the afternoon. Furthermore, the importance we attribute to private property may be a symptom of greed or selfishness, or of a now useless instinct instilled in us in the course of evolution. That we regard private property as important is not enough to show that it really is important. We have been wrong in the past about the importance of magic, the divine right of kings, or not sparing the rod in the upbringing of children. Maybe we are wrong about private property as well. I will now give reasons for thinking that we are not mistaken about the importance we attribute to it.

---

[4] For an excellent discussion of the complexities of how property should be understood, see Jeremy Waldron, *The Right to Private Property* (Oxford: Clarendon Press, 1988), part 1.

[5] This way of understanding the right to private property is indebted to A. M. Honoré's now classic "Ownership," in *Oxford Essays in Jurisprudence*, ed. A. G. Guest (Oxford: Oxford University Press, 1961).

II. The Importance of Private Property

The importance of private property is that it enables us to control how we live. A good society must be committed to the protection of the right to private property, because a society is made good by protecting the conditions on which the well-being of its members depends. Moreover, I am supposing that having control of one's life is one of these conditions. Private property, according to this view, is an indispensable means of control.

By control I mean directing how one lives. This is done by forming intentions, having the opportunity to carry them out, and then doing so. The intention needed for control must be uncoerced by external pressures or internal compulsions that are either irresistible or unacceptably costly to resist. The opportunity to carry out intentions depends on favorable external conditions, such as order, prosperity, peace, and so forth, and on possessing the necessary resources. The resulting action must be judged by the agent as an acceptable way of achieving the intended result. Private property is a necessary part of this process, because it provides the needed resources.

By control, therefore, I do not mean domination. Control does not involve lording it over others, imposing one's will on the political system of one's society, or being obsessed with the minute details of daily life. To control one's life is to be one's own master, not to be at the mercy of the will or kindness of others, not to depend on the state or some collectivity for the necessary resources, to make decisions for oneself, and to live with the consequences. Private property is a means to this kind of control, because the intentions we form, the opportunities we seek, and the activities we engage in are centrally concerned with the satisfaction of our needs.

Some of these needs, as we have seen, are the primary needs of subsistence. Their satisfaction is a minimum condition of our well-being, but, of course, we have many different needs beyond subsistence. Among them are the needs for psychological and financial security; relief from drudgery; interesting and rewarding work; a good marriage; and possessing the tools of one's trade, such as a first-rate instrument for a concert violinist, books for a scholar, a well-lit studio for a painter, a good stove for a chef, or reliable equipment for a rock climber. In addition, we need some privacy and enjoyable distraction from work; we need a car to travel to work and to shop, decent housing to live in, a computer to keep records and communicate with others; and so forth. I will refer to these needs jointly as secondary.

Primary and secondary needs are alike in that their satisfaction is a requirement of our well-being, but they also differ because all human beings have the same primary needs, whereas we differ in what secondary needs we have. The prolonged frustration of any of our primary needs is incompatible with well-being, but this is not so with respect to secondary needs. Only the frustration of many of our most important secondary needs makes well-being impossible. Calling these needs "primary" and "secondary" is not intended to suggest that the former are more important than the latter. Soul-destroying work, being prevented from pursuing our chosen profession, an unhappy marriage, or prolonged insecurity are as incompatible with well-being as starvation or sleeplessness. The satisfaction of both primary and secondary needs is essential for our well-being, but we can satisfy them only if we have the required resources, and that is why the right to private property is indispensable for controlling how we live.

If we think of the right to private property as the right to means of control, then doubts about its importance can be seen as groundless. I have no idea whether the importance we attribute to it is based on an instinct. But if we suppose that it is, any doubt about its continued usefulness in the contemporary world is obviously misplaced. Our well-being depends as much on our resources as the Cro-Magnon men's did. The difference between us is only in the kind of resources we need.

As to the charge that the importance we attribute to the right to private property is a symptom of greed, it clearly is so for some people who are obsessed with possessions. Equally clearly, however, it is not so for numerous others who want just as much as they need for controlling how they live, with a little extra, perhaps, as a margin of safety. Nor need the importance we attribute to the right be a symptom of selfishness. We may use our resources to acquire a skill that will benefit others, to improve the life of our family, to support a worthy cause, to invest in the business of others, and, of course, to pay taxes, a considerable portion of which funds welfare programs. Recognizing the importance of the right to private property, therefore, may be a symptom of public spirit, love, or business acumen, not just of selfishness. The importance we attribute to it is often a symptom of prudence, which used to be regarded as a virtue, and not of greed or selfishness, which a defender of the right to private property can readily acknowledge as a vice.

But what about those saintly or fanatical ascetics who enjoy what they insist is well-being, even though they refuse to own property? That they can do so is clear, since they have done it. What they cannot do is to live without resources. If they survive, it is because they depend on other people who share their resources with them out of the goodness of their heart, which may or may not be misguided. The ascetics' refusal to own private property no more calls into question the importance owning it has for others than the renunciation of sex by celibates casts doubt on its importance for those who are otherwise inclined.

There still remains the point that recognizing the importance of property for well-being is not the same as recognizing the importance of *private* property for well-being, because property may be owned by a collectivity or by the state. Why should the private ownership of property be important? Because it allows us to control how we live, whereas collective or state ownership would take control from us and transfer it to others. If this happened, forming and executing intentions would no longer be up to us, but become subject to the approval or disapproval of those who distribute the resources we need. This would be a morally unacceptable interference with liberty and would destroy our well-being, since no one acting on behalf of a collectivity or a state could possibly know nearly as well as we ourselves do what secondary needs we have and what would be an adequate satisfaction of them. No society committed to the well-being of its members could be in favor of depriving them of the control of how they live. Since that control depends on the right to private property, collective or state ownership is not a viable option, as we know from the dismal failure of all Communist regimes.

The reasons against collective or state ownership are not reasons against a society's limiting in various ways the right to possess and use private property. There is obviously need for such limits, because a society must coordinate its members' efforts to control their own lives. Appropriate limits make it illegitimate to possess and use material resources in ways that prevent others from doing the same. The scarcity of resources necessitates additional limits, because resources often have to be competed for and this has the unavoidable consequence that the resource acquisition of one person prevents the acquisition of others. The terms of legitimate competition must be set, and this further limits what individuals can do to obtain and use the resources they need to control how they live. We inevitably chafe under such limits, but if they are reasonable and no more extensive than what is needed to make the possession and use of private property secure, then we should recognize their necessity and stay within them.

It may be thought that the just-completed explanation of the importance of the right to private property is also an adequate justification of it. This would be a mistake, because the explanation tacitly presupposes one or another much too simple and far too problematic justification, as I will now proceed to show. These justifications will be familiar to those who have thought seriously about the right to private property. I will not examine them in detail, because what I find problematic are not the details, but the justifications' overall strategy. I will state the justifications briefly and explain why I believe that they do not yield the needed support for the right to private property. These proffered justifications are based on interest, entitlement, and utility.

8 JOHN KEKES

III. Interest-Based Justifications and Their Problems

Interest-based justifications proceed in the following way.[6] Human beings have needs, and it is in their interest to satisfy them. Doing so depends on having the necessary resources and on being able to use them as they see fit. The right to private property is the right to have and control the use of resources individuals require for satisfying their needs. The justification of this right is that it serves everyone's interest. Since a good society must protect its members' well-being, and since the right to private property is essential for their well-being, a good society will provide legal protection for that right.

There are two serious problems with this attempted justification. The first is a consequence of human fallibility. Individuals may be wrong to have a need they rightly feel they have (e.g., for murdering rivals); or they may feel a need they in fact do not have (e.g., hypochondriacs for medical treatment); or they may not feel a need they should feel (e.g., the ignorant for education). Individual well-being, therefore, does not depend on satisfying the needs people feel they have, but on satisfying the needs they really have. If the justification of the right to private property is the interest of individuals, then a good society will not leave it to the discretion of individuals to control the use of their resources, since they may use them contrary to their interests. Why should a good society protect the rights of individuals to misuse scarce resources? Much more needs to be said, therefore, to justify the right to private property than merely that it enables individuals to satisfy their needs. But the more that is said, the less control will be left to individuals, and the more tenuous the right will become. A good society, therefore, may well conclude that the collective or state ownership of property better serves the interests of its members than private ownership, or that there are often good reasons for interfering with the right to private property. And this conclusion, of course, shows the failure of the interest-based justification.

The second problem is that this justification assumes that the required resources are available and the problem is only who should control them. But this assumption is false. The resources have to be produced before they can be controlled. If their control is left to the discretion of those who produce them, then, given the ever-present scarcity of resources and the partiality of the producers, many people will lack the resources they need. If the control of resources is taken from those who produce them, why would reasonable people produce them?

Neither problem is unsolvable, of course. My point in calling attention to them is to show that much more is required for solving them than

---

[6] Some interest-based attempts at justification are Ronald M. Dworkin, *Taking Rights Seriously* (Cambridge, MA: Harvard University Press, 1977); and Neil MacCormick, *Legal Rights and Social Democracy* (Oxford: Clarendon Press, 1982).

a simple appeal to needs and to the importance of satisfying them. For needs and satisfactions must be limited, and setting reasonable limits unavoidably appeals to considerations other than the judgments of individuals about their needs and interests. There are complex moral, economic, legal, and psychological issues that must be considered, and their respective importance must be weighed in order to decide what limits are reasonable. The interest-based justification of the right to private property is much too simple for that. It founders on the problem of limits.

IV. ENTITLEMENT-BASED JUSTIFICATIONS AND THEIR PROBLEMS

The entitlement-based justification of the right to private property has several versions, distinguished mainly by what they base entitlement on. According to the earliest version, individuals are entitled to a piece of property if they mix their labor with a generally available resource and if, after they have done so, enough is left of the resource for others to do likewise if they wish.[7] Those who acquire the right to a piece of property in this manner can sell, exchange, or bequeath it. Other people, then, may acquire a right to it if they receive it from the original owner by one of these means.

This justification has great intuitive appeal, because it leads us to think of the well-deserved rewards of hard work and skill. If out of driftwood I found lying on a beach I build a beautiful table, who but I would have a right to it? And if I decide to give it as a birthday present to my daughter, then who but she could claim to have a right to it? There is no doubt that this justification holds good in some cases, but a little thought shows that it does not hold in many others. To begin with, it is virtually impossible to trace the chain of ownership back to the original acquisition of, say, a piece of land. Moreover, if it is traced back as far as we are likely to be able to go in the undocumented past, we frequently find that it was acquired by dispossessing its earlier owner by force. Virtually all nations presently in existence began by killing or subjugating the native population. On an entitlement-based theory, then, no one can claim legitimate possession of any land presently owned in these nations.

Next, suppose I hire a person to build a house for me and he does. He mixes his labor with it, and he may do it very well, but he certainly does not acquire the right to the house. The house is mine, even though I have neither mixed my labor with it nor acquired it from someone who did so. The builder is entitled to payment for his labor, but not to anything more. Take another case. I buy a lottery ticket, win a sum of money, invest it in

---

[7] John Locke, *Second Treatise of Government* (1690) (Indianapolis, IN: Hackett, 1980).

a mutual fund, and the money grows. I am clearly entitled to the proceeds, but I have done nothing remotely resembling mixing my labor
with the money I won. For these reasons, among others, contemporary
defenders of an entitlement-based justification tend to ignore the past and
concentrate on present possession.[8]

They also begin with intuitively appealing cases, such as Robert Nozick's
Wilt Chamberlain example.[9] Chamberlain is a great basketball player, and
people willingly pay again and again a lot of money to see him practice
his artistry. He becomes wealthy and he is entitled to his wealth. He
cheated no one, he delivered what people expected, everyone was better
off, and no one was worse off. He has a right to do what he pleases with
the money he has earned: he can spend it, invest it, give it away, leave it
to his children, use it to support a cause he believes in, and so forth. Who
could reasonably doubt that he has the right to possess and use what he
has acquired in this way? A critic could.

A critic might say, to begin with, that the case has intuitive appeal only
to those who share the conventions on which the case rests, but these
conventions are deplorable, sharing them is a sign of corruption, and a
society would be better off without them. One of these conventions is the
commercialization of sports. It is a bad thing for a society, the critic might
argue, that a great athlete like Wilt Chamberlain sells his talent for money.
He does with basketball what prostitutes do with sex. Perhaps people
should be allowed to pay money for either, but surely a society should not
encourage it, and we should not model the right to private property on
such dubious cases. And it is not just Wilt Chamberlain who demeans
himself, the critic may say. Those who pay to watch him also do so,
because by finding enjoyment in the passive observation of an endlessly
repetitive activity, they betray a great vacuum in their inner lives.

Now my point is not that such a critic is right to condemn commercial
sports. The point is that he is right to claim that the Wilt Chamberlain case
rests on conventions it presupposes, but does not justify. This entitlement-
based justification takes for granted the conventions involved in acquisition, but the acquisition of possessions in conformity with prevailing
conventions does not by itself entitle people to what they possess. Two
further cases will strengthen this point.

Following the collapse of Communism, many ex-Communist states
privatized previously state-owned enterprises, which were expropriated
from their legitimate owners when the Communists took power. After the
collapse, laws governing privatization were enacted, the expropriated
enterprises went up for sale, and anybody who had the money could bid
for them. However, the only people who actually had the money were

---

[8] See, for instance, Robert Nozick, *Anarchy, State, and Utopia* (New York: Basic Books,
1974).
[9] Ibid., 161–63.

members of the Communist elite who expropriated the enterprises in the first place. Thus, the old discredited Communist elite transformed itself into the new super-rich capitalist elite. They acquired their new possessions in accordance with the recently established conventions. There is surely something wrong with these new conventions if they allowed such blatant injustice. No reasonable person could say that members of the Communist elite have a right to such possessions.

Take another case. Consider an ordinary person without any great talent. He earns a living doing a low-paying job and supports his wife and three young children. On his way home from work, he is killed in a freak accident for which no one could be blamed. His family is now destitute. Would a good society not be remiss in protecting the well-being of its members if it did not tax the earnings of the talented Wilt Chamberlain and use the funds to support those who through no fault of their own are destitute? The reason for doing so may be pity, fellow-feeling, or charity, but it need not be. It may simply be prudence; for destitution that follows from misfortune creates needs that must be satisfied in some way. If society does not help the destitute satisfy these needs, then crime is a natural option, and if there is a lot of it, the society will be destabilized, and the right to private property will be endangered. Once again, no reasonable person could say that the talented Wilt Chamberlain should not be taxed so as to avoid these consequences.

The problem with this entitlement-based justification is that the conventions that entitle people to their possessions need to be examined and justified. But they cannot be justified on the basis of entitlement, because that would simply assume that the conventions appealed to have been justified, and that, of course, is precisely what is in question. The justification of the conventions, therefore, must proceed in some other way. Regardless of what that way is, the need for it is a conclusive reason for thinking that the entitlement-based justification of private property is insufficient. People do not and should not have a right to all of their possessions. But to draw a reasonable distinction between possessions to which people ought to have a right and those to which they ought not is a complex question that cannot be settled by appealing to prevailing conventions. Perhaps the prevailing conventions should not prevail. The entitlement-based justification, therefore, is too simple to solve the problem of legitimate possession.

V. UTILITY-BASED JUSTIFICATIONS AND THEIR PROBLEMS

Defenders of utility-based justifications postulate a good they take to be essential for human well-being and then argue that the protection of the right to private property is a necessary condition of the efficient pursuit of the postulated good. Versions of this justification differ, because different theorists postulate different goods. The version I will discuss here has liberty and prosperity as the goods.[10]

The argument for this version has a constructive and a critical component. The constructive component aims to show that liberty is necessary for our well-being, because it enables us to decide how we want to live and allows us to choose without interference between the available alternatives. Liberty should be curtailed only to prevent interference with the liberty of others. The constructive component also aims to show that prosperity is similarly necessary, because it enlarges the scope of liberty and frees us from the necessity of providing what we need for subsistence. By protecting the right to private property, a society enables its members to create prosperity and produce the resources needed for the meaningful use of liberty. The critical component of the argument shows that collective or state ownership of property will not create the needed prosperity and that it leads to an unjustifiable restriction of liberty.

In my opinion, the utility-based justification is correct in both its constructive and its critical claims, but nevertheless falls short of providing an adequate justification of the right to private property. The fundamental reason for this is that, although it is undoubtedly true that liberty and prosperity are necessary for our well-being, it is also true that there are other goods necessary for our well-being. Liberty, prosperity, and these other goods routinely conflict, and there may be strong reasons for curtailing liberty and prosperity in order to secure the other goods. Some examples of the other necessary goods are education, justice, order, peace, public health, security, and stability.

One of the most obvious features of contemporary politics is that liberty can be used and prosperity can be pursued in ways detrimental to these other necessary goods. It is similarly obvious that protecting these other goods may require curtailing liberty and prosperity. Goods we rightly recognize as necessary for our well-being often conflict. The reasonable resolution of these conflicts is to balance the conflicting goods so as to have as much as possible of all the goods we need. It cannot be reasonably supposed that when liberty and prosperity conflict with one or more of these other necessary goods, then liberty and prosperity should always take precedence over them. The circumstances in which it is reasonable to curtail liberty and prosperity are those in which it is reasonable to curtail the right to private property.

What are these circumstances? They are, for example, those in which the right to private property is used in ways that endanger public health, such as the discharge of industrial waste into rivers, advertising cigarettes to adolescents, or selling unsafe cars. Other circumstances include instances

---

[10] There are numerous defenders of this version. Perhaps the best-known representative is Friedrich A. Hayek, *The Constitution of Liberty* (Chicago: University of Chicago Press, 1960); and Hayek, *The Mirage of Social Justice*, volume II of *Law, Legislation, and Liberty* (Chicago: University of Chicago Press, 1976).

when the right to private property threatens security, such as selling sophisticated weapon systems to terrorists, or using scarce resources needed for defense to produce more profitable luxury goods. Or when it undermines order, such as financing lawyers who specialize in securing the acquittal of criminals on technicalities, or publishing newspapers that malign public officials by spreading misleading innuendos about their private lives that skirt but skillfully avoid libel. Or when it puts stability at risk, as, for example, when it results in great inequalities between those who possess private property in abundance and those who barely have enough for subsistence. These examples, of course, can be multiplied.

Defenders of the utility-based justification may respond by acknowledging the necessity of these other goods for human well-being, but arguing that liberty and prosperity should still take precedence over them because these other goods can be pursued only by people who have the freedom to make choices and who have the necessary resources. And these are the conditions that liberty and prosperity provide. I think this response is correct, but it still fails to show either that liberty and prosperity should have precedence over the other goods when they conflict, or that the right to private property should not be curtailed. For just as the pursuit of other goods presupposes liberty and prosperity, so the pursuit of liberty and prosperity presupposes, among other things, education, justice, order, peace, public health, security, and stability.

In our complex contemporary circumstances, prosperity cannot be achieved without having a workforce that has at least basic skills, and liberty cannot be meaningfully pursued unless there is a general understanding of the alternatives among which we can choose. Both presuppose education. In an anarchic society, everyone is at risk, liberty is severely curtailed by the necessity of self-protection, and prosperity cannot be enjoyed, because no one's private property is safe. The liberty and prosperity we cherish are possible only because there is adequate order and security in our society. When we use our liberty to make choices, we make predictions about how the various alternatives open to us would be likely to affect us in the future, and in seeking prosperity we assume that what we acquire now we can continue to hold in the future. These predictions and assumptions presuppose stability. In the midst of war and epidemic, everyone's well-being depends on commandeering resources, providing necessary services, and severely restricting the liberty of choices about medical care and travel. Our present enjoyment of liberty and prosperity is possible only because public health is protected and peace is maintained.

These rather obvious observations make clear that the goods necessary for our well-being are interdependent and mutually presuppose and strengthen one another. The utility-based justification is correct to insist that the right to private property must be protected if we are to have a free and prosperous society. But it is mistaken in forgetting that the pursuit of these important goods conflicts with the pursuit of other important goods, that the reasonable resolution of such conflicts requires balancing the important goods, and that achieving a reasonable balance is possible only if we resign ourselves to having less liberty and prosperity than we would like in order to secure other important goods, albeit they too to a lesser extent than we would like. This is the problem of balancing goods, and the utility-based justification of the right to private property is too simple to cope with it.

VI. Complex Justification

I conclude that the attempted justifications of the right to private property based on interest, entitlement, and utility are inadequate. I say inadequate, not wrong, because they are right to stress the importance of the interest we all have in satisfying our needs, the importance of having resources to which we are entitled, and the importance of enjoying liberty and prosperity. They are also right to stress the importance of private property for all this. But they nevertheless fail to justify the right to private property, because they cannot cope with the problem of how to set reasonable limits to that right, how to identify legitimate possessions, and how to balance important goods. We need a complex justification for that. The one I will now propose and try to defend combines what I take to be right in the three simple justifications, overcomes their inadequacies, and replaces an assumption which they share (and which leads them astray) with a more realistic one. The upshot is that the right to private property can be justified, but its justification is much less philosophical, general, and theoretical and much more practical, concrete, and political than has been traditionally supposed.

The fundamental reason why the interest-, entitlement-, and utility-based justifications of the right to private property are too simple is that they share the assumption that there is some one thing—perhaps a canonical principle, or a conclusive theory, or a highest good—that makes the justification adequate. They disagree about what that thing is, but they agree that an adequate justification must be based it. The complex justification rejects this assumption for three reasons. One is that the right to private property is a bundle of rights and the components of the bundle need to be justified differently. These components are the *possession, use,* and *limits* of private property. The second reason is that the various rights to private property must be justified differently in different contexts. It is highly unlikely that property's justified possession, use, and limits would be the same in feudal, revolutionary, post-Communist, ex-colonial, tribal, impoverished, affluent, agrarian, industrial, authoritarian, and democratic societies. And the third reason is that an adequate justification must cope with the problems of setting reasonable limits, identifying legitimate possessions, and balancing goods. These problems, as we have seen, introduce serious complexities. I will proceed by showing how possessions, uses, and limits may be justified in our context, that is, in contemporary, affluent, industrial, and democratic societies.

The justification of the possession of private property begins with accepting much of the entitlement-based justification. Possession, as opposed to use within limits, is justified if a piece of private property has been acquired legitimately. The legitimacy of its acquisition depends on conformity to prevailing conventions. The problem with the entitlement-based justification is that it presupposes, but does not justify, the prevailing conventions, which, of course, may be unacceptable for numerous reasons. The complex justification, therefore, must do what the entitlement-based one fails to do. How, then, can the prevailing conventions be justified?

The first step is to remind ourselves of just how plausible at least some of these conventions are. Take those involved in agreements, for example. Two parties make a formal or informal agreement to the effect that one will do a job, lease an apartment, or sell a car, and the other will pay wages, rent, or the purchase price. The performance of the first creates an entitlement to a possession that the second should transfer to the first. Or consider conventions involved in relationships. Parents should finance the education of their children; married couples should share their resources; investors should get a share of the profit; executives should not run companies mainly for their own benefit. Such relationships create entitlements to what their explicit or implicit terms specify. A large part of these entitlements is constituted by the unspoken conventions in the background. These conventions are obvious and well-known to people of normal intelligence who live together in the context of a society. The obviousness of the conventions, however, may just show that they are customary and prevalent in the context, but not that they are justified.

The second step is to show what would justify them. My claim is that they are justified if they have become traditional, if people conform to them voluntarily, and if they are important for the well-being of those who conform to them. By traditional conventions I mean ones that have endured for a considerable length of time, measured in decades rather than months, and are so widely known as to be taken for granted by the vast majority of people in that context. In the appropriate situations, the majority of people naturally and spontaneously follow the conventions, and they rightly expect others to do the same. If this expectation is not met, and it may not be, then its violation is widely regarded as blameworthy or as requiring an excuse.

Traditional conventions may endure as a result of coercion that makes the failure to conform too costly for most people. One indication of voluntary conformity is that people conduct themselves according to the conventions in the absence of coercion. Another indication is that although there are political, legal, or social avenues for challenging and attempting to change the conventions, the avenues are not followed. A further indication is that even though people could leave the society in which the conventions prevail, they do not and they continue to follow them in appropriate circumstances. None of this requires a conscious, articulated approval of the conventions. Most people who conform to them voluntarily may do so without having given (or wanting to give) the matter serious thought. They bought the goods, so they pay for them. They made an agreement, so they stick to it. They borrowed a car, so they return it.

Voluntary conformity, however, may just indicate habit, indoctrination, or that it is easier to go with the current than to swim against it. There may be a good reason for such conformity, however, even if this reason is not uppermost in the minds of those who conform. The good reason is that by conforming to the traditional conventions, people can acquire and control the resources they require to satisfy their primary and secondary needs. The reason, then, why the conventions have become traditional and why people conform to them without being coerced is that their well-being depends on it. They do not question or feel the need to justify the conventions, because they can afford to take them for granted.

There is, of course, no society in which all prevailing conventions about the ownership of private property are in this happy state. Some of the conventions are routinely questioned, and then they need to be justified, reformed, or abandoned. This is what happened to primogeniture, to the custom of a husband controlling his wife's property, or to the practice of imprisoning those who have defaulted on a debt. And this is what may be happening in America now concerning inheritance and capital gains taxes, although the 2008 election and the financial crisis have made this unclear. In some cases, it may happen that most of a society's conventions are questioned and their justifications are found wanting. Then the society in which this happens is disintegrating, and it is on the brink of revolution, as France was in 1789 and Russia in 1917.

The essential point in the present context is that according to the complex justification, the possession of a piece of private property is legitimate if the property has been acquired in accordance with traditional conventions to which voluntary conformity continues to be widespread, because such conformity is rightly assumed to be a condition of the well-being of those who live together in a particular society. This justification resolves the problem of legitimate possession on which the entitlement-based justification foundered. But it is nowhere near the end of the matter, because it says nothing about the justified uses and limits of legitimately possessed private property.

I turn next to how the complex justification resolves a problem that arises in the context of the utility-based justification of the right to private property. That justification, it will be remembered, is that liberty and prosperity are important goods, because they are necessary for our well-being. They jointly require the protection of the right to private property, because it is the right to the resources that provide us with the means to control how we live. Making use of the right to private property, therefore, is one way in which we enjoy the advantages of liberty and prosperity.

The problem with this justification is not with any of its claims, which I think are correct, but with its failure to take into account other claims that are no less plausible. As we have seen, these other claims are made on behalf of goods other than liberty and prosperity that are also necessary for our well-being. Some of them are education, justice, order, peace, public health, security, and stability. The problem is that the enjoyment of these goods often requires limiting liberty and prosperity, and, with them, limiting the right to private property. We need to know what limits are reasonable and how to balance the conflicting claims of all the important goods we need for our well-being. In this way, the problems of balancing goods and setting reasonable limits to the claim of each good are closely connected.

It is clear, I hope, that it would not be a reasonable resolution of these problems to assume that one or two of these goods is always more important for our well-being than any of the others. For there are reasonable disagreements about the respective importance of acknowledged goods, and these disagreements should not just be ignored. There may be, and have been, numerous circumstances in which order (e.g., illegal immigration), public health (e.g., pollution), or security (e.g., terrorism), for instance, justified some restrictions of liberty and some decrease in prosperity. But if the problems cannot be reasonably resolved by attributing overriding importance to one of the goods we obviously need for our well-being, then how can they be resolved?

I propose the complex justification as a reasonable resolution of both problems together and as an improvement over the utility-based justification. This reasonable resolution depends on bearing in mind three considerations. First, the reasonable resolution of conflicts among important goods rarely involves an all-or-none decision. Usually it is a matter of deciding how much of each good we can have, so we will typically have to make a decision about the extent to which we can have one without endangering the other. The protection of security may require restricting liberty by requiring everyone to carry forgery-proof identification. Or the protection of public health may require stringent curbs on pollution, which will raise the cost of goods, and reduce prosperity. The decision, then, does not usually involve choosing one or the other, but deciding how much of each we should have.

Second, a reasonable resolution cannot be to decide once and for all which good or goods should have priority over the others. The avoidance of this arbitrariness does not mean that we could not or should not decide that one good is more important than another in a particular context. Arbitrariness enters only if we decide to maintain the same order of priority in other, not yet encountered, contexts. It may be that security is more important than liberty in a context where liberty is already extensive and the threats against security are serious. But if, in another context, liberty is already curtailed and the threats to security are negligible, then their priority should be reversed. Reasonable conflict-resolutions vary with contexts. They exclude only context-independent resolutions and acknowledge the necessity of assigning temporary priority to one of the conflicting goods in a particular context.

Third, at any given time in a society there are many goods whose necessity for well-being is generally recognized. These goods form a system, and the system of goods is always more important than any of the particular goods that jointly constitute it. Reasonable conflict-resolutions, therefore, have a standard to which they can appeal. This standard is the respective importance of the conflicting goods for the protection of the system of goods as a whole. Whether a particular conflict-resolution is reasonable does not, then, depend on which of the conflicting goods is more important for well-being in a particular context. It depends, rather, on deciding which of the conflicting goods is more important for the protection of the whole system of goods.

An approach to conflict-resolution that takes into account only the respective importance of the conflicting goods is bound to go wrong, because it fails to consider the effect of the resolution on the other goods that form the system. This is just what the utility-based justification failed to do. My proposed complex approach takes into account how the whole system of goods would be affected by a particular conflict-resolution. This approach is just as concerned with well-being as the utility-based one, but it recognizes that at any time, in any context, well-being depends on the protection of many goods, not just on one or two of them.

The complex justification, therefore, resolves the problems of finding a reasonable balance of goods and setting reasonable limits to the pursuit of goods in the same way: by appealing to the standard constituted by the system of goods. A reasonable balance is one that best protects the system of goods in a particular context, and a reasonable limit is one that restricts one, or perhaps both, of the goods in order to protect the system of goods. Liberty and prosperity, and with them the right to private property, may be reasonably limited if doing so is necessary for securing the other goods on which well-being also depends.

It may be objected that the complex justification does precisely what it criticizes the utility-based justification for doing: arbitrarily assigning priority to a particular good and resolving conflicts in its favor. But this objection rests on a misunderstanding of the standard to which the complex justification appeals. The standard is not a particular good, but all the goods forming a system. And the appeal to it is not arbitrary, because the goods that form the system are recognized as necessary for well-being in the context of a particular society. No one can reasonably suppose that education, justice, order, peace, public health, security, and stability, to which we may add liberty and prosperity, are arbitrarily regarded as goods. The serious question about them is not whether they are really good, but which of them should have priority when they conflict. It is this serious question that is answered by the complex justification.

Another objection may be raised against the complex justification: namely, that politicians competing for scarce resources cannot be expected to consider the wider consequences of the outcome of their competition. They need to prevail then and there, in order to serve the interests of the people who elected them and to remain in power. It is much too demanding that they should take a wider view, which may actually require them to go against the interests, including their own, that they are expected to represent. This is unfortunately true of many politicians, but it is not an objection to the complex justification. For what that justification aims to provide is a reasonable approach to conflict-resolution. That many politicians are shortsighted and insufficiently reasonable is not exactly news, nor is it an objection to the approach I favor. It would make political life less corrupt if politicians would make it a habit to consider the implications of what they are doing for the well-being of their country, rather than merely for their own and perhaps their constituents' well-being.

We have now seen how the complex justification justifies the possession of private property and the limits on its use. From this, it is but a small step to providing a justification for the remaining component of the right to private property: its actual use. Private property provides resources which we can use to satisfy our needs. As the interest-based justification rightly claims, it is in our vital interest to have a right to the use of private property. What the interest-based justification fails to note is that we may misuse the private property we have by satisfying needs that should not be satisfied and by not satisfying needs that we should satisfy. What specifically constitutes the misuse of private property, and how can it be avoided?

The number of ways in which people can and have misused their private property is large and depressing. They may be led to such misuse by self-deception, stupidity, addiction, neurosis, vindictiveness, fanaticism, taking unreasonable risks, and so on and on. Legal and political strictures against misuse cannot possibly take into account the countless individual ways in which people may waste their resources by using them contrary to their own interests. Protection of the right to private property must proceed, therefore, by thinking of interests in impersonal terms, that is, as interests that any normal adult in a particular context is going to have. The misuse of private property, then, may be understood as using it in ways that violate other people's interests impersonally conceived.

We can go a step further in specifying the ways in which the interests of others may be violated by the misuse of private property by drawing on what I have already said about justified possessions and limits. To misuse private property is to use it in ways that prevent others from trying to acquire private property legitimately, or to use it in ways that interfere with how others use their legitimately acquired private property. The reasonable use of private property, then, is within limits that strengthen rather than weaken the system of goods on which everyone's well-being depends in a particular context. Legitimate acquisition and reasonable limits, then, define an area of discretion within which people should have the right to use their private property in any way they see fit. If they use it within their area of discretion, they may still misuse it, of course, but they can blame only themselves if their interests thereby suffer. The proper business of politics and law is to protect individuals' right to private property, to protect them from interference by others, not to protect them from being harmed by themselves.

VII. CONCLUSION

In summary of this account of complex justification, it may be said that the justification of the right to private property depends on justifying its possession, use, and limits. Possession is justified if it has been acquired legitimately in accordance with prevailing conventions that are traditional, voluntarily adhered to, and serve the well-being of those who conform to them. Limits are justified if they are set by the system of goods on which everyone's well-being depends. And uses are justified within each individual's area of discretion.

It may be said in favor of this justification that it explains the importance of private property by interpreting it as the means of controlling resources we need for our well-being. This justification avoids the problems that beset the entitlement-, utility-, and interest-based justifications, and it offers a separate justification of the possession, use, and limits of private property. It is a mixture of old and new components. The old ones are the defensible portions of the entitlement-, utility-, and interest-based justifications; the new ones are the interpretation of private property as a means of control and the recognition that different aspects of private property need to be justified differently.

Philosophy

CLASSICAL NATURAL LAW THEORY, PROPERTY RIGHTS, AND TAXATION*

By Edward Feser

I. Introduction

The aim of this essay is to put forward an exposition and defense of a classical natural law theory of property rights and taxation. As the "natural law" label indicates, the view to be propounded holds that the right to private property is a natural right in the sense of being grounded in nature rather than human convention. The underlying natural law theory is a "classical" one in the sense that its understanding of nature is classical rather than modern. That is to say, it is *essentialist* rather than nominalist insofar as it holds that things instantiate natures or essences that are neither the inventions of the human mind nor mere artifacts of human language; and it is *teleological* rather than mechanistic insofar as it holds that things have final causes or ends toward which they are naturally directed.

These metaphysical commitments are definitive of the "classical realist" tradition in philosophy represented by such thinkers as Plato, Aristotle, Augustine, and Aquinas, along with many other Scholastic philosophers. The modern philosophical tradition inaugurated by the likes of Descartes, Hobbes, Locke, and Hume is defined, more than anything else, by its rejection of these commitments in favor of a mechanistic and (usually) nominalistic conception of the natural world. Modern "natural law" theories are those which attempt to reformulate the idea of natural law in terms that either take on board, or at least do not challenge, this modern nonteleological and nominalistic conception of nature. Hence, Locke, who is often classified as a natural law theorist but who vigorously rejects the Aristotelian metaphysics of the Scholastic tradition, grounds his doctrine of rights not in human nature or final causes, but in God's ownership of us.[1] Hence, the "new natural law theory" of contemporary writers like Germain Grisez, John Finnis, and Robert P. George eschews the Aristotelian-Thomistic metaphysics of the Neo-Scholastic natural law theorists of the late nineteenth and early twentieth centuries, in favor of an attempt to ground traditional

* I thank Ellen Frankel Paul and the other contributors to this volume for their comments on an earlier version of this essay.

[1] See Edward Feser, *Locke* (Oxford: Oneworld Publications, 2007), for an account of the differences between Scholastic and Lockean conceptions of natural law.

doi:10.1017/S0265052509990021

21

natural law conclusions in a theory of practical reason that is neutral vis-à-vis the metaphysical dispute between classical and modern philosophers.[2] Other theories having no connection at all to the classical metaphysical tradition also sometimes go under the "natural law" label.[3] From the classical natural law theorist's point of view, all such theories appear to be "natural law" theories in name only, insofar as nature per se really plays no normative role in them (and couldn't, given that the moderns' conception of nature as devoid of teleology or final causes effectively strips nature of any intrinsic value or purpose). Be that as it may, since these theories certainly differ radically from the classical theory in their basic metaphysical and methodological assumptions, it is important to keep these differences in mind when evaluating arguments purportedly based in "natural law." Much confusion can and often does arise when critics of classical natural law theory unwittingly read into it metaphysical assumptions that only a modern natural law theorist would accept, and vice versa.

II. Metaphysical Foundations

One example of such confusion is the assumption that any natural law theory must commit the "naturalistic fallacy" by failing to take note of the "fact/value distinction." For there can only be a "fact/value distinction," and thus a "fallacy" in deriving normative conclusions from factual premises, given something like a modern mechanistic-cum-nominalistic conception of nature.[4] No such distinction, and thus no such fallacy, exists given a classical essentialist and teleological conception of the world.

Consider, to begin with, a simple example. It is of the essence or nature of a triangle to be a closed plane figure with three straight sides, and

[2] For a useful account of the differences between the classical and "new" natural law theories, written from a classical point of view, see David S. Oderberg, "The Metaphysical Foundations of Natural Law," in H. Zaborowski, ed., *Natural Law and Contemporary Society* (Washington, DC: Catholic University of America Press, 2008).

[3] For example, the libertarian theorist Randy Barnett characterizes his position as grounded in "natural law" because it takes account of general empirical facts or "natural laws" about human biology, psychology, and social organization. See Randy Barnett, *The Structure of Liberty: Justice and the Rule of Law* (New York: Oxford University Press, 1998), 4–12. One problem with this characterization is that it makes the "natural law" label vacuous, since surely every moral theorist, including those who explicitly reject natural law theory, would claim to take account of such general empirical facts.

[4] And there may not be, even then; for the "fact/value distinction," though still (usually unreflectively) accepted by many contemporary philosophers, has been criticized by philosophers not necessarily sympathetic to classical metaphysics. See, e.g., Hilary Putnam, *The Collapse of the Fact/Value Dichotomy and Other Essays* (Cambridge, MA: Harvard University Press, 2004). Criticisms by writers who are sympathetic to classical metaphysics include Christopher Martin, "The Fact/Value Distinction," in David S. Oderberg and Timothy Chappell, eds., *Human Values: New Essays on Ethics and Natural Law* (New York: Palgrave Macmillan, 2004); and David S. Oderberg, *Moral Theory: A Non-Consequentialist Approach* (Oxford: Blackwell, 2000), 9–15.

anything with this essence must have a number of properties, such as having angles that add up to 180 degrees. These are objective facts that we discover rather than invent; certainly, it is notoriously difficult to make the opposite opinion at all plausible. Nevertheless, there are obviously triangles that fail to live up to this definition. A triangle drawn hastily on the cracked plastic seat of a moving bus might fail to be completely closed or to have perfectly straight sides, and thus its angles will add up to something other than 180 degrees. Indeed, even a triangle drawn slowly and carefully on paper with a Rapidograph pen and a ruler will contain subtle flaws. Still, the latter will far more closely approximate the essence of triangularity than the former will. It will be a *better* triangle than the former. Indeed, we would quite naturally describe the latter as a *good* triangle and the former as a *bad* one. This judgment would be completely objective; it would be silly to suggest that we were merely expressing a personal preference for angles that add up to 180 degrees, say. Such a judgment simply follows from the objective facts about the nature or essence of triangles. This example illustrates how an entity can count as an instance of a certain type of thing even if it fails perfectly to instantiate the essence of that type of thing; a badly drawn triangle is not a non-triangle, but rather a defective triangle. At the same time, the example illustrates how there can be a completely *objective, factual* standard of goodness and badness, better and worse. To be sure, the standard of goodness in question in this example is not a *moral* standard. But from the point of view of classical natural law theory, it illustrates a general notion of goodness of which moral goodness is a special case. And while it might be suggested that even this general standard of goodness will lack a foundation if one denies, as nominalists and other antirealists do, the objectivity of geometry and mathematics in general, it is (as I have said) notoriously *very* difficult to defend such a denial.

Many contemporary philosophers (and not just philosophers) are coming to see how difficult it is plausibly to deny the reality of essences in other domains. Let us look at another simple example, one that brings us closer to the notion of a distinctly moral conception of goodness. Philippa Foot, following Michael Thompson, notes how living things can only adequately be described in terms of what Thompson calls "Aristotelian categoricals" of a form such as *S's are F*, where *S* refers to a species and *F* to something predicated of the species.[5] To cite Foot's examples, "Rabbits are herbivores," "Cats are four-legged," and "Human beings have thirty-two teeth" would be instances of this general form. Note that such propositions cannot be adequately represented in terms of either the existential or the universal quantifier. The proposition "Cats

---

[5] Philippa Foot, *Natural Goodness* (Oxford: Clarendon Press, 2001), chapter 2. The relevant essay by Michael Thompson is "The Representation of Life," in Rosalind Hursthouse, Gavin Lawrence, and Warren Quinn, eds., *Virtues and Reasons: Philippa Foot and Moral Theory* (Oxford: Clarendon Press, 1995).

are four-legged," for instance, is obviously not saying, "There is at least one cat that is four-legged." But neither is it saying, "For everything that is a cat, it is four-legged," since the occasional cat may be missing a leg due to injury or genetic defect. Aristotelian categoricals convey a *norm*, much like the description of what counts as a triangle. Any particular living thing can only be described as an instance of a species, and a species itself can only be described in terms of Aristotelian categoricals stating at least its general characteristics.[6] If a particular S happens not to be F—if, for example, a particular cat is missing a leg—that does not show that S's are not F after all, but rather that this particular S is a *defective* instance of an S.

In living things, the sort of norm in question is, Foot tells us, inextricably tied to the notion of teleology. There are certain *ends* that any organism must realize in order to flourish as the kind of organism it is, ends concerning activities like development, self-maintenance, reproduction, the rearing of young, and so forth; and these ends entail a standard of goodness. Hence (again to cite Foot's examples), an oak that develops long and deep roots is to that extent a good oak, and one that develops weak roots is to that extent bad and defective; a lioness that nurtures her young is to that extent a good lioness, and one that fails to do so is to that extent bad or defective; and so on. As with our triangle example, it would be silly to pretend that these judgments of goodness and badness are in any way subjective or reflective of human preferences. Rather, they have to do with objective facts about what counts as a flourishing or sickly instance of the biological kind or nature in question, and in particular with an organism's realization of (or failure to realize) the ends set for it by its nature.

It might, of course, be suggested that such teleological language can always be reduced to descriptions couched in nonteleological terms. Widespread though this assumption is, however, there is surprisingly little in the way of actual argumentation in its favor, and much to be said against it. To be sure, Darwinian theory famously suggests a way of accounting for adaptation in a manner that dispenses with anything like goal-

---

[6] As Foot notes, questions about the evolutionary origin of a species can largely be set aside here, for the point of an Aristotelian categorical is to describe a species as it actually exists at a point in time, whatever its origins. One might still wonder, however (as Gerald Gaus did in commenting on an earlier version of this essay), whether the existence of such borderline cases as evolutionary transitional forms, which would seem to be indeterminate as to their essence, casts doubt on biological essentialism. But it does not. As David Oderberg points out, characterizing such forms as indeterminate presupposes a contrast with forms which are not indeterminate (such as the evolutionary ancestors and descendants of the forms in question), and thus does not entail that there are no biological essences at all. Furthermore, given the general arguments in favor of classical essentialism, there is no reason to doubt that even such borderline cases do, in fact, have essences of their own, different from the essences of the forms with which we are contrasting them. See David S. Oderberg, *Real Essentialism* (London: Routledge, 2007), chapter 9, for a detailed discussion of this issue.

directedness or final causality.[7] But the adaptation of organisms to their environments is only one small (albeit important) aspect of the natural world, and the question is whether there is any reason to believe that teleology can be *entirely* or even *mostly* dispensed with in our understanding of nature. The answer, I would submit, is that it cannot be. Every attempt to eliminate teleology in one domain seems, at most, merely to relocate it elsewhere, leaving it "grinning residually up at us like the frog at the bottom of the beer mug," as J. L. Austin famously said of another problematic phenomenon.[8]

This is a large topic, which I have addressed at length elsewhere.[9] Some general remarks will suffice for our purposes here. Certain common misconceptions about the nature of final causes form one of the main obstacles to acknowledging their reality. It is often thought, for example, that to attribute a final cause to something is necessarily to attribute to it something like thought or consciousness and/or something like a biological function. It is then concluded that anyone committed to the reality of final causes must believe such absurdities as that asteroids and piles of dirt (or whatever) somehow play a role within the larger universe that is analogous to the role a heart or kidney plays in an organism, and that they are at least dimly conscious of doing so. But this is a complete travesty of the Aristotelian notion of final causality. In fact, the Aristotelian view has always been that most teleology or final causality is not associated with consciousness or thought at all, and that biological functions constitute only one kind of final causality among others.

The heart of the Aristotelian "principle of finality" is, as Aquinas put it, that "Every agent acts for an end."[10] What is meant by this is that any-

---

[7] On one currently popular account of how this might work, to say (for example) that the kidneys existing in such-and-such an organism have the "function" of purifying its blood really amounts to something like this: Those ancestors of this organism who first developed kidneys (as a result of a random genetic mutation) tended to survive in greater numbers than those without kidneys, because their blood got purified; and this caused the gene for kidneys to get passed on to the organism in question and others like it. To say that an organ's function (now) is to do X is therefore shorthand for saying that it was selected for by evolution because its earliest ancestors did X. There are several well-known difficulties with this sort of account, however. For example, it seems to imply that an organ that did not arise through natural selection could not have a function; yet it is surely at least theoretically possible that organs with genuine functions could arise through means other than natural selection. Related to this, the account seems to imply that we cannot know the function of an organ until we know how it evolved; yet it is obvious, even to someone who knows nothing about evolution, what functions eyes, ears, and many other bodily organs serve. For further discussion of this issue, see Edward Feser, *The Last Superstition: A Refutation of the New Atheism* (South Bend, IN: St. Augustine's Press, 2008), 248–57.

[8] J. L. Austin, "Ifs and Cans," in his *Philosophical Papers*, 3rd ed. (Oxford: Oxford University Press, 1979), 231. Austin's topic was the analysis of the verb "can."

[9] See Feser, *The Last Superstition;* and Edward Feser, *Aquinas* (Oxford: Oneworld Publications, 2009).

[10] Aquinas, *Summa Theologiae*, translated by the Fathers of the English Dominican Province as *The Summa Theologica*, 5 vols. (Notre Dame, IN: Christian Classics, 1981), I.22.2.

thing that serves as what Aristotelians call an efficient cause—that which brings about a certain effect—is directed toward production of that effect as its natural end or goal. The cause "points to" that effect specifically, rather than to some other effect or to no effect at all; or, in other words, when *A* is the efficient cause of *B*, that is only because *B* is the final cause of *A*. For example, a match "points to" or is "directed at" the generation of flame and heat specifically, rather than frost and cold, or the smell of lilacs, or a nuclear explosion. That is the effect it will naturally bring about when struck, unless prevented in some way, and even if it is never in fact struck, it remains true that it is that specific effect that it always "aimed at." As Aquinas argued, unless we acknowledge the existence of finality in this sense, we have no way of explaining why efficient causes have exactly the effects they do rather than other effects or no effects at all. In short, efficient causality becomes unintelligible without final causality.[11]

Notice that there is nothing in this line of thought that entails that matches or other efficient causes carry out "functions" in the biological sense. To say that final causality pervades the natural world is *not* to say that atoms and molecules, rocks and trees, are somehow related to the world as a whole as biological organs are related to the organism whose organs they are. Functions of the sort that biological organs serve exist only where physical systems are organized in such a way that the parts of the system are ordered to the flourishing of the whole, as in living things. Most of the teleology that Aristotelians would attribute to nature is not like this, but involves merely the simple directedness of a cause of a certain type toward the generation of a certain effect or range of effects. Notice also that there is no implication here that the causes in question are typically conscious (as the match of my example obviously is not). Other than human beings and animals, they typically are not conscious at all. The Aristotelian claim is precisely that things can be directed toward certain ends or goals even if they are totally incapable of being conscious of this fact.

Now it is by no means only Neo-Scholastics and other old-fashioned Aristotelians who would defend essences and teleology today. One finds a hint of final causality even in the work of the materialist philosopher David Armstrong, who suggests that in order to explain intentionality— the human mind's capacity to represent the world beyond itself—his fellow materialists ought to consider the dispositions physical objects possess (such as the disposition glass has to break, even if it never in fact shatters) as instances of a kind of "proto-intentionality" or "pointing

---

[11] That there is something to what Aquinas is saying here should be obvious to anyone familiar with the history of philosophical debate over causation since David Hume. I would submit that Humean puzzles about efficient causality arose precisely because of the early modern philosophers' decision to abandon final causality. See the works cited in note 9 for elaboration of this suggestion.

beyond themselves" toward certain specific outcomes.[12] Similarly, the late George Molnar defended the idea that the causal powers inherent in physical objects manifest a kind of "physical intentionality" insofar as, like thoughts and other mental states, they point to something beyond themselves, even though they are unlike thoughts in being unconscious.[13] Molnar was representative of a movement within the philosophy of science toward what Brian Ellis has called a "new essentialism," the view that the standard mechanistic and empiricist interpretation of physical science simply does not hold up in light of the actual discoveries of modern science or the facts of scientific practice.[14] Ellis and Nancy Cartwright, another prominent "new essentialist," are forthright about the neo-Aristotelian character of their position.[15] Actual experimental practice, Cartwright argues, shows that the hard sciences are in the business of discovering, not mere Humean regularities, but the hidden natures or essences universal to, and the causal powers inherent in, things of a certain type. "The empiricists of the scientific revolution wanted to oust Aristotle entirely from the new learning," but, Cartwright judges, "they did no such thing."[16]

As the work of Foot and Thompson indicates, many contemporary thinkers are prepared to acknowledge the continuing applicability of Aristotelian concepts in biology no less than in physics. To take another example, the philosopher of biology André Ariew has noted that even given that Darwinian evolution undermines William Paley's famous design argument, "it does not follow that Darwin has debunked natural teleology altogether," for "Aristotelian teleology is an entirely different sort."[17] Though natural selection might suffice to explain the adaptation of an organism to its environment, there is also the question of the internal development of an organism, and in particular of what accounts for the fact that certain growth patterns count as aberrations and others as normal. Here Aristotle would say that there is no way to make this distinction apart from the notion of an end toward which the growth pattern naturally points: normal growth patterns are those that reach this end;

[12] D. M. Armstrong, *The Mind-Body Problem: An Opinionated Introduction* (Boulder, CO: Westview, 1999), 138–40.

[13] George Molnar, *Powers: A Study in Metaphysics* (Oxford: Oxford University Press, 2003).

[14] See Brian Ellis, *Scientific Essentialism* (Cambridge: Cambridge University Press, 2001); and Ellis, *The Philosophy of Nature: A Guide to the New Essentialism* (Chesham: Acumen, 2002).

[15] It should be noted that Ellis and Cartwright, unlike some of the authors to be cited later, do not extend their neo-Aristotelianism to biology, but confine it to physics. A more thoroughgoing Aristotelianism is defended in Oderberg, *Real Essentialism*, and in David S. Oderberg, "Teleology: Inorganic and Organic," in A. M. Gonzalez, ed., *Contemporary Perspectives on Natural Law* (Aldershot: Ashgate, 2008).

[16] Nancy Cartwright, "Aristotelian Natures and the Modern Experimental Method," in John Earman, ed., *Inference, Explanation, and Other Frustrations: Essays in the Philosophy of Science* (Berkeley and Los Angeles: University of California Press, 1992), 70.

[17] André Ariew, "Teleology," in David L. Hull and Michael Ruse, eds., *The Cambridge Companion to the Philosophy of Biology* (Cambridge: Cambridge University Press, 2007), 177. For Paley's design argument, see William Paley, *Natural Theology* (C. Knight, 1836).

aberrations (clubfoot, polydactyly, and other birth defects, for example) are failures to reach it. Ariew seems to allow that there is nothing in Darwinism that undermines this sort of argument for final causes within biology. The biologist J. Scott Turner is even more explicit that accounting for the phenomena in question requires attributing an unconscious "intentionality" to biological processes.[18]

The persistence of teleological thinking within biology is perhaps most clearly evident from the way in which biologists describe DNA. Accounts of the function of this famous molecule regularly make use of such concepts as "information," "code," "instructions," "data," "blueprint," "software," "program," and the like, and there is no way to convey what DNA does without something like them. But every one of these concepts is suffused with intentionality, that is to say, with the notion of a thing's pointing to something beyond itself in the way our thoughts do—in this case, to an organism's physiological and behavioral traits, including those determining the species or kind it belongs to. Of course, no one would claim that DNA molecules literally can be said to think. But the notion of something which points to some end or goal beyond itself despite being totally unconscious *just is* the Aristotelian notion of final causality. As the biophysicist and Nobel laureate Max Delbrück once wrote, if the Nobel Prize could be awarded posthumously, "I think they should consider Aristotle for the discovery of the principle implied in DNA," and "the reason for the lack of appreciation, among scientists, of Aristotle's scheme lies in our having been blinded for 300 years by the Newtonian [i.e., mechanistic or nonteleological] view of the world."[19] More recently, the physicist Paul Davies has complained of the contradiction implicit in biologists' use of informational concepts that entail meaning or purpose while purporting at the same time to be committed to a completely mechanistic picture of the world. Recognizing that such concepts are indispensible, his solution appears to be at least tentatively to suggest giving up mechanism, asking: "Might purpose be a genuine property of nature right down to the cellular or even the subcellular level?"[20]

It should go without saying that human action is perhaps the most obvious example of a phenomenon that it appears in principle impossible

[18] J. Scott Turner, *The Tinkerer's Accomplice: How Design Emerges from Life Itself* (Cambridge, MA: Harvard University Press, 2007).

[19] Max Delbrück, "Aristotle-totle-totle," in Jacques Monod and Ernest Borek, eds., *Of Microbes and Life* (New York: Columbia University Press, 1971), 55.

[20] Paul Davies, *The Fifth Miracle: The Search for the Origin and Meaning of Life* (New York: Simon and Schuster, 1999), 122. Peter Godfrey-Smith is one philosopher of biology who resists the idea that genes encode for phenotypic traits, but even he concedes that they encode for the amino acid sequence of protein molecules in a way that involves semantic information. Though he does not draw the lesson, this would seem all by itself to concede the reality of something like Aristotelian teleology. See Peter Godfrey-Smith, "Information in Biology," in Hull and Ruse, eds., *The Cambridge Companion to the Philosophy of Biology*.

CLASSICAL NATURAL LAW THEORY

to account for in nonteleological terms.[21] (As Alfred North Whitehead once said, "Those who devote themselves to the purpose of proving that there is no purpose constitute an interesting subject for study.")[22] Then there is human thought, which, even apart from the actions it sometimes gives rise to, manifests intentionality or "directedness" toward something beyond itself and is thus as problematic for a mechanistic picture of the natural world as teleology is.[23]

Much more could be said in support of the classical teleological and essentialist picture of the natural world; and, again, I have in fact said much more in support of it elsewhere. To forestall irrelevant objections, I should perhaps also emphasize that the view in question has nothing whatsoever to do with "intelligent design" theory, creationism, or other such bogeymen. It is not William Paley, but Aristotle, who I would suggest stands vindicated by the philosophical and scientific trends I have been describing.[24] Given those trends, there is at the very least a powerful case to be made for the view that ends or goals toward which things are directed by virtue of their essences pervade the natural order from top to bottom, from the level of human thought down to that of basic physical particles. It follows that defectiveness, "missing the mark," or failure to realize a natural end or goal also pervade the natural order—as does the opposite of this circumstance, namely, that feature of things which Foot has aptly labeled their "natural goodness."

III. Natural Law

It is but a few short steps from natural goodness to natural law, as classically understood; and the other steps are very easily taken. Aquinas famously held that the fundamental principle of natural law is that "good is to be done and pursued, and evil is to be avoided," such that "all other precepts of the natural law are based upon this."[25] That "good is to be done, etc." might at first glance seem to be a frightfully difficult claim to

---

[21] Two important recent defenses of this thesis are G. F. Schueler, *Reasons and Purposes: Human Rationality and the Teleological Explanation of Action* (Oxford: Oxford University Press, 2003); and Scott Sehon, *Teleological Realism: Mind, Agency, and Explanation* (Cambridge, MA: MIT Press, 2005).

[22] Alfred North Whitehead, *The Function of Reason* (Princeton, NJ: Princeton University Press, 1929), 12.

[23] My own view is that an explanation of intentionality in purely materialistic-cum-mechanistic terms is impossible in principle. See Edward Feser, *Philosophy of Mind: A Short Introduction* (Oxford: Oneworld Publications, 2005), chapter 7, for a survey and defense of various arguments for this position; see also chapters 5 and 6 of Feser, *The Last Superstition*.

[24] Far from being Aristotelian in spirit, Paley's "design argument" and the "intelligent design" theories that have succeeded it essentially concede the idea that the physical universe is *inherently* mechanistic or nonteleological. Such arguments are thus as radically different from the theistic arguments of an Aristotelian like Aquinas as modern "natural law" theories are from classical natural law. See the works of mine cited in note 9 for discussion of this issue.

[25] Aquinas, *Summa Theologiae* I-II.94.2.

justify, and it certainly does not seem to be a very promising candidate for an axiom on which to rest an entire moral theory. For isn't the question "Why should I be good?" precisely (part of) what any moral theory ought to answer in the first place? And isn't this question notoriously hard to answer to the satisfaction of moral skeptics? Hasn't Aquinas therefore simply begged the most important question at the very start of the inquiry?

Properly understood, however, Aquinas's principle is not only *not* difficult to justify, but is so obviously correct that it might seem barely worth asserting. Aquinas is not saying that it is self-evident that we ought to be morally good. He is saying, rather, that it is self-evident that whenever we act we pursue something that we take to be good *in some way* and/or avoid what we take to be evil or bad *in some way.* And he is clearly right. Even someone who does what he believes to be *morally* bad does so only because he is seeking something he takes to be good in the sense of worth pursuing. Hence, the mugger who admits that robbery is evil nevertheless takes his victim's wallet because he thinks it would be good to have money to pay for his drugs; hence, the drug addict who knows that his habit is wrong and degrading nevertheless thinks it would be good to satisfy the craving and bad to suffer the unpleasantness of not satisfying it; and so forth. Of course, these claims are obviously true only on a very thin sense of "good" and "bad," but that is exactly the sense Aquinas has in mind.

Now you don't need the metaphysics of natural goodness described in the previous section to tell you that Aquinas's principle is correct. Again, it is just obviously correct, as everyone knows from his own experience. But that metaphysics does help us to understand *why* it is correct. Like every other natural phenomenon, practical reason has a natural end or goal toward which it is ordered, and that end or goal is just whatever it is that the intellect perceives to be good or worth pursuing. This claim too is obvious, at least if one accepts the metaphysical view in question. And now we are on the threshold of a further conclusion that does have real moral bite. For if the metaphysical view described earlier is correct, then like everything else in the world, human beings have various capacities whose realization is good for them and whose frustration is bad, as a matter of objective fact. A rational intellect apprised of the facts will therefore perceive that it is good to realize these capacities and bad to frustrate them. It follows, then, that a rational person will pursue the realization of these capacities and avoid their frustration. In short, practical reason is directed by nature toward the pursuit of what the intellect perceives to be good; what is *in fact* good is the realization or fulfillment of the various capacities and potentials definitive of human nature; and, thus, a *rational* person will perceive this and, accordingly, direct his actions toward the realization or fulfillment of those capacities and potentials. This, in essence, is what the moral life consists in. Natural law ethics as a body of substantive moral theory is just the formulation of general moral principles on the basis of an analysis of the various human capacities in question and the systematic working out of the implications of those principles. So, for example, if we consider that human beings have intellects and that the natural end or function of the intellect is to grasp the truth about things, it follows that it is good for us—it fulfills our nature—to pursue truth and avoid error. Consequently, a rational person apprised of the facts about human nature will see that this is what is good for us and thus will strive to attain truth and to avoid error. And so on for other natural human capacities.

Things are more complicated than this summary perhaps lets on. Various qualifications and complications will need to be spelled out as we examine the various natural human capacities in detail, and not every principle of morality that follows from this analysis will necessarily be as simple and straightforward as "Pursue truth and avoid error." But this much is enough to give us at least a general idea of how natural law theory determines the specific content of our moral obligations. It also suffices to give us a sense of the *grounds* of moral obligation, that which makes it the case that moral imperatives have categorical rather than merely hypothetical force. The hypothetical imperative (1) "If I want what is good for me, then I ought to pursue what fulfills my natural capacities and avoid what frustrates them" is something whose truth is revealed by the metaphysical analysis sketched in the previous section. By itself, it does not give us a categorical imperative, because the consequent will have force only for someone who accepts the antecedent. But the proposition (2) "I do want what is good for me" is something that is true of everyone by virtue of his nature as a human being, and is in any case self-evident, since it is just a variation on Aquinas's fundamental principle of natural law. Thus, the conclusion (3) "I ought to pursue what fulfills my natural capacities and avoid what frustrates them" is unavoidable. It does have categorical force because (2) has categorical force, and (2) has categorical force because it cannot be otherwise given our nature. Thus, both the content of our moral obligations and their obligatory force are determined by natural teleology.[26] As the natural law theorist Michael Cronin has written, "In the fullest sense of the word, then, moral duty is natural. For not only are certain objects natural means to man's final end, but our desire of that end is natural also, and, therefore, the necessity of the means is natural."[27]

---

[26] Hence, from a classical natural law point of view, the problematic status of moral obligation in modern moral philosophy is a symptom of the moderns' abandonment of final causes. In general, from a classical point of view, many philosophical problems often characterized as "perennial" or "traditional" (e.g., the mind-body problem, the problem of personal identity, puzzles about causation, and many others) are in fact merely by-products of the moderns' adoption of a mechanistic philosophy of nature, and do not arise, or at least do not arise in so puzzling a form, on a classical metaphysical picture. See Feser, *The Last Superstition*, chapter 5, for development of this idea.

[27] Michael Cronin, *The Science of Ethics, Volume 1: General Ethics* (Dublin: M. H. Gill and Son, 1939), 222.

IV. Natural Rights

We are rationally obliged, then, to pursue what is good for us and avoid what is bad, where "good" and "bad" have, again, the senses described in our discussion of the metaphysical foundations of classical natural law theory. Hence, we are obliged (for example) to pursue the truth and to avoid error, to sustain our lives and our health and to avoid what is damaging to them, and so on (ignoring, as irrelevant to our present purposes, the various complications and qualifications that a fully developed natural law theory would have to spell out). The force and content of these obligations derive from our nature as human beings.

It is part of that nature that we are *social* animals, as Aristotle famously noted. That is to say, we naturally live in communities with other human beings and depend on them for our well-being in various ways, both negative (such as our need not to be harmed by others) and positive (such as our need for various kinds of assistance from them). Most obviously, we are related to others by virtue of being either parents or children, siblings, grandparents and grandchildren, cousins, and so forth. Within the larger societies that collections of families give rise to, other kinds of relationships form, such as that of being a friend, an employee or an employer, a citizen, and so forth. To the extent that some of these relationships are natural to us, their flourishing is part of what is naturally good for us.

For example, as Foot writes, "like lionesses, human parents are defective if they do not teach their young the skills that they need to survive." [28] It is part of our *nature* to become parents, and part of our *nature* that while we are children we depend on our own parents.[29] Accordingly, it is simply an objective fact that it is good for us to be good parents to our children and bad for us to be bad parents, just as it is (even more obviously) an objective fact that it is good for children to be taken care of by their parents. The satisfaction good parents often feel and the sense of failure and frustration bad parents feel obviously give us confirmation of this judgment, but it is important to emphasize that classical natural law theory does not regard the often fluctuating subjective feelings and desires of individuals to be what is most fundamental to an analysis of what is good for them. To be sure, there is at least a rough and general correlation between what is good for us and what we want or find pleasant, and on a classical natural law analysis, our tendency to find some things pleasurable and other things unpleasant is one of nature's ways of getting us to do what is good for us and avoid what is bad. Still, feelings and desires

---

[28] Foot, *Natural Goodness*, 15.

[29] As a fully worked out natural law account of the matter would show, this does not entail that every human being is under an obligation to become a parent, but it does entail that if someone does become a parent, he is obligated to be a good one, with everything that that implies.

are not infallible. It is good for us to eat, which is why we like to do it, but obviously this does not entail that it is good for us to follow every impulse we have to eat; the heroin addict finds it pleasurable to take drugs, but it does not follow that it is good for him to give in to his desire to take them; and so forth. For a variety of reasons—ignorance, stubbornness, irrationality, peer pressure, addiction, habituated vice, genetic defect, mental illness, and so on—people sometimes do not want what is in fact good for them, and even want what is not in fact good for them, their natural desire for the good being oriented away from its proper object. The fact remains that what really is good for them is defined by their nature as human beings, and thus by the sorts of biological and metaphysical considerations summarized earlier. Subjective feelings that would incline us to act contrary to our nature must themselves be judged defective, and must be regarded as something we have a moral duty to strive against and try to overcome. Hence, the existence of sadistic parents or the occasional "deadbeat dad" who has no regrets does nothing to undermine the truth of the judgment that their behavior is contrary to their nature and thus bad for them, just as the existence of a sickly squirrel who has been conditioned to prefer sitting in a cage eating toothpaste on Ritz crackers to scampering about the woods looking for acorns does not undermine the judgment that the squirrel's behavior is contrary to its nature and thus bad for it.

Now if it is good for a parent to provide for his children, then given that we are obliged to do what is good for us, it follows that a parent has an obligation to provide for them. Similarly, since given their need for instruction, discipline, and the like, it is good for children to obey and respect their parents, it follows that they have an obligation to obey and respect them. But an obligation on the part of a person A toward another person B entails a right on the part of B against A.[30] It follows in turn, then, that children have a *right* to be provided for by their parents, and parents have a *right* to be obeyed and respected by their children. And since the obligations that generate the rights in question are obligations under *natural law* (rather than positive law), it follows that they are *natural* rights, grounded not in human convention but in human nature. Other obligations we have under natural law toward various other human beings will similarly generate various other natural rights. At the most general level, we are all obliged to refrain from interfering with others' attempts to fulfill the various moral obligations placed on them by the natural law. For as Austin Fagothey puts it, "man cannot have such obligations unless he has a right to fulfill them, and a consequent right to prevent others from interfering with his fulfillment of them."[31] The most *basic* natural

---

[30] Note, however, that the weaker the obligation is, the weaker is the right generated by it. (Cf. the distinction between perfect rights and imperfect rights discussed below.)

[31] Austin Fagothey, *Right and Reason*, 2nd ed. (St. Louis: The C. V. Mosby Company, 1959), 250. Cf. Oderberg, *Moral Theory*, 53–63.

right is the right to do what we are obligated to do by the natural law. Hence, everyone necessarily has a natural right not to be coerced into doing evil. There are also many things that are naturally good for us even if we are not strictly obligated to pursue them, such as having children. This particular example is, according to classical natural law theory, the foundation for the natural right to marry.[32] And, of course, we cannot pursue any good or fulfill any obligation at all if our very lives could be taken from us by others as they saw fit; thus, the natural law entails that every human being (or at least every innocent human being) has a right not to be killed.[33]

If classical natural law theory entails the existence of natural rights, it also entails that there are very definite limits on those rights. To be sure, a right to a significant measure of personal liberty is clearly implied by the natural law, given that the natural differences between individuals in terms of their interests, talents, upbringing, and other personal circumstances, and in general the complexities inherent in the human condition, entail that there are myriad ways in which human beings might concretely realize the capacities and potentials inherent in their common nature, and each person will need to be free to discover for himself which way is best for him. Nonetheless, this freedom cannot possibly be absolute, for while there is much that the natural law allows, there is also much that it forbids as absolutely contrary to the human good, and rights only exist to allow us to fulfill the human good. Thus, as one classical natural law theorist has put it, "the rights of all men are limited by the *end* for which the rights were given";[34] and, therefore, to cite another, "there can never be a right to that which is immoral. For the moral law cannot grant that which is destructive of itself."[35] Natural rights have a *teleological* foundation, and cannot exist except where they further the purposes they serve.

It is important to emphasize that this does not entail the institution of a totalitarian "morality police." As Aquinas famously emphasized, the fact that the natural law *morally* prohibits something does not suffice to show that governments should *legally* prohibit it.[36] The point is, rather, that no one can coherently justify his indulgence of some vice on the grounds that he has a *natural right* to indulge in it, or that it would be

[32] Explaining exactly how and why this is the case (and what the implications are for the debate over "same-sex marriage") would require an excursus into the classical natural law approach to sexual morality, which is beyond the scope of this essay. Readers interested in an exposition of this approach are directed to chapter 4 of Feser, *The Last Superstition*.

[33] For classical natural law theory, this rules out abortion and euthanasia but not capital punishment or just wars. For a useful recent explanation of why this is the case, see David S. Oderberg, *Applied Ethics: A Non-Consequentialist Approach* (Oxford: Blackwell, 2000).

[34] Celestine N. Bittle, *Man and Morals* (Milwaukee, WI: Bruce Publishing Company, 1950), 293; emphasis added.

[35] Thomas J. Higgins, *Man as Man: The Science and Art of Ethics*, rev. ed. (Milwaukee, WI: Bruce Publishing Company, 1959), 231.

[36] Aquinas, *Summa Theologiae* I-II.96.2.

intrinsically unjust to prevent him from doing so. The idea of a "natural right to do wrong" is an oxymoron. But there still might be many reasons of a prudential or even moral sort for government to tolerate certain vices; for instance, enforcing laws against them may be practically impossible, or may inadvertently do more harm than good.

Both the existence of natural rights and their limitations derive from their teleological foundation, and neither can be made sense of apart from it. From a classical natural law point of view, this is precisely why the very notion of natural rights has been so problematic in modern philosophy, given its mechanistic or anti-teleological metaphysical orientation. For example, John Locke, famously critical of Aristotelian Scholasticism, cannot give natural rights an essentialist-cum-teleological foundation, and so must appeal directly to God's will for us. Locke's famous thesis of self-ownership turns out to be a kind of shorthand for talk about the leasehold rights over ourselves that God has granted us, with God ultimately being our true "owner." The result is that Locke's "defense" of natural rights is really a denial of them: strictly speaking, for Locke it is God who has all the rights, not us, and our obligation not to harm others derives not from any rights they have, but rather from our duty not to damage what belongs to God. As we will see (in Section V), Locke's rejection of final causes poses particular problems for his theory of property.[37]

Contemporary Lockeans, who eschew Locke's theology, are even more hard-pressed to find a way to justify the claim that we have rights that are in some interesting sense "natural." For instance, Robert Nozick's notion of self-ownership, though more robust than Locke's, is also (and notoriously) even less well-grounded.[38] Certainly, self-ownership cannot by itself serve as the foundation of a theory of natural rights, since the concept of ownership *presupposes* the notion of rights. Nozick's appeal to Immanuel Kant's principle of respect for persons only raises the question of *why* we should respect persons as such, and while the classical natural law theorist can answer this question in terms of a robust metaphysics of human nature, those who reject that metaphysics (as Nozick, and indeed Kant himself, would) have no clear answer—at least, again, if their intention is to show that our basic rights are truly *natural* rights.

If the existence of natural rights becomes problematic for Locke and Lockeans, it is in the work of Thomas Hobbes and his successors that we see most clearly how the limitations the classical natural law theorist would put on our rights are undermined when a teleological metaphysics is abandoned. In the Hobbesian state of nature, everyone has a right to do

[37] It causes him many other problems too; for discussion of these problems, see Feser, *Locke.*

[38] Robert Nozick, *Anarchy, State, and Utopia* (New York: Basic Books, 1974). Edward Feser, *On Nozick* (Belmont, CA: Wadsworth, 2004), chapter 3, offers a sympathetic discussion, though it was written at a time when I believed (as I no longer do) that Nozick's theory of rights could be grounded in a classical natural law approach to moral theory.

anything he wants, without any limitations whatsoever. Of course, that is precisely because Hobbesians do not see us as *naturally* having "rights" in the moral sense at all, morality being the result of a kind of contract between rationally self-interested individuals. Even when the contract is made, though, the rights that result seem inevitably to have very little in the way of restrictions upon them, at least in the thinking of contemporary contractarians inspired by Hobbes.[39] The reason is that it is not any objective natural end that our rights are meant to further on a contractarian account, but rather whatever subjective desires or preferences we happen to have, whether or not these desires or preferences are in line with any purported natural ends. The contract that rationally self-interested individuals would agree to, then, is essentially a nonaggression pact, each party granting the others the "right" to be left alone to do whatever they want to, so long as they are willing to reciprocate. If such a right has very little in the way of restrictions on it, however, that is, again, precisely because it is not natural but (in the relevant sense) conventional.

Of course, contractarians themselves would not regard either the conventional status of rights or the lack of restrictions as a problem for their theory. But contractarian theories also famously face the problems of explaining (1) why we should attribute even conventional rights to the weakest members of society (who have nothing to offer the stronger parties to the proposed "contract" in return for being left alone) and (2) why we should suppose that even every rationally self-interested individual would sincerely agree to such a contract in the first place (since some might prefer to take their chances in a Hobbesian war of all against all, or opt for the life of a free-rider who benefits from others' abiding by the contract while he secretly violates it whenever he knows he can get away with doing so). Contractarians have offered various responses to these difficulties, which typically involve inventive appeals to various less obvious ways in which the strong might benefit from leaving the weak alone, or in which even a rational misanthrope might benefit from sincerely abiding by the terms of the contract. At the end of the day, however, the contractarian can give no *rational* criticism of someone who fully understands the benefits that would accrue to him by agreeing to the social contract and treating others as if they had rights, but nevertheless refuses to do so. The most the contractarian can say is, "Better keep an eye on *that* guy, then," for he might do the rest of us harm. He does not do *himself* harm, though, on a contractarian analysis; and in denying others their rights, he does not deny them anything they really had objectively in the first place.

For the classical natural law theorist, by contrast, such a sociopath *does* do himself harm, and also fails to perceive the objective facts about oth-

---

[39] See, e.g., Jan Narveson, *The Libertarian Idea* (Philadelphia, PA: Temple University Press, 1988).

ers. As Foot puts it, "free-riding individuals of a species whose members work together are just as *defective* as those who have defective hearing, sight, or powers of locomotion."[40] If we look at the evident facts of human experience through the lens of an essentialist metaphysics, we can see that a certain measure of fellow-feeling is, like bipedalism or language, natural to human beings and, thus, objectively good for every human being simply by virtue of being human, whether or not certain specific individuals fail, for whatever reason, to realize this.

V. Property Rights

Much more could be said about the classical natural law theory of natural rights, but our interest here is in the right to private property in particular, so let us turn at last to that. The best-known defenses of private property in contemporary philosophy, those of Locke and Nozick, start with some version of the thesis of self-ownership and work from it to a defense of private property in general, their strategy being to show that if as self-owners we own our own labor, then we must also have a right to the fruits of our labor. Does classical natural law theory recognize anything like the thesis of self-ownership?

Yes and no. On the one hand, if the thesis of self-ownership is taken (as it seems to be by Nozick) to entail the virtually unlimited right to do with ourselves just anything we want, then classical natural law theory obviously cannot endorse the thesis. For if, as classical natural law theorists would typically hold, illicit drug use, prostitution, suicide, and other so-called "victimless crimes" are inherently immoral, then for reasons stated already there can be no natural right to do such things. Moreover, as Fagothey has argued, "since in the exercise of any right the subject always subordinates the matter [i.e., that which the right is a right to] to himself and uses it as a means to his own end, it follows that the matter of a right can never be a person."[41] Fagothey's point is that since every human being already has certain ends set for him by nature, he cannot possibly be entirely subordinated to the ends of another, which he would be if he were owned by another; and Fagothey's immediate aim is to argue against the legitimacy of chattel slavery.[42] But this argument might

---

[40] Foot, *Natural Goodness*, 16; emphasis in the original.

[41] Fagothey, *Right and Reason*, 243.

[42] It is sometimes claimed that classical natural law theory supports the moral legitimacy of slavery, but this is highly misleading at best and at worst slanderous. What natural law theorists have held is that, since it is obviously morally unproblematic for one person to come to owe another this or that particular service as a matter of right, it is in principle possible that someone could come legitimately to owe another service for some prolonged period of time, perhaps even a lifetime. For example, such servitude might be imposed as a punishment for a crime. But this is a far cry from chattel slavery, slave hunting, allowing children to be born into slavery, etc., all of which are condemned by natural law theory as intrinsically immoral. (Hence, the African slave trade could not be justified in terms of

seem to rule out self-ownership as well, since if each human being has certain ends set for him by nature, he not only could not legitimately use another person, but also could not use himself, for just *any* ends he happens to have—as it seems he could do if he could be said to be his own property.

On the other hand, it is hardly unusual to speak of someone as owning something even if it is also said that he cannot do just whatever he likes with it. Though I have no right to stab you with my knife, it does not follow that the knife is not my property. Though I have no right to conduct dangerous experiments on radioactive materials in my garage, lest I accidentally blow up the neighborhood, it does not follow that I do not own my garage. Similarly, even if there are limits on what I can legitimately do with myself, it would not follow from that fact alone that there is no sense in which I own myself.[43] Ownership involves the possession of various rights over a thing—the right to use it, the right to sell it, the right to exclude others from using it, and so forth—and even if someone does not have every possible right one could have over a thing, it will still be plausible to say that he owns it as long as he possesses a sufficient number of these rights. Of course, as it stands, that is somewhat vague. But it suffices to make the point that as long as natural law theory allows that an individual has, over himself and his faculties, certain key rights, such as the right to decide how to employ his labor, the right to life and to bodily integrity, and the right to a significant measure of personal liberty—and the theory would indeed affirm rights of this sort—then perhaps this will suffice to show that natural law theory entails that individuals are, in *some* significant sense, self-owners.

However, given the qualifications which, as we have seen, would have to be put on self-ownership from a natural law point of view, it is also probably true that the idea of self-ownership ceases to be very interesting. For that idea is, of course, most commonly employed by libertarians seeking to undermine every form of paternalistic morals legislation and redistributive taxation in one fell swoop, as violations of the right of self-ownership; and such a strategy obviously becomes impossible on classical natural law theory. The point is not that natural law theory entails that all or even any redistributive taxation is legitimate—we have yet to address that issue—nor, as I have already noted, is it to say that the theory necessarily entails that there should be laws against vices indulged in privately. The point is, rather, that given the qualifications the theory

---

classical natural law theory.) Moreover, the consensus among recent classical natural law theorists is that even the more limited form of servitude natural law allows in principle is so morally hazardous that in practice it cannot be justified.

[43] Indeed, even Locke says that we cannot legitimately commit suicide or sell ourselves into slavery despite our ownership of ourselves, though in his case this is precisely because talk of "self-ownership" is, for Locke, really a kind of shorthand for talk of our leasehold rights over what is ultimately God's property rather than ours.

would place on self-ownership, the concept of self-ownership can no longer serve as a "magic bullet" that *automatically* takes down everything the libertarian wants to rule out. If self-ownership is far from absolute in the first place, then in order to know whether I either have a moral right to do this or that, or ought at least to be allowed legally to do it whether or not it is immoral, it will not suffice to shout, "I own myself!" One will have to investigate, on a case-by-case basis, how the act in question either helps, hinders, or is neutral vis-à-vis the realization of what natural law entails is good for me; whether a law against it would, even if it is bad for me, do more harm than good, all things considered; and so forth. That I own my home does not by itself settle whether I can sink a well in my back yard, tear my house down and build a skyscraper on the lot, put up a guard tower manned with sentries carrying grenades and machine guns, and so on. Private property rights are simply more complicated than that. Similarly, even if there is some sense in which I can be said to own myself, that does not *by itself* show that I can inject myself with heroin, become a prostitute, sell my bodily organs for profit, or whatever.

Thus, from a natural law point of view, self-ownership per se would not seem to be a promising basis on which to build a political philosophy, including a theory of private property rights. Still, like Locke and Nozick, many classical natural law theorists have argued that a right to private property follows from a consideration of (among other things) our natural powers, and labor specifically. Indeed, to a large extent, the classical natural law case for private property overlaps with the case made by classical liberal and libertarian property theorists. The difference—and it is a significant one—is in the way this case is informed by a classical essentialist-cum-teleological metaphysics and by the moral implications we have already seen to follow from that metaphysics.

By nature, human beings obviously need natural resources in order to survive. But acknowledging that fact is consistent with holding the view that they ought to be allowed only the *use* of natural resources rather than ownership of them, or the view that natural resources ought to be collectively owned. Of course, there are very serious and well-known practical problems both with a situation where natural resources are left in the commons and with any system of collective ownership à la socialism and communism. But that would by itself show only that private property has certain practical advantages, not that there is a natural right to it. So how does classical natural law theory show that such a right does in fact exist?

The case begins by noting that the institution of private property is something toward which we are *naturally suited* and which we even *require* for our well-being.[44] With respect to the former point, we can note, first,

---

[44] A particularly thorough presentation of the classical natural law case for private property can be found in Michael Cronin, *The Science of Ethics, Volume 2: Special Ethics* (Dublin: M. H. Gill and Son, 1939), chapter 4, which has informed my discussion here. (In addition,

that an individual human being's intellect and will make it possible for him (unlike the lower animals) to take permanent occupation and control of a resource and to use it for his personal benefit; and such occupation, control, and use is precisely what private property consists in.[45] Furthermore, in doing so the individual inevitably imparts something of his own personality to the resources he transforms, insofar as the particular properties a resource takes on as a result of his use and transformation of it reflect his personal intentions, knowledge, talents, and efforts. As Michael Cronin colorfully puts it, considered just as such, "a machine is very little more than crystallized human thought and energy."[46] In our very use of external resources, then, we tend unavoidably to put into them something that is already ours (which is, of course, something Locke also emphasizes in his talk of "mixing our labor" with external resources).

Thus, our inherent faculties naturally orient us toward private ownership. But such ownership is also necessary for us. It is necessary for us, first of all, as individuals. An individual's personal capacities and potentials cannot be exercised and realized, respectively, without at least some stable body of resources on which to bring his efforts to bear; the freedom of action required in order to do this cannot exist unless he has permanent access to at least some of those resources; and as the experience of individuals in even the most egalitarian societies attests, human beings have a natural desire for at least something to call their own, and cannot be happy if this desire is frustrated.

Ownership is also necessary for us as families. We are naturally ordered toward the having of children; and, as we have seen, for classical natural law theory this entails an obligation to provide for whatever children we have, not only materially but spiritually, that is, with respect to their moral upbringing, education, and the like. Furthermore, as is well known, classical natural law theory entails that large families will inevitably tend to be the norm, given what the natural law tells us with respect to sexual morality (though this is, again, not something there is space to get into here). As children grow to adulthood and have families of their own, they tend to need assistance from their parents in starting out; there are other relatives (aunts and uncles, cousins, and the like) to whom, in some circumstances, we might also owe some assistance under natural law, even if our obligations here are not as strong as our obligations to our

---

chapters 5–8 contain a lengthy critique of socialism.) Also useful are Bittle, *Man and Morals,* chapters 16 and 17; Fagothey, *Right and Reason,* chapters 28 and 29; and Higgins, *Man as Man,* chapters 17 and 18.

[45] Classical natural law theorists also typically add that since what is less perfect exists for the sake of what is more perfect, inanimate resources, plants, and animals exist for the sake of man. But the hierarchical conception of reality this presupposes is an aspect of classical metaphysics that I do not have space here to expound or defend. For a general account, see Feser, *Aquinas.*

[46] Cronin, *Special Ethics,* 120. Of course the "little more" (namely, the natural resources out of which a machine is made) is important too. I will have more to say on this presently.

own children; and there are always emergencies that need to be planned for as far as possible. As the fundamental social arrangement, for the sake of which others (such as states) exist, it is also crucial that the family maintains a significant measure of independence. These considerations entail that heads of families need to be able to amass large amounts of wealth to which they have permanent rights of use and transfer.[47]

Finally, private ownership is necessary for the good of the larger societies that tend naturally to form out of groups of families. Here the sorts of considerations favoring private property famously adduced by Aristotle and Aquinas become particularly relevant. The incentives to labor are massively reduced where the laborer is not allowed to reap its fruits, which drastically limits the amount of wealth available for the use of society at large; economic and social planning are far more efficient when individuals are able to look after their own property than when things are held in common (a point Ludwig von Mises and F. A. Hayek have developed in illuminating detail); and social peace is more likely when individuals each have their own property than when they must debate over how best to use what is held in common.[48]

If our natural capacities are ordered toward private ownership, and if the fulfillment of those capacities and of our moral obligations under natural law requires such ownership, then it follows, given the justification of natural rights outlined above, that the natural law entails a natural right to private property. So far, though, this establishes only the general institution of private property. We need to say something more to determine how a title to this or that *particular* resource can come to be acquired by this or that *particular* individual. That is to say, we need a theory of "original appropriation" or "initial acquisition."

The tendency of classical natural law theorists of property is to find the origin of such appropriation in first occupation. Taking occupation of a previously unowned resource is *necessary* for ownership because unless one first takes hold of a resource, nothing else can be done with it at all, including the carrying out of any other procedure that might be claimed to be necessary for appropriation. In particular, one cannot "mix one's labor" with a resource until one has first taken hold of or occupied it, for which reason classical natural law theorists tend to reject Locke's theory of appropriation at least as an account of the *fundamental* means by which ownership gets started. Taking occupation is also (apart from a qualifi-

---

[47] As Cronin notes, it is irrelevant that some individuals might not in fact have families, for the conclusions of natural law follow from the normal case, from what our nature inclines us to. Thus, insofar as even those who happen not to have children nevertheless have an inherent or natural tendency toward family life, they will retain whatever natural rights flow from this particular aspect of human nature. Ibid., 123–24.

[48] Cf. Aquinas, *Summa Theologiae* II-II.66.2. For the arguments of Mises and Hayek, see Ludwig von Mises, *Socialism*, 2d ed. (New Haven, CT: Yale University Press, 1951); and F. A. Hayek, "The Use of Knowledge in Society," in Hayek, *Individualism and Economic Order* (Chicago: University of Chicago Press, 1948).

cation to be noted presently) *sufficient* for ownership because it suffices to enable one to fulfill the ends for which natural law theory tells us the right to property exists in the first place.[49]

Though not as fundamental as first occupation, labor nevertheless also has a crucial role to play in the story of how property comes into being. As I noted above, for classical natural law theory, to labor over a resource is, as it were, to put into it an impress of one's own personality, and thus something one already has a right to. Furthermore, most of the value that comes to exist in a transformed resource derives not from the resource per se but from the labor put into transforming it. As Cronin puts it, "with the exception of a mere fraction of our present wealth, the riches of the world are entirely a result of human labour" (where he is clear that what he has in mind is "labour in its broad sense—not mere manual labour").[50] Hence, the more one has put one's labor into a previously unowned resource of which one takes first occupation, the *stronger* or more *complete* is one's property right to that resource.

This naturally brings us to the question of the limits on the right to private property, which are implied by the suggestion that a property right can be more or less strong or complete. As with natural rights in general, the right to private property has a teleological basis, namely, the role it plays in enabling us to realize our natural capacities and fulfill our obligations under natural law; and, as with natural rights in general, this right is limited by the very teleological considerations that ground it. As what has already been said clearly implies, the right to private property, like our other natural rights, cannot possibly be so strong that it would justify us in doing what is contrary to the natural law. Hence, there can be no *natural* right to use our property for intrinsically immoral purposes. As before, this does not by itself entail that government must or even should regulate our private exercise of our rights so that it conforms to the standards of natural law. But it does entail that there can be no natural law basis for libertarian arguments to the effect that outlawing strip clubs and drug dens (or whatever) is *necessarily* a violation of the natural right to private property.

There is, however, another limitation on the right to private property, one that is more directly related to its specific teleological grounding. As we have seen, for classical natural law theory, property exists in the first place in order to allow individuals to realize their natural capacities and satisfy their moral obligations by bringing their powers to bear on external resources. Hence, if property rights were so strong that they would

---

[49] What *counts* as first occupation? Does an explorer who merely sets foot on the edge of a vast continent thereby come to occupy the whole thing? I would argue that the mark of genuine occupation of a resource is some significant measure of *control* over it. Cf. my discussion of this issue in "There Is No Such Thing as an Unjust Initial Acquisition," *Social Philosophy and Policy* 22, no. 1 (2005): 56–80.

[50] Cronin, *Special Ethics,* 127.

justify some people in using their property in a way that undermined the possibility for others to fulfill their natural ends and moral obligations, then the very point of the institution of private property would be undermined. To take an extreme but clear example, if some one person or group of persons acquired a monopoly over some crucial resource (such as land or water) and refused access to those who did not have this resource, or allowed them access only under onerous conditions, then it is obvious that the institution of private property would allow some individuals to fulfill their natural ends at the expense of the ability of others to fulfill theirs. Clearly, then, the right to private property cannot be so strong as to justify such a circumstance.

What does this limitation imply in practice? The most obvious implication is that individuals in circumstances of what Cronin calls "absolute distress" have a right to the use of the resources of others, where the paradigm examples would be the starving man in the woods who takes food from a cabin, or a window washer who grabs a flagpole to break his fall from a building, or someone fleeing robbers who can only escape by running through someone else's back yard.[51] Someone in circumstances like these is not guilty of theft or the like, because for actions like the ones in question to count as theft, etc., the cabin owner or flagpole owner or homeowner would have to have such an *absolute* right to his property that he could justly refuse to allow others to use it even in the circumstances in question; and, according to natural law theory, no one could possibly have so absolute a property right. For the same reason, if some resource (say, the only remaining source of water in an area stricken by drought) became "absolutely necessary . . . to save the community or part of it from extinction," then any individual who had heretofore privately owned that resource would have an obligation in justice to relinquish it.[52]

Here classical natural law theory is committed to something analogous to what the libertarian philosopher Eric Mack calls the "self-ownership proviso" on the use of resources, which "requires that persons not deploy their legitimate holdings, i.e., their extra-personal property, in ways that severely, albeit noninvasively, disable any person's world-interactive powers."[53] I say "analogous" rather than "identical" because, for reasons already stated, classical natural law theory is probably not best thought of as basing its theory of property rights on self-ownership per se, and because it is not clear that Mack would allow for a case where an owner

---

[51] Ibid., 135.
[52] Ibid., 136. Given the improvements an owner might have made to a resource, or his personal economic stake in it, compensation might be called for in such a case.
[53] Eric Mack, "The Self-Ownership Proviso: A New and Improved Lockean Proviso," *Social Philosophy and Policy* 12, no. 1 (1995): 186–218, at 187. See Feser, "There Is No Such Thing as an Unjust Initial Acquisition," for a development and defense of Mack's proviso, though I would now qualify much of what I said in that essay in light of the views expressed in this one.

would have to relinquish his property, as opposed to merely allowing others to use it (though the distinction between taking and merely using blurs in the case of something like a source of water, which people use precisely by taking some of it). Like Mack, though, natural law theory is less concerned with the initial appropriation of resources (the focus of Locke's famous provisos) than with how they are used after they are acquired.[54] Moreover, as it is for Mack, the key to the issue for classical natural law theory is the possibility of bringing what Mack calls our "world-interactive powers" to bear on the world, since the point of the institution of private property is precisely to allow us to fulfill the natural end of these powers.

In this connection, we should note that classical natural law theorists would argue that their metaphysical commitments allow them to make sense of what they and Lockeans (like Mack) have in common in a way that strict Lockeans cannot. For to speak (as Mack does) of our "powers" as "essentially" "world-interactive" is to say something that naturally suggests an Aristotelian essentialist-cum-teleological metaphysics; certainly, it is hard to see how we could *literally* have "powers" that are, of their essence, oriented or directed toward the external world on a modern mechanistic or anti-teleological metaphysics, and if this talk is not meant literally then its import needs to be explained. Similarly, Jeremy Waldron has noted that it is hard to see why Locke should think that putting one's labor into a resource would give one a property right in that resource, any more than dropping one's diamond into a vat of cement would give one a property right in the cement, unless we think in teleological terms.[55] But how could Locke appeal to the teleology of labor, or of natural resources, when he denies the existence of Aristotelian final causes? Indeed, how can he even ground a *natural* right to property by appeal to the concepts of labor, natural resources, etc., when for Locke the essences of things (including, if he is to be consistent, the essences of labor, natural resources, and indeed of human beings themselves) are man-made or conventional rather than natural? The mechanistic metaphysical picture of the world to which Locke and his successors tend explicitly, or at least implicitly, to be committed seems to undermine the foundations of their political philosophy. Yet to try to avoid these difficulties by adopting an Aristotelian metaphysics would entail committing oneself to the classical natural law theory that flows from it, and thus ceasing to be a Lockean—or so I would argue.[56]

---

[54] Note, however, that Cronin indicates that a person could not justly appropriate for himself a previously unowned resource that was known *in advance* to be necessary for the continued existence of the community. Cronin, *Special Ethics*, 136.

[55] Jeremy Waldron, *God, Locke, and Equality* (Cambridge: Cambridge University Press, 2002), 159. Nozick famously gives a similar example in *Anarchy, State, and Utopia* (p. 175), though without drawing the teleological lesson.

[56] Again, see Feser, *Locke*.

VI. Taxation

The question of the limits that classical natural law theory would put on the right to private property naturally brings us at last to the issue of taxation. There is no way this subject can be treated adequately without discussing the natural law understanding of the nature of the state and the basis of its authority, and that is obviously beyond the scope of this essay. Suffice it to say that classical natural law theory rejects the classical liberal idea that the state is artificial, a product of human convention, and regards it instead as a natural institution to which we owe allegiance whether or not we consent to it. At the same time, natural law theory regards the state as existing only to serve the interests of its citizens, and only with respect to those functions that private citizens cannot carry out on their own. Hence, the natural law theorist is committed to the idea of limited government, though given what was said earlier the limitations in question would no doubt not be severe enough to satisfy contemporary libertarians. In any event, whatever taxes would be required to fund the legitimate functions of government are taxes that the classical natural law theorist would hold us to be obligated in justice to pay.[57]

Beyond this, some further general remarks can be made in light of the theory of property rights sketched above. Other than those limits on the use of one's property that are entailed by one's general obligation not to employ what one owns for evil purposes (e.g., as a drug den or brothel or whatever), we saw that the main limitation, and the one that entails the possibility that one might, under certain circumstances, be morally required to relinquish (or at least allow others to use) one's property, had to do with cases where a more absolute right to ownership would undermine the very point of the institution of private property. But how can we be required *in justice* (not merely in charity) to give up our property rights even in these cases, especially since, as we have seen, it is our talents and energies that are primarily responsible for the existence of the objects owned in the first place, and since in using our talents and energies we have put something of ourselves into the products of our labor? As Cronin argues, the answer to this question must lie in the fact that we are never *entirely* responsible in the first place for the existence of the things we produce, since we must always make use of natural resources which we did not create and which start out unowned by anyone.[58] For if others have at least *some* claim over these preexisting resources even before we transform them with our labor, that claim will persist even after we do so—even though the claim is so weak that it will require us to relinquish our property rights only under certain exceptional conditions. That others

---

[57] From this and what is said below, it should be clear that I have moved away considerably (though not completely) from the position I defended in Feser, "Taxation, Forced Labor, and Theft," *The Independent Review* 5, no. 2 (2000).

[58] Cronin, *Special Ethics*, 135.

46   EDWARD FESER

do have such a claim is entailed by the reason for which property rights
exist in the first place, namely, to allow us to bring our capacities to bear
on external natural resources so that we might fulfill the ends and obligations set for us by natural law.[59]

These various considerations would appear to suggest what we might
call a *Natural Law Proviso* on the use of property, according to which an
individual has a natural right to use whatever property he acquires either
via first occupation or by trade, gifts, wages, inheritance, etc.,[60] in any
way he wishes, provided that (i) he does not use his property in a manner
that is directly contrary to the general moral obligations imposed on us by
the natural law, and (ii) he allows those who lack resources sufficient even
for the possibility of the fulfillment of their own natural capacities and
obligations to use or take ownership of his property *to the extent and in the
manner that* their particular circumstances (and his own) dictate.

This is a very rough formulation; a more complete treatment would no
doubt require some tightening up, such as the addition of further qualifying phrases. It seems to me, however, that it is a useful first approximation, and that it gives us a basis for determining the grounds and
limitations set by natural law for taxation and for governmental regulation of the use of private property. What sort of regulation and taxation
might this proviso justify, at least in principle? Much more than libertarians would be happy with, but also, it seems to me (and contrary perhaps
to first appearances), much less than egalitarians would be happy with.

The implications of the proviso's first clause should be evident from
what has been said already. If there can be no natural right to use one's
property for intrinsically immoral purposes, then it seems at least in
principle allowable for government to regulate property to prevent this,
at least where such use might have a dramatic negative impact on public
morality. (Again, whether this is advisable in practice in any particular
case is a separate issue.) The qualification that it is uses that are "directly"
contrary to natural law that are ruled out by the proviso is added to
forestall governmental interventions that are so draconian that they would

---

[59] Hence, the claim that natural resources start out unowned needs to be qualified; everyone has at least this minimal claim over them. But this does not entail anything like initial
common ownership of resources, because it does not entail that we all collectively have all
the rights constitutive of ownership, such as the right to exclude others from a resource, the
right to sell it, the right to transform it, the right to destroy it, and so forth. These rights only
come into existence with respect to specific resources once they are acquired via occupation
by specific individuals.

[60] The "transfer" of property via such means—as Nozick famously calls it in order to
distinguish buying, inheriting, etc. from what he describes as the "initial acquisition" of
previously unowned resources—does not appear to be considered more problematic by
classical natural law theorists than it is by Nozick, since once a resource is justly acquired
it would seem to follow automatically that an owner, precisely *qua* owner, can transfer it to
others in any way he wishes (in general, anyway; see note 63 below). This is no doubt
because, like Nozick, classical natural law theorists are uninterested in preserving any
overall *pattern* of wealth distribution per se, even if they are more inclined than Nozick is
to see in this or that particular case of economic distress the possibility of injustice.

effectively undermine the institution of private property. Thus, for example, it is reasonable (if one accepts the standard natural law attitude toward illicit drug use and sexual morality) to hold that no one has a natural right to use his property as a public opium den or brothel. And it would be absurd to suggest that a government that forbade such uses was totalitarian, or threatened the very institution of private property. Nonetheless, it is another thing altogether to hold that no one has a natural right to sell a home or rent an apartment to someone he believes will be carrying out this or that immoral activity in it *in private*, or to suggest that a government could enforce a prohibition on such selling or renting practices without endangering the integrity of the institution of private property.[61] Such selling or renting practices would of themselves involve at most *indirect* cooperation in immorality, which natural law theorists regard as sometimes permissible in light of the principle of double effect.[62]

The second clause of the proposed proviso is what would justify the starving man in the woods taking food from a cabin and similar uses or seizures of another's property in emergency situations. It is also what would justify the taxation required for the necessary functions of government (national defense, courts of law, etc.), since from a classical natural law point of view, the very existence of the community, and thus the possibility of its members' fulfilling the ends set for them by nature, depends on the state's performance of these functions. Again, though, an adequate treatment of this issue would require a detailed exposition of the natural law theory of the state.

It seems clear that the second clause of the proviso would also justify taxation for the purposes of funding some measure of public assistance for those in absolute distress who are incapable of either finding work or getting help from family members and friends. For these circumstances would seem to be relevantly similar to those in which the starving man in the woods finds himself. Bureaucratic inefficiency, fraud, and welfare dependency are potential problems here, but they are problems of practical implementation rather than moral principle. Governmental regulation to prevent monopolies on natural resources crucial to the existence of the community (such as water) would also seem obviously justifiable, and though there are, here as elsewhere, practical problems whose solution requires a sound understanding of economics, they do not entail that such regulation would be unjust per se.[63]

---

[61] I do not mean that owners have no *right* to refuse to rent or sell to such a person. They may refuse if they see fit. The claim is rather that there is no *absolute obligation* to refuse to sell or rent to him.

[62] For a recent defense of the principle of double effect, argued from a classical natural law point of view, see Oderberg, *Moral Theory*, 86–126.

[63] There is also the thorny question of the "just wage," a concept central to classical natural law thinking about economics and social justice. This is too big a topic to deal with here, but two general points can be made. First, the natural law conception of property rights definitely entails that it is *in principle* possible for the market wage to diverge from the

Would the second clause of the Natural Law Proviso require a more extensive system of "welfare rights," such as governmental provision of health care, education, and the like? It does not seem to me that it would, at least not by itself. Property as we know it is the result of two factors, natural resources on the one hand (such as land, water, plants, animals, minerals, etc.) and the labor and ingenuity of specific individuals on the other. Following Cronin, I have suggested that it is the fact that everyone has at least a general claim to the former that justifies putting some limitation on the right to private property. But there is no general claim to the latter; that is to say, no one has a claim in justice to the labor, ingenuity, etc. of a particular individual except that particular individual himself (as well as those to whom he has certain specific obligations under natural law, such as his children). The things a human being needs in order to stay alive and thus to have the possibility of fulfilling his natural capacities and obligations—namely, food, water, basic shelter, clothing, and the like—are included among natural resources, or at least require only the most rudimentary effort to produce. As a Lockean might say, these things exist even in a state of nature, before property rights have been established and even before anyone has exerted much or any labor or ingenuity at all. Hence, it is plausible to hold that those with no access to these basic resources have a right to public assistance to the extent needed to feed, clothe, and shelter themselves until they can once again become economically self-sufficient. However, education and health care are *not* naturally existing resources like food, water, etc. They exist only because of the highly specialized labor and ingenuity of particular individuals. But in that case they are not among the natural resources to which everyone has a general claim under natural law, and thus they are not the sort of thing access to which could plausibly be guaranteed as a matter of justice by the Natural Law Proviso.[64]

---

just wage. To take the most obvious sort of example, someone who legally buys up all the land and businesses in some geographical region, making it impossible for others to support themselves through farming and the like and leaving himself the only possible employer, would be committing an injustice against those whom he employed at mere subsistence wages, even if they "freely" consented to these wages. Second, what this entails *in practice* is not at all obvious. For real-world conditions are almost never anywhere close to this cartoonish example, and the further they diverge from it, the less clear it is that the market wage really has diverged from the just wage. Thus, while the moral principle that the market wage and the just wage can diverge seems to me obviously correct, it seems equally obvious that *by itself* this principle tells us very little where practical policy measures are concerned.

[64] Would the proviso entail that natural resources beyond food, water, etc.—in particular, land, raw materials, and the like—should be redistributed so that as many people as possible might become as self-sufficient as they might have been in the state of nature, as the "distributism" of Hilaire Belloc and G. K. Chesterton would seem to require? No, for at least two reasons. First, if such resources are susceptible of being redistributed as often as doing so would allow yet more people to be self-sufficient, it is hard to see how those holding them could really be said to have private ownership of them. Second, as David Schmidtz has emphasized, appropriation of natural resources is not a zero-sum game. While it diminishes

There is, to be sure, a *weaker* right to these things under natural law, just as there is a right to economic and other assistance more generally. Given that we are social animals by nature, we have various obligations to one another that derive not only from family ties, but also from being friends, fellow citizens, or even just fellow human beings. Hence, just as others have a right to be treated by us with courtesy, respect, and the like in our everyday dealings with them, so too do they have a right to our assistance when they are in distress, simply by virtue of being friends, fellow citizens, and fellow human beings (with the strength of these rights varying according to how close our relationship is to the people in question). But it does not follow from this that our obligations here are the sort that ought to be met through taxation for the purposes of funding extensive social programs, any more than the fact that everyone has a right to be treated courteously entails that government has a duty to throw me in jail if I am rude to someone. There is a distinction traditionally drawn in rights theory between *perfect* rights—those which uphold the very possibility of morality, entail absolute obligations, and are paradigmatically the sorts of rights governments ought to enforce—and *imperfect* rights, which tend merely to support morality and entail only some lesser degree of obligation, and which governments need not enforce. The right of an innocent person not be killed is obviously a perfect right, while the right to be treated courteously is obviously only an imperfect right. And while there is obviously a strong case to be made for the claim that we have an imperfect right to be aided by others when in distress vis-à-vis health care, education, and the like, the Natural Law Proviso does not seem to entail that we have a perfect right to such assistance.[65]

It is also important to keep in mind that in a society whose ethos is deeply influenced by the principles of classical natural law, families will tend to be much larger and more stable, religious and other social institutions intermediate between the family and government will be stronger and have a greater role in people's everyday lives, and in general the "individualist" mentality of modern liberal societies will be absent. The circumstances in which individuals would be unable to find assistance from sources other than the government would, accordingly, be extremely rare. But this raises another possible justification of

---

the stock of raw materials that can be "initially acquired" (in Nozick's sense), it increases the stock of wealth that can be owned, and it is the latter which matters with respect to self-sufficiency. Hence, though a starving farmer whose crops have failed and whose cattle have died due to drought may own his land outright, and a middle-class office worker may live his entire life well-fed in a rented apartment, it does not seem plausible to suggest that the former is more self-sufficient than the latter. See David Schmidtz, "The Institution of Property," *Social Philosophy and Policy* 11, no. 2 (1994): 42–62.

[65] When Aquinas famously says that the ownership of property ought to be private but its use common (*Summa Theologiae* II-II.66.2), what he seems to mean is not that those in need of assistance have (in general) a perfect right to my property, but rather that they have an imperfect right to it. For if they had a perfect right to it, it is hard to see in what sense ownership would be truly private. Cf. Cronin, *Special Ethics*, 134.

a right to at least minimal assistance when in distress vis-à-vis health care and the like. I have argued that the Natural Law Proviso does not imply an obligation in justice for government to provide such assistance; our rights against others to assistance in obtaining these specific things are at most imperfect. But suppose the ethos of a society is informed by natural law principles in the way I have just described. Suppose, in particular, that the individuals who make up such a society are in general so united in their basic values that the majority of them are willing to accept taxation for the purposes of aiding those relatively rare individuals who have no recourse to family, friends, etc., in obtaining decent health care, education, and the like. Again, they are not *obligated* in justice to accept such taxation. But *may* they do so? It seems to me that they may, even if there is a minority of individuals who would not agree to such taxation, but who are "outvoted." For even this minority has an imperfect obligation to provide assistance; and while the usual reason for not enforcing imperfect obligations is that doing so would be impractical or draconian, that consideration does not seem to apply in this case. For the policy in question would not be like a policy of punishing rude people through force of law, which, far from making ordinary life more pleasant, would make it intolerable. The policy in question would simply be one of collecting a relatively small amount of extra tax money to aid a relatively small group of people in unusually difficult circumstances. That is surely workable.

A further possible justification of a right to assistance when in distress vis-à-vis health care and education would be to hold that such assistance falls under the "public good" that the state is obliged to provide for under natural law. The operative principle here is that of *subsidiarity,* according to which the more central authorities within a society should not carry out any functions that can be performed by the less central ones, though the more central authorities should carry out those that cannot be performed by the less central ones. To the extent that those in distress vis-à-vis health care and education simply have no other recourse, a right to assistance would arguably follow, if not from the Natural Law Proviso by itself, then at least from that proviso together with the classical natural law theory's conception of the state and its proper functions.

The *extent* of governmental assistance such a right would justify is another question, and here I will end with three points. First, what classical natural law theory strictly requires and strictly rules out in the way of practical policy is much less than many partisans of various political persuasions would like. What it strictly requires is a system of private property rights that are robust but not absolute. What it strictly rules out, accordingly, are socialism at one extreme and *laissez-faire* libertarianism at the other. Between these extremes, though, there is wide latitude for reasonable disagreement among classical natural law theorists about how best to apply their principles, and these disagreements can largely be settled only by appeal to prudential matters of economics, sociology, and practical politics rather than fundamental moral principle.

Second, it would be a mistake to conclude from this that a classical natural law theorist ought always to favor policies that fall exactly midway between these extremes. As any good Aristotelian knows, although any virtue is a mean between opposite extremes, one extreme can sometimes be a more serious deviation from virtue than the other is. Natural law theory takes the family to be the fundamental social unit, which puts it at odds with both the excessive individualism of the libertarian and the collectivism of the socialist. But the family is obviously closer to the level of the individual than it is to the level of the "community" or "society" as the socialist tends to understand those terms, namely, as referring to the entire population of a modern state. Furthermore, while classical natural law theory is concerned both with affirming the right to private property and with meeting the needs of those who lack resources of their own, there is a clear sense in which the former concern is analytically prior, at least where questions of justice (as opposed to charity) are concerned. For the theory starts by affirming the right to property and only afterward addresses the question of how that right might be limited. There is a presumption in favor of a person's having a right to what he owns even if that presumption can sometimes be overridden. In these ways, it seems clear that the classical natural law approach to property rights is at least somewhat closer to the libertarian or individualist end of the contemporary political spectrum than it is to the socialist or collectivist end.[66]

Third, it needs to be emphasized that the sort of assistance through taxation that I have countenanced here essentially involves *emergency aid to those in distress*, not only in cases where the Natural Law Proviso strictly requires such aid (e.g., for someone in danger of death by starvation) but also where it merely allows it or where the "public good" functions of government kick in (e.g., for someone unable to afford education or health care). It does *not* follow from this that government could legitimately provide education and health care to its citizens *in general*, either through cash payments funded via taxation or (even less plausibly) by directly providing educational and health services itself. While the issues involved here are complex, it seems clear that given its emphasis on private property, the independence of the family, and subsidiarity, there is at the very least a strong *presumption* implicit in classical natural law theory against the social democratic approach to these matters and in favor of private enterprise.

---

[66] This seems clear at least where questions of *economic justice* are concerned. On non-economic questions, most libertarians and socialists are probably equally distant from classical natural law theory. And where charity rather than justice is concerned, I suppose socialists might claim to be closer than libertarians are to classical natural law theory, though in my view it is by no means obvious that socialism is really motivated by charity.

VII. Conclusion

Though the devil is in the empirical details, then, the classical natural law approach to private property does give us substantial moral principles to guide our economic, sociological, and political-scientific inquiries. And in its essential conservatism, it is, I should think, exactly what we would expect from a theory rooted in Aristotelianism: A mean between extremes. Moderate. Unexciting. And true.

Philosophy, Pasadena City College

THE NATURAL RIGHT OF PROPERTY*

By Eric Mack

I. Introduction

In this essay, I defend the ascription to individuals of a natural, that is, original, nonacquired, right of property. I seek to build a case for such a right as one component within a plausible rights-oriented classical liberal doctrine. The signature natural right of any rights-oriented classical liberalism is the right of self-ownership. This is the original, nonacquired right of each individual to do as she sees fit with that which comprises her own person (e.g., her bodily parts, her mental faculties, her energy, and her skills).[1] Thus, my defense of the inclusion of a natural right of property within a plausible rights-oriented classical liberalism is a defense of affirming this natural right *along with* the natural right of self-ownership. I shall, in fact, maintain that we have the same good reasons for ascribing to each person a natural right of property as we have for ascribing to each person the natural right of self-ownership.[2] The reader will be on the right track if he or she suspects that the natural right of property is going to turn out to be something like an original, nonacquired right—possessed by each individual—to engage in the acquisition of extrapersonal objects and in the disposition of those acquired objects as one sees fit in the service of one's ends. A bit more strictly speaking, it is going to turn out

* This essay is a sequel to an earlier and quite different essay in which I also attempt to articulate and defend a natural right of property. See Eric Mack, "Self-Ownership and the Right of Property," *The Monist* 73, no. 4 (October 1990): 519–43. I thank Ellen Paul and the other contributors to this volume for their helpful comments on an earlier draft of this essay.

[1] In saying that natural rights are nonacquired rights, I mean that these rights are not acquired by any specific performance on the part of the right-holder and also are not acquired as the correlatives of obligations acquired by other parties through their specific performances. This is consistent with recognizing that we are, as Locke puts it, "born to" these rights, even though we are not "born in" them. As Locke sees it, we come into these rights as we come into rational agency. See John Locke, *Second Treatise of Government*, in *Two Treatises of Government*, ed. Peter Laslett (Cambridge: Cambridge University Press, 1960), section 55.

[2] In speaking of rights, I will at least for the most part be speaking of compounds of moral liberties and claim-rights. Bekah's self-ownership right is composed of (a) her moral liberty to do as she sees fit with that which makes up her person (her bodily parts, her energy, her skills), and (b) a claim-right against others' interfering with the exercise of that liberty. Correlative to that claim-right is an obligation on the part of others not to interfere with Bekah's exercise of that liberty. Similarly, Bekah's right to the acorn she has just picked up from the (unowned) forest floor is composed of (a) her moral liberty to do as she sees fit with that acorn, i.e., her having no obligations to others to dispose of the acorn in any particular way, and (b) a claim-right against others' interfering with her exercise of that moral liberty.

doi:10.1017/S0265052509990033
© 2010 Social Philosophy & Policy Foundation. Printed in the USA.

to be something like an original, nonacquired right *not to be precluded from* engaging in the acquisition and discretionary disposition of extrapersonal objects.[3]

In building the case for such a right, the key conjunction of intuitive ideas is that individuals have a basic moral claim—I shall refer to it as an ur-claim—to be allowed to pursue their own good in their own way, and that, since acquiring and exercising discretionary control over extra-personal objects is at least close to essential to agents' pursuing their own good in their own way, part of the proper codification of this ur-claim is the right of all agents not to be precluded from engaging in the acquisi-tion and discretionary disposal of extrapersonal objects. Such a natural right *of* property is not to be confused with a natural right *to* property— which would be an original, nonacquired right to some specific extra-personal objects or to some share of extrapersonal objects. A natural right *to* property—e.g., the natural right of joint ownership over the Earth— would be the sort of substantive right over extrapersonal objects which classical liberals hold can only exist as an acquired right, that is, as a right which has arisen through one or more agents' chosen interactions with the extrapersonal world. Thus, while this essay affirms a natural right *of* property, it denies that there is any *natural* right *to* property. (Classical liberals also deny the existence of any *acquired* right of joint ownership over the Earth; persons have not interacted with the extrapersonal world and each other in ways that would generate this right.)

My first main claim in this essay is that there is a natural right *of* property—or, more guardedly, the claim is that the reasons which support the affirmation of a natural right of self-ownership comparably support a natural right of property. There is a second main claim as well. This is that the natural right of property takes the form—or can take and has taken the form—of a right not to be precluded from participation in *a practice of private property* through which individuals can acquire and exercise dis-cretionary control over extrapersonal objects. Here the contrast is between what we may call the "inherent-feature conception" and the "practice conception" of how an agent's action generates a property right for that agent over some extrapersonal object. Under the inherent-feature concep-tion, any action that generates a property right for the actor in the extra-personal object with respect to which she has acted must have some inherent feature in virtue of which the actor acquires that property right. The most famous exemplification of an inherent-feature conception is found in John Locke's account of the generation of (initial) property rights in extrapersonal objects. According to that account—which we shall con-sider a bit more, shortly—each rights-generating action has the inherent

[3] Jerry Gaus has provided me with the interesting suggestion that the natural right of property is, even more strictly speaking, a Hohfeldian natural normative power to make things one's own.

feature of being labor-mixing; and it is in virtue of this feature that each such action generates a right over the object with respect to which the agent has labor-mixed. Under a practice conception, actions that generate property rights for the actor may do so in virtue of their being actions of the sort which a justified practice of property specifies as rights-generating. Here the right-generating force of the action descends from the practice and the practice's justification, rather than arising from some feature inherent in the action. Practices are themselves artifacts. A practice of private property is a device that extends the ways in which agents can, through their actions, generate property rights. Because any practice of private property is a body of conventions, and numerous different bodies of conventions may be justified as devices for extending the ways in which agents can, through their actions, generate property rights, the practice conception can accommodate the fact that the ways in which agents can establish property rights are highly conventional.[4] My hope is that this all ties together because it is the natural right of property which requires that individuals not be precluded from participating in a practice of private property and which ultimately explains why individuals who are deprived of particular extrapersonal objects that they have acquired in accord with the rules of a practice of private property are wronged by that deprivation.

I attempt to defend these two main contentions with a series of inter-connected and (I hope) mutually supportive lines of argument. First, in Section II, I offer a sketch of a top-down argument for a really basic moral claim—a moral ur-claim—on behalf of each individual against all other individuals (and groupings of individuals) to be allowed to live her own life in her own chosen way, to be free of interferences by those individuals (or groupings) which prevent her from exercising her capacities as she sees fit in the pursuit of her own ends. I argue that this ur-claim or the reasons we have for accepting it support both the natural right of self-ownership and the natural right of property. Given what is involved in the human endeavor of living one's life and exercising one's capacities in the pursuit of one's ends—namely, purposive action in and through the world of extrapersonal objects—the right of self-ownership articulates only some of the implications of the ur-claim to be allowed to live one's own life in one's own way. I maintain that the natural right of property articulates further implications of our ur-claim to live our world-interactive

---

[4] I shall be focusing throughout on *initial* acquired property rights, not rights that one acquires through the transfer of objects that, until the transfer, are the property of others. As we move along, I shall not bother to repeat the "initial." My case against an inherent-feature account of property rights and for a practice account would be strengthened if we were to look at which sort of account better deals with rights-conveying *transfers* of already right-fully held extrapersonal objects. I should add that, in speaking of individuals' acquired property rights, I do not at all intend to rule out various associations of individuals—e.g., communes, unions, firms, or churches—as possible possessors of such rights. I am simply taking ordinary workaday individuals as the paradigm possessors.

lives free of disruptive interference. As an indication that the codification of this ur-claim involves more than a natural right of self-ownership, I point to the natural right to have promises that have been made to one and contracts that have been made with one kept as a further part of the articulation of that ur-claim. Indeed, I draw upon the idea that in a number of important ways the natural right of property stands to particular acquired rights to property as the natural right to have promises and contracts kept stands to particular acquired promissory and contractual rights.

Second, in Sections III and IV, I seek to employ Locke—our prime historical exemplar of a self-ownership-affirming classical liberal—first as an ally and then as a foil, to advance my main contentions. Section III provides a very stylized statement of Locke's case for ascribing natural rights to individuals. I maintain that the implications of the reasons Locke presents are only partly codified in a natural right of self-ownership. In addition, I argue that Locke himself takes a further implication of his reasoning about persons' basic moral claims to be that persons have natural rights against being precluded from making portions of the Earth their own. As is well known, Locke *says* that God has given the Earth "to mankind in common." [5] However, as I discuss further in Section III, Locke immediately sets out to explain why he does not mean that there is anything like original joint-ownership of the Earth. That is, he does not mean to assert that there is a (substantive) natural right *to* property. As we shall see, especially when we look at Locke's discussion (in his infrequently read *First Treatise of Government*) of why the natural right of joint-ownership is to be rejected, Locke disavows this natural right *to* property precisely because it would sanction precluding individuals from making portions of the Earth their own. Moreover, I suggest that Locke's affirmation of this additional natural right *of* property comports well with his basic endorsement of the propriety of each individual's pursuing his own happiness and self-preservation through the employment of his own person and the natural materials which stand available for human use. In short, I argue that the reasons Locke offers for natural rights support both a right of self-ownership and a natural right *of* property, and that Locke actually appeals to the latter right in his most extensive discussion of why there is no natural right *to* property.

In Section IV, however, I turn from Locke as ally to Locke as foil. In this section, I recount Locke's labor-mixing conception of the creation of property rights and argue that it provides the correct explanation only of a special subset of acquired property rights. I maintain that the crucial defect of this account is precisely that it directs us to search for some inherent feature whose presence in each action we judge to be rights-generating explains why that action is rights-generating. In contrast, I

---

[5] Locke, *Second Treatise*, section 25.

advance a practice conception of property according to which specific actions generate rights to extrapersonal objects by being actions in accord with the rules of a justified practice of private property. A property right is generated not in virtue of a feature inherent in the action, but rather by the action's being an appropriate move within a justified practice. Crucial to the justification of any practice of private property, and to individuals' having rights to what they have acquired in accordance with the rules of the practice, is people's natural right to such a practice of private property—or more guardedly, people's natural right not to be precluded from participating in such a practice, should a practice be available. In short, I argue that the deficiencies in Locke's labor-mixing account support the adoption of the practice conception rather than the inherent-feature conception of rights-generating action.

Sections II and IV appeal to the idea of a practice of private property and to a practice conception of rights-generating acquisitions. The idea is that, through the creation of rule-constituted practices of private property, individuals are enabled to transcend the limitations of natural (e.g., labor-mixing) rights-generating acquisition of extrapersonal objects. A practice of private property is an artificial means that expands the capacity of individuals to gain morally protected possession of and discretionary control over portions of the extrapersonal world. My focus on the *practice* of private property and my appeal to certain parallels between the practice of private property and the practice of promising suggests a type of account of particular property rights and particular promissory rights which is in competition with my own. According to this competing "social practice" account, the rights and correlative obligations that arise when individuals interact under the aegis of a rule-constituted practice are to be explained entirely by the rules of that practice; the rights and correlative obligations that arise are not (even in part) to be explained by some independent, natural norm which itself stands outside of and supplies normative significance to the practice. Thus, for example, the promissory right that arises when Josh promises Bekah that he will supply her with a fried turkey, is generated by their interactions within the *game* of promising. We do not have to appeal to any freestanding norm—namely, a principle of fidelity or a natural right to have promises made to one kept—in order to explain the rise of Josh's promissory obligation to Bekah. Similarly, the friend of social practice accounts will hold that particular property rights that arise through individuals' engagement within a practice of property are not at all to be explained in terms of any freestanding natural right of property. Thus, the social practice response concludes, my appeal to practice undermines my affirmation of such a natural right of property. Hence, in Section V, I must myself undermine the social practice view. If I can do that, I can use the premise that property rights do arise through individuals' engagement in a practice of private property, conjoined with the premise that such rights arise only because some independent, natural norm supplies normative force to the results of that practice, to conclude that there is a natural right of property.[6]

II. The Individualist Ur-Claim and the Natural Right of Property

Let us survey at least some of the underlying considerations that rights-oriented classical liberals give—or should give—for affirming an original right of self-ownership. Rights-oriented classical liberalism depends, I believe, on an embrace of a robust form of moral individualism. Crucial to that individualism is the thesis that each person's good is the ultimate rational end of that individual's actions. As far as goal-rationality is concerned, each person's good is that which she is rational to promote. (This is consistent with one individual's good or aspects of one individual's good being partially constitutive of another individual's good.) The moral individualist starts here with the most noncontentious claim about practical rationality—namely, that individuals have reason to promote their utility—while avoiding contentiously narrow conceptions of what an individual's utility consists in. Moral individualism takes seriously the separateness of persons. It does this not merely by denying that there is some supra-individual "social entity" whose good is the object of rational social principles, but also, and more importantly, by denying that any sort of concatenation of the good of individuals constitutes a common substantive end which individuals at large have reason to serve even at the cost of their own individual good. There is, according to this moral individualism, no common substantive end—no "higher" good—for the sake of which it is rational for individuals to sacrifice their own well-being.

However, it does not follow from *Bekah's* having good reason not to impose losses on herself to advance the good of others or her having no obligation to impose such losses on herself, that Bekah is *wronged* by others when *they* impose losses on her which she is not obligated to impose upon herself. To hold that Bekah is wronged by others when they impose such losses upon her—that is, to hold that some principle of (natural) rights or (natural) justice protects her against such impositions—is to go well beyond the assertion that each individual has good reason not to impose such losses upon herself and even the assertion that each has good goal-oriented reason to resist the imposition of losses on her by others. It is to go from the moral individualist's central contention about the good (that each individual has a good of his or her own which he or she has reason to promote) to his central contention about the right (that

---

[6] For attempts at a similar move from promissory or contractual rights to natural rights, see H. L. A. Hart, "Are There Any Natural Rights?" reprinted in Jeremy Waldron, ed., *Theories of Rights* (Oxford: Oxford University Press, 1984), 77–90; and Eric Mack, "Natural and Contractual Rights," *Ethics* 87, no. 2 (January 1977): 153–59.

each individual has claims against others not to be interfered with, in certain ways, in the course of his or her value pursuits). The crucial and difficult task for a moral individualism which includes interpersonal constraints on how individuals may treat others in the course of their pursuit of their own ends is to explain how the affirmation of such constraints is supported by—albeit, not entailed by—each individual's having in her own well-being an ultimate rational end of her own.

Here is one way in which lines of support might run. That other persons also have rational ends of their own to which they sensibly devote their actions, capacities, and lives is a striking (normative) fact which marks other persons off from objects like (unowned) sharp pieces of stone or (unowned) acorns which one sensibly views as means available for one's own use in the advancement of one's own ends. It would be odd for this sort of striking fact about others not to have *some sort* of directive import for oneself—just as it would be odd for the fact that one has ultimate rational ends of one's own not to have *some sort* of directive import for others. It would be odd if the fact that other persons have ends of their own which they are rational to promote did not itself matter to one—if it did not itself make a difference with respect to how it is reasonable to conduct oneself in one's interactions with others. After all, it seems that reasonable conduct toward entities of a certain sort has to reflect or be marked by cognizance of the striking and distinguishing facts about entities of that sort. Yet the difference made in how one has reason to conduct oneself toward others by the fact that they also have rational ends of their own cannot plausibly be seen as due to their ends standing alongside one's own ends as objects of one's rational promotion. For those ends are *their* (respective) rational ends—not one's own; and, as ends for those others, they are not imbued with an agent-neutral value which summons all rational agents to their promotion. What, then, is left as a sensible reflection in one's conduct toward others of the fact that they are beings with rational ends of their own? What is left is one's eschewing treating these other value-seeking beings as though they are—as lots of other entities are—material which one is morally at liberty to employ for one's own purposes. These beings do not stand as morally available means to one's own ends. The appropriate fundamental *interpersonal* regulative norm for a kingdom of beings each of whom has in his own well-being an ultimate end of his own—and, thus, is a normatively independent being—calls upon each of us to respect the independence of others by allowing others to live their own lives—to pursue their own ends—in their own chosen ways. This is the ur-claim on behalf of each individual against all other individuals (and groupings of individuals) to be allowed to live her own life in her own chosen way, to be free of interferences by those individuals (or groupings) which prevent her from exercising her capacities as she sees fit in the pursuit of her own ends.

Here is a slightly different tracing of lines of support. A first step toward morality taking seriously the separateness of persons is its affirming for each person a moral liberty not to volunteer for subjugation to the ends of others, that is, a moral prerogative not to impose sacrifices on oneself for the sake of others' ends. But the affirmation of a *bare* liberty not to volunteer for subjugation—a *naked* prerogative not to impose sacrifices on oneself for the sake of others' ends—leaves each other agent morally at liberty to impose such subjugation (or sacrifices) upon one. Moreover, each one of us is pervasively vulnerable to others exercising this prospective moral liberty to subordinate us to their purposes, that is, to impose sacrifices upon us to advance their ends. For these reasons, a morality that takes only that first step of affirming a liberty or prerogative not to subordinate oneself to the ends of others advances hardly at all toward genuinely taking seriously the separateness of persons. If morality is to make a significant advance in taking seriously the separateness of persons, a second step is required: namely, the inclusion within that morality of *constraints* against others' interference with one's exercise of that liberty or prerogative. A morality will genuinely take seriously the separateness of persons only if it clothes the liberty or prerogative it ascribes to each individual not to subordinate himself to the ends of others with a moral claim against others' precluding his exercise of that liberty or prerogative. This is our now familiar ur-claim to be allowed to live one's life in one's own chosen way.

The natural right of self-ownership is part of the articulation or codification of this ur-claim. Since it is one's person which has rational ends of its own, one's person is excluded from the set of objects which are (or at least begin as) morally available as means to others' ends. A moral liberty of doing as one sees fit with one's own person—a liberty that others are obligated to respect—is central to a moral code that takes its cue from the claim of each individual to be allowed to live her own life in her own chosen way. Perhaps everything necessary to a full articulation of the ur-claim could be inserted (shoe-horned?) into a capacious characterization of this right of self-ownership. This would be one way of dividing (or not dividing) things; and I am not unalterably set against such a project. Nonetheless, I am inclined to think that we get a clearer picture of the range of implications of the reasons which support a non-capacious right of self-ownership if we do not insist that each of these implications is part of an all-encompassing right of self-ownership. Clarity may be served by restricting what we understand an agent's right of self-ownership to be to that agent's right over that which comprises his person, while recognizing additional rights of the agent that share an underlying rationale with that noncapaciously conceived right of self-ownership.

Consider this well-known passage from Isaiah Berlin's "Two Concepts of Liberty," which offers an argument quite similar to my first tracing of the case for the ur-claim to be allowed to live one's own life in one's own way:

> [T]o lie to men, or to deceive them, that is to use them as means for my, not their own, independently conceived ends, even if it is for their own benefit, is, in effect, to treat them as sub-human, to behave as if their ends are less ultimate and sacred than my own. In the name of what can I ever be justified in forcing men to do what they have not willed or consented to? Only in the name of some value higher than themselves. But . . . there is no value higher than the individual. Therefore to do this is to coerce men in the name of something less ultimate than themselves—to bend them to my will, or to someone else's particular craving for (his or their) happiness or expedience or security or convenience. I am aiming at something desired (from whatever motive, no matter how noble) by me or my group, to which I am using other men as means. But this is a contradiction of what I know men to be, namely ends in themselves.[7]

The ultimacy of the value available within each individual life makes it unreasonable—in "contradiction" to the facts—for anyone to use other men as means. Although it departs from terminology with which Berlin would feel comfortable, it does no substantive violence to Berlin's passage to say that one implication of its argument is a right of self-ownership. No man is a means to any other man's ends—although each is a means (is morally available to himself as a means) to his own ends.

Yet the passage takes off from the fairly specific intuition that individuals have a (natural) claim against being lied to and deceived. Moreover, this apparent right against being lied to or deceived is part of what the passage seeks to justify as another part, one might say, of the codification of the really basic claim of each individual against being subordinated to the will of others. My point here is threefold: (1) Something like a right not to be lied to or deceived is an implication of the arguments that Berlin and I offer. (2) Something like a right of self-ownership is an implication of these same arguments. (3) There is no good reason to attempt to subsume the right not to be lied to or deceived under the right of self-ownership. One can be precluded from living one's own life in one's own way by being deprived of discretionary control over the elements that comprise one's person. One can *also* be precluded from living one's own life in one's own way by being lied to or deceived. One reason it is important to be prepared to see distinguishable ways in which persons can be precluded from living their own lives in their own chosen ways is that this opens the door to seeing that being precluded from acquiring and exercising discretionary control over extrapersonal objects is another

---

[7] Isaiah Berlin, *Four Essays on Liberty* (Oxford: Oxford University Press, 1969), 137.

way of having one's claim to be allowed to live one's own life in one's own way violated. Precluding Bekah from acquiring and enjoying discretionary control over extrapersonal objects infringes upon her claim to live her life in her own chosen way because, for human beings (of which Bekah is one), life is lived through the acquisition, transformation, and utilization of extrapersonal objects.

Insofar as one adopts the practice conception of rights-generation—in contrast to the inherent-feature conception—one will cast the natural right of property as the original, nonacquired right not to be precluded from participation in a rule-constituted practice through which entitlements to extrapersonal objects are acquired (and transferred and relinquished, etc.). Given the right of self-ownership, however, that natural right of property cannot be a positive right that others must deliver such a practice to one if such a practice is not already available to one. For the natural right of self-ownership rules out persons' being born to positive obligations to deliver goods or services or desirable practices to others. Individuals who found themselves in an environment bereft of a practice of private property and who could create such a practice would violate no right of one of their number who yearned to participate in a practice of private property if they simply sat around and twiddled their thumbs instead of constructing the yearned-for practice. If the yearner had a right to have such a practice be made available to him, that right would forbid those thumb-twiddling individuals from exercising their self-ownership.

Three premises connect the ur-claim that each individual is to be allowed to live her own life in her own chosen way with this natural right of property. The first of these is that almost all human life, almost all human goal-pursuit, takes place in and through the purposive acquisition, transformation, and utilization of objects in the extrapersonal world. We are not merely embodied beings; we are beings whose lives are mostly lived in and through the physical world that exists beyond the outer surface of our skin. The second premise is that individuals' living their own lives in their own chosen ways in and through the purposive utilization of objects in the extrapersonal world is greatly facilitated by their acquiring and exercising ongoing assured discretionary control over extrapersonal objects—in contrast to individuals' having merely a liberty temporarily to put objects to use. The third premise is that the possibilities for individuals' acquiring and exercising ongoing assured discretionary control over extrapersonal objects is greatly extended by the presence of a rule-constituted practice of private property. A practice of private property is an artificial extension of the means available to individuals to acquire, enjoy, and exercise discretionary control over portions of the extrapersonal world.

I should add that I do not mean here to suggest that, when such a rule-constituted practice of private property arises, it does so through people's intentionally constructing it. Rather, such practices are characteristically collations of evolving customs, conventions, and judicial rulings which tend to survive and be reinforced by their (typically only dimly perceived) tendency to enable people with their own ends and ambitions to live peacefully and productively with one another. Such practices are the results of human action, but not of human design. They are artifacts, just as practices of promising or contracting are. But we will be misled if we think that such artifacts must appear—or even typically do appear—as anyone's or any group's foreseen invention.[8]

Rule-constituted practices of private property will vary in how successfully they fulfill their function of creating an environment in which individuals can (more readily) acquire, enjoy, and exercise discretionary control over (and transfer and relinquish, etc.) extrapersonal objects. We can identify several features of such a practice that will contribute to its fulfilling this function. The practice will be *coherent* insofar as the entitlements generated by acting in accordance with its rules are compossible. It will be *transparent* insofar as the entitlements generated under it can be readily identified. It will be *comprehensive* insofar as it facilitates the establishment of private rights over all extrapersonal objects (except for those objects, if any, which are not appropriate candidates for private ownership). A more moralistic and difficult to formulate feature is that the practice must be *inclusive*. All persons must be equally eligible to participate in the practice. I will say—with somewhat less than total precision—that a practice of private property is *justifiable* if and only if it instantiates these features to a reasonably acceptable extent. The more precise formulation of the natural right of property under consideration is that it is a right not to be precluded from participation in a justifiable practice of private property. Of course, the maintenance of one justifiable practice will preclude individuals from participation in *other* justifiable practices that might be instituted. *That* sort of precluding will not count as a violation of the right not to be precluded from participation in a justifiable practice of private property.[9]

We may anticipate that the right not to be precluded from living under a justifiable rule-constituted practice of private property would be subject to violation at two quite different levels. At the more general level, individuals would suffer violations of this right if they were precluded from establishing such a practice or from entering into participation in such an established practice. At the more specific level, individuals who have entered into the practice—for example, by acquiring extrapersonal objects

---

[8] The only barrier to thinking of such rules as legal rules is the mistaken tendency to think that legal rules have to arise via legislation, that law requires a (legislating) lawmaker. For the classic rejection of this view and defense of the view that systems of law emerge unintended from custom, convention, and judicial rulings, see F. A. Hayek, *Law, Legislation, and Liberty, Volume 1, Rules and Order* (Chicago: University of Chicago Press, 1973).

[9] A practice will realize the features that make it justifiable *to a reasonably acceptable extent* only if there is not another practice that could be instituted (given the world as it actually is) that would realize those features to a significantly greater extent.

in accordance with the rules of the practice—would suffer violations of this right if they were treated by others in ways that violated rules of the practice—for example, if those objects were taken from them. Alternatively, in these cases, we might more naturally say that the individual's acquired property right to that extrapersonal object would be violated; but we must appeal to the individual's natural right not to be precluded from participation in a justifiable practice of private property to explain the existence of that individual's acquired property right. (Recall my intention to consider and reject the social practice view.)

III. Locke on Natural Rights and the Natural Right to the Earth

Locke's own arguments for ascribing original, nonacquired rights to persons is at least highly congruent with the lines of argument traced above in support of the ur-claim on behalf of each individual that he be allowed to live his own life in his own chosen way.[10] On Locke's view, although everyone's happiness is, in some abstract sense, part of the good, each individual's own happiness is the part of the good that he is rational to promote.[11] Each individual can, therefore, be said to exist for purposes of his own; and, in this strong sense, no individual exists for any other individual's purpose. We are not merely naturally morally equal; we are all by nature morally "equal and independent" agents.[12] For Locke, this implies not merely that no individual is naturally required to submit to subordination to others, but also that others are naturally required not to subordinate that individual to themselves. It is not merely that each individual is naturally at liberty to decline to volunteer for (and naturally at liberty to resist) subordination to the will of others; it is, further, that others are naturally obligated not to dispose of this individual for their purposes—"as if we were made for one another's uses."[13] That Bekah is an equal and independent being who exists for her own purposes does not merely defeat the proposition that Josh has a *right* to subordinate her to his (noble or ignoble) ends; it also defeats the proposition that Josh is *at liberty* to treat her in this way. Thus, Josh is obligated not to treat her in this way and, correlatively, Bekah has a right—a right founded on her natural equality and independence—against the subordination of her person to the will of Josh (and all others).

---

[10] In this discussion, I pass by many complications in the explication of Locke—including his assertion that we are all the property of God and, ultimately, exist for God's purposes. For a discussion of some of these complications, see chapters 2 and 3 of my *John Locke* (London: Continuum Publishing, 2009).

[11] John Locke, *An Essay Concerning Human Understanding*, ed. A. C. Fraser (New York: Dover, 1959), book II, p. 341.

[12] Locke, *Second Treatise*, section 6.

[13] Ibid.

It may well be that the implications of this argument—similar as this argument is to the arguments traced in my previous section—are only partially codified in a natural right of self-ownership. It is noteworthy that when Locke presents his main arguments for natural rights in chapter II of the *Second Treatise,* he formulates his conclusion more broadly, and not specifically in the language of self-ownership. He tells us instead that "no one ought to harm another in his Life, Health, Liberty, or Possessions,"[14] and that no one may "unless it be to do Justice on an Offender, take away, or impair the life, or what tends to the Preservation of the Life, the Liberty, Health, Limb, or Goods of another."[15] The presence of "Possessions" and "Goods" in these formulations is especially striking since Locke has not yet presented his famous labor-mixing theory of rights to extrapersonal possessions and goods. Perhaps this provides some basis for thinking that we can read into Locke some sort of a *natural* right with respect to external holdings—a right that is reflective of the necessary role of extrapersonal objects in the human pursuit of happiness and self-preservation.[16]

In addition, we should note an explicit way in which Locke does not hold that the right of self-ownership is the one and only natural right. Almost in passing, Locke affirms an original, nonacquired right of persons to have promises made to them and contracts made with them kept: "For Truth and keeping of Faith belongs to Men, as Men, and not as Members of Society."[17] It seems to be in virtue of this natural claim that specific promises and contracts that men make with one another are binding in the state of nature. It is because of this background right that the contracts men make to exit the state of nature have binding force. Since the breaking of promises or contracts, like acts of lying and deceit, are ways of subordinating others to one's own purposes, it seems likely that the right not to be subjected to such treatment can be taken to be a further implication of the arguments that also yield the right of self-ownership.

Locke goes on to offer an account of the rise of acquired rights over extrapersonal objects. A necessary background presumption of Locke's account of rightful initial appropriation by individuals is that the Earth itself—the totality of raw materials that stand before mankind—is origi-

---

[14] Ibid.

[15] Ibid.

[16] Elsewhere in the *Second Treatise* (section 57), Locke offers an important argument against the (Hobbesian) view that our moral freedom consists just in our moral liberties. Locke argues to the contrary that any moral freedom worth its salt requires that others be morally excluded from suppressing one's exercise of one's moral liberties. ("For who would be free, when every other Man's Humour might domineer over him?") When Locke formulates the conclusion of this argument, we get the very broad claim that each man's natural liberty is "a *Liberty* to dispose, and order as he list, his Person, Actions, *Possessions, and his whole Property,* within the Allowance of those Laws under which he is, and therein not to be subject to the arbitrary Will of another, but freely to follow his own" (emphasis added).

[17] Locke, *Second Treatise,* section 14.

nally unowned, and hence available for individual use and appropria-tion. This seems to be a reasonable enough starting-point; for the burden of proof seems to rest on those who would assert that persons do have nonacquired rights over this raw material. However, Locke puts himself in a position from which he has to argue against at least one version of the proposition that there is an original, nonacquired right to the Earth. Locke's explicit target throughout the *Two Treatises of Government* was the author-itarian doctrines of Sir Robert Filmer;[18] and one of the important claims advanced by Filmer was that Adam, through donation from God, was the original (human) owner of all the Earth. When Locke sums up his argu-ments against this claim by Filmer, he does so by saying that God has given the Earth not to Adam but, rather, to mankind in common.[19] That is, in his eagerness to oppose Filmer, Locke *seems* to accept the view that there is a natural right of joint-ownership over the Earth. This appearance creates a serious problem for Locke qua champion of individual owner-ship because he accepts the entirety of the following argument offered by Filmer.[20]

(1) If the Earth is originally jointly owned by all mankind, then unanimous consent among those owners is necessary for any individual ownership of portions of the Earth to arise.
(2) No such unanimous consent among mankind has ever occurred or is ever going to occur.
(3) Therefore, if the Earth is originally jointly owned by mankind, no individual ownership of portions of the Earth has ever arisen or will ever arise.

In *seeming* to affirm original joint-ownership, then, Locke *seems* to commit himself to the idea that no individual ownership of portions of the Earth has ever arisen or will ever arise.

To get around this problem, Locke has to argue against the proposition that the Earth is originally jointly owned by mankind. Then he can say that, of course, he cannot reasonably be construed as meaning *that* when he says that God gave the Earth to all mankind in common.[21] Indeed, he must be construed as simply meaning that "no body has originally a private Dominion, exclusive of the rest of Mankind, in any of [the extra-personal objects], as they are thus in their natural state."[22] In the *Second*

[18] See Sir Robert Filmer, *Patriarcha and Other Writings* (1680), ed. Johann Sommerville (Cambridge: Cambridge University Press, 1991). Locke's sustained critique of Filmer is, of course, to be found in the surviving portion of Locke's *First Treatise* in his *Two Treatises of Government*.
[19] Locke, *Second Treatise*, section 25, and *First Treatise*, section 40.
[20] Filmer, *Patriarcha*, 234.
[21] Locke also has to go on to give an account of the appearance of property rights which does not depend on consent. See Locke, *Second Treatise*, section 25.
[22] Ibid., section 26.

Treatise, Locke argues that given the correctness of Filmer's argument, if all individuals were joint-owners of the Earth, then "Man [would have] starved, notwithstanding the Plenty God has given him."[23] That is to say, everyone who would behave with propriety (i.e., who would abide by others' joint-ownership rights) would have to simply sit and starve.[24] For Locke, this reduces the joint-ownership thesis to absurdity. For each individual with propriety pursues his self-preservation; and each at least typically pursues his self-preservation through the use or appropriation of a portion of "the Plenty" God has given to man. The positive claim Locke seems to be making here is that, given the propriety of each man's pursuit of self-preservation and the necessity of using or appropriating portions of nature in order to achieve self-preservation, each man must be *at liberty* to use or appropriate a portion of the Earth; since each must have this natural liberty to use or appropriate without asking leave of or being subject to the will of others, there cannot be an original joint-ownership of the Earth. Hence, again, Locke's statement that God gave the Earth to all mankind in common cannot be meant to assert the original joint-ownership of the Earth.

Locke's more extensive discussion in his *First Treatise* of man's original normative relationship with nature is cast in terms of a *right* of self-preservation and a consequent *right*—not merely a *liberty*—of men to use the "Creatures" which have been presented to them. (Locke speaks of rights to "Creatures" because he is tracking Filmer's presentation, which is cast largely in terms of God's purported donation to Adam of all the *Creatures* of the Earth.) Presenting matters in terms of God's plan for how human life should be conducted, Locke points to the "strong desire of self-preservation" which God has planted in man and to God's having "furnished the World with things fit for Food and Rayment and other Necessaries of Life." All this evinces God's design "that Man should live and abide for some time upon the Face of the Earth [and not] perish . . . after a few moments continuance."[25] Because men with propriety pursue self-preservation through the use or appropriation of the raw materials furnished to them, "Man had a right to a use of the Creatures. . . ."[26] And here it is because men have *a right* to a use of these creatures—and the fruits of the Earth and portions of the Earth—that there cannot be an original joint-ownership which would morally preclude the exercise of that right.

The remainder of section 86 from the *First Treatise* deserves to be quoted in full for its affirmation of a natural right with respect to extrapersonal objects:

[23] Ibid., section 28.
[24] Of course, even remaining on the spot one finds oneself on would be a violation of others' joint-ownership rights.
[25] Locke, *First Treatise,* section 86.
[26] Ibid.

> For the desire, strong desire of Preserving Life and Being having been Planted in him, as a Principle of Action by God himself, Reason, *which was the Voice of God in him,* could not but teach him and assure him, that pursuing that natural Inclination he had to preserve his Being, he followed the Will of his Maker, and *therefore had a right to make use of those Creatures,* which by his Reason or Senses he could discover would be serviceable thereunto. And *thus Man's Property in the Creatures was founded upon the right he had, to make use of those things, that were necessary or useful to his Being.*[27]

Locke repeats this claim in the next two sections. In section 88, he tells us: "The first and strongest desire God Planted in Men, and wrought into the very Principles of their Nature being that of Self-preservation, that is the Foundation of a right to the Creatures, for the particular support and use of each individual Person himself." In section 87, we are told that all individuals have "an equal right to the use of the inferior Creatures, for the comfortable preservation of their Beings . . ." and that "Every Man has a right to the Creatures, by the same Title *Adam* had, *viz.,* by the right every one had to take care of and provide for their Subsistence. . . ."

However, it seems that if the right to the creatures (or other raw materials) is an emanation of the right of each individual "to take care of and provide for their Subsistence," the former right must be a right not to be prevented from acquiring and retaining some creature (or other raw material), rather than a right to some specific creature (or raw material) or some share of creatures (or raw materials). Furthermore, no such natural right *to* property would be compatible with Locke's claim that "no body has originally a private Dominion, exclusive of the rest of Mankind, in any of [the extrapersonal objects], as they are thus in their natural state."[28] Nor does Locke give any indication that he thinks the natural right with respect to raw materials that he asserts in the *First Treatise* involves anyone's having a natural nonacquired property in any particular thing or share of things. Rather, and very strikingly, in section 87 of the *First Treatise* he tells us that it "shall be shewn in another place"—obviously, the property chapter of the *Second Treatise*—how an individual can make "himself a Property in any particular thing." Thus, the natural right with respect to property which we have in virtue of our right to pursue "comfortable preservation" must be a right not to be blocked from acquiring and retaining discretionary control over extrapersonal objects. We have that right not to be precluded from making things our own as an emanation of our right to pursue comfortable preservation, because beings like ourselves at least typically need to acquire and exercise control over

---

[27] Ibid.; emphasis added on the phrase "therefore had a right to make use of those Creatures," and in the last sentence of the quotation.

[28] Locke, *Second Treatise,* section 26.

extrapersonal "things fit for Food and Rayment and other Necessaries of Life" in order to advance our comfortable preservation.

Thus, on the standard reading of Locke, in virtue of the propriety of each individual's pursuit of comfortable preservation, each individual has a natural *liberty* to use and appropriate raw material, while on the reading which attends to Locke's *First Treatise* passages, in virtue of that propriety, each individual has a natural *right* to use and appropriate raw material. What difference, if any, does this difference make? And, if it does make a difference, does that difference provide a reason to affirm the bolder *First Treatise* assertion?

Imagine a number of hunter-gatherers who are endowed with rights of self-ownership and a *liberty* of using or appropriating natural materials, and who are hunting and gathering in an area furnished "with things fit for Food and Rayment and other Necessaries of Life." Let us presume that there are no violations of self-ownership (or of the right to have promises kept) among these hunter-gatherers. And, more directly on point, let us presume that none of the uses and (minor) appropriations of raw material engaged in by any of these hunter-gatherers affects what is available for the use and (minor) appropriation of others. Perhaps this is because each individual's use or appropriation is like one individual taking a drink out of a river. "No man could think himself injured by the drinking of another man, though he took a good draught, who had a whole river of the same water left to quench his thirst." [29]

Now suppose a scientifically advanced and malicious Trickster comes along and simply sprays every bit of raw material with a coating that makes it impossible for any of our hunter-gatherers to use or appropriate the material. If, in addition to their rights of self-ownership and promise-fulfillment, the hunter-gatherers have only a natural liberty to use or appropriate raw material, then the Trickster does not wrong them. For that natural liberty would only be a matter of no one else's having a natural right over that raw material which morally precludes the hunter-gatherers from its use or appropriation. There is no violation or denial of their natural liberty in the Trickster's exercise of his liberty to spray the coating on all that raw material. The Trickster's spraying does not take away this natural liberty from the hunter-gatherers; it only (!) precludes them from engaging in uses or appropriations. Nor (it seems) does the Trickster's action violate any right of self-ownership possessed by the hunter-gatherers. For the Trickster is very careful not to trespass upon their persons. He fastidiously avoids expropriating any of their bodily parts or skills or self-owned labor. If, nevertheless, one thinks that the Trickster does wrong the hunter-gatherers through his precluding them from engaging in any use or appropriation of the raw material, one has to think that these individuals are also endowed with a natural right *of*

---

[29] Ibid., section 33.

property, that is, a natural right not to be precluded from acquiring and exercising discretionary control over portions of previously unowned material.[30] Since it is reasonable to think that the Trickster wrongs them, it is reasonable to think that the hunter-gatherers (and, hence, people at large) are endowed with this further natural right.

Actually, the argument by way of this example proceeds too quickly. However, correcting for this will enhance the case for the natural right of property. The argument proceeds too quickly because it ignores an alternative *Lockean* explanation for the wrong done by the Trickster. This is that the Trickster violates the Lockean proviso, which requires that one leave "enough, and as good" for others.[31] So this wrong is to be explained on the basis of the validity of such a proviso, rather than on the basis of a natural right of property.[32] To slip past this difficulty, we need a Trickster who does not violate this proviso but still wrongs individuals in a way that is best described as a violation of their natural right of property. Let us return, then, to our hunter-gatherers and allow them to proceed merrily in their hunter-gatherer ways. This includes the presumption, which we already made above, that among themselves these agents do not violate the Lockean proviso. Whatever use or (minor) appropriation any one of them engages in is like taking that draught from the river. But now suppose that some of these individuals set themselves to move beyond hunting and gathering to an agricultural existence. It is this move, as Locke realized, which marks the transition from a world that is pretty much innocent of property to a world that is chock-full of property. As Locke points out, the movement of individuals (or households) from non-propertied hunter-gatherer existence to propertied agricultural existence does not pose the threat of violating the "enough, and as good" proviso. For individuals (or households) seeking comfortable preservation by way of a propertied agricultural existence need less in the way of raw materials—especially less land—than do individuals (or households) seeking comfortable preservation by way of a non-propertied hunter-gatherer existence. "And therefore he that incloses land, and has a greater plenty of the conveniences of life from ten acres, than he could have from a hundred left in nature, may truly be said to give ninety acres to mankind. . . ."[33]

---

[30] A trickier Trickster might allow individuals to acquire extrapersonal objects and then spray them with a coating that makes their disposition uncontrollable.

[31] Locke, *Second Treatise*, section 33.

[32] I shall not pause here to investigate where precisely such a proviso might fit into a rights-oriented classical liberal doctrine. I examine this issue in Eric Mack, "The Self-Ownership Proviso: A New and Improved Lockean Proviso," *Social Philosophy and Policy* 12, no. 1 (1995): 186–218; and in section 5 of Mack, "Self-Ownership, Marxism, and Equality: Part I," *Politics, Philosophy, and Economics* 1, no. 1 (February 2002): 75–108, and section 3 of Mack, "Self-Ownership, Marxism, and Equality: Part II," *Politics, Philosophy, and Economics* 1, no. 2 (June 2002): 237–76.

[33] Locke, *Second Treatise*, section 37.

Suppose that the Trickster steps in now with a modified device which sprays whatever raw material any aspiring agriculturalist sets out to acquire as property with a coating that renders it unfit for that agent's use. (The coating does not prevent hunter-gatherer-style use of the raw material, so if the aspiring agriculturalist gives up his aspiration, he can revert to unimpaired hunting and gathering.) By employing his modified device, the Trickster prevents individuals from engaging in all the acquisition of property that is involved in moving beyond the hunter-gatherer mode of interaction with extrapersonal objects. Once again, however, the spraying does not, strictly speaking, trespass upon the persons seeking to make the transition to an agricultural way of life. And now the spraying does not itself violate anyone's claim to have enough and as good raw material left for his use. If, nevertheless, one thinks that the Trickster's use of the modified device does wrong the aspiring agriculturalists—and surely one will think this if one thinks that individuals have a basic claim to live their own lives in their own way—one must think that this is because they possess a natural right not to be precluded from acquiring property in previously unowned raw materials.[34] If a less scientifically advanced Trickster comes along and prevents the aspiring agriculturalists from proceeding with their appropriations by credibly threatening to kill or imprison anyone who betrays his hunter-gatherer heritage or the Trickster's socialist five-year plan, that Trickster too would be a violator of their natural right of property.

IV. Locke on Self-Ownership and the Investment of Labor

It is only when Locke sets out in chapter V of the *Second Treatise* to explain the rights of individuals to their acquired estates that Locke invokes self-proprietorship as an implication of his earlier and main arguments for natural rights. Instead of staking out the broadly restrictive rule that no one may "harm another in his Life, Health, Liberty, or Possessions,"[35] Locke now tells us that "every Man has a *Property* in his own *Person*. This no Body has any Right to but himself."[36] Each agent's right to his own labor then comes along as an implication or aspect of each agent's self-ownership. "The *Labour* of his Body, and the *Work* of his Hands, we may say, are properly his." Absent (uncoerced) alienation, each laborer's labor is "the unquestionable Property of the Labourer."[37] Moreover, when an individual mixes his labor with some unowned physical material, he "annexes" that which is naturally his own to that material, and this removes

---

[34] Notice that this conclusion is independent of any specific view about what sorts of actions on the part of the aspiring agriculturalists would generate for them particular rights over specific extrapersonal objects.

[35] Ibid., section 6.

[36] Ibid., section 27; emphasis in the original.

[37] Ibid.; emphasis in the original.

the labored-upon object (or the material that comprises the object) from the commons and makes it the property of the laborer. Locke writes as though the annexing itself does the crucial work; it sounds as though once the labor is annexed to the unowned material, the laborer's right to the labor flows over to that material. We are left to wonder why this flow takes place. Still, Locke is usually and reasonably read more charitably than this.

On the more charitable reading, to say that an agent mixes his labor with (or annexes his labor to) some unowned material is to say that the agent invests some aspect of his industriousness in the purposive trans- formation of some unowned material. To some non-negligible degree, the agent puts some productive aspect of himself into that material. Since that productive aspect is not itself a physical part of the agent, we do not have literal mixing or annexing. Rather, we have an investment of the agent's effort, skill, or insight. The change in the condition of the (previously) unowned material counts as an investment and not a relinquishment of his effort, skill, or insight because that effort, skill, or insight is directed toward some anticipated change in the material. So the hunter invests a portion of his owned labor in the stick that he sharpens to make a hunting spear and in the rabbit that he tracks and spears with the sharpened stick. When such a transformation through labor investment occurs, the result- ing object cannot be taken from the agent without taking from him his (still owned) invested labor. Because (1) taking the object from him with- out his consent would take that invested labor from him without his consent, and (2) taking that invested labor from him without his consent would violate his self-ownership, it follows that (3) taking the labor- invested object violates the agent's rights, and (4) we can say that the agent has a right to that object. One way of expropriating another's labor is to coerce her—for example, through a threat of bodily injury—to per- form some labor for you, for example, to sharpen a stick that one already possesses into a spear. Another way is to wait for someone to engage in that labor and then make off with the labor-invested object. It is because the two methods of expropriation are at least close to being on a moral par, that the labor-investing agent ends up with a right to the object in which he has invested his labor.

Given my agreement with Locke's affirmation of self-ownership, I find this Lockean labor-investment story to be highly persuasive—as far as it goes. My only problem with the story is its limited range of application. What I mean by this is that there are many cases in which it is reasonable to say that an individual has through her actions acquired a right over some extrapersonal object and yet the acquisition of the right cannot plausibly be said to be a matter of labor investment. Take, for example, the case of an individual who acquires a right over forty nice raw acres by placing forty stakes around the boundary of those acres, or the case of an individual who acquires a right to the gold flakes that can be obtained through panning a certain segment of a stream by spending some time panning in that stream segment for gold and filing a claim at the local mineral rights registry office. In these cases, we can *say*—and it is sometimes tempting to say—that the agent invests his labor in the forty acres or the stream segment by driving in those stakes or by panning and filing that claim. But such statements will simply raise the questions: (1) Why do these actions count as labor-investing, if they do count as labor-investing? And (2) if we count these actions as labor-investing because we count them as rights-generating, must we not have a distinct (non-labor-investment) explanation for their being rights-generating? As my questions suggest, I think that any disposition to describe these actions as labor-investing comes from the combination of our taking them to be rights-generating actions and our desiring to retain the doctrine that (initial) property rights arise through labor investment. Whether or not we indulge the latter desire, the real and pivotal issue is what sort of non-labor-investment explanation (if any) is available for our taking these actions to be rights-generating.

In case one is still tempted to describe the stake-driving as an instance of labor investment, here is a more concrete way of making the point that what is really at stake is what non-labor-investment explanation (if any) can be given for the driving of the forty stakes giving rise to the driver's right to the forty acres. If driving in the forty stakes counts as investing labor in the forty acres, then it seems that driving in thirty-eight stakes should count as .95 times as much of a labor investment and, hence, .95 times as much of a rights-generating action—giving rise to .95 times as much of a right to the forty acres. Yet driving in thirty-eight stakes does not count as .95 times as much of a rights-generating action as driving in forty stakes. Hence, driving in the forty stakes does not yield the right to the forty acres by way of the labor investment involved in that action.

How, then, does the driving in of the forty stakes generate a property right to the forty acres, if it does generate that right? It seems that driving in forty stakes generates that right if and when driving in forty stakes is a recognized way of acquiring a right to that acreage within an established (and justifiable) practice of property acquisition. The appropriate response to someone who expresses puzzlement about what our stake-driver is doing is: "This is one of the ways in which a property right (in land) is established around here." Our responder might well continue:

It used to be—in some conjectural past age—that in order to establish a property right over any unowned extrapersonal object (or aspect of such an object), one had to invest one's labor in it in as literal a way as is possible. For instance, one would have to clear those forty acres of boulders and stumps and otherwise prepare the land for cultivation. We still think of this as the *natural* way of acquiring such rights. And, of course, we still acknowledge the property right of anyone who does so mix his labor with some previously unowned material. Nonetheless, somehow, over time, other ways of acting with respect to particular sorts of extrapersonal objects have come to be recognized as further ways of acquiring rights over those objects. Perhaps at first the further recognized ways of establishing property rights were all in some way analogous to the natural ways—as driving in stakes is analogous to turning the earth in preparation for planting or to fencing off an area for pasturing livestock. Presumably, at first, the physically analogous modes of acquisition also had to have the feature of naturally marking off the acquired material from other (non-acquired) material. But, quite conveniently, artificial means of marking off acquired material—filing survey information at the registry office—have come into existence and have been incorporated into newly recognized (and less natural yet) ways of establishing property rights. All this is most fortunate, because there are now ways of establishing property rights over certain objects (or aspects of objects)—e.g., rights over segments of streams (at least insofar as discretionary control of those stream segments is needed to extract gold from them)—even though it is hard to see how these rights could be established by natural, labor-investing procedures.

When we encounter the stake-driving and the registry of the segment of the stream cases, our judgment that the property right in question cannot plausibly be thought to be grounded in labor investment is not accompanied by disbelief in the property right. The explanation for this is that we are at the same time informed of the procedures—the stake-driving and the panning plus registration—through which our agents have acquired the forty acres or the stream segment; and we take these procedures to be part of a recognized (and justifiable) practice of private property. "This is one of the ways in which a property right (in land) is established around here." Our disposition is to think that there does not need to be some feature which is inherent in the agent's individual action—namely, the feature of being a labor investment—which grounds the agent's right to the object of his action. Rather, we think that the rights-generating force of the agent's individual action derives from the action's being in accord with such a justifiable practice—a practice whose suppression would violate people's claim to live their own lives in their own ways as that claim is codified in the natural right of property. Thus, the problem with the labor-investment theory is not so much that it does not broadly enough vindicate particular property rights, but rather that it encourages us to search for an inherent feature in each action that generates a property right in virtue of which that right arises, and hence it directs us away from appreciating how a practice of private property provides people with artificial ways of generating such rights. Relative to the range of objects (or aspects of objects) to which it is valuable for persons to be able to acquire property rights, there is a scarcity of natural (practice-independent) rights-generating actions. The evolution of practices of private property fills this gap. Such practices satisfy a mostly inchoate demand for further ways for individuals to establish property rights and thereby to secure their possession of and discretionary control over extrapersonal objects.

It is instructive here to compare Locke's labor-mixing account of just initial acquisition and Robert Nozick's neo-Lockean historical entitlement conception of justice in initial acquisition.[38] Nozick seems to have serious doubts about whether labor-investment *ever* accounts for the generation of a property right. Might not all laboring be like pouring your can of tomato juice into the ocean? Rather than acquiring a right to the new mixture, you may simply relinquish what you previously had a right over. So, without this being his conscious motivation, Nozick shifts to what I have been calling a "practice conception" of the generation of initial property rights. That is, he shifts to an account which turns on the thought that what matters is that acquisition take place in accordance with the procedures of a recognized and justifiable practice of private property. Nozick does not say what those procedures are. Perhaps he senses that under a practice approach there need be no inherent feature of the rights-generating action in virtue of which the right is generated, and hence that there is no such feature which he must identify. Nozick does recognize, however, that he needs to provide a reason for endorsing his historical entitlement approach against all competing end-state and pattern conceptions of justice in holdings. And this is the point at which he appeals to good old-fashioned Lockean self-ownership. For Nozick's crucial claim is that, in contrast to the historical entitlement doctrine, all end-state and pattern doctrines make some individuals the partial owners of others, and therefore all such doctrines are to be rejected for contravening self-ownership.

Yet why is it that, for example, John Rawls's difference principle institutes partial ownership for the least advantaged over the talented or energetic? The tax collector merely shows up and trucks off x percent of the corn that talented Bekah has grown and harvested, and y percent of the beef that energetic Josh has raised and cured, and delivers that corn and beef to Harry. The system institutes Harry's ownership over that seized corn and beef. But on what basis can it be said that this amounts to instituting Harry's partial ownership *of Bekah and Josh*? To say this, one has to say that part of what they own *as self-owners* is seized by the tax collector; and that part must be the labor they have invested in the corn or the beef. But, then, Nozick's attempt to provide a reason for favoring his historical entitlement view over all end-state and pattern views relies upon precisely the doctrine upon which he wants not to rely, namely, the

[38] Robert Nozick, *Anarchy, State, and Utopia* (New York: Basic Books, 1974), esp. 149–83.

labor-investment view.[39] My point here, of course, is not that no justification can be given for the historical entitlement practice view but, rather, that the appropriate justification is the invocation of the natural right of property.

V. Practices and Independent Justifying Norms

My focus on the practice conception of property-rights-generating actions—combined with the parallels I have drawn between, on the one hand, particular property rights and the natural right of property and, on the other hand, particular promissory rights and the natural right to have promises made to one kept—calls to mind a competing view about promissory rights and, by extension, about property rights. The competing view about promissory rights is that they are creatures of persons' participation in the rule-constituted practice of promising. Bekah enters into the game of promising by, for example, saying to Josh, "I promise you that I will do z," and, having so entered the game, Bekah falls under the rule of the game according to which if one says "I promise you that I will do z," one is obligated to the addressee to do z. This "social practice" view of particular promissory obligations and (correlative) rights is a competitor to the view of particular promissory obligations and (correlative) rights with which I have aligned myself, because it takes the generation of a promissory right to be fully explained by reference to the practice through which it arises. The explanation makes no reference to any practice-independent norm, for example, a natural right to have promises made to one kept. By extension, a friend of the social practice view may maintain that, if one is going to take seriously the notion of a practice of private property and of particular property rights arising through individuals' making plays within that game of property, one should similarly take the resulting property rights to be fully explained by reference to the practice through which they arise. One should not think that those particular acquired rights are tied to an independent, nonacquired right of property.

There is one disanalogy between the promissory rights case and the property rights case which might well allow one to accept the social practice view with respect to the former and reject it with respect to that latter. In the promissory case, an agent obligates *herself* through her participation in the promissory practice, while, in the property case, an agent would have to be said to obligate *others* (indeed, all other persons) through her participation in the property practice. At first blush anyway, it seems more likely that an agent could obligate herself to others by making

---

[39] In his section on "How Liberty Upsets Patterns," Nozick also argues that, unlike the historical entitlement theory, all end-state and pattern theories must condemn as unjust outcomes that arise innocuously from distributions that they institute in the name of justice. See ibid., 160–64.

certain moves within a rule-constituted practice than that she could obligate others to herself by making such moves. However, I shall not take this easy way out—both because I favor the rejection of the social practice view even in its most promising application, and because explaining my basic reason for rejecting the social practice view helps me refine this essay's claims about property rights.

Rather than engage in an extended critique, let me indicate quite baldly the basis on which I would reject the social practice account of promissory rights and obligations. What makes an agent's failure to fulfill her promise an instance of her wronging the recipient of the promise is not her transgression of some rule that is partially constitutive of the practice. Rather, what makes that failure wrongful is the manner in which she treats the recipient through the conjunction of her making and then failing to abide by the promise. Her promising provides the agent with an opportunity to treat the recipient in this manner; but the wrongfulness of treating the agent in this manner is not itself a creature of the promising activity. That this manner of treating another is wrongful is independent of the promising practice. This view is supported by there being cases in which an agent inflicts the same wrongful treatment upon another without having created the opportunity for that wrongful treatment through plays made within the promising game. This shows that the wrongfulness of the type of treatment inflicted through breaking promises is not itself a product of the promising practice.

For instance, suppose that Josh is on a beach that is about to be submerged by a rising and dangerous tide. He is thinking of escaping by running down the beach—across a point that will very soon be flooded—to the only staircase leading up the surrounding cliffs. Before he sets out, however, he sees Bekah gesturing to him and lowering a rope ladder to him from a near point on the cliffs. Relying upon that ladder still being there when he arrives at it, Josh heads toward it and forgoes the chance of crossing over to the foot of the staircase. As he approaches the rope ladder, Bekah pulls it up and waves.[40] The wrong-making feature of Bekah's conduct is her manipulation of Josh through deception (rather than, e.g., through the imposition of force or the threat of force); and this, I take it, is also the wrong-making feature of her failing to fulfill her earlier promise to Josh to do z. If we think that in both cases Bekah's conduct violates Josh's rights (rather than merely lowers social utility), it must be because we believe that Josh possesses a right against Bekah not to be subjected to manipulation through deception. Such a right may be thought of as a part of the codification of Josh's ur-claim not to be precluded from living his life in his own chosen way—a partial codification

---

[40] This is a slightly modified version of an example supplied by Neil MacCormick in "Voluntary Obligations and Normative Powers I," *Proceedings of the Aristotelian Society, Supplement* 46 (1972): 59–78.

which is a bit more general than the right to have promises that have been made to one kept.

In explaining my rejection of the social practice view as it applies to the case of promising, I have appealed to the idea of a wrong-making feature of promise breakings—a feature in virtue of which they are violations of rights. By extension, I should be prepared to identify the wrong-making feature of acts which seize from people holdings that they have acquired in accordance with a (justifiable) practice of private property or which deprive them of discretionary control over those holdings. The wrong-making feature of those actions is the precluding of the holder from pursuing his own ends through his chosen disposition of those extra-personal holdings. The independent norm which explains why such actions are violations of the holder's right is the natural right not to be precluded from acquiring and employing extrapersonal objects as one sees fit in the service of one's ends. That such interferences with persons' possession and chosen employment of the holdings they have acquired under a (functional) practice of private property has this inherent wrong-making feature is consistent with my denial that there must be some inherent feature in all property-rights-generating actions in virtue of which they engender such rights.

VI. Conclusion

There is a natural right not to be precluded from acquiring and exercising discretionary control over extrapersonal objects—although there is no natural right to any particular extrapersonal objects or any share of such objects. More guardedly, if it is reasonable to affirm a natural right of self-ownership, it is also reasonable to affirm this natural right of property. The affirmation of this original right involves no specification of the sorts of actions through which individuals will acquire property rights in extrapersonal objects. While it is plausible that labor investment is a natural way of generating such acquired rights, the emergence of practices of private property also provides individuals with artificial ways of generating property rights. Depriving individuals of possession of or discretionary control over what they have acquired in accordance with the procedures for acquisition specified within an existing (and justifiable) practice of private property violates their natural right not to be precluded from acquiring and exercising discretionary control over extrapersonal objects.

Philosophy, Tulane University

PROPERTY AND JUSTICE*

By David Schmidtz

I. Introduction

It is natural to assume that theorizing about property should be grounded in a foundation of theorizing about justice, and not vice versa. That is, philosophers should theorize about justice first, and only then think of themselves as in a position to theorize about what can legitimately become a person's property.

I have become skeptical about this. This essay explains why and sketches an alternative. I now see justice as something that can and does evolve in a given society. Moreover, as I see it, one driving factor of such evolution consists of facts about how judges, legislators, and cultures contingently respond to a particular history of litigation in particular and conflict in general.

Section II characterizes property rights, arguing that a property right first and foremost is a right to say no to proposed terms of exchange.[1] Section III discusses an inherent practical limit of the right to say no. Section IV argues that this limited right, and its correlative duty to respect prospective trading partners, is the key to getting real production, real cooperation, and real community off the ground. Later sections consider what this has to do with justice, arguing that our philosophical theorizing about justice needs to answer to our legal, economic, and historical theorizing about property, at least as much as the other way around, lest our philosophical theorizing have no reliable implications for what situated flesh-and-blood citizens owe each other (or what society's basic structure owes citizens) in their everyday lives.

II. The Concept of Property

According to Wesley Hohfeld, the crucial difference between a mere liberty and a full-blown right is this: I am at *liberty* to use P just in case I

* I thank Dean Donald Weidner and his colleagues at Florida State College of Law for honoring me with the opportunity to teach their first-year Property course in the fall of 2007. Their trust, encouragement, and unstinting collegial support inspired this essay. Thanks also to the Earhart Foundation for their support on this and various related projects. For comments, I thank Jason Brennan, Michael Bukoski, Chris Freiman, Keith Hankins, Kate Johnson, Ben Kearns, Mark LeBar, Dan Russell, Daniel Silvermint, John Thrasher, Jennifer Zamzow, and Matt Zwolinski.
[1] See David Schmidtz, "Property," *Oxford Handbook of the History of Political Philosophy*, ed. George Klosko (Oxford: Oxford University Press, 2010), for a reworking of some material from Section II.

doi:10.1017/S0265052509990045
79

have no duty to refrain from using P. I have a *right* to P just in case I am at liberty to use P, *plus* others have a duty to refrain from using P.[2] The difference between a mere liberty and a full-blooded property right is that a liberty, in this technical sense, is a nonexclusive right. A proper right implies a right to exclude other would-be users: a right to say no.

William Blackstone called property the "sole and despotic dominion which one man claims and exercises over the external things of the world, in total exclusion of the right of any other individual in the universe."[3] In practice, though, property rights in Anglo-American law have always been hedged with restrictions. The dominion to which Blackstone refers is real, but limited by easements, covenants, nuisance laws, zoning laws, regulatory statutes, and customary understandings of the public interest.

Today, the term 'property rights' generally is understood to refer to a bundle of rights that could include rights to sell, lend, bequeath, use as collateral, or even destroy. (John Lewis generally is regarded as the first person to use the "bundle of sticks" metaphor, in 1888.)[4] The fact remains, though, that at the heart of any property right is a right to say no: a right to exclude non-owners. In other words, a right to exclude is not just one stick in a bundle. Rather, property is a tree. Other sticks are branches; the right to exclude is the trunk.

Why must we see it this way? Because without a right to say no, other rights in the bundle are reduced to mere liberties rather than genuine rights. For example, I could own a bicycle in a meaningful sense even if, for some reason, I have no right to lend it to your friend. (That is, this particular tree is missing the "right to lend" branch.) By contrast, if I have no right to deny you permission to lend it to your friend, then I do not own the bicycle in any normal sense. Thus, there is a conceptual reason why, among the various sticks that make up property, the right to exclude is the core.

This does not settle what, if anything, can *justify* our claiming a right to exclude, but it does clarify the topic. When we ask about *owning* a bicycle as distinct from merely being at liberty to use it, we are asking about a right to exclude.

Exactly what protection is afforded by the right to say no is a separable issue. Property P normally is protected by a *property rule*, meaning no one may use P without the owner's permission. In some cases, we might instead say that P is protected by a *liability rule*, meaning no one may use P without compensating the owner. In a third kind of case, P might be protected by an *inalienability rule*, meaning no one may use P *even with* an

---

[2] Wesley Hohfeld, *Fundamental Legal Conceptions* (New Haven, CT: Yale University Press, 1964; first published in two parts in 1913 and 1917).

[3] William Blackstone, *Commentaries on the Laws of England* (Chicago: University of Chicago Press, 1979; first published 1765), book II, chapter 1.

[4] John Lewis, *Law of Eminent Domain* (Chicago: Callaghan and Co, 1888).

owner's permission. This is how Guido Calabresi and A. Douglas Melamed analyze the ways of giving property rights their due.[5]

The takings clause of the U.S. Constitution's Fifth Amendment specifies that private property may not be taken for public use unless just compensation is paid. In Calabresi and Melamed's terms, the takings clause affirms that even when a compelling public interest precludes respecting a private property right by treating it as protected by a property rule, the public must still respect the right to the extent of treating it as protected by a liability rule.[6]

The policy rationale for protecting property with property rules is that when a resource's only protection is liability rules, control of the resource is, for all practical purposes, concentrated in the hands of the bureaucrats who decide to treat one thing rather than another as a compelling public interest, and who make mistakes at other people's expense.

One rationale for liability rules is that sometimes it costs too much, or is impossible, to avoid impinging on someone's property. Or, in the case of torts, the impinging has already occurred, and the question is how to undo the wrong while acknowledging that the impinging was accidental rather than deliberate. (Where a property rule would require us to get advance permission from every owner on whom we impose a risk of accidental trespass, a liability rule requires instead that we compensate owners after the fact if we should accidentally damage their property.) One rationale for an inalienability rule is that there are forms of property so fundamental that we might cease to be persons in the fullest sense if we were to sell them. We may, for example, regard my kidney or my vote as my property, yet deny that this gives me any right to sell such things. In this respect, we would then be treating my right as inalienable.

---

[5] Guido Calabresi and A. Douglas Melamed, "Property Rules, Liability Rules, and Inalienability: One View of the Cathedral," *Harvard Law Review* 85 (1972): 1089–1128.

[6] *Spur Industries v. Del Webb*, 494 P.2d 700 (Ariz. 1972) is a notorious case in which housing developer Del Webb sued neighboring feedlot operator Spur industries, alleging that Spur's operation was a noxious nuisance that was damaging property values and making neighborhood life unpleasant. Spur Industries had been operating long before Del Webb showed up, though, which is part of the reason why Del Webb was able to buy the land so cheaply in the first place. The basic principle of common law is that if a party moves to the nuisance, as Del Webb did, then it has no complaint. Yet the judge ruled that although Del Webb per se did not have a case, Del Webb's customers were "the public" and the public has a right to be protected against noxious and potentially unhealthy nuisances. Thus, the judge ruled for Del Webb, granting an injunction against feedlot operator Spur Industries. Remarkably, the court held that winning plaintiff *Del Webb* had to compensate *Spur*, not the other way around. The court judged that Spur's property claim was valid but that (because the feedlot was a public nuisance) Spur could be forced to move, with compensation, because Spur's property right was, in effect, protected by a liability rule rather than a property rule. Interestingly, the case was settled within a month of the publication of Calabresi and Melamed's article; the judge had not read it. For further information, see almost any casebook on property. I have used Thomas Merrill and Henry Smith, *Property* (New York: Foundation Press, 2007).

82   DAVID SCHMIDTZ

III. Property's Practical Limits

The right to say no is stringent but by no means absolute. The right to say no is an institutional structure that facilitates commerce, that is, commerce in the broadest sense. When people have a right to say no, and to withdraw, they can afford to live in close proximity and to produce and prosper, without fear. The right to say no enables people to come to market and celebrate the fruits of their productivity, spreading the goods across a store window for all to see, without fear that the goods will simply be taken.

However, the right to say no is not a weapon of mass destruction. It does not put people in a position to gridlock the system. The right to say no is meant to be a right to decline to be involved in a transaction. It is not a right to forbid people in general to transact. For example, in many cases, judges have to affirm, as utterly basic to the concept of property, that owners have a right to exclude—to post a "No trespassing" sign. But does flying over someone's land at ten thousand feet count as trespassing? In the case of *Hinman v. Pacific Air Transport* (1936), a landowner, Hinman, sued an airline (Pacific Air) for trespass.[7] Hinman wanted the court to affirm his right to stop airlines from flying over his property. Hinman cited the ancient doctrine of *ad coelum*, which says that he who owns the soil owns it from the heavens to the depths of the earth.

The court was in a predicament, for the right to say no is the backbone of the system of property that, in turn, is the backbone of cooperation in a society of self-owners. Yet much of property's ultimate point is to facilitate commercial traffic, and ruling that landowners could veto the emerging airborne commercial traffic would have been a kind of red light that would gridlock traffic, not facilitate it. So the judge had to find a way to rule in favor of the airline without destabilizing the whole system of property. There were truths the judge was trying to track: about what institutional framework enables people to live well together, about what enables people to mind their own business, and about what would empower people to hold each other for ransom without conferring any compensating power or incentive to make a positive contribution.

The plaintiff relied heavily on *ad coelum*, but the court ruled that *ad coelum* isn't true, and never was. Subsequent readings were silent on this nuance, so far as I can tell, finessing the need to pronounce on *ad coelum* by interpreting air traffic as having a *navigation easement*, held by the public in theory and administered by the federal government in practice, which wasn't a radical departure from traditional law regarding easements.[8] Whatever else is true, though, the right to exclude was not the thing to give up, and in fact the practical instances of the right to exclude

---

[7] *Hinman v. Pacific Air Transport*, 84 F.2d 755 (9th Cir. 1936).
[8] See, e.g., *United States v. Causby*, 328 U.S. 256 (1946).

that had a history of mattering to people were left pretty much undisturbed by the *Hinman* decision.

It would be a manner of speaking, at best, to say that the court in *Hinman*, in coming to a verdict, was discovering a natural law. The court was trying to discover *something*, though, and what it was trying to discover was closer to laws of nature than to legislation. That is, the court was trying to discern the laws and economics of human coordination—realizing that the point of the rule of law is to enable people to prosper, and that the basic prerequisite of people prospering is that people be able to produce and then to trade. Moreover, the air traffic industry was a potentially revolutionary experiment in pushing the frontier of people's ability to produce and trade. The judge also realized that giving every landowner a right to treat air traffic as a trespass would throttle air traffic, because the cost of an airline transacting with every potential rent-seeking property owner on the ground would be prohibitive.[9]

None of these facts are artifacts of legislation. There may have been no fact of the matter about what *ad coelum* really meant—no fact of the matter about whether landowners had a right to forbid people to pass over their land at ten thousand feet. Before the advent of air travel, no legal dispute had ever brought the issue to a head. There had not yet been philosophical debate that needed to be resolved in one way rather than another. Once air travel emerged, though, and once landowners filed suit against airplanes for trespass, that was when someone had to decide what *ad coelum* entailed (or discover what it *ought* to entail, by discovering what it *needed* to entail to be part of a system that helps people live together).

To be clear, it should be a rare event when judges step back to ask what property is for. Property is supposed to settle what is within one's jurisdiction and what is not. If it is settled that X is your property, then you are the one who gets to decide what X is for. When we get to the parking lot at the end of the day, you drive home *that* car and I drive home *this* one, period. When the institution of property is working well, no discussion is needed. Judges need to step back to ask what property is for when and only when the institution is not working well—when litigants run into a question that the institution has not yet evolved to answer.[10]

Another thing to note is that, even given that justice has to answer to principles of traffic management, so as to enable people to move forward, the fact remains that to move forward, people need to look backward, to a degree, in order to secure conditions for reliable trade. For example, one has to do a routine title search when transferring title to real estate. One

[9] Schmidtz, "Property," discusses the Hinman case as an example of a decision driven by the imperative to limit transaction costs—namely, the various costs (transportation, packaging, advertising, and so on) of getting a product to market and then into the hands of customers—to manageable levels.

[10] I thank Matt Zwolinski for pressing for clarification here.

need not go back to the Middle Ages in search of histories of nonconsen-
sual transfer. A routine title search is more modest, going back to a point
where title appears to have been uncontested. A title insurance company
then takes on the risk of warranting that it has done due diligence and
that the title being transferred is good.[11]

One further important clarification: It is (or, in any case, should be) no
part of classical liberal theory that the right to property implies a correlative duty to roll over and die rather than trespass on someone's land. For
the system to be stable enough to last, respecting the property system has
to be a good option for just about everyone, including those who arrive
too late to be part of the wave of first appropriators. And in order for
respecting the system to be a good option for just about everyone, it has
to be true that just about everyone has good options regarding how to
make a living within the system.

IV. Property Rights as a System of Traffic Management

The main theses of Stephen Holmes and Cass Sunstein's *The Cost of
Rights* (1999) are that rights depend on government and rights cost money.[12]
They do not argue, but I would argue, that it is because rights are so costly
that people who seriously believe in rights as a framework for revering
persons as ends in themselves do not believe in *lots* of rights.

Consider that the whole point of fences, and of rights, is to *get in the
way*. Or to use a different metaphor: rights are like traffic lights.[13] A mere
liberty is a green light. A full-blooded *right* is a green light combined with
a correlative red light. Some rules are better than others at unobtrusively
enabling people to get on with their business. Traffic lights facilitate traffic
movement not so much by turning green as by turning red. Without

[11] Michael Walzer has asked me where I stand on issues of rectificatory justice. What are
we to do about the histories of unjust expropriation that we find everywhere we look? There
comes a time when it is too late and such histories cannot be undone. When it is too late to
make victims whole, rectificatory justice has to be about something else. It has to be about
enabling people to repair broken relationships, reconcile, forgive, understand exactly where
their culture has been and where they resolve never to be again, so that they can get on with
their lives together. So my answer to Walzer is that he was correctly interpreting my view:
our need to be able to coordinate and cooperate, going forward, shapes the interpretation of
all principles of justice, including principles of rectificatory justice. See Linda Radzik, *Making Amends* (New York: Oxford University Press, 2009); and Charles Griswold, *Forgiveness*
(New York: Cambridge University Press, 2007).
[12] Stephen Holmes and Cass R. Sunstein, *The Cost of Rights: Why Liberty Depends on Taxes*
(New York: Norton, 1999), 15. To elaborate, "Property rights have costs because, to protect
them, the government must hire police officers" (ibid., 146). The government takes responsibility, at considerable expense, in three ways: first, when it pays the officers; second, when
it trains the officers to respect the rights of suspects; third, when the government monitors
police (and other public officials, presumably) so as to deter rogue officials and generally
minimize corruption (ibid.).
[13] Jason Brennan and I elaborate on the traffic light and traffic management metaphors in
David Schmidtz and Jason Brennan, *A Brief History of Liberty* (Oxford: Blackwell Publishers,
2010).

traffic lights, we all in effect have a green light, and at some point traffic increases to a point where the result is gridlock. By contrast, a system in which we take turns facing red and green lights is a system that keeps us out of each other's way. Of course, the system itself gets in the way when it presents us with a red light, but almost all of us gain in terms of our overall ability to get where we want to go, because we develop mutual expectations that enable us to get where we want to go more peacefully and more expeditiously.

We can see from this that we do not want *lots* of rights, for the same reason we wouldn't want to face red lights every fifty feet. We want the most compact set of lights that enables motorists to know what to expect from each other, and thereby get from point A to point B with minimal interference. By getting in our way to some degree, well-placed traffic lights, like well-placed property rights, liberate us, and help us stay out of each other's way.[14]

Holmes and Sunstein's basic point is, as they say, obvious. Rights are indeed costly. (More generally, they could have said, government is costly — since what they mean by rights is essentially tied to government.) Their point is important, too, for a reason they leave unmentioned: namely, the cost of various alleged rights is one key way for theorists to sort out which rights ought to be taken seriously, for many alleged rights are *prohibitively* costly. The implication is that we cannot afford to teach people to think they have the hugely expensive ones.

Property rights are, among other things, red lights that tell you when the right to use the intersection belongs to someone else. Red lights can be frustrating, especially as a community becomes more crowded, but the game they create is not zero-sum. When the system works, nearly all of us get where we are going more quickly, safely, and predictably than we otherwise would, in virtue of having been able to coordinate on a system that enables us to know what to expect from each other.

Commercial traffic consists of people coordinating in a thick sense of undertaking elaborate projects together, and in a thin sense of staying out of everyone else's way as they pursue their respective projects. To secure coordination in a thin sense, people need some common understanding of torts and property. To secure coordination in a thick sense, people need a common understanding of their right to say no and also of new obli-

---

[14] When I speak of putting people in a position where they know what to expect from each other, this may seem to privilege the status quo. I am of two minds about this. First, I think the often-expressed concern about privileging the status quo often is misplaced. Acknowledging that we start where we actually start is a bias in a sense, because it rules out places we cannot get to from here, but it is not an arbitrary bias. If we rule out options on the grounds that we cannot get there from here, we are ruling them out for good reason. Second, if there is anything conservative about this approach, it is the thinnest kind of conservatism. The point is that we start from where we are, not that we have any reason to stay where we are. Wherever we want to go, if we are serious, then we will take seriously questions of whether we can get there from here, and if so, how.

gations created by freely saying yes. Thus, they need common understandings of contract as well as of tort and property.

V. JUSTICE

What about the pedestrians, one might ask?[15] That is a crucial respect in which the traffic-light metaphor radically understates the benefit of a successful property regime. Literal traffic lights are working well when people manage to stay out of each other's way, but commercial traffic management must pass a far more stringent test. Commercial traffic's aim is not merely to be accident-free but to bring people together. Rising commercial traffic is a boon, not a drag. The ultimate secret of progress and prosperity is the cooperation of multitudes. Commercial traffic—the trucking and bartering of multitudes—is a community's lifeblood, enabling children to grow up to become *drivers*.

Not every would-be motorist gets a car at the same time, but commercial traffic's point is to produce and disperse the means of participating in the market.[16] Ensuring that everyone gets a car on the same day, or at the same age, is not the point. If, instead, we were to insist on a distributive principle such as "no one gets cars or computers or kidney transplants until there is enough for everyone to be guaranteed one at the same time," that would be the sort of red light that gridlocks a system, bringing progress to a crashing halt. That red light has no place in a community's system of traffic management, no place in its system of property, and therefore no place among its principles of justice, because that sort of red light cannot coexist with people having reason to live in that community.[17]

The traffic management function of property conditions what can count as justice, given that whatever we call justice has to be compatible with people prospering, which means it has to be compatible with the system of property that enables people to prosper. If whatever we choose to call justice is not compatible with property, then we have no reason—indeed, no right—to take so-called justice seriously.

We have reason not to treat justice the way philosophers have treated it in recent decades, as a matter of distributing shares. Some philosophers even ask us to imagine rational contractors coming to a table to divide the

---

[15] I thank Daniel Bell for the question.

[16] I suppose age would be one of the best demographic predictors of car ownership, as it is of income in general, and for the same reasons. It takes years to accumulate capital, including the most valuable job skills.

[17] Egalitarian theorists such as Richard Arneson (in a series of articles on the various currencies of egalitarianism, and on alternatives that simply prioritize the claims of the destitute), and Thomas Christiano, in *The Constitution of Equality* (Oxford: Oxford University Press, 2008), and *The Rule of the Many* (Boulder, CO: Westview Press, 1996), are helping to take political philosophy to places it has never been before. Each in his own way seems to be developing principles of egalitarian justice that are not recipes for gridlock—that could be implemented in ways that would unleash producers without leaving young pedestrians permanently on the outside looking in.

economic pie. Bruce Ackerman is candid enough to refer to what contractors come together to distribute as manna from heaven.[18] In the real
world, though, the stuff that would-be distributors want to distribute
tends to be a product of lifetimes of work. Intuitively, it is not just—and,
to say the least, is not the *essence* of justice—to ignore the fact that what
distributors want to distribute is not manna but is in fact produced by
other people. Holmes and Sunstein get at this fact, albeit inadvertently,
when they stress that rights cost money.[19] More precisely, pie costs money;
it sits on a table awaiting division only if someone paid the cost of creating it and then getting it to the table.

I see real justice as a response to whole persons, especially persons as
producers of pie, and most definitely not just as a response to persons as
stomachs—that is, as mere consumers of slices of pie. To respect producers, we have to respect what they have produced, and what they have
plowed into production.[20] (We have to give up on theories that ask us to
pretend not to be able to tell the difference between people who contrib-
uted to a given production process and people who didn't.) So we have
to talk about what we have reason to regard as theirs, rather than as
someone else's.

Holmes and Sunstein repeatedly present their thesis that rights cost
money as refuting libertarians and conservatives. They scoff at "the *libertarian fiction* that individuals who exercise their rights, in the classic or
eighteenth-century sense, are just going about their own business, immac-
ulately independent of the government and the taxpaying community." [21]
Conservatives are supposed to be similarly oblivious to the cost of rights.
In Holmes and Sunstein's words, "Conservatives, for their part, may
prefer to keep quiet about—or as their rhetoric suggests, may be oblivious
to—the way that the taxes of the whole community are used to protect the
property rights of wealthy individuals." [22]

Not once in Holmes and Sunstein's book is the most important corollary of the truism that rights cost money even mentioned. Namely, there
is a world of variation in what particular rights cost, and some of the
rights-claims that government has granted cost *a lot*.[23]

---

[18] Bruce A. Ackerman, *Social Justice in the Liberal State* (New Haven, CT: Yale University Press, 1980), 31.

[19] Holmes and Sunstein, *The Cost of Rights*, 15.

[20] John Rawls was ahead of his time in insisting that we must not think of the pie as fixed and must construct our redistributive principles with a view to the fact that what people produce will depend on the extent to which we treat their product as their property. Rawls also, unfortunately, insisted that people's productive capacities were among the morally arbitrary properties of persons that did not figure directly into the question of what they rightfully could claim as their due (from society's basic structure). See John Rawls, *A Theory of Justice* (Cambridge, MA: Harvard University Press, 1971), 74–75.

[21] Holmes and Sunstein, *The Cost of Rights*, 29; emphasis added.

[22] Ibid., 25.

[23] It seems the "libertarian fiction" is a fiction written *about* libertarians, not *by* them, which may account for why (aside from two sentence fragments on page 1 of *The Cost of*

When we are trying to articulate principles of justice that we have reason to take seriously in a world like ours, one way to start is with an understanding of what our world is like, and of which institutional frameworks promote our thriving in communities and which do not. If we start this way, we can sort out alleged principles of justice by asking which ones license mutual expectations that promote our thriving and which ones do otherwise.

A priori reasons for endorsing principles of justice generally are not good enough. A good enough reason would be something like this: to endorse *this* way of applying *this* principle in *this* kind of circumstance is to support institutional frameworks that position us to play positive-sum games that make no one worse off, or that at worst limit negative externalities (noise pollution, say) to levels and kinds widely accepted as a reasonable price of living in communities.

A. Creation myths

Holmes and Sunstein refer to "the obvious truth that rights depend on government."[24] But Holmes and Sunstein are smart enough to know that this is not obvious, and readers should not let themselves be intimidated. Let me quote the paragraph from the beginning: "The Declaration of Independence states that 'to secure these rights, Governments are established among men.' To the obvious truth that rights depend on government must be added a logical corollary, one rich with implications: rights cost money."[25] Notice that the Declaration *denies*, rather than states as obvious, that rights depend on government. The Declaration says that part of what can justify establishing a government is its efficacy in securing rights: the explicit point is to *secure* rights, not to create them.

Legal rights admittedly are creations in some sense, but there remain truths about which legal rights ought to be created and which ought not. Holmes and Sunstein say:

Rights, ascribed to contemporary policy experts Charles Murray and David Boaz) no libertarians are ever cited. Nowhere do Holmes and Sunstein acknowledge that the classical liberals to whom they allude (without ever naming them, and frankly I doubt they have anyone specific in mind) are the most cost-conscious rights theorists who ever lived. (It would make sense to at least mention Friedrich Hayek, James Buchanan, Richard Epstein, Thomas Sowell, Daniel Shapiro, Scott Arnold, Jan Narveson, Robert Sugden, or even left-libertarian Hillel Steiner, just to name a few.) Holmes and Sunstein write: "Some of those who wince at the very mention of the cost of rights may distrust close inquiry into the tradeoffs that rights enforcement inevitably entails" (ibid., 177). Holmes and Sunstein insinuate that classical liberals and conservatives are the ones who wince, but nothing could be further from the truth. Classical liberals have always done more than anyone to warn us that few alleged rights are worth the cost. Holmes and Sunstein themselves do not actually do anything in this regard. Their only reason for belaboring this theme is that it is the closest thing they have to an argument that rights are created by government, and that it is the government's prerogative to decide what we owe government in virtue of such protection.

[24] Holmes and Sunstein, *The Cost of Rights,* 15.
[25] Ibid.

A liberal government must refrain from violating rights. It must "respect" rights. But this way of speaking is misleading because it reduces the government's role to that of nonparticipant observer. A liberal system does not merely protect and defend property. It defines and thus *creates* property. Without legislation and adjudication there can be no property rights in the way Americans understand the term.[26]

Since they mention misleading ways of speaking, it seems fair to note that Holmes and Sunstein are speaking of how *they* understand the term, which has little or nothing to do with how "Americans" understand the term. Holmes and Sunstein acknowledge that a liberal government must refrain from violating rights, yet their view entails that the all-too-easy way for a government to ensure that it does not violate rights would be to eschew creating inconvenient rights in the first place. I observe that there have been Americans—including judges, legal theorists, and founding fathers—who understood the term differently.

I would not deny Holmes and Sunstein's premise that property would, on balance, be more insecure if governments were not in the business of protecting it. That property would be *nonexistent* in the state of nature, though, is either false or an empty tautology, depending on whether we treat property as legal rules that only governments can create, or as forms of possession that neighbors respect by spontaneous village custom. Property in the latter sense is an institution that governments sometimes recognize, ratify, and clarify. On this reading, there is nothing trivial about what governments can bring (and what governments at their best do bring) to systems of property, but there is nothing primordially fundamental about it either.[27]

More generally, if rights and correlative duties are true claims about how moral agents ought to be treated, then the idea that such truths do not exist until governments say they exist just isn't credible.[28] The idea that rights would not be *enforced* without government is closer to being

---

[26] Ibid., 60; emphasis added.

[27] Holmes and Sunstein write: "No sharp line can be drawn between markets and government: the two entities have no existence detached from each other" (ibid., 69). Likewise, Liam Murphy and Thomas Nagel write that because "[t]here is no market without government and no government without taxes . . . [i]t is therefore logically impossible that people should have any kind of entitlement to all their pretax income." Murphy and Nagel, *The Myth of Ownership* (New York: Oxford University Press, 2002), 32. My best guess from the context is that this is a maximally provocative way of saying that governments do not function well in the absence of a price mechanism and markets do not function well except in the context of enforceable contracts.

[28] Even the idea that laws are exclusive creatures of government is hard to believe unless it is stipulated to be so by definition. Mutual understanding and coordination, based on mutual acknowledgment of one another's possessions, has always been mostly a spontaneous matter, just like language, not generally or primordially a creation of government. And such coordination does, in fact, give rise to expectations that community members treat

plausible. Still, even that weaker claim is dubious. Our ancestors were marking and defending territory long before there were governments. Even today, most protection and enforcement is not governmental but is instead in private hands. Normally, we call government police not to prevent crimes but to fill out forms and otherwise deal with the aftermath.

As the infrastructure of coordination and cooperation emerges, one of the services in scarce supply will be basic physical security. People do not come to the market unless they are confident that they will survive the trip (or at least that making the trip is safer than staying home). Eventually, ordinary producers not only make the trip, they begin to feel *so* secure that far from *concealing* the value of what they possess (to limit the extent to which they are targets for robbers), they begin to *openly advertise* the fruits of their productivity. When that happens, there has been a minor miracle. Society has progressed to a point of being able to secure an expectation that such fruits will be transferred only by consent.

B. What plumbers do well

Having (for better or worse) defined rights as basic interests that government can protect,[29] Holmes and Sunstein suppose that

> [i]t is perfectly obvious that people cannot lead decent lives without certain minimal levels of food, shelter, and health care. But calling the crying need for public assistance "basic" may not get us very far. A just society would ensure that its citizens have food and shelter; it would try to *guarantee* adequate medical care; it would strive to offer good education, good jobs, and a clean environment.[30]

Here are two responses. First, suppose we grant that the proper way to evaluate societies is by asking whether they empower and enable people to lead decent lives together. How then would we evaluate plumbers? We might ask the same sort of question: namely, do plumbers make us better off? But we would not use that question as a template for a plumber's *job description*. A job description would be narrower and would have something to do with plumbing. Suppose, then, that we call a plumber to fix a faucet, but decline to turn over to the plumber the jobs of feeding and clothing us and providing us with health care. Would we thereby be failing to take "crying needs for plumbing assistance" seriously? No. We simply recognize that a plumber's job description—a plumber's particu-

---

as legitimate, with at least as much status within communities as the sorts of expectations that later in human history come to be created by governments as well.

[29] Costs "will be understood to mean budgetary costs and 'rights' will be defined as important interests that can be reliably protected by individuals or groups using the instrumentalities of government" (Holmes and Sunstein, *The Cost of Rights*, 16).

[30] Ibid., 120; emphasis added.

lar way of making us better off—does not encompass everything. Nor should it. Why not? Because if plumbers had a license to do everything (without customers' consent! without needing to say in advance what the service will cost!), we would live worse lives, not better ones. The point is, if we decline to turn over a given job to the plumber, it *may* be because we fail to see how important the job is. A more likely explanation, though, is that we decline precisely because we *do* see how important the job is.

C. Guarantees

My second response is to recast Holmes and Sunstein's basic point: *guarantees* cost money. As they say, people need food, shelter, and occasionally medicine. It is neither obvious nor even true that people in any analogous way need guarantees.[31] Nor is it comparably obvious that justice has much to do with guaranteeing that citizens will, like it or not, have to pay the price of meeting other people's needs but not their own.[32]

Thus, people who clamor for guarantees should stop and ask whether the guarantees they envision, in the hands of ordinary government administrators, will actually make people better off. Are such guarantees guaranteed to make people better off? Why don't we need *that* to be guaranteed as a prerequisite of having any right to start issuing guarantees?

Better yet, why don't we need at least to be guaranteed that issuing such guarantees won't make poor people *worse* off? If guarantees are so important, we should clamor for *that* guarantee first, and clamor for additional guarantees only after getting that one.

Holmes and Sunstein say that "a theory of rights that never descends from the heights of morality into the world of scarce resources will be sorely incomplete, even from a moral perspective."[33] I could not agree more. We must look at patterns of results, and once we see the pattern, we should take the hint. For a start, we can measure how much a society has achieved, along one uncontroversially important dimension, by looking at life expectancies. In 1900, life expectancy in the U.S. was forty-seven years for white males, and thirty-three years for black males. By the year

[31] Echoing Holmes and Sunstein, Murphy and Nagel write: "Few would deny that certain positive public goods, such as universal literacy and a protected environment, that cannot be *guaranteed* by private action, require government intervention" (*The Myth of Ownership*, 6; emphasis added). What a curiously old-fashioned approach this seems to be, as if there were no gap between finding a theoretical imperfection in private provision and clinching the case for public provision. Perhaps Murphy and Nagel assume that public provision has a record of perfection in these areas. More likely, they assume that public providers need not achieve perfection, because public providers (and only public providers) have their hearts in the right place, which suffices to make public provision just.

[32] If there were one thing people needed from a government, it would be to give some teeth to the right to say no. And the right to say no won't have teeth except under a government that treats possessions as presumptively legitimate—defeasible, of course, but not in fact defeated in normal cases.

[33] Holmes and Sunstein, *The Cost of Rights*, 18.

2000, life expectancy was seventy-five years for white males and sixty-eight years for black males.[34] This represents an incredible achievement. Whether the U.S. government ever *guaranteed* that people would live that long is beside the point.

Prosperity's foundation is productivity, and productive societies are always the ones that do not overdo the guarantees.[35]

D. *The meaning of life well lived*

To theorize about justice and do it well, we need to start by considering what it takes for people to prosper in communities. However, a judge need not know every facet of that genuine ideal of justice to say something about justice in a given case. All a judge needs to know is that commercial traffic management is a prerequisite of achieving that ideal on any non-question-begging interpretation, and that some kinds of property rights are a prerequisite of effective commercial traffic management. A judge has to see that litigants come before the court with their own visions of the good life. Usually the visions are compatible, but the litigants have incompatible views about their right to pursue their vision in a given way. A judge's job is to resolve the conflict. A judge never needs to know the details of people's visions of the good life, but in hard cases a judge does need to keep in mind that the job of the court is to clarify the rights-of-way at issue in such a way that people such as these litigants in circumstances like theirs will be able to get on with pursuing their own visions, and will be able to do so in peace, assisted by a verdict that clarifies what people like these litigants reasonably can expect from one another. In metaphorical terms, we need to know that our system of traffic management is helping people get where they want to go, accident-free. We do not need to know or to evaluate the details of where they want to go.

What it means to prosper is somewhat (although only somewhat) underdetermined by theory, but communities work out the details. For one thing, people will not prosper together unless they come up with a system that does not require consensus on the details. To prosper, people need to agree on who has jurisdiction, that is, who gets to make the call. The point of property rights is to settle who gets to make the call. That is part of the explanation of why liberal societies are places of rising prosperity (and also of why measures of prosperity tend to be controversial).

Which kinds of property rights enable people to prosper together? In a nutshell, the kind that can evolve to internalize evolving externality prob-

---

[34] See http://www.elderweb.com/home/node/2838, citing data from the U.S. Census Bureau's Current Population Reports.
[35] Aiming at near-universal literacy is one thing. Aiming to eradicate polio is one thing. I am open to arguments that such aims are altogether legitimate, even at significant cost. Even so, the aim itself is the thing. Guarantees are neither necessary nor sufficient.

lems while securing the opportunity and incentive to produce, invent, and otherwise help a society make progress. In most times and places, this will mean a mixed regime in which important bits of property are held by the public but in which the primary means of production are in private hands. That kind of mixed regime has been tested repeatedly in practice. Evidently, and for well-known reasons, it just works better.[36]

Worldly principles of justice are principles of conflict resolution and conflict avoidance. They define and codify legitimate mutual expectations and articulate ideals about what is involved in being a good neighbor in a particular community. A principle can and does work better if it responds to the realities of where people happen to be, and points the way to something better *starting from where they are.* And making progress from where they are is most imperative when where they are is not already fair and just.

If asked whether plumbers help us live well together, we might say, "Of course, so far as plumbing goes." The indeterminacy of what is to count as living well would not trouble us in that circumstance. Why not? Partly because such a question sounds ordinary rather than technical, and we know what the words mean well enough to have no trouble with them in ordinary conversation. Another part of the explanation is that what plumbers contribute to society is concrete and specific enough that no warning bells go off. We know what they contribute, and we know that the contributions of the ones who do an honest job are straightforwardly positive, even if limited. So, if we asked whether traffic lights help us live well, that too would have a straightforward answer. Lights that are well-placed and function reliably do indeed help motorists live well. I suppose we could say much the same of property rights. Some rights (but not others) internalize externalities, effectively enshrine a right to say no, help people stay out of each other's way, help people feel secure enough to take the risk of investing in cooperative ventures, and so on.

Property rights don't do everything for us, any more than traffic lights or plumbers do. Traffic lights don't cure cancer. (Perhaps property rights do in a sense cure cancer if and when they help us find whatever we are hoping to find when we come to the market, including opportunities to do research, and to buy and sell what we discover in the process. Perhaps there is nothing that property rights cannot ultimately help us do. On any given day, though, property rights will not be a panacea.) They will help secure our possessions well enough to make it safe for us to be a part of the community. That is a lot, but it isn't everything.

---

[36] See, e.g., Robert C. Ellickson, "Property in Land," *Yale Law Journal* 102 (1993): 1315–1400; Carol Rose, "Possession as the Origin of Property," *University of Chicago Law Review* 52 (1985): 73–88; Carol Rose, "The Comedy of the Commons: Custom, Commerce, and Inherently Public Property," *University of Chicago Law Review* 53 (1986): 711–87; and Elinor Ostrom, *Governing the Commons: The Evolution of Institutions for Collective Action* (Cambridge: Cambridge University Press, 1990).

If we could conceive of people more or less in isolation, then living well for them would consist of being self-sustaining in a quite literal sense. As trade begins to emerge, though (which is another way of saying, as *communities* emerge), there emerges with it the opportunity to be self-sufficient not by producing enough directly to meet one's own needs so much as by producing enough to meet *other people's* needs. As a rule, the people we think of as more or less self-sufficient members of a community come nowhere near to producing enough to meet their own needs (in the way a hermit would need to do). They do not even try. Instead, they go to the market to offer their plumbing or cancer-curing services to other people, and after a series of trades they go home with plenty of food for their families, typically without producing a grain of food.

Yet people cooperate only if they establish adequately understood and mutually acceptable *terms* of cooperation. The possibilities multiply when people become able to give their word, create mutual expectations, and count on agreements being kept. Being able to count on one another makes possible the rule of law, which enables people to trust each other even more, giving up on the idea of being self-sufficient and instead becoming especially skillful at making their neighbors better off in particular ways. The division of labor thus vastly expands the opportunity to be served by, and in turn to be of service to, vast multitudes. In an advanced commercial society, one can produce for customers whom one will never meet. One may be only dimly aware of their purposes, and indeed of their very existence; one knows only that sales are good. Someone somewhere must deem the product worth paying for, and that is all that an ordinary producer needs to know. On such foundations are modern society and our unprecedented modern prosperity built (a prosperity undreamt of as recently as a century ago, even by science fiction writers).

VI. What Property Is For

When I taught the first-year Property course at Florida State College of Law, I was fascinated to imagine what it must have been like to have been in the judges' shoes in the cases we studied. Judges found themselves having to resolve competing claims, and in the more interesting cases, each side brought to bear relevant and weighty moral and legal desiderata. Typically, it would have been superficial to interpret the conflict as between, say, justice and utility. The claims were competing claims of justice, and the judge was in a position of having to interpret the rival claims so as to render them "compossible."[37] A judge might face a case

[37] The term 'compossible' is most often associated with Hillel Steiner. I think the idea comes originally from Leibniz, but Steiner fruitfully applied it to theories of rights. The idea of rights being compossible is that it cannot be true that a person both does and does not have a claim to X. When rival claims are not compossible, then at least one of the rival claims has to be incorrect, or in any case must be reinterpreted or repudiated so that the rival claims

where the plaintiff claims a right to run a school unmolested, complaining that the defendant has no right to interfere. The judge looks at how the defendant is alleged to have interfered and says yes or no. If the interference took the form of running a superior school that "steals" the plaintiff's customers, the judge throws out the suit. Why? Because the plaintiff's customers are not the plaintiff's property, so "stealing" them is not really stealing. If the interference instead took the form of firing guns into the air and frightening parents into removing children from the school, then the judge rules for the plaintiff, because that sort of disturbance is an intentional trespass, aimed at making the plaintiff's parcel a less desirable location for a school. It deliberately sabotages the operation of the school with no constructive purpose in view.

A. Before justice

All this suggests that, at least in hard cases where judges aim not merely to apply principles of justice but to articulate them (sometimes for the first time), judges have to make decisions about where to locate property's edges, and in the process settle whether justice sides with this litigant rather than that one.

The details of justice in a given time and place are not specifiable by armchair philosophy. The substance of justice is partly a product of contingent pressures of actual dispute resolution. No one needs to know whether flying over someone's land at ten thousand feet counts as trespassing until actual disputes come before a court. We could see this as an epistemological issue—saying there are eternal truths that we learn by going to court. I am not sure that much of practical significance rides on this, but I find it more realistic to interpret the issue as metaphysical: there is *no truth of the matter* about what the law is until litigants force the issue, creating a need for a ruling and a common understanding. Indeed, sometimes there is no uniquely determinate truth about what the law ought to be. (Sometimes rulings are like deciding whether distances will be measured in miles or kilometers, or whether people will drive on the left or the right.) The only determinate truth is that a decision has to be made one way or another, so people can get on with their lives with a better idea of what to expect from each other.

Even natural law theorists would acknowledge that the edges of the concept of property are underdetermined by theory. Edges must be defined

no longer contradict each other. Where I disagree with Steiner is in thinking that this truth is more fruitfully regarded as a contingent truth than as a necessary one. I think judges and legislators affirm rights claims all the time that turn out not to be compossible, and, as I see it, compossibility in a system of rights is an achievement, not a given. Judges, legislators, and other agents have to work to make sure that rights claims are compossible *enough* to enable agents to avoid conflict while still taking seriously their rights as affirmed by judges and legislators.

and refined by practice and custom, and sometimes by judges confronting newly evolving edges of the traffic management problems that property rights are supposed to solve. Often, there are right and wrong answers to how edges need to be defined so as to settle current disputes, enable people to get on with their lives, and avoid disputes in the future. To return to the flyover case, a landowner's right to say no, essential though it may be to land ownership, would have been a recipe for gridlock had it been taken to entail that airlines generally need permits from individual landowners to have a right to fly.

In *Hinman*, the nature and value of commercial traffic settled the question of where to locate the boundaries of rights and justice, not the other way around. The judge was trying to take rights seriously. He succeeded. His verdict left us with a system of rights that we could *afford* to take seriously. He took a system that had come to be inadequately specified relative to newly emerging forms of commercial traffic, and, in a predictable, targeted, not overly clever way, made the system a better solution to the particular problem confronting his court.[38]

Property's normative roots are to be found less in philosophical theorizing about justice and more in whatever the truth of the matter happens to be in a given time and place about what it takes for people to be able to prosper together. The latter discussion turns on facts about what it takes to induce and inspire people to be productive, that is, to identify and meet needs, not only their own needs but also the needs of the people around them.

The point here is not that justice is unneeded or unimportant. In particular cases, we want it to be true that justice is the most important thing, or perhaps the only important thing. But reaching a point where justice holds sway in that manner is an *achievement*. Judges in hard cases don't have such principles to appeal to; by hypothesis, they begin with principles that are silent on the issue at hand. They need to articulate, discover, extend, or in any case decide what justice says in the kind of case they are facing, and (in a precedent-driven system, at least) if they rule well, they will make similar cases easier to resolve in the future.

If the principles of justice are to be compatible with people getting what they need, then they must be compatible with people getting what they

[38] Avner de-Shalit has asked me about the status of principles of justice that in particular cases fail to fit nicely into a system of traffic management. There are no guarantees. Quite the contrary. Judges face such cases from time to time and have to make decisions nonetheless. What often seems to guide them, and I would say rightly so, is a desire to avoid doing anything that appears too creative. They want their rulings to be what people would or should have expected under the circumstances. The law does a better job of managing traffic, other things equal, to the extent that it is predictable. Sometimes the justice of a ruling is controversial. Sometimes it would have been controversial regardless of which way the judge ruled. Sometimes the ruling is a net loss for society in a particular case, and sometimes, nonetheless, the ruling is correct—insofar as it is fair, it is what people should have expected, and it is in keeping with the kind of overall rule of law that keeps the traffic moving as smoothly as can be reasonably expected.

need from a property system, because people do after all need a property framework, and they need it to function in a particular way. (They likewise need a traffic management system, and need it to function in a particular way.) If an alleged principle of justice rules out what people need to do to coordinate expectations, internalize externalities, and secure their possessions well enough to make it safe for them to look for ways to make their customers better off, then people need to keep looking for principles of justice that they can afford to respect. By analogy, if an alleged principle of justice ruled out doing what people needed to do to meet their dietary needs, then people would have to keep looking for principles of justice they could live with.

B. Property as theory-laden

Scholars such as Gerald Gaus sometimes claim that it is basic to any liberal philosophy that there is a presumption against coercion, and thus that coercion has to be justified.[39] Critics reply (at least in conversation) that the presumption against coercion is theory-laden, and in particular presupposes a controversial conception of property and especially of self-ownership.[40]

Alternatively, one might argue that society sets prices, thereby determining the remuneration of particular skills sets, and therefore ought to use redistribution to make amends for setting so high a price on, say, the services of the most talented entertainers. On the one hand, if it were customers who were responsible for deciding whether to pay that high a price, out of their own pockets, then it would not be society's business. In that case, society did not calculate prices at all, so it did not miscalculate either. There is nothing to feel guilty about. On the other hand, if society is the true owner of the money, and for that matter the talents, then (and only then) the question of how to distribute becomes very much society's business. Some of the things Gaus would call coercion—some of the

---

[39] Gerald Gaus, "Coercion, Ownership, and the Redistributive State: Justificatory Liberalism's Classical Tilt," elsewhere in this volume.

[40] Here is a common view that in a subtle way denies the liberal premise of self-ownership. Holmes and Sunstein say that the ACLU (American Civil Liberties Union) is tax exempt, "which means its activities are partly financed by the public." Holmes and Sunstein later say that "a tax deduction is a form of public subsidy" (The Cost of Rights, 21, 66). If this is meant as a substantive claim, though, it is indefensible. The truth is that if a dollar belongs to George Washington, and George uses that dollar to finance project X, then George is subsidizing project X. But if the dollar that Patrick Henry is investing in the ACLU belongs to Patrick, then it is Patrick's dollar, not George's, that is subsidizing the ACLU, and we do not change that fact by noting that George is powerful enough to take it from Patrick but decided not to. To say that the tax deduction is a public subsidy is to presume, rather than to argue, that the public owns the dollars that it sometimes declines to take from Patrick. Perhaps there is an argument for this, but to assert without argument that deductions are subsidies is to try to bully readers into not asking for the argument. Thus, there is a basic choice, and a defining choice for liberalism: Does George need to justify taking Patrick's possessions, or does George need to justify not taking them?

things that call for justification—would not be coercion at all. They would simply be a matter of an agent (the state) deciding how to allocate resources that the agent has every right to allocate.

Perhaps the critics are wrong. But if the critics are right, what follows? In particular, if I cannot justify my possession, does that entail that someone else has a better claim to my possession than I do? Or is it the case that the king (or the state) does not *need* a better claim, so long as he can convince himself that there is some problem with *my* claim? Perhaps no one has a better claim than anyone else. Would that leave the king (or the state) at liberty to settle the question with raw power?[41]

Philosophers Liam Murphy and Thomas Nagel write: "The state does not own its citizens, nor do they own each other collectively. But individual citizens don't own anything except through laws that are enacted and enforced by the state."[42] I wonder, which is it? Who owns a citizen's body, if not the state, not the "people," and not individual citizens either? Perhaps there is a fourth alternative: *no one* owns the citizen's body. *No one* holds a right to say no. But if no one has an exclusive right to a citizen's body, and therefore no one has a correlative duty not to seize that body, that is not liberalism. It is not even civilization.

Property is in some ways conventional, but that is not to call it arbitrary. We may decide arbitrarily to drive on the right rather than on the left, but once a decision is made, the further decision to respect a convention of driving on the right is not arbitrary. And property conventions are less arbitrary than that. There are compelling (even if not universally decisive) reasons to treat a given crop's grower as the crop's owner rather than, say, tying ownership to being the next person to introduce crop disease, or being the next to seize the throne.

Gaus is right; there really is something basic about his premise that coercion is the paradigm of what requires justification, as a straightforward claim and also as a characterization of what is involved in being a liberal. If coercion did not need justifying, not much would. I would add (realizing this is somewhat alien to Gaus's own approach) that *if* Gaus's premise required defense, a defense would be ready to hand. (It is not part of my view that Gaus's premise requires a defense, only that a non-question-begging defense is in fact available.) Namely, people have a record of prospering together when they treat each other as self-owners,

---

[41] Murphy and Nagel say that "we cannot be said to deserve outcomes for which we are in no way responsible. Thus, to the extent that market outcomes are determined by genetic or medical or social luck (including inheritance), they are not, on anyone's account, morally deserved. Since nobody denies that these kinds of luck at least partly determine how well a person fares in a capitalist economy . . ." (*The Myth of Ownership*, 32). But to be lucky is not to be "in no way responsible." What cuts against being deserving is not being lucky, but rather being *merely* lucky. See my "How to Deserve" (1982), updated in Schmidtz, *The Elements of Justice* (Cambridge: Cambridge University Press, 2006), and in Schmidtz, *Person, Polis, Planet: Essays in Applied Philosophy* (New York: Oxford University Press, 2008).

[42] Murphy and Nagel, *The Myth of Ownership*, 176.

and thus treat the coercing of other selves—disposing of their possessions without their consent—as the paradigm of what needs justifying.

VII. Conclusion

One familiar way of theorizing about justice and ownership starts with ideal theory, meaning that we assume a world of perfect compliance, then decide what the principles of justice should be in that world. Some theorists, for example, start with intuitions about how much inequality justice permits, formulate a theory that underwrites those intuitions, then infer what sort of redistribution is needed to keep our evolving wealth distribution in compliance with justice by the lights of that theory. Then our job as moral philosophers is done, as we turn the resulting compliance problem over to experts at implementing policy. Let them learn from experience how many police it takes, with what legal powers, to implement justice so conceived. In short, do the philosophy first; save the social science for later. That is one way.

A second way to talk about justice in ownership starts by picturing a world of human beings as they actually are, and then says that the first virtue of social institutions is that they help such beings live together, realizing the best of the potential benefits while avoiding the worst of the potential costs of community life. After we have such a picture in front of us, we go on to say that alleged principles of justice, if they are to have any place in society, must find their place within—must facilitate rather than thwart—the growing of such beneficial institutions, including property institutions. Before we formulate principles of justice, we first draw conclusions about which principles are compatible with growing institutions, norms, and expectations that people need to live by if they are to live well together. Thus, if an alleged principle of justice (such as "People should not have to pay for basic human needs") rules out our using a price mechanism to distribute bread, and if a price mechanism is the only way to distribute bread without starvation and without turning the central distributor's subjects into a groveling underclass, then we know we have no duty, indeed no right, to try to impose that alleged principle of justice on our fellow citizens. If justice is not the only (or even the first) virtue of institutions, or of persons, then not everything that matters is a matter of justice.[43] My claim in this essay is that *figuring out* what else matters can be an essential step in determining what justice itself is about.

Think of the choice between these two ways of theorizing about justice in terms of direction of fit. The first approach says that our world ought to fit our theory of justice, and "you can't make an omelet without breaking a few eggs." The second says that our theory of justice ought to fit our

---

[43] See John Tomasi, *Liberalism Beyond Justice* (Princeton, NJ: Princeton University Press, 2001).

world, and "you can break a lot of eggs and still not have an omelet." This second approach treats functioning property institutions as morally fundamental and justice as derivative. Philosophy has tended to choose the first path, which empowers us to begin (and end) with philosophy, without all the hard slogging through law, economics, history, and other disciplines before we can even start philosophizing. In a way, this is understandable, but still, it is time for a change.

This has been an essay in the how and why of nonideal theory: in particular, how and why principles of property come first and principles of justice second. Ownership conventions, and property law as it develops under the pressures of case-by-case dispute resolution, tend to become touchstones for conflict mediation down through generations. These conventions (and property law itself) remain imperfect, retaining vestiges of adaptations to ancient problems that no longer exist; yet still they work, coordinating expectations so as to make it easier for people to live together.

Philosophy, University of Arizona

PROPERTY AND RIGHTS

By Jan Narveson

I. Introduction

Eric Freyfogle, in his recent book *On Property*, introduces the subject as follows:

> Today's conflicts over property have arisen chiefly because of changes taking place in American society. Some of the changes are demographic (we have more people), some are economic (we are wealthier overall and have new technology), some aesthetic (we want our landscapes to look better), and some intellectual or cognitive (we understand more how nature works and want to respect its ecological functioning). These [changes] . . . are calling us to revise the rights that landowners possess, and, once again, to draw new lines between the individual owner and the community, between individual liberty and democratic governance.
>
> . . . Private property is basically just a tool. It is a governance arrangement that exists because life with it is better than life without it. Just so, life with well-crafted ownership rules can be a good deal better than life with poorly shaped ones.[1]

This passage poses a general question about private property: Do the basic ideas of property need revision, or are there fundamental ideas here that are still valid and applicable? I will defend the apparently unpopular thesis that there are such ideas. I will do so despite agreeing with Freyfogle about the basic status of private property: it is indeed "a tool," and property rules are intended to make life a "good deal better." But putting it that way raises important questions: What if certain ways of drawing the lines of ownership would benefit some at the expense of others? If we set about redrawing lines and redefining property rules, what principles are there to guide us? I propose to defend what we might call the "classic" view of property. On that view, property is a unitary concept, explicable as a right over the thing owned, against others who are precluded from the free use of it to which ownership entitles the owner. We can attack many difficult issues in the light of these classic ideas, rather than finding altogether new ones. To that end, I will both restate and defend the classic

[1] Eric Freyfogle, *On Private Property* (Boston, MA: Beacon Press, 2007), xxi. Freyfogle is Professor of Law at the University of Illinois.

doi:10.1017/S0265052509990057

view, and will illustrate the view by applying it to the discussion of some important problems in property theory.

II. Property: The General Story

The general story is clear enough. We have property because we need it, or at least want it, or, most likely of all, want things that require property notions and rights in order for us to have them. Moreover, we have the institution of property rights because we are particular people, vulnerable to various interventions by other people, and not happy at the prospect of continual incursions from them. For human beings, drawing lines around stable things and designating them as "belonging" to certain individuals as such, and thus not belonging to others, is just what is necessary to enable us to get on successfully with our lives.

Property is exclusionary. To say that x "belongs" to A is to say that others not identical with A are not to use x without A's permission. Others are, in short, excluded from the sort of unilateral voluntary utilization of x that was enjoyed by A at the time of his initial acquisition of x. A is in charge: A becomes the authority on the use of x, and thus has the authority to exclude others who would make competing use of x. This I take to be a matter of definition.

On that point, we must make a further distinction, following Jean-Jacques Rousseau (among others).[2] This is the distinction between *possession* and *ownership*. 'Possession' is understood here as a purely descriptive relation between the possessor and the thing possessed, while 'ownership' is understood as a normative concept. If, after stealing it, I am in possession of your BMW, I am able to use it without your permission, though I have no right to do so. Likewise, if you own the BMW, then you are normatively permitted to use it without anybody else's say-so, though it does not follow that you are actually in a position to do so. Ownership, then, is entitlement to possession, which is to say, entitlement to use the thing oneself and to exclude others from using it. Ownership is also transferable, being a set of alienable rights. These rights are not only alienable but decomposable, so that one can transfer a part of one's rights, or transfer one's rights temporarily, and so on, to designated other parties. What makes ownership ownership is that the owner has the normative authority to do these things.

---

[2] Rousseau's distinction is found in his *Social Contract,* chapter 8: "What man loses is his natural freedom and an unlimited right to everything that tempts him and that he can get; what he gains is civil freedom and the proprietorship of everything he *possesses*. . . . [O]ne must distinguish carefully . . . between *possession*, which is only the effect of force or the right of first occupant, and *property*, which can only be based on a *positive title*." See Jean-Jacques Rousseau, *On the Social Contract (with Geneva Manuscript and Political Economy)*, trans. Judith R. Masters (New York: St. Martin's Press, 1978), 56; emphasis added.

III. Self-Ownership and Liberty: The Latter Not Founded on the Former

Many authors have treated 'self-ownership' as a basic concept, from which comes our general right of liberty; in turn, all other property stems from that general right. I think this view is mistaken. But there are different reasons why one might think it is mistaken. One thought would be that the concept of ownership is logically inapplicable to the self. Another would be that the idea of ownership of the self is morally objectionable. A third view would be that although neither of the first two objections can be sustained, it is also not the case that the ownership of anything else that can be owned *comes from* self-ownership.

The first view holds that the concept of 'ownership' does not *apply* to oneself. On the face of it, though, it seems as though the concept does. For to say that one owns anything is to say that others may not use it without one's permission. To say that one "owns oneself" is to say that others may not use one's *self* without that self's permission. Why, then, would there be a problem?

Those who object to such talk complain, especially, that in the case of our selves, the notion of being able to market those selves, transfer their ownership at will, and the like, does not apply. But those complaints are not obviously correct. Among the larger issues discussed among libertarians, for example, is the issue of whether voluntary slavery would be permissible. If it would be either permissible or not permissible, however, then transferring ownership of oneself is evidently being treated as at least logically possible. Thus, slavery as normally understood surely appears to be a case in which person *A* is owned by person *B: A* does not get to do with *A* whatever *A* chooses, being instead compelled to do what *B* chooses. This does not seem to be such a stretch; indeed, it seems to be the natural way to describe the situation. Whether slavery is normatively shipshape is, of course, an issue—if perhaps a dead one by now. But how could it ever have been an issue if the notion of ownership of selves doesn't even make sense in the first place?

Voluntary slavery is, of course, tricky. For one thing, it sounds like a contradiction in terms, slavery being quintessentially involuntary. For another, it is difficult to see what's in it for the voluntarily enslaved person. My hiring myself out to do a job for someone, in return for payment, makes so much sense as to be paradigmatic of the whole idea of employment. My "selling" myself into slavery suffers from an obvious problem: it's hard to see how I could be in a position to collect if slaves have no authority over themselves; the slave owner could simply prevent the now-enslaved person from collecting, ever. And there are other issues. For example, what if the voluntarily enslaved person has a change of mind, or heart, and wishes to withdraw? If the contract of slavery specified conditions for termination, the previous problem would obtain; that is, the owner could simply prevent the enslaved person from suing for the enforcement of the contract. If this problem did not obtain, if the enslaved person had the option of suing, then would we not have to say that the individual in question was not quite a slave? Slaves ordinarily so called had no such options, after all.

The voluntary slave could perhaps make a contract calling for payments or other compensation to someone other than the slave (e.g., to his wife). In such cases, there might be legal enforcement of the condition as well. There is still a question about the moral acceptability of any such thing, and a question about whether a rational being could contemplate binding himself thus; but neither of those points casts doubt on the applicability of the terminology of ownership in the context of slavery. And we do read of the Roman era and others in which slaves could accumulate income and buy their release from that condition.[3]

If self-ownership were self-evident, it is hard to see how there could ever have been such a thing as slavery. If I own myself, then you don't, and if that is self-evident, you not only don't but *can't*. Yet slavery was practiced in a wide range of human societies, for a very long time. All this suggests that the ownership of persons by themselves is conceptually possible, and is basically on a par with the ownership of any other things that can be owned.

The second view is that talk of self-ownership is morally objectionable. This objection, of course, is partisan: that is to say, whether we are going to hold that people do indeed *own* themselves depends on what we think of freedom. People can ruin their own lives, or so we think. But even if we grant that, there is the question whether they have the *right* to do so. And there is, at least, a considerable weight of popular opinion behind the libertarian's view of the matter: the right to "go to hell in a handbasket" is one that we can defend without in the least endorsing any individual's choice to take that path.

In any case, I argue here for the third alternative: that, while self-ownership is both coherent and morally defensible, it is not helpful to suppose that the general right of property is *founded* on self-ownership. The argument that property is so founded would hold that the general

---

[3] According to the Public Broadcasting System Web site on Rome (http://www.pbs.org/empires/romans/empire/slaves_freemen.html): "Another difference between Roman slavery and its more modern variety was manumission—the ability of slaves to be freed. Roman owners freed their slaves in considerable numbers: some freed them outright, while others allowed them to buy their own freedom. The prospect of possible freedom through manumission encouraged most slaves to be obedient and hard working. . . . Formal manumission was performed by a magistrate and gave freed men full Roman citizenship. The one exception was that they were not allowed to hold office. However, the law gave any children born to freedmen, after formal manumission, full rights of citizenship, including the right to hold office."

On the idea of buying out of slavery in the modern setting of Sudan, see Kwame Anthony Appiah and Martin Bunzl, eds., *Buying Freedom* (Princeton, NJ: Princeton University Press, 2007).

right of *liberty* stems from self-ownership, and that the right of property follows from that general right. The problem here is fundamental. There seems to be an idea in the literature that the general principle of liberty, as in John Stuart Mill and John Locke, *rests on* the notion of self-ownership as its foundation.[4] But the preceding analysis should make it clear that this cannot be so. To act is to *use oneself* in some way—to put oneself into motion in some direction or other. Being at liberty means that one acts as one's own self directs, rather than as some other self directs; it therefore means that one *uses oneself* as one directs. The moral thesis of self-ownership asserts that this liberty is rightful. But if one wants to claim that people "by nature" *own themselves,* then one is simply proclaiming their general freedom to do as they please—which is exactly the libertarian principle itself, neither more nor less. The libertarian principle may be unfounded, but it cannot coherently be said to be founded *on* self-ownership, for to say that is to say that it is founded on itself.

IV. Self-Ownership and Self-Possession

Perhaps what is meant by the claim that the general right of liberty is *founded on* self-ownership is something else: what we may call *self-possession.* Recalling our distinction between ownership, which is moral, and possession, which is descriptive, we can see that it is plausible to say that people "by nature" *possess* themselves. Individuals, we may say (and I would say) are essentially "souls," that is, personalities, minds. The point of self-possession talk would be that each individual is built in such a way that the decision-and-control parts of the individual's mind are connected with a certain body, and with the rest of the same mind, in a manner enabling that particular decision center to exercise (to whatever extent) direct control over that body. That is what makes us call it "his" (or "her") body and mind.[5] Paralysis might disable some of the connec-

---

[4] Robert Nozick, *Anarchy, State, and Utopia* (New York: Basic Books, 1974), takes this approach. G. A. Cohen, *Self-Ownership, Freedom, and Equality* (Cambridge: Cambridge University Press, 1995), takes Nozick to be doing so; see esp. chap. 3, "Self-Ownership, World Ownership, and Equality," 67–91. Will Kymlicka, *Contemporary Political Philosophy: An Introduction* (Oxford: Oxford University Press, 1990), 103–25, discusses the notion that liberty is founded on self-ownership at some length. My disagreement with much of Kymlicka's treatment would take too long to explain here. Note that I do not take these writers to suppose that either Locke or Mill themselves took the principle of liberty to be founded on self-ownership. Locke thinks that it is founded on reason, whatever that is supposed to mean, and Mill thinks that it is founded on utility.

[5] In so saying, I disagree with G. A. Cohen, who proposes that self-ownership is *fully reflexive,* so that "what owns and what is owned are one and the same, namely, the whole person" (Cohen, *Self-Ownership, Freedom, and Equality,* 69). I do not think that pure reflexivity makes sense, metaphysically speaking. What does make sense is the control of the rest of us by our proprietarily so-called "selves," that is, the consciously deliberating, willing, and feeling parts of our minds. This may be a metaphysical issue of little import—apart from its connections to, say, slavery. And in any case, I cannot discuss the issue further in the present essay.

tions that normally obtain; external interference might make normal control difficult or impossible. But still, it is a fact about people that they can get their bodies moving on the say-so of the decision-and-command-making faculties that define those people as the particular persons they are (however those faculties are to be conceived).[6]

Nevertheless, it of course does *not* follow from the fact of possession that we have a particular *normative* status in doing either some or all of those things that we can by nature do. If there is anything to the idea that getting from 'is' to 'ought' is a problem, this is surely a case in point. Let *A* be ever so competent to decide to do this or that, the question whether he *ought* to do it, or even has a *right* to do it is logically open, as the foregoing discussion of slavery makes clear. It is a matter of substantive moral principle to say that he does have such a right or obligation. No amount of sheer description of how the human frame is put together will suffice to establish any normative claim about the relation between decision-and-command-making faculties and the associated self.

V. Property: Public and Private

Discussions of property tend almost exclusively to be discussions about the legitimacy, extent, and nature of *private* ownership. This is understandable, but it has to be pointed out that there is no inherent reason why ownership cannot be public as well as private.

Using land as our prime example, we can distinguish three categories of ownership here:

(a) "Common" in the sense that there is *no* ownership;
(b) "Common" in the sense that there is *collective* ownership by some group or other; and
(c) Private ownership in the usual sense, that is, ownership by a person as such—one person (normally, or in the first instance), or else sets of persons who, in some specified arrangement, share control over the thing owned by them.

Each of these categories plays an important role in political communities. To be sure, the first and third categories, no ownership and private ownership, are prima facie nonpolitical. More precisely, we can distinguish between moral and political types of ownership (or senses of the term 'ownership') and can then note that the case for *A*'s being taken to be the legitimate owner of *x* may be exclusively moral, or it may be political and legal in the sense that the question is whether *A*'s possession

---

[6] Perhaps minds are entirely physical, in which case perhaps there is a literal location for the decision-making parts of the mind. That metaphysical question is of no special concern in this connection, interesting though it may be in its own right.

of *x* is recognized and upheld in law or in the political structure of the community in question. I claim that the moral sense of ownership is the basic one, so that what we are discussing here is essentially moral, but with important and pervasive connections to the legal and political realm.

It is part of the logic of society, as we may put it, that ownership must begin with non-ownership, and that the beginnings of ownership must be by some process of acquisition. But how does this work? It is to this question that I now turn.

VI. FROM SELF-OWNERSHIP TO THING-OWNERSHIP?

Moral and social philosophers have long been concerned about the status of property in respect of things external to the self—though more recently, and interestingly, they have also been concerned about things such as intellectual property, which is (in a sense) not external, though its connections with what is external are very strong. We will see that the very nature of intellectual property (as an interface between the internal and the external) makes it important for the subject of ownership of "externals" in the more usual sense. Meanwhile, the situation has been, generally speaking, that many philosophers are inclined to accept some such thesis as self-ownership, but are disinclined to accept, without considerable qualification, ownership of things. The qualification in question is substantial. For if we suppose that whatever people earn by their work, with conditions of payment negotiated by parties acting voluntarily, counts on the face of it as *theirs*, then rates of taxation running from 30 to 50 percent[7] would seem to fly rather strongly in the face of accepting private ownership with any sort of robust conscience.

Why the concern? What makes theorists hesitate to accept that people can fully *own* various bits of the world? 'Fully owning' would mean that the owners may do whatever they want with the things in question so long as it does not violate the same rights of other persons, rights to themselves and to *their* property. But to say this is not to say very much until we are reasonably sure just which rights they have, and that is less than obvious. As a general principle, though, we can certainly say that the right not to be harmed by others is paramount here. And, as another very relevant fundamental principle, we can say that the notion of 'harm' must in the end be determined by the interests of the person in question, *as that person sees them.*[8] Thus, we have David Gauthier's lucid formulation, that

---

[7] Current federal income tax rates in the United States do not quite reach the 50 percent level, but they do in Canada, where I live, and in some countries in Europe. In any case, adding up various taxes and charges that amount to taxes (at the municipal, state, and federal level) will yield total tax levels on this order even in the United States.

[8] Malcolm Murray analyzes this, brilliantly, as a matter of acting with the consent of the individual affected. See Malcolm Murray, *The Moral Wager* (New York: Springer, 2007), esp. chap. 6.

A is not to pursue his interests by thwarting those of *B*, unless there is no other way for *A* to avoid damage to himself.[9] Each person is a sort of barrier, or boundary, to each other person, not to be crossed without that person's permission, actual or implied.

Keeping this in mind, we need to ask: Why is the acquisition of property such a contentious issue? The reason is that appropriators of bits of the world, insofar as they engage in such appropriation, are accused of a sort of *theft*. It will be said that such acquisition cuts into the natural supply of resources available, in principle, to all, and that it deprives the excluded from a liberty they previously had. Thus, Freyfogle writes:

> [L]et's consider what really happens when a person becomes first owner of a tract of land and puts up no-trespassing signs around the perimeter. . . . The landowner, to be sure, has gained greater freedom over this exclusive piece of land. The owner's liberty has gone up. At the same time, everyone else's liberty has gone down.[10]

So when individual *A* acquires bit of land *x* in what appears to be a condition of wilderness, no other persons being present, theorists like Freyfogle have a surprise for him: people in general *do* have a claim on this land, despite their absence—indeed, despite the fact that, in most cases, they have not even been born yet. This thesis, which is apparently affirmed even by the otherwise sensible Locke,[11] evidently presumes that, somehow, everything basically *belongs* to everyone, where 'belongs' is taken in a strongly normative sense. For if it did not belong to them, how could the person who takes it be accused of taking it *from them*? So understood, this thesis is among the more intriguingly subversive bugbears of social philosophy.

To claim that everything "belongs to everyone" is, on the face of it, to claim that each person has the "right" to exclude every other person from the use of everything, that is, of *any natural object whatever*. This seems to be a textbook example of utter nonsense at work. Consider any thing, *x*: the claim implies that person *A* has the right to exclude *B* from use of *x*; yet, on this idea, person *B* in turn also has the right to exclude *A* from the use of *x*. So *A* may compel *B* to desist from using *x*, thus leaving *A* free to use it, but meanwhile *B* may also compel *A* to so desist, thus leaving *B* free to use it. Thus, the claim models the "condition of nature" according to Thomas Hobbes, where "every man has right to every thing." [12] But

---

[9] David Gauthier, *Morals by Agreement* (New York: Oxford University Press, 1986), 205.

[10] Freyfogle, *On Private Property*, 7.

[11] There is some dispute about Locke's intentions here. But in saying "God, who hath given the World to Men in common . . ." (*Second Treatise of Civil Government*, sec. 26), he certainly leaves the impression that everyone has a claim to the land, one which needs to be overturned by argument (which he tries to provide).

[12] Thomas Hobbes, *Leviathan* (New York: E. P. Dutton, 1950), chap. XII, p. 107.

in the usual sense of the term 'right', what one has by right others (by that very fact) do *not* have, and thus the right-holder may legitimately defend his right, others being in the wrong. Obviously, to try to make this universal is simply nonsensical, as we have just seen. No coherent assertion about rights can be derived from this claim.

Any such claim, then, if it is to make any sense, has to be understood collectively. So understood, there is the usual problem that collectives do not have minds, and thus some kind of internal structure of command and control must be envisaged here. And what will that be? One tradition identifies it with the will of the King, who personifies "the community" — whether I or you happen to go along with that identification or not. Persons of liberal persuasion, in turn, will interpret the command-and-control structure democratically: the collective will make decisions about what to do with its estates by majority rule. For all x, then, the majority decides what is to be done with x and by whom. Yet majority rule is the very juggernaut against which individual rights are typically asserted in the first place: a *right* is what a mere majority does *not* get to overrule. Rights are a *constraint against* the majority, rather than a status that is entirely theirs to decide.

Whether those who agree with Freyfogle are correct in holding that the excluded individuals are somehow harmed by the first-comer's ownership of things is a crucially important question, and I will argue that they are not harmed. My reasons are as follows.

To begin with, if the idea is that excluded individuals are being harmed in the particular way that property owners are harmed by robbery, then the idea can be denied straight off. To say that excluded individuals are thus harmed is, really, to deny that there is such a thing as "property" — that natural items ever *can* be "acquired" — since, of course, for anyone to acquire anything is, logically, for others to be excluded from future use of it by the acquirer. But since, by hypothesis, the excluded individuals already "own" the things in question, they cannot be so excluded. And since ownership is, by definition, rightful use with power to exclude, it is a plausible inference that the situation of supposed "universal ownership" is a situation of universal uselessness.

Next, we observe that notionally, at least, "first-comers" are precisely people operating in a hypothetical environment in which no others are or have been around to acquire claims arising from previous use. Thus, by hypothesis, there simply is no one there to be "harmed," unless the question is begged by simply proclaiming the possession of rights over things by all, prior to and independent of any use anyone makes of the things in question, and in the absence of any reasons for the proclamation.[13] That

---

[13] For further discussion, see Ann Levey, "Liberty, Property, and the Libertarian Idea," in Malcolm Murray, ed., *Liberty, Games, and Contracts* (Burlington, VT: Ashgate Publishing Co., 2007), 147–56; see also my comments on her arguments (ibid., 231–34).

can hardly qualify as an "argument" for the claim that those rights are *due to* the harms to these individuals that would be caused by prior occupation.

Finally, we may ask whether possible future acquirers are indeed deprived of a liberty, as Freyfogle claims. I argue that they are not. We are all at liberty, given an environment in which there is unacquired potentially useful stuff lying around, to *attempt* to acquire some of it. We still have this liberty even though others have used the same liberty successfully in acquiring this or that bit of stuff. But we are not morally at liberty to acquire what others already have, and we are not automatically entitled to any particular bit of the Earth, or indeed to any of it at all. We must either earn what we have, by making or discovering or occupying it, or else be given it by someone else who legitimately has it. Now, first-comer *A* does not prevent *B* from *attempts* to acquire something; he merely, by being there first, prevents *B* from becoming the possessor of this already-possessed thing. Since nothing can be wholly owned by more than one independent party, the fact that occupancy by one person prevents occupancy by others obviously cannot visit a "harm" in the sense of a deprivation of something the others could also have had. For they "could have had" the thing only if someone else did not have it. Obviously, there cannot be a universal right to all things. There can only be a right to exert oneself in the pursuit of one's goals, given the similar right of others. And the acquisition of something one would like to have had, by someone else, does not deprive one of that right. Nor does it deprive one of the thing itself, which of course one did not have before. This means, therefore, that acquisition does not visit harms on others.

Meanwhile, of course, most finders of things do not operate in an uninhabited environment, and when they do not, there are others "around," with possible claims to be considered and cleared before acquisition by a particular individual can be legitimate. Most ownership issues will require negotiation and agreement at some point, leading to the adoption of more specific rules about many matters. Yet one of the premises that has to strongly influence the formulation of such rules is that an individual's use and occupation of some bit of nature, in the evident absence of others making competing claims by their presence at the time, gives that individual's property claim a very strong priority over any other claims. Possession, as the saying goes, is nine points of the law. In state-of-nature cases, make that virtually ten.

VII. The Positive Argument for Liberty — and, Therefore, Property

The idea of self ownership—that is, of a general right to liberty—is rooted in our particularity and our individuality. Persons are separate: one person's purposes are not another's; there is no necessary normative output from A's interests to B's. Consequently, when the pursuit of interests is to be curtailed by consideration of the interests of others, this will have to be due to aspects of *interaction*, specifically the impinging of some persons on others in such a way as to create a potential for cooperatively derived mutual benefit—or the reverse. This provides genuine reason, seen from each agent's internal point of view, for restricting one's own pursuit of benefit: the reason is simply that we stand to do better with such restrictions than without them, *provided*, of course, that others accept such restrictions as well.

This abstract result seems to be viewed with alarm by many theorists, who apparently suppose that morals must require self-abnegatory altruism. The trouble with that, however, is that selves are the only beings with interests; they are, normatively speaking, *all we have*, and therefore, negating them means, on the face of it, abandoning the whole point of being someone in particular—as we all are, after all. If the point is generalized, then it raises the problem that if *my* self means nothing, why should anybody else's mean something? If the satisfaction of some self doesn't count, independently of who provided the sources of that satisfaction, then the point of altruism is as completely defeated as the initial self-interest to be abnegated.

Our individual persons and pursuits are what we have, and the general principle of liberty protects us in being the persons we are, doing what we want to do, and thus acquiring what we can and want to acquire, compatibly with the similar right of others.

VIII. Original Acquisition *Is* Exchange

Once things are acquired, their owners, having the right to do whatever they wish with the acquired items, provided they do it peaceably in relation to any others encountered, may proceed to exchange. Exchange, if voluntary, is for mutual benefit: A exchanges his x with B's y because A prefers y to x and B prefers x to y; otherwise, the exchange would not voluntarily take place. Thus, both benefit from the exchange. Persons acquiring the sort of property (e.g., land) that can be improved by making it more productive of things (e.g., crops), the rights to which can be transferred from one person to another, will most likely proceed to just such exchanges, given the familiar story of diverse abilities and tastes as well as diverse resources.

What needs to be appreciated is that the situation leading to "original" acquisition is itself actually one of exchange. Each of us, as Hobbes puts it, "lays down" his or her liberty to interfere and "despoil" in exchange for similiar forbearance by others. The benefit of peace is a strictly public good: A can *only* get it from B, and B from A. Both are better off with it than without it, and so, if these value assessments are right, peace will be sought by reasonable people as a fundamental good and, indeed, the precondition of all other goods, *including* that of acquired property. When *A* allows *B* to acquire, and *B* allows *A* to acquire, they are trading liberties.

This provides an underpinning for taking the point of view of the "social contract": self-imposed restriction of one's pursuits will be motivated by those very pursuits, in view of the ways that others relate to one. Classically, the social contract idea has led to major emphasis on what have come to be called "negative" rights: the agreement to refrain from inflicting damage on the other person, in return for a similar resolution on the other's part. Despite being negative, these rights are benefits in relation to what could otherwise be expected. They are, indeed, enormous benefits from the point of view of nearly anyone. If the social contract works, we are all safe from each other's capability of inflicting all manner of losses, up to and including death: we receive the benefit of being able to count on being alive tomorrow and next year, insofar as death could result from the intentional activities of others. For all of us, being alive is a necessary condition for accomplishing anything we are interested in—even suicide, which requires that its subject be alive to commit it. But more generally, being free from the predation of others, and not just having one's life intact, is a necessary condition for our accomplishing anything at all. The social contract recognizes this, in the ways made familiar by Hobbes and Locke: The "First Law of Nature," Hobbes writes, is to "seek peace" and resort to violence only when peace is not available from others.[14] Locke, in his very similar version of "the Law of Nature," has Reason telling us that "no one ought to harm another in his Life, Health, Liberty or Possessions,"[15] with a subsequent reference to people's "Lives, Liberties and Estates, which I call by the general Name, *Property*."[16] That all this should be reasonably accounted "property" is what I shall argue further below. The general case of being able to use one's body and mind implies the slightly more restricted case of being able to use them to manipulate, fashion, and transform various bits of the world into bits more to one's liking and more conducive to flourishing and longevity.

IX. THE BASIC REASON FOR PROPERTY

Property is closely bound up with negative rights. Indeed, it essentially is a negative right (or several?)[17] itself. To own something is for others to be required to keep off. They are already, we are supposing, required to

---

[14] Hobbes, *Leviathan,* chap. XIV.

[15] Locke, *Second Treatise of Civil Government,* sec. 6.

[16] Ibid., sec. 123.

[17] It has been popular to maintain that ownership is essentially a "bundle" of distinguishable rights, as if they had nothing to do with each other. For further discussion of this view, which I dismiss as a confusion, see Jan Narveson, *The Libertarian Idea* (Philadelphia, PA: Temple University Press, 1988; republished, Peterborough, Ontario: Broadview Press, 2001), 64; see esp. note 6 on p. 342.

keep off *you*. You have property only if others are required to keep off *it*, unless you permit them to use it. So we can now pursue the central question of how to get from "you" to "it." What connects them? I believe that the answer is not very far to seek, even if it isn't exactly staring us in the face.

Ownership is a normative relation with three terms: (1) you, the owner; (2) whatever you own; and (3) everybody else. It is *not* a relationship between you and the thing owned, simpliciter. This seems not to have been appreciated by some writers, and one can only suppose that the reason is that from the point of view of the owner, it might look that way. But to think that is to confuse possessions with property. When I merely have something in my grasp, that has no immediate entailments for what anyone else ought to do, though it might have implications for what they would need to do if they are to get it out of my possession. But as soon as someone else makes a claim to the thing, I need to show that my possession of it is not only a fact but also *legitimate*—that my claim is reasonable, and thus to be respected. That means that the relation between me and that thing has to be claimed by me in such a way as to imply that you, and others, are morally (or, as may be, legally)[18] required to keep off. That is what is meant by insisting that ownership is three-termed, not two-termed. To fail to recognize this is to deny ownership any potential for resolving any normative problems. It can resolve such problems only if *A*'s ownership has reasonably clear implications concerning what *B*, *C*, and so on may or may not do.

X. All Rights Are Rights to Act

There is another point to emphasize about the nature of rights: rights all fundamentally concern *actions*. A "right to a thing" is a right to do something with it. My rights against you are rights that you do or not do certain things to me, and, similarly, that I do or not do them to you. Any assertions about rights "to things," as we are accustomed to putting it, are assertions about what we may do in relation to each other, with or to or about the things in question. Rights enable us to tell each other where to get off—where to desist from doing what one might like to do (or perhaps not only to desist, but to do something else quite specific instead). Rights, then, relate the will of the right-holder to the wills of all others. The right-holder may do this or that, and this means that others are normatively required to refrain from or to do something. On the general liber-

---

[18] I mean 'legally' in the sense of called for by some actual body of law. The general point of view of this essay is the classic one in this respect as well—that positive law is properly subordinate to morality, which has often enough, as by Aquinas, been dubbed 'moral law.' Possession used to be said to be nine points of the law; in recent times, however, public intervention is so pervasive that the need for sharply distinguishing positive law and moral law is now evident.

tarian view, the rights in question are, as I have said, fundamentally negative: they say what others are *not to do*, but not, basically, what they are *to do*.

Thus, the question is: Which facts about my possession of various things are such as to supply relevant premises for normative claims against the activities of others? To this, the libertarian has a general answer. Libertarianism proclaims that we all have a general right to liberty, and to have that right is, precisely, to have a right that others refrain from interfering with, negating, or undermining that liberty (i.e., interfering with, negating, or undermining the course of action, or inaction, that the rightholder has in mind to engage in). Libertarianism, in short, is essentially the affirmation of a general right against the initiation of force and the use of fraud by others against any person.

Why should we accept such a view? To begin with, I have denied that the hypothesis of a general collective ownership of everything natural has any rational standing. Instead, there is only (1) *us*—people—a bunch of organisms possessed of and animated by minds, and of various powers, including the power to communicate with each other, and in enough contact with each other to present potential problems for (as well as potential benefits to) each other; and (2) a whole lot of natural stuff which, so far as it goes, has no normative status whatever. What does have normative status is (or stems from) *us:* our lives, our actions, our interests.

Taken by themselves, however, our individual assertions of value have little purchase against others. To arrive at principles for us all, we must ask what we, collectively, might stand to benefit from and what we might stand to lose from. Abstractly, the case is pretty straightforward: what we each want is whatever is good for ourselves (at least), and what we want to avoid is what is bad for ourselves. So a general prohibition of actions that tend to undermine our welfare is called for, and a general endorsement—but not a flat requirement—of what tends to promote our various welfares is also called for.

How, then, do we get to property? In brief, the answer is that many of our actions involve the use of various bits of the world outside of ourselves. We want to be able to engage in those actions successfully, and to do this requires, generally, that others not intervene to upset those trains of actions, given the plans governing them. Successful actions "require" this in the straightforward sense that noninterference is a logically necessary condition of their success: if you stop me from doing x, then I don't do x, by definition; but x here is, by hypothesis, the very thing I wanted to do.

This can generate misunderstanding, in one important respect. Obviously, many of our actions involve others, and many involve the joint use, by ourselves with others, of assorted material objects, spaces, and processes. A few actions might involve many others. But in virtually all of these cases, it is possible to distinguish between those *in* the group of persons acting together and those *not* in that group, with the latter, usually, vastly exceeding the former in size. In those cases, persons outside the group can often act to prevent or greatly increase the difficulty of successful performance by those inside, including oneself. Here, too, property rules will often be necessary, or at least useful. A group of condominium owners (for example) needs freedom from a lot of external intervention, and each of its members has an interest in that freedom. The point generalizes: just as every individual is to have a right of liberty as against every other individual, so too every group, however small, has such a right against every other, however large.

The question from my individual point of view is: How do I induce you to refrain from such interferences? The proposed answer is that I make a very general deal, or arrangement, or agreement, with you: You refrain from interfering with me, in regard to certain bits of the world, and I refrain from interfering with you in your use of certain other bits of it. This is the proposed answer because, given that we are both capable of such interferences, mutual refraining is of mutual benefit for us. We both do better in the absence of such interference: with rights, we do as well as our own powers and our relation to our environment and to each other will enable us to do. This result is far superior to what we would be able to achieve under a regime where interference, by all and sundry, is common and expected (because it is not prohibited).

XI. Property-Respecting as a Moral Duty

The moral dimension of all this is that, for full effect, we want this tendency to refrain from interference to become a strong internal commitment: we want everyone to have an internally monitored aversion to such interfering activity, a disposition to ask before we encroach, and not to proceed without assurance of (or reason to expect) an affirmative answer. The general possession of such a disposition is, I propose, to our maximum mutual advantage. I say "maximum" mutual advantage because this arrangement permits the widest range of potentially useful action on the part of each individual: if we ask for more, it will, by definition, be at the expense of someone else. Moreover, that expense is uncompensated, since if it were compensated to the satisfaction of the affected persons, an imposed restriction on those persons' powers would be unnecessary. For we suppose that we will do what benefits ourselves, and a deal from you leaving me better off does benefit me—but it also benefits you, since you need not have made it, but did so. Hence, we would voluntarily accept such a deal if it were offered, and so, mutual benefit ensues.

All that said, we very often know those with whom we interact well enough that we can, in many cases, anticipate permission from them for what would otherwise be infringements of their rights. Sometimes what I want of yours is trivially costly to you: the cost to you of my asking for it, even when that would be easy to do, exceeds the cost to you of parting with the items in question. Sometimes we are friends and are disposed to help each other out, and sometimes we are neighbors, whose utility profiles are familiar enough to each other that we have developed mutually beneficial patterns of borrowing and trading various helpful things. And so on. But for all these things to work properly, the baseline has to be the general negative right to oneself and one's things, and a habitual respect for them by (preferably) everyone.

XII. Original Acquisition

The preceding exposition emphasizes that the acquisition of things is the beginning of property rights. In the course of action, we use things, and if nobody else is already doing so, then the way is clear for us to use them, and to insist on the right to continue to use them. We do not need to justify our acquisition of x by demonstrating that it will best serve the public good if *we* are allowed to use it rather than someone else—even though that is, quite often, true. The point is that people being able to use what was previously unused, at will, enables a better-off society. Indeed, it enables that better-off society even in the (presumably numerous) cases in which there is someone out there who might make better use of it than the person who becomes the owner. That is because, on the face of it, the new acquirer, A, adds value, while subtracting none from anyone else. (A is prohibited from doing the latter.) If someone else, B, comes along and undoes A's good work, then B negates this addition of value; and he or she thereby also undoes the pristine Paretian quality of A's activities. I refer here to the criterion of Pareto efficiency, according to which an outcome is Pareto-efficient if it makes no one worse off and at least one person better off. Those who acquire property are better off, and those who don't are not worse off—they are only in whatever condition they were in before (namely, without possession of the thing that the envisaged new acquirer acquires). Of course, this sets the stage for further improvements due to exchanges of property.[19]

The argument here does not appeal to views about interpersonally compared utility; nor does it appeal to a supposed "intrinsic value" of liberty. The claim that the libertarian argument requires some such premise is made, for example, by John Christman in *The Myth of Property*, where he writes:

> Freedom construed in the non-normative sense is defined as the absence of restraints in the carrying out of a person's desires, and none of those key terms—"restraints," "persons," or "desires"—is

[19] See Jan Narveson, "The Invisible Hand," *Journal of Business Ethics* 46, no. 3 (2003): 201–12.

understood as a moral notion. . . . Hence, since non-normative freedom refers to *any* acts by persons free of restraints, the concept of
freedom itself does not distinguish between being free to hit others
with baseball bats and being free to make political speeches in a
public park. . . . So the moral evaluation of allowing such freedom to
flourish is not provided by the concept itself. . . .

But recall that a separate premise—that liberty of this sort (construed non-normatively) has intrinsic value—will be included in arguments linking negative liberty (L1) and liberal ownership. This value,
moreover, must be intrinsic, since it would not do to say that liberal
ownership protects liberty but the value of liberty is merely instrumental. . . . Certainly the "freedom" to do the act, intrinsically and by
itself, has no value whatsoever to the agent. For unless the absence of
external physical restraints facing the agent in some way enhances
the possibility that she will achieve something she wants to achieve,
such an absence can have no value for the person. That is, L1 has no
value except for its power to allow or bring about other things, such
as L2, L3, or some other good for the agent. . . . [Christman defines
liberty (L2) as "the relative absence of restraints and the presence of
resources enabling agents to carry out their actual desires"; and L3 as
"the relative absence of restraints (L1) and the presence of resources
enabling agents to carry out their *critically appraised* desires."][20]

What this seems to amount to is that we are not interested in liberty
except insofar as its absence is a restriction on something we want to do
because we value it. The reason for attributing "intrinsic" value to liberty
is found there: ordinarily we do what we do because we value something
enough to do it, as a way of achieving or promoting that value. If that is
Christman's point, he is certainly correct. But why does he think this is a
problem for the libertarian? It is true that if *I* am prevented from doing
something that I have no interest in doing anyway, then my liberty to do
it is not of much interest to me. But suppose I later become interested in
doing it, as well I might? Do I not have reason to prefer a system which
does not deprive me of that liberty in advance? I think it's obvious that I
do, even though I might be ready to trade it off for something more
important. But, of course, doing that is not trading off liberty *tout court*: it
is trading off a particular liberty to do a particular kind of thing, and we
do that all the time. Trading off our general liberty (e.g., by putting
oneself into slavery) is, on the face of it, a very different matter. In short,
our liberty matters because our lives matter. A necessary condition of
doing anything is that one was not prevented from doing that thing.

---

[20] John Christman, *The Myth of Property* (New York: Oxford University Press, 1994), 73–74.
For Christman's definitions of L2 and L3, see ibid., 68 (emphasis in the original). Christman
is Associate Professor of Philosophy at Pennsylvania State University.

There is nothing "iffy" or problematic about affirming the importance of liberty, even though it is hardly an "intrinsic" value.

There is sometimes talk of comparing liberty: we want to say that someone's liberty has been enhanced or the reverse, and also that some people have more liberty than others in some places or at some times. On this matter of "comparative" liberty, when someone sees himself to be better off, that involves a comparison, of course; but it need not be a comparison between his own utility state and that of others. Rather, it involves a comparison between two states of himself or, more precisely, two possible states of himself, between which he is to choose. The moral rule about property that I am proposing is required by the criterion of mutual benefit from interaction: an acquisition must not make someone else *worse off* as compared with what he or she would enjoy in the absence of that acquisition. Here no interpersonal comparisons of utility are necessary; nor do we compare the "amount" of liberty enjoyed by A relative to B. Rather, each person's liberty is to be respected by the other (and any relevant others). In many cases, acquisition is not interactive in the sense that A's taking possession of some item x involves affecting someone else, B, in some way (apart from the fact that A's acquisition means that B is no longer able to acquire *that particular item*). When no such interaction occurs, the original complaint of the socialist, as we may call him—that acquisition robs the nonacquirer—is pointless, since it is logically impossible for both of two people to acquire the same item. Thus, there is no relevant complaint on that score: we cannot reasonably complain about what is logically impossible. If A's action left B without something that B previously possessed, that would be another matter. In such cases, assuming that B's previous possession of the item was not, in its turn, at the expense of others, then B's permission must be secured by A before A can take possession. However, in the case of *initial* acquisition, A deprives no current possessor of anything. On the one hand, then, he does not inflict any injury on B. On the other hand, someone's *now* taking x from A *would* inflict a harm on A. A currently both has it, and wants it; he prefers this to not having it, else he would part with it voluntarily— and for that, B needs but ask. What we term 'theft' is, therefore, the infliction of a harm: it makes the victim worse off than he was in the status quo prior to the thief's act. Were the thief not to engage in thievery, of course, his condition would be the same as it was in the status quo. Thus, theft is, as should be no surprise, action at someone else's expense. It is Pareto-inferior to its alternative.

XIII. Is "Initial Acquisition" a Useful Concept?

Of course, it might be objected that initial acquisition is an empty category, since everything now *is* owned by someone or other. But that is not entirely true even in the most ordinary sense; and in two further respects—both very significant—it is quite the reverse of true.

I deal first with the ordinary sense in which it is not true that initial acquisition is an empty category. Every now and then someone leaves various objects—"junk," leftovers, and so on—with the intention of simply abandoning his own right to them. In this case, they go to whomever happens upon them and wants them, thus having precisely the status that natural things have in the social contract account. Cases like this are rare, of course, but far from nonexistent, and certainly not impossible. Some uncharted areas of the world remain as well, and some areas that have been abandoned by previous inhabitants. Of course, all such areas are claimed by some state or other by now, complicating the inquiry. If we argue that states ought to grant maximum freedom to their inhabitants, however, then the rule of first users can be applied by states in such areas, and this too would be a nontrivial domain for the application of the first-use idea.

I turn now to the two more significant senses in which it is not true that initial acquisition is an empty category. The first of these concerns the extremely important case of *ideas*—intellectual property, as it is now called, including also artworks, scientific discoveries, and inventions. The creator of an invention or a work of art, or an original author, produces something altogether new. While this creation may involve paper, computers, canvas, and so on as material components or production aids, the created work is not identical with any of those. Given that it is the product of its creator and has not previously been in the possession of anyone, we can say, at least prima facie, that authors and artists do acquire rights in their work by original acquisition. (There are, to be sure, serious difficulties. One major difficulty is that, unlike the case with discovering a particular bit of the Earth, it is logically possible for two different persons to come up with the same idea, independently. In the case of scientific discoveries, this is not only logically possible but happens quite often. I discuss this topic further below.)

Second, there is the extremely fundamental case of *self*-possession. No one owns Louisa Jones prior to her first appearance, and she neither creates nor is given possession of herself. Nor does anyone relevantly create her. Parents, in a sense, *produce* her, but they do not and cannot *create* her: they don't work out a blueprint and make up a person out of prior stuff well put together. Insofar as anyone does that, nature does it, and neither parents nor anyone else can claim any entitlement to a child on the basis of natural possession. Rather, as soon as she counts as a person at all (this being, to be sure, a disputed matter) she is also the possessor of that person "by nature" (as I argued in Section IV), but not by nature the *owner* (as I argued in Sections II and III).

All these cases, ranging from trivial to critically important, show that the category of initial acquisition is not by any means an empty one. Of course, this last case, self-ownership, leans on the others. I possess myself by "getting there first," by finding myself to be in control of various bits of a certain body and mind, and intimately affected by their various changes of condition; that is what makes me their possessor. It is also what creates my interest in liberty: those of us sympathetic to the liberal view of morals will also declare this prior possession to be a good ground for awarding moral ownership as well.

XIV. Problem Cases

The theory of original acquisition gets us somewhere, but it falls far short of self-evidently answering all questions. The general point of view of this essay is that the principles of social morality are indeed social rules, and not "natural" ones. They are not genetically implanted in our minds, but must be worked out in the course of life, and especially of social life, that is, in the course of interaction with others. Nevertheless, we make these rules not arbitrarily but in the light of reason, or more precisely, reasons. We have good reason to want not to be damaged or interfered with, but we also have good reason to get along with our fellows. Rules on these matters, I suggest, have the support of reason in that *it would be a good idea for each individual to agree* to certain general rules about these matters, provided that one's fellows also subscribe to those rules. Obviously, there is the interesting theoretical problem that some may not "subscribe," and the practically much more serious problem that some who profess to subscribe do not in reality do so. Just how enforcement costs factor into the moral computation is a difficult and important question, which I cannot explore in any serious depth here.

The need for enforcement measures and their administration, and the inevitable vagueness and variability of what is agreed upon, mean that the rules can, to some extent, be arbitrary. Still, they cannot be entirely arbitrary, nor even very much so. In particular, the rules cannot simply be the arbitrary edicts of some strongman or, for that matter, some deliberative body. Considerations exist to guide any such bodies or rulers if they mean to be addressing us as reasonable beings. The arguments of the foregoing sections are intended to be examples of this: they are meant to pick out basic features of our situations and ourselves, attention to which leads us to adopt certain rules and not others. The question about original acquisition to be explored here is: How do we decide just what it is we have acquired when we do so in a "natural" way? That is, how do we do this when we do not have preexisting clear boundaries to form natural baselines for mutually beneficial agreed-upon exchanges?

The cases we want to focus on to begin with are cases of acquisition of land, water, and mineral resources. I will look especially at land, in part because of its importance: the acquisition and ownership of land has been the subject of most military conflicts since time immemorial, as well as of local disputes among individuals and small groups. A special feature of land for this purpose is that it is readily divided into parcels, with definite locations and areas, and generally stays put (though earthquakes and volcanic activity may alter things; and water, of course, is a lot trickier in this respect). This characteristic of land, along with its usefulness, makes it a plausible subject for theorizing about ownership. We may well suppose that if lands puts us in intractable difficulties, things look bad for property in general.

In the subsections below, then, I will consider several problems that confront the property rights theorist. The general point of view from which I will pursue these problems has been set forth above. Rights to property are part of rights to action, that is, rights to do what we want to do—what we take to be the pursuit of the best life we can manage. This pursuit often involves or requires reliable use of various stably identifiable and definable "things," and when it does, there is an interest that our use of these things be stable and identifiable. This, given the enormous potential for conflict and competition, requires rights, absent which we will not be able to pursue our interests effectively in the social environment in which we all live. But that is all. There is no further source of "natural" rights. Rights to things are as natural as our interests, but those, after all, are to a very large extent malleable and socially shaped. And the existence of other people is natural, so far as we are concerned—that is, their existence is due to features of our social environment that are largely beyond our own control—and so we need to shape the rules by which we will relate to those other people as best we can.

With that in mind, let us consider several sources of difficulty for property rights. Property rights work very well when applied to real estate and to material objects, ranging from very small (but not microscopically small) to large (but not astronomically large). They work for land because that is what we walk around on. When we instead walk on other surfaces, someone has created those surfaces, invariably as the result of arrangements with various others, and thus we have ample evidence to go on in tracking the relevant rights. When objects are visible and manipulable, they become both convenient to use and easy to transfer to others. But when these characteristics are lacking, things can get difficult. In the following seven subsections, I discuss some principal areas in which difficulties arise.

A. Subsurface rights

One very serious difficulty, given today's interest in oil and other minerals, pertains to the issue of just what one owns by virtue of owning, say, an acre of land. If a well drilled though a certain surface, previously acquired by Smith, strikes water ten feet or a hundred feet down, we have little hesitation in assigning the water rights to Smith, the owner of the land at the surface. But suppose that oil is struck at four thousand feet below the surface, after much technically demanding and ingenious calculation by others? However owner Smith might have conceived his purchase, he is unlikely to have any inkling of what exists at such a depth, let alone any intention to seek it out and use it.

The nature of the problem suggests a solution. Who struck the oil and how did he find it? Suppose that person, Jones, drills holes on the surface of Smith's land. In this case, Smith gets to charge Jones for the right to do so, surely. (Or does he? Not if he is so unfortunate as to live on self-owned land in British Columbia, it seems. There, without your knowledge, a stranger can buy the right to explore beneath the surface of your land, and then leave lots of holes and debris around in the process.)[21] But suppose that Jones drills at an angle from an adjacent area owned by Brown (who permits him to drill) or by no one? We must then ask, first, whether any future externalities might occur that significantly affect Smith's property, as they surely might. Insofar as they do, Smith will have a case for compensation. Second, we must note that Smith is in a position to point out that it's a lot cheaper to drill straight down than sideways, and he can make an offer advantageous to Jones. Beyond that, however, I don't see that Smith has any obvious "natural" claim to rights, as it were, all the way down. One might also note that for such examples, there is the problem that all places on the surface of the Earth are such that if you go straight down, they will all meet at the center. Then what? Clearly we cannot simply extrapolate from the situation on the surface.

We can also mention the potential for pollution of groundwater, undermining of buildings, infestations of pests, microbes, or parasites, and so on. Solutions to such problems are contingent on the right solutions to the problem of subsurface rights. If Smith has clear title to some volume of earth, he also has the right that others not infest it or render it incapable of fulfilling his purposes in acquiring it, insofar as those purposes are themselves peaceable.

It seems to me that this last is not appreciated by Freyfogle, who points out, correctly enough, that "absolute ownership" is impossible, if we suppose this to include the right to exterminate the neighbors' prairie-dog population when those little beasts are attracting predators which feed on the prairie dogs but also attack other people's pets.[22] Such claims are the

---

[21] The Province of British Columbia's Mineral Tenure Act of 2002 permits this. See Kendyl Salcito, "'War Brewing' over Mining Rights in Rural BC," http://thetyee.ca/News/2006/06/14/MiningRights/. As a case in point, one Bruce Essington, who "lives in a tarp-covered bread truck on the side of Bluenose Mountain . . . has bought rights to about 150 acres of his neighbours' land. For \$50." And "Essington was not charged for repeatedly scrawling 'free miners lic.' in blue paint on private property and removing 'For Sale' signs at the entrance of Kurt Yakelashek's driveway, for snooping around the property at night, or for leaving piles of beer cans around the grounds."

[22] Freyfogle, *On Private Property*, 20; the prairie dog example is discussed on pp. 1–2.

stock in trade of critics of liberal rights, who take such rights to be a license to a free-for-all. But that is the pre-moral Hobbesian state of nature, and not the converting of liberty into a *right*. Such conversion is engaged in precisely for the purpose of blocking the free-for-all, and thus enabling persons to benefit from their activities. What I advocate here is the general recognition of the individual right to own property—ownership that is compatible with ownership by others. Thus, my right to what I own cannot extend to a right to destroy, damage, or interfere with anything that belongs to my neighbor. Often it is difficult to respect this, as when one has predatory animals on one's own land, while the neighbors have attractive prey for the predators. But what makes a solution to this problem both necessary and possible is recognition of the antecedent rights of the respective parties.

Of course, the libertarian will favor private methods for resolving conflicts in this area, and will deplore initiatives such as those of the province of British Columbia, initiatives that deny owners of surface land any priority in rights concerning what might lie beneath it. Development of mineral resources should not bypass people's rights.

B. Air rights

Suppose we worry about what's in the air above? Here we need to distinguish two quite different contexts. On the one hand, there is pollution, and especially (in point of theoretical interest) noise pollution. I will address those separately below. On the other hand, there is the analogue to the previous case concerning areas beneath the surface. Perhaps the air contains noxious gases. Perhaps the air above A's land in particular, for some reason, has more of these gases than that above B's, so A might try to clean up "his" air by extracting cleaner air from over B's land. Perhaps A is concerned about his sunlight being blocked by proposed neighboring tall buildings. Perhaps A is even concerned about changes in climate brought about, he supposes, by B's lax behavior regarding CO_2 emissions. What now?

Someone occupying a bit of land is often able to do something about other persons' proposed alterations of the situation overhead—but, beyond a small distance, not usually very much. Some of the things those other people could do to the space overhead matter to him. But how much, and why? Because concerns of this kind are unusual and the potential for action is normally very limited, one important part of the answer is that these matters will be negotiable. We just have to see what turns up and then try to sort it out, building from the preexisting interests of those concerned. Paramount among those interests, no doubt, will be the health of the persons below; this anchors questions about air rights in the rights of the landowners below (particularly their rights in their own bodies). In time, a history of mutually agreeable dispute settlements will be formed, and that will provide a basis for the negotiations in question.

C. Aesthetic issues

In public, it is easy for anyone to do something that some or many others won't like, even though what is done does not physically impinge on those others. Unattractive people generate negative externalities as they go about in public: we dislike to look at them, yet we do nothing to earn their unpleasurable presences. Likewise, attractive people generate positive externalities quite liberally, without the rest of us having done anything to deserve this pleasure. These externalities are (usually) minor — but an ugly house or garden next door can constitute quite a substantial source of negative utility. Is our general principle of liberty to be understood to imply that we may not annoy our fellows by subjecting them to experiences they find aesthetically displeasing? Obviously, given the wide variation in tastes among human beings, this will have its difficulties. In general, we shall have to say that the principle does not have this implication. But, obviously, this rather strongly raises the question of just what our proclaimed ownership of self amounts to in these important contexts. May people bother us all they please with impunity? Surely not. But if not, then criteria need to be formulated for defining the legitimate limits on the bothersome activity. At some point, the bothered person may be moved to relocate, an option that is always available to a property owner (or occupant). But though available, it might also be very expensive. The question is: At what level of bother should we say that the botherer "compelled" the botheree to move?

Aesthetic issues shade off into health issues, of course. Noxious odors are unpleasant, but they are also quite likely to have bad effects on the lungs or other organs of those who smell them. The question is whether the aesthetic objections have moral weight *independently* of the health issues. Many of us have always disliked cigarette smoke, but it wasn't until the surgeon general's report came out that we nonsmokers got some freedom from the tyranny of smoke in public stores, hallways, and other public areas. Should we have been able to get redress or protection of this kind?

The case of noise pollution, as we might call it, is perhaps more pressing yet. Beyond some threshold, noises can damage the ear, and even beneath that threshold, they can annoy, sometimes enormously. What is the relevant natural baseline here? The old saw has it that my right to use my fist terminates at your nose. Does my right to use my voice terminate at your ears? Are we entitled to dead silence on the part of those we meet? Or are they entitled to make noise to their hearts' content? (The case with regard to speech, as such, is rather different. There, content is everything, and the main requirement is that what is heard is heard voluntarily, in the sense of not *in*voluntarily. Usually we can avoid unwanted speech; the speaker who refuses to be put off is invading the intellectual space, not just the acoustic space, of his reluctant audience.)

Reciprocity will take care of some problems here. I can respond to your unwanted noises by making noises that you don't want to hear; reciprocal silence is preferable, or sounds that we both like. And if I can't respond, then what? A further source of assistance lies in the ownership of spaces. If I own the space into which you project your noise, I can build sound-proof walls (perhaps), or withdraw far enough (if I own enough space) that you are now happily beyond sonic reach. We can wear earplugs, though, unfortunately, they eliminate both the unwanted noises and those we would really like to hear, and they can be uncomfortable and inconvenient.

We are entitled to nonviolence. But are we entitled, in general, to nonan-noyance? We characterize our general rights as rights to freedom or lib-erty, which suggests the freedom to *do* as we please. Nonetheless, the point of characterizing this as a right is that all have it, and this implies a duty to respect the freedom of others, which, in turn, means that we may *not* just do whatever we please. We are not Robinson Crusoe, and rarely is there no one within vocal or visual (or olfactory) reach. We also differ from one another, enormously, and imposing rules that make sense to all is a challenge. The key is finding the right baselines from which appropriate negotiations may proceed. In part, those baselines can be identified using rights to spaces, such as buildings and land. That will solve some problems, allowing all parties to do as they please in terms of emitting noises or creating visual surfaces out of visual and aural reach of all potentially nonconsenting others. It will solve more problems as tech-nology advances and as the command over resources of all relevant par-ties increases: for example, the development of soundproof walls and floors between adjacent parties in apartment buildings and condos con-siderably increases the scope for activities that might otherwise be trou-blesome. When neighbors cannot afford such things, however, they will have more difficulty, and their only options will be negotiated solutions that are less satisfactory. Some of the problems thus generated will require a distributive solution, as in R. B. Braithwaite's ground-breaking essay, where the trumpet-playing neighbor and the silence-loving neighbor divide the time in some ratio, giving optimal relative utility to each.[23]

D. *Offense and opinions*

If we have some right not to be subjected to noise, ugliness, and the like, then what about our souls? Are we also protected from insult, or

---

[23] R. B. Braithwaite, *The Theory of Games as a Tool for the Moral Philosopher* (Cambridge: Cambridge University Press, 1954). Braithwaite was for a long time Professor of Moral Philosophy at Cambridge.

the intrusion into our acoustic environs of unwanted opinions? Take, for instance, the case of offense: Are we allowed to insult and vilify the religious beliefs of others, in their presence? Suppose I claim that B's religious beliefs are a conceptual mess—incoherent, obscure, inconsistent, and out of touch with anything remotely resembling evidence. Is that an insult? I might be able to illustrate just how his beliefs do have all those putatively undesirable properties. Is it insulting even to mention such shortcomings? There is a serious need to determine how rights—whose rights, over what—yield a reasonable solution to the problems that can be created by such situations. One obvious point is that no one owns the laws of logic, and no one owns, as we might put it, the truth. We do own our own ears and tongues, however, and we own various spaces. The latter fact enables us to decide, quite often, who is speaking "out of turn." In A's house, B is an invited guest, and A sets the terms regarding what may or may not be said. But A does not determine what is true and what is false, nor what is good reasoning and what is not. Truth and good reasoning are not subject to private possession, to the exclusion of others, and, therefore, they are not things that it is sensible to regard as anyone's property. Henry Sheffer discovered the Sheffer stroke, but he did not thereby come to own it.[24]

Thus, we can say that insofar as people are interested in coming to know about some subject, they submit themselves to the rules of logic and the disciplines of inquiry. If we want to know whether p, then anyone with relevant evidence or reasoning can provide that evidence and reasoning, and the exclusion of persons in possession of such resources is prima facie irrational. But insofar as the point of a communication is sheer vilification or psychological pain, it is subject to the same arguments as all other attacks on possessions. We shall want to uphold a right not to be subjected to that kind of "communication"—with the usual caveat that it, or something close to it, may in fact be deserved on some occasions.

It is often said that people have a right to believe whatever they want. There is a sense in which that is clearly false, and another in which it is plausible. What is false is that we *can* "believe whatever we want"; we believe what seems to be true, and wanting to believe something else will get us nowhere. Nor is it true that we are *entitled* to our beliefs. Many of them are unjustified, and, in intellectual terms, we are not entitled to them. (In philosophy, it is often appropriate to say, "I may agree with what you say, but I deny your right to say it!") So the right in question is

---

[24] Professor Sheffer discovered that all of the standard operations in the propositional calculus (or truth-functional logic) can be defined in terms of the function that amounts to "not p and q," nowadays referred to as the 'NAND' operator, short for 'not both . . . and. . . .' In fact, Charles Sanders Peirce discovered this thirty years earlier, but did not publish it. Sheffer's "discovery" (which there is no reason to think he plagiarized from Peirce) was published in 1913. H. M. Sheffer, "A Set of Five Independent Postulates for Boolean Algebras, with Application to Logical Constants," *Transactions of the American Mathematical Society* 14 (1913): 481–88.

moral, and not intellectual. Many beliefs have moral implications, and a person who propounds such beliefs while having only bad reasons (or no reason) to support them may indeed be accused of a moral shortcoming.

E. Inheritance

If I own something, I decide who gets it if I want to part with it. But what becomes of my property after my own death? Does ownership include the right to decide who will inherit? Western countries have, in general, said that it does, but have at the same time imposed various levels of estate taxes and death duties. Are those taxes infringements of rights that we should think we have?

All taxes may be such infringements, of course. Income taxes, property taxes, and all the others are imposed against the wills and, prima facie, the interests of many. The question here is whether inheritance is special in some way. Many have thought that it is, but in two opposite ways. Some think it obvious that inheritance is entirely illegitimate, since, after all, the dead, as such, can have no rights. Many others have thought it obvious that whatever else we may be able to do with our property, we should certainly be able to leave it to our children (for example). Indeed, many people work as hard as they do to accumulate property precisely in order to make their children better off than they themselves were. So who's right?

First, it is clear that the persons who make decisions about inheritance are alive: when I choose to leave something of mine to someone after I die, it is a living person who makes that choice. Others act as administrators, for example, and will be bound by agreements to carry out my instructions after my death. However, it might be argued that they should not feel so bound, on the ground that, after my death, I am no longer on the scene and therefore not a person whose will must be respected.

It could be argued, plausibly, that to be denied the right to direct the disposition of one's property after one's death is counterproductive, depriving society of an important incentive for individuals to produce more than they otherwise might. But although I believe this is a good argument, it is an indirect one. A direct argument would purport to show that it is part of the idea of ownership that one has this right. Is it?

The owner of x decides what happens to x: he or she has veto power over uses of x. Now, all these uses are future uses, in the most relevant sense. Property is inherently enduring: instantaneous ownership makes no sense. On that ground alone, we should side with the pro-inheritance position, prima facie. Moreover, the "indirect" argument becomes a direct one when we appreciate the force of the point that all rights are rights to act, with rights of ownership being an identifiable subset of such rights. The act of handing property over to kin or to deserving art galleries or to hospitals in Africa, and so on indefinitely, is a straightforward extension of this general idea.

Whether inheritance taxes and the like can be justified at all depends on whether taxes in general can be justified. All taxes infringe on rights, and to justify the imposition of taxes, one needs to demonstrate that the infringement is justified. If such a justification can be found for other taxes, then it might also be found for inheritance taxes. I will not address the matter further here, except to note that finding such justifications is not easy.

F. Public property

I noted at the outset the distinction between the "commons" in the sense of what is not owned at all, and the "commons" in the sense of property owned by "the public." The difference is that in the former case, there are no rules governing the commons, whereas in the latter, the rules are set by the public, somehow. But how?

When the sovereign or the legislature lays down rules about the use of "its" lands, minerals, or whatever, is it making law ex nihilo? Is it just asserting the (perhaps altogether arbitrary) will of the government? Or if not, then what is going on here?

Moreover, I have referred just now to "the public," but, in fact, land is often claimed by a great number of different publics—villages, cities, provinces, nation-states, and many nonpolitical organizations. If we talk of what is owned by "the public," then, we are either idealizing or generalizing. Generalizations are rather unsafe in view of the enormous differences among the numerous publics that, in fact, claim ownership of this or that bit of geography. Our generalization would have to be very thin to cover all cases. The safest generalization is the one that does no more than define the notion of property for publics. That definition is derived from our general definition: to own is to have the right to exclude others from use of the owned item. In the case where the relevant public is relatively small, so that it is one group among others, then the members of the group, as collective owners, would have the right to exclude persons from other groups, though this does not often happen any more at local levels.

But if we say that the world is owned by everyone in common, there would seem to be no one left to exclude, so where do we go from there? The answer is that we would have to distinguish between the individual acting privately, as an individual, and the individual acting in his role as a citizen or member of the public. In the latter capacity, we can pass legislation to prohibit private actions of various kinds by all. For example, we can collectively decree that land may not be privatized—however much we might, as individuals, want to possess this or that piece of land to the exclusion of others. Alternatively, we might collectively decree that land *may* be taken into private possession, with rules regarding how that is to be done, limits to the amounts or kinds of land or mineral resources that may be possessed by any one individual, and so on. Whether it is rational to go in for such collective ownership depends on whether the returns to collectivization are higher than people could get acting independently. In many contexts, we may be sure, the returns are, on the contrary, far lower, as in China's agricultural regime under Mao, which led to massive starvation. Possibly, the returns for collectively owned national parks are more satisfactory.

In saying this, I do not intend a retraction of the individualist assumptions that underlie this essay. When we are members of a relevant collective, it remains true that the individuals within the collective have the relevant rights, and they must decide whether and in what ways they will support any kind of "collective" undertakings. The point I want to make is merely that we could have good reason to engage in some collective activity. This is activity where we can recognize the benefit of having general rules for the use of collectively owned items; the benefit associated with these rules gives us reason to support them.

Recognition of the wide range of possible patterns of exclusion prompts us to distinguish a wider and narrower sense of 'public.' Legislation, including moral legislation, is inherently public: it concerns rules for all (that is, for all persons that lie within the relevant jurisdiction, morality having as its basic domain everyone there is). In a narrower sense, however, we will distinguish between items owned by the public and items owned by individuals as such. The former might include public parks, government buildings, Social Security funds, and so on, while the latter will include privately owned land and buildings, privately acting firms, and so on. Then the question is: Should there be anything in the former category? The Stalinist will say that everything should be in it, with nothing left for individuals; the anarcho-capitalist might say that nothing should be in it, with everything to be owned by individuals or privately acting groups. In all but universal practice, though, there is a mix of the two types, along with complex rules identifying restrictions on each kind of ownership. Which is best depends on careful analysis. I incline toward the anarcho-capitalist end of the spectrum. But I do not think this can be settled *a priori*.

The economist Randall Holcombe observes that "[s]peculation on the nature of anarcho-capitalism has typically proceeded under the assumption that all property in anarcho-capitalism would be privately owned."[25] But he goes on to argue that the assumption "is not justified because property can come to be owned in common . . . and libertarian ethics would not allow the private appropriation of such common property."[26] As a plausible example, he observes that "[t]he ocean is available in common to all men, to use Locke's language, but crossing it in a ship does

---

[25] Randall Holcombe, "Common Property in Anarcho-Capitalism," *Journal of Libertarian Studies* 19, no. 2 (Spring 2005): 3–26. Holcombe is DeVoe Moore Professor of Economics at Florida State University.
[26] Ibid., 3.

not cause that person to become the owner of the ocean, and others could legitimately come later and use the same ocean."[27] The example is well chosen: it illustrates the plausibility of the idea of common property, and it also raises, even in this ideally chosen case, the point that nation-states do privatize to some extent. States will declare that waters lying within specified distances of their shorelines lie within their territorial domain, and might, on some occasions prohibit occupation of those waters by foreign ships. The same is true of air spaces. In addition, of course, ponds, small lakes, and even portions of streams have been and are privately owned by individuals, not to mention by political entities below the level of nation-states. The question is, then, why we might want to retain a category of "commons"—even if we accepted, as Holcombe does, the arguments for anarcho-capitalism.

What is the rationale for retaining any public property? Or is there one? I believe there are two plausible answers to this, which work in tandem. On the one hand, in most communities there are areas that traditionally have been in the "commons" category, and it is arguable that privatization would violate the rights of the people who live in those areas and use the common property in question in ways that respect the similar rights of fellow users. On the other hand, it can be useful to have common property. Holcombe points to the example of paths and roads in a community that has considerable amounts of private property. These paths and roads are used by people generally, to get from one private place to another. "Simply traveling over a piece of land is not sufficient to say one has combined his labor with the land and therefore is the owner. The paths became thoroughfares, and became valuable, because of their common use by many people. Thus, they are not owned by a single owner but are owned in common."[28] The example is persuasive. It is in the interest of private businesses that members of the public generally be able to travel unimpeded to their places of business. Similarly, private home owners will want friends, guests, sharers of goals being pursued by several persons, and so on, to be able to arrive at their doors without substantial cost.

In turn, as with the ocean, business owners and private parties would prefer, if possible, that thieves and murderers be excluded from these public paths and roads. And in cases where there is considerable traffic, there might need to be rules of the road, even for pedestrians. Additionally, there may be problems of maintenance. Paths through woods and fields are, to an extent, self-maintained: frequent walking on the same path assures that it won't be overgrown. But it may be that travel is promoted by the installation of hard surfaces, and then what? Schemes for cost-sharing will need to arise, and these have typically taken the form of taxation, with all its attendant problems. Holcombe does not discuss

[27] Ibid., 5.
[28] Ibid., 8.

"the interesting policy question of how this common property would be controlled and maintained."[29] What stands out is that acceptance of the general case for private property does not preclude recognition of some extent of common property as well. Indeed, we might view any particular commons as the joint property of a set of individuals, membership in the set being determined mainly by occupation of adjacent areas, with guest privileges, as it were, accorded to visitors from beyond the borders (however imprecisely defined) of that community.

Freyfogle notes that the doctrine of liberty led to arguments for both opening and closing land to private ownership. "Capitalist tendencies, then, pushed in both directions: keeping lands open and closing them."[30] He is correct, but the moral is not that the idea of liberty is either wrong or incoherent. Rather, it is that our interests in having open access to land conflict with other interests in using land that require exclusion, and this creates a need for negotiation among parties pursuing each of these interests. If those who hunt and forage in a certain area have it all their way, then those who would build and manufacture in that area cannot have it all their way, and vice versa. Property rights always entail the right to exclude, but who is excluded and from what depends on what the occupants want to do on the lands (or with the other things) in question. However, it is never true that the whole human race, going indefinitely into the future, has claims to be regarded. The homestead idea continues to be significant: it is the loose set of people already in the area who are excluded by the builders of markets and factories, and the latter who are excluded if the former's interests prevail. If, as we may suppose is the usual case, the hunters and gatherers came first, then those who would settle and produce need to clear it with the others—but they don't need to compensate the human race in general.

One plausible way for builders to effect (at least partial) compensation for previous occupants or users of the land would be for the builders to give up their right to hunt and forage in exchange for the others giving up their right to do so on this particular piece of land. Another way, soon available when manufacturing and farming increase the "social dividend," is for the builders/homesteaders to buy the right to the land from the others, though that is not so easy to do when the group who hunt and forage is indefinite and sizable, as with the American natives. In principle, there should be a point at which the hunters and gatherers are exactly compensated, we may surmise. Moreover, we can argue, as capitalists have for so many centuries, that growth in farming and manufacturing, and entrance into the exchange economy, will ultimately benefit the hunters and gatherers far more than enough to "compensate" them. Eventually, specified areas will be set aside for hunting and other wilderness

---

[29] Ibid., 3–4.
[30] Freyfogle, *On Private Property*, 55.

activities, not to be privatized further. But of course such areas *are* privatized in the sense that they are devoted to the interests of a specific group (hunters, say) to the exclusion of would-be individual privatizers.

Are there plausible micro rules for the use of common property? Surely there are. In the first place, as I have noted here, common property is used for specified purposes, and thus any use by an individual that tends to render the item unusable for those purposes, or significantly more difficult to use, is ipso facto to be regarded as a "misuse." Those who misuse common property are subject to requirements to restore the area to the status quo prior to their misuse of it, and perhaps to penalties for failure to make the appropriate amends. In the second place, of course, the general moral rule of nonharm always applies: we are not to molest others on the public roads, for example. More specifically, we should do what best enables each user to use the common property in the way he or she wishes, within the constraints of common use. (Thus, on the highways, people should be able to go at varying speeds, in a manner compatible with safety and comfort.)

G. Intellectual property

The basis of modern economic civilization is the vast fund of ideas from innumerable innovators—engineers, entrepreneurs, designers—who enable us to produce so much more of what we want with so much less labor, or who make our labor so much more interesting. In what sense, if any, should we say that the discoverer or engineer or architect, say, who comes up with a good idea "owns" it? In principle, the answer is easy enough. Just as the agricultural worker enables the fruit to emerge, so the entrepreneur enables us to enjoy a well-built home or car, and so on. Assembly-line workers do not copyright their products; how do intellectual workers differ? Presumably, they differ in this way at least: they produce something that no one else does, or perhaps even could. They also produce it before anyone else.

In part, this suggests the homesteading principle: I thought of it first, so it's mine. Yet if someone else thinks of it second, and is ready to impart it to others at a lower price than I am, why should he not be able to do so? Is that anything like his stealing my car to resell it at a bargain price? Surely not. The problem is that thoughts are universals. A thought is A's insofar as it is in A's mind, or originated by A. The very same thought can be in the minds of indefinitely many others, and can even be originated by many others. This makes it difficult to establish ownership rights on a close analogy with rights to solid property.

Thoughts have economic value only if they are imparted to others, or used to produce things that are of interest to others. In the latter case, patent rights are relevant and would presumably absorb the costs of design and research. What about the former case, though? If we copyright ideas, does that mean that others are required to stop thinking about those things? Or to pay a price if they do? This would clearly be an unsatisfactory conclusion, since the origination of these ideas takes place in individual heads, taking nothing from others.

A distinction has to be made between ideas, as such, and writings, as such. In the case of writings, such as books and articles, other people are overwhelmingly unlikely to write just the same things, beyond a few words. Instead, original thinkers need to publish, and if they accuse others of stealing their ideas, they must provide evidence that the others have done so. Original writers may establish copyright, and then the question is who will prosecute (and how) if their works are replicated by others without permission. If it is easy to replicate others' work, and difficult to detect when people replicate others' work without permission, the question of where we go from here is not an easy one to answer in practice.

I do not propose to discuss the matter further here. Rather, the general point is that here, again, we have plausible claims by first-comers against other plausible claims by idea-consumers, such as readers, the scientifically curious, and those interested in making practical use of others' ideas. The search is on for an optimal mix, taking into account advancing replicative technology, the march of knowledge, and consumer interests. Even so, however, the same old principles—principles of first occupancy or use, and defense of self against incursion—are what ground the actions of those who wish to defend intellectual property rights.

XV. Conclusion

The classic theory of property has it that the person who first undertakes use of some hitherto unowned bit of the world should thereby be credited with a right to use it, and that others are to be excluded from activities that prevent the first users from realizing their ends. But this right is to be universalized, and thus the first users, likewise, are not to use their property in ways that undermine the activities of others, who are using other things in other ways.

A distinction between possession and ownership is essential, then. First possession is to be protected, and the category of ownership is precisely that of reasonably protected possession. Possessors possess things in order to use them, for pursuing their various purposes. And the purposes are wide-ranging indeed. Thus, there are potential conflicts, and these are to be resolved by negotiation from the baseline of first occupancy or use (these being really the same, in the end), together with the specific profiles of proposed new uses by those concerned. In turn, third parties are not to be harmed in the process, and we may also describe this prohibition on harm in terms of property, attributing to each person ownership of the body and mind possessed by that individual by nature.

Thus, we need not deny that, in detail, the rules of property will change over time, given emerging trends in technology, demographics, and consumer interests. But the changes in rules called for by these emerging trends would make basic principles more precise, rather than discarding them and starting over; so far as I can see, the basic principles would remain intact. First possessors have rights to what they possess; those who come later must negotiate further uses of what is already owned. Ownership is always the right to exclude, but the patterns of exclusion will be dictated by the varying interests and situations of the negotiating parties.

The proprietarian outlook has what seems to me to be an enormous advantage: it keeps the individual intact, never subordinating anyone to the "general good," except in the sense that the general good is, indeed, the general liberty. Maximization of the general liberty has to proceed by optimization, and it is easy to make the mistake, as some advocates of property rights do, of supposing that people have rights to specific things that entail what amounts to a setting-aside of the rights of others. But rights are not to be set aside; rather, they are to be refined by negotiation against a background of basic rights, established by initial possession. That the result is a society that works better for all is, I think, an altogether plausible thesis.

Philosophy, University of Waterloo

EMBODIMENT AND SELF-OWNERSHIP*

By Daniel C. Russell

I. Introduction

Suppose that I find myself believing that we own ourselves, that we are "self-owners." How does that belief constrain my further commitments in political thought? The received view is that it does not constrain them very much: committing to self-ownership leaves open a swath of philosophical options broad enough to be bordered by socialism on the left and radical forms of libertarianism on the right. How could such diverse groups all carry the same banner of self-ownership?

Part of the story is that a right of self-ownership is actually a bundle of rights, and different thinkers describe the bundle differently. Even so, however, there is broad agreement that self-ownership involves the right to control oneself, the right to exclude others from control of oneself, immunity from expropriation of these rights, the power to transfer these rights, and rights to compensation for infringement of these rights.[1] Likewise, different thinkers offer different moral considerations to ground the right of self-ownership. But this too can be only part of the answer, since at the core of self-ownership is generally the basic idea that persons do have rights, and that in order to have rights a person must not be a part of any other person's bundle of goods, in Hillel Steiner's phrase, so that each person's bundle of original property rights must include, at least, himself.[2] The normative thrust of the notion of self-ownership, wherever we find it, is the idea that one ought to be able to live one's life without interference.[3]

A more penetrating answer, I think, is that there is considerable disagreement over the relation between owning one's person, on the one hand, and owning parts of the extrapersonal world—the world outside

* I would like to thank Richard Arneson, Tom Christiano, Ed Feser, Jerry Gaus, Mark LeBar, Eric Mack, Fred Miller, Jan Narveson, Dave Schmidtz, and the other contributors to this volume, for their comments on an earlier version of this essay. Thanks also to Ellen Paul for her helpful editorial comments.

[1] For fairly typical discussions, see Peter Vallentyne, "Libertarianism," *The Stanford Encyclopedia of Philosophy,* revised 2006, sec. 1; Robert Taylor, "Self-Ownership and the Limits of Libertarianism," *Social Theory and Practice* 31, no. 4 (2005): 465–482, at 466–67.

[2] Hillel Steiner, *An Essay on Rights* (Oxford: Blackwell, 1994), 231.

[3] See Douglas Rasmussen and Douglas Den Uyl, *Norms of Liberty* (University Park: Pennsylvania State University Press, 2005), 209; and Eric Mack, "How to Derive Libertarian Rights," in Jeffrey Paul, ed., *Reading Nozick: Essays on Anarchy, State, and Utopia* (Totowa, NJ: Rowman and Littlefield, 1981), 288.

doi:10.1017/S0265052509990069
135

one's physical silhouette—on the other. As one moves to the left on the political spectrum, these issues become increasingly separate, as self-ownership is said to remain untouched despite even radical restrictions on the control one may justly claim over parts of the extrapersonal world, such as the earning of wages or the private owning of capital. And the issues come apart again, in a different way, the farther one moves to the right, where self-ownership is said to remain intact even when the control of extrapersonal goods by others leaves some people with little or no such control. The diversity of the adherents of self-ownership is ultimately attributable to the common view that one's position on self-ownership is one thing, and one's position on extrapersonal property quite another.[4]

I argue here that these two issues are anything but distinct. More precisely, I argue that one can hold them to be distinct only by adopting a particular conception of the self, one which I will argue is independently implausible. The alternative view of the self that I sketch here has two central features: (1) the self is not just one's psychology and power of choice, but extends also to one's physical person; and, more provocatively, (2) the reasons that the self extends to one's physical person are *also* reasons that the self extends into the world beyond one's person. Such a self I shall call an "embodied" self. My aim in this essay is to examine the notion of owning an embodied self, and in particular to examine how commitment to that kind of self-ownership constrains one's further commitments about other sorts of ownership. It should be clear already that ownership of an embodied self would leave far fewer options open than the received view would have us think, since there is no clean line separating the self so understood from the extrapersonal world.

For the purposes of this essay, and given the limits on space, the present discussion is restricted in two main ways. First, although I occasionally touch on the rationale for the self-ownership thesis, I do not try to defend that thesis here. That thesis is, of course, controversial, but my present aim is the more modest one of exploring where that thesis leaves one, once one has accepted it. Second, I limit that exploration to where self-ownership leads within libertarianism. Libertarianism itself has a left and a right, and seeing how self-ownership and property ownership come apart on either side of this spectrum is, I hope, suggestive of how these issues might come apart on the right and the left more generally.

I argue for two main claims in this essay. One is that the major forms of libertarianism are committed to importantly different conceptions of the self. If the self is embodied in the sense I sketched above, then to own a self *is* (among other things) to have the right to control parts of the extrapersonal world. In particular, I argue that far-right libertarians who reject any provisos on property—"no-proviso libertarians," for short—

---

[4] See, e.g., Philippe Van Parijs, *Real Freedom for All* (Oxford: Oxford University Press, 1995), chapter 1.

reject an embodied conception of the self in considering the case of "have-nots," and that so-called "left-libertarians" reject it in their discussion of what "haves" owe to others. I argue that there is exactly one form of libertarianism—what I shall call simply "right-libertarianism"—that commits to an embodied conception of the self, for haves and have-nots alike. If I am correct, then committing to self-ownership constrains one's commitments regarding extrapersonal property in ways that depend crucially on one's conception of the self. This result is significant, as it reveals how great a difference the conception of the self makes for libertarian positions on the ownership of extrapersonal goods, a difference that so far has not been sufficiently appreciated among libertarians themselves.

The other claim I defend is that the right-libertarian's conception of the self is the more plausible one. Space does not permit a full-blown defense of that conception of the self, but I do hope to clarify why I find right-libertarianism to be more plausible in this respect than either of its two libertarian rivals. Simply put, I see no reason to agree that the self includes one's physical person but deny that it includes parts of the extrapersonal world, such as loved ones or cherished projects. On the contrary, the rationale for understanding the boundaries of the self to include the body seems to be equally a rationale for including things beyond the body within the boundaries of the self.

I begin in Section II with a discussion of these three broad forms of libertarianism and their differences. These remarks will be brief and programmatic, since I shall explore each of these forms of libertarianism more closely in Sections IV through VI. But before taking that closer look, I shall say more about the notion of an embodied self in Section III.

II. LIBERTARIANISM: LEFT, RIGHT, AND FAR RIGHT

One thing is clear: all libertarians as such are committed, at the very least, to the thesis that persons own themselves. What sets different camps of libertarians apart from each other has to do with how self-ownership rights license property in extrapersonal goods. We can state these differences as differences with respect to the so-called "Lockean proviso" on ownership—that one must leave "enough and as good" for others, in some sense—which on its broadest interpretation is a constraint on how much control of the extrapersonal world self-owners can rightfully claim. More specifically, I shall understand the proviso as, broadly, a "fair share" proviso.[5] On such a broad interpretation, the Lockean proviso can be seen

---

[5] See Jan Narveson, "Original Appropriation and Lockean Provisos," *Public Affairs Quarterly* 13, no. 3 (1999): 205–27, at 214–15, who says that it is possible to read the proviso more narrowly as a ban on interfering with the use of extrapersonal goods already underway. But this strikes me as a theory of property—viz. that engaging with some such good is sufficient to gain title to it—rather than a constraint on property. In any case, even Narveson (p. 222)

either as a restriction on initial appropriation (as in Locke himself) and thus on what one can *own*, or as a restriction on the *use* of what one owns, or both (as in Robert Nozick's theory). Put another way, the proviso can either limit how much one can own or it can limit how extensive one's rights of ownership in a thing can be. (As we shall see in Section VI, my own concern is with the proviso understood as one on use.) In any case, the proviso rules out practices that would exclude others from a stake in the extrapersonal world, either by appropriating too much of that world or by using ownership claims to exclude others from it. The main differences between libertarians concern (1) whether the Lockean proviso has egalitarian implications and (2) whether there really is any place for the Lockean proviso after all.

One form of libertarianism, which I shall call simply "right-libertarianism," holds that ownership of extrapersonal property (either its acquisition or its use) is subject to a Lockean proviso, but that the proviso has no egalitarian implications. Nozick is one example of such a right-libertarian, as is Eric Mack, who confines the proviso to use rather than acquisition. Right-libertarians are set apart from those even farther on the right—"no-proviso libertarians"—who deny that there is any Lockean proviso on either acquisition or use. Some representative no-proviso libertarians are Jan Narveson, Douglas Rasmussen and Douglas Den Uyl, and Murray Rothbard. Finally, "left-libertarians" hold that there is a Lockean proviso on the acquisition of property, and that this proviso, properly understood, has important egalitarian implications. Here one thinks of philosophers like Michael Otsuka, Hillel Steiner, Peter Vallentyne, and Philippe Van Parijs.

In what follows, I argue that both no-proviso libertarianism and left-libertarianism must reject the embodied conception of the self, albeit for different reasons. In particular, since no-proviso libertarians claim that the poverty of have-nots leaves their self-ownership untouched, they must hold that control of one's person is a separate matter from control of goods outside one's person, and thus they cannot countenance an embodied conception of the self in the case of have-nots. So too, left-libertarians must reject such a conception of the self in order to argue in the case of the haves that self-ownership is untouched despite the demand on them to make compensation for controlling parts of the extrapersonal world (and in this way to fund egalitarian schemes). If these conclusions are correct, then it seems clear that an embodied conception of the self, for haves and have-nots alike, means both that there must be a Lockean proviso and that the proviso cannot incorporate an egalitarian conception of justice. This conjunction of claims, of course, is exactly what right-libertarianism holds.

acknowledges that the "original intent" of the proviso has to do with fair shares. See also Robert Nozick, *Anarchy, State, and Utopia* (New York: Basic Books, 1974), 176.

III. Embodiment

"Self" is said in many ways, so I begin by pointing out that in discussing the self I mean to discuss what some philosophers call "psychological identity."[6] Psychological identity is to be distinguished from both metaphysical identity and personal identity, which concern the conditions under which one remains the same individual or the same person, respectively.[7] Psychological identity, rather, is an agent's first-personal sense of himself—a sense of what person one is, of one's nature or character, of one's options and abilities, and of one's place in the world. It is in this sense of the self that engaging in certain ongoing activities, projects, and relationships is an essential part of oneself.

The starkest alternative to the embodied conception of the self is what I have elsewhere called the "formalized" conception.[8] On the formalized conception, a self is fundamentally a particular, unique psychology. Here we can think of the self as the dimension of the person that engages in choice and practical reasoning. The actions of this self are performed in relation to the world around it, but the self and its actions remain always distinct from that world, strictly speaking. On such a view, ongoing activities and projects are seen as patterns of selection and response with respect to the world around one, and such patterns can continue unabated even when the particular details of one's worldly circumstances change (hence the description of such a self as "formalized"). Consequently, a formalized self is less vulnerable to serious interruption or upheaval brought about by external or even bodily changes: I may lose a leg or its use, say, but while this may be a serious and distressing loss, its impact is mainly on what particular projects I can engage in, not on who I am. It does not even impact what I can do, on a formalized understanding of doing: if what I do, really, is to direct my will in a certain way—so as to act well, say—in relation to the world around me, then I can continue to do the same in my new circumstances, too. If something stops me, it is not the loss per se.

Perhaps the clearest philosophical example of such a view comes from the ancient Stoics, who went so far as to define even the act of walking not in terms of what the legs do, but in terms of what the willing, selecting

[6] See Marya Schechtman, *The Constitution of Selves* (Ithaca, NY: Cornell University Press, 1996); Catriona McKenzie, "Personal Identity, Narrative Integration, and Embodiment," in Sue Campbell, Letitia Meynell, and Susan Sherwin, eds., *Embodiment and Agency* (Philadelphia: Pennsylvania State University Press, 2009). Identity of this sort corresponds also to what Richard Sorabji calls sometimes "persona" and sometimes "identity"; see Richard Sorabji, *Self* (Chicago: University of Chicago Press, 2006).

[7] On self-ownership and personal identity, see Edward Feser, "Personal Identity and Self-Ownership," *Social Philosophy and Policy* 22, no. 2 (2005): 100–125.

[8] Daniel C. Russell, "Happiness and Agency in the Stoics and Aristotle," *Proceedings of the Boston Area Colloquium in Ancient Philosophy* 22 (2009): 83–112. This section draws on several of the arguments I made in that article.

mind does.[9] The self, on this view, is one's will, and in this spirit, when Epictetus imagines someone threatening to fetter him, he replies, "What are you saying, man? Fetter *me?* You will fetter my leg; but not even Zeus himself can get the better of my choice."[10] Notice that Epictetus does not reply merely, "Go ahead, fetter me—I can take it; I will still conduct myself well; you won't break my will." His reply is more radical—that *he cannot* be fettered, because he *is* only his will. Such a conception of the self was also crucial to the Stoics' conception of virtue. Virtuous activity, on the formalized Stoic view, is the activity of selecting and reacting well with respect to one's circumstances, whatever they may be. Such a view also supported the Stoics' surprising position that the activities of the virtuous are invulnerable to circumstantial changes, and that the happiness of the virtuous person, which consists in such activities, is therefore beyond the reach of bad luck. But formalized conceptions of the self are found in many places even today, such as in the view, well attested in twentieth-century cognitive science and psychology, that a person's sense of identity and individuality is fundamentally psychological, a sense of a distinct personality related to the body as to something that the personality controls.[11]

However, twentieth-century studies of how people relate to their bodies also began to suggest that the earliest sense of individuality is a sense of physical rather than psychological distinctness, and that bodily motion is not the result of a person's controlling a body, but of a self that is aware of itself as a body.[12] Such findings suggest that the self is not only a selector and controller, but indeed is partially constituted by its physical form and its particular repertoire of capacities for moving through and engaging the physical world.

Such an understanding of the self is also strongly suggested in cases of substantial bodily change. For instance, psychologists have observed a significant correlation between limb loss and depression.[13] This depres-

---

[9] Seneca, *Letters* 113.23. See Julia Annas, *Hellenistic Philosophy of Mind* (Berkeley: University of California Press, 1992), 99–100.

[10] Epictetus, *The Discourses*, ed. Christopher Gill, trans. Robin Hard (London: Everyman, 1995), 1.1.23; italics in the original.

[11] For discussion, see Shaun Gallagher, "Dimensions of Embodiment: Body Image and Body Schema in Medical Contexts," in S. Kay Toombs, ed., *Handbook of Phenomenology and Medicine* (Dordrecht: Kluwer, 2001).

[12] See Gallagher, "Dimensions of Embodiment"; and Maurice Merleau-Ponty, *Phenomenology of Perception*, trans. Colin Smith (New York: Routledge, 2002). See also Mark Johnson, *The Mind in the Body* (Chicago: University of Chicago Press, 1987), who argues that rationality and meaning involve "image-schematic structures of imagination that are extended and figuratively elaborated as abstract structures of meaning and patterns of thought," and as such are among the "principle means by which the body (i.e., physical experience and its structures) works its way up into the mind" (pp. xxxvi–xxxvii).

[13] Bruce Rybarczyk, David L. Nyenhuis, John J. Nicholas, Susan M. Cash, and James Kaiser, "Body Image, Perceived Social Stigma, and the Prediction of Psychological Adjustment to Leg Amputation," *Rehabilitation Psychology* 40, no. 2 (1995): 95–110; J. M. Behel, B. Rybarczyk, T. R. Elliott, J. J. Nicholas, and D. L. Nyenhuis, "The Role of Perceived Vulner-

sion cannot in general be explained as resulting from the trauma of the violence that resulted in limb loss, since depression does not differ significantly between surgical and accidental amputations.[14] A better explanation is that the loss of a limb is often experienced as a kind of loss of self, a change that many patients find understandably difficult to endure. This hypothesis is bolstered by reports of the experience of loss of limb use, as in the case of degenerative diseases like multiple sclerosis. Such changes obviously affect one's sense of one's present possibilities for engaging the world and relating to other people, as well as the changing amounts of time required for acting. But they also affect one's sense of connection with one's past self, as it becomes increasingly difficult to identify oneself with a person who used to move in ways now impossible. Perhaps even more tragically, these changes have a significant impact on one's ability to project oneself into the future, since as degenerative diseases progress, one continues to lose various modes of being in the world.[15] Notice that in virtue of such changes, the entire structure of intentional agency changes as well.[16]

On this conception of the self, then, the self includes one's sense of practical and physical possibilities—that just is a part of the sense of what person one is. This is what it means to say that one's particular embodiment is part of the self. As one philosopher has put it, one's legs are not just objects in the world to which one is specially attached, but are indeed "the possibility of walking, running, playing tennis," so that a loss of body function "represents a modification of the existential possibilities inherent in the lived body." [17]

The idea that the self includes one's sense of practical possibilities seems to be the best rationale, and perhaps the only rationale, for thinking that the self includes one's body. But notice that, *for exactly the same reason,* the self as a psychological identity would also include one's sense of participation in particular ongoing activities, projects, and relationships. After all, the sense of one's practical and physical possibilities obviously cannot be restricted to that part of the physical world within the boundary of one's skin. My sense of my place in the world is radically altered if I lose my legs or their use, but surely the loss of a partner, or a career, or a community, can have precisely the same effect. If I were to lose the people closest to me, for instance, the task of rebuilding my life would not be one of finding new people in relation to whom to act and select, but the

---

ability in Adjustment to Lower Extremity Amputation," *Rehabilitation Psychology* 47, no. 1 (2002): 92–105.

[14] Isao Fukunishi, "Relationship of Cosmetic Disfigurement to the Severity of Posttraumatic Stress Disorder in Burn Injury or Digital Amputation," *Psychotherapy and Psychosomatics* 68, no. 2 (1999): 82–86.

[15] See S. Kay Toombs, "Reflections on Bodily Change," in Toombs, ed., *Handbook of Phenomenology and Medicine.*

[16] I thank Mark LeBar for this way of putting the point.

[17] Toombs, "Reflections on Bodily Change," 254.

much more radical task of redefining who I am going to be, of constructing a new self. Simply put, if my leg represents one set of possibilities of
my embodied existence, then so too does my wife. Therefore, if psychological identity includes the body, then it also seems to include one's
sense of participation in particular attachments—one's relationships,
projects, and ongoing activities. This is what I shall mean, then, in saying
that psychological identity and the activities in which it consists are
"embodied": the boundaries of the self include one's body as well as—and
for the same reason—certain parts of the extrapersonal world.

On an embodied conception of the self, then, one's activities are not
things that one does in relation to the world, but how one occupies and
engages that world as a physical, worldly being. The self's ongoing activities, projects, and relationships can therefore be interrupted or termi-
nated altogether by circumstantial changes: to lose a leg—or a spouse, or
a career—on this view, is to lose forever a particular way of being in the
world, leaving one to find a new self to be. As a result, a person's happiness and well-being are more vulnerable to circumstantial changes,
since the person's identity and activities depend so crucially on the particular ways he or she inhabits the world.

It is this embodied conception of the self that I think is the more plausible one, for the reasons just given—although, again, limitations of space
do not permit a more thorough demonstration of this claim. It is worth
pointing out, though, that it is a commonplace of the libertarian conception of self-ownership that to own oneself includes *at least* the possession
of control rights over one's physical person. It is, of course, possible for
even a formalized self to acquire such control rights, for instance by
bargaining for them within an original position.[18] For the libertarian,
however, control rights over one's person are not rights for self-owners to
acquire, but rights in which self-ownership *consists.* The libertarian is willing to demonstrate that, given self-ownership, one can also come to own
parts of the world beyond one's person. What the libertarian does not do,
however, is to argue from the ownership of the self to the ownership of
one's person, as though these were different issues—as indeed they are
taken to be on the formalized view.[19] The self that the libertarian takes to
be owned, then, must at least include the whole physical person.

Nonetheless, an important disagreement among libertarians—as I intend
to show in the rest of this essay—concerns whether these control rights
end at the boundary of the skin. As I argue now, although no-proviso
libertarians and left-libertarians alike accept that the self includes the

---

[18] Indeed, note that the self behind John Rawls's veil of ignorance is stripped down even
further than the formalized self as I have described it here. See John Rawls, *A Theory of Justice*
(Cambridge, MA: Harvard University Press, 1971).

[19] For the idea that having rights like those associated with self-ownership is not the same
thing as having those rights in virtue of being a self-owner, see also Steiner, *An Essay on
Rights,* chapter 7, esp. 231, 245.

body, nonetheless they cannot accept the embodiment of the self in parts of the extrapersonal world. These libertarians therefore adopt a third view of the self, which we can call the "quasi-embodied" conception. For their part, right-libertarians disagree with both no-proviso libertarians and left-libertarians in embracing the embodied conception of the self and rejecting the quasi-embodied conception. Furthermore, since I argued above that the rationale for thinking of the self as including a body is equally a rationale for thinking of the self as including parts of the extra-personal world, the attempt to drive a wedge between embodiment in the body and embodiment in the extrapersonal world should seem at least prima facie implausible.

In what follows, I shall focus on how an embodied conception of the self bears on the libertarian's attitude toward the Lockean proviso, broadly construed, and thus on these different forms of libertarianism. I begin by arguing that no-proviso libertarianism, by rejecting the Lockean proviso, cannot accept the embodied conception for have-nots (Section IV). I then turn to left-libertarianism, whose egalitarian interpretation of the Lockean proviso is incompatible with the embodied conception for haves (Section V).

IV. No-Proviso Libertarianism

My aims in this section are twofold. First, I argue that given an embodied conception of the self, self-ownership requires that there be a Lockean proviso on ownership. I do so by arguing that no-proviso libertarianism can reject the Lockean proviso only by rejecting an embodied (as opposed to quasi-embodied) conception of the self, at least in the case of have-nots. More precisely, I aim to show that without a Lockean proviso, the self-ownership that remains intact for the very poor is one that must be separated from the ability to control parts of the external world. My other aim is to argue that the embodied conception of the self yields an independently more plausible account of the nature of the use of extra-personal goods and what counts as infringing such use (when compared to the quasi-embodied conception).

No-proviso libertarians hold that while the welfare of the disadvantaged may be a matter of moral urgency, still it is not a matter of *justice*— that is, a matter that could license the introduction of coercively enforceable obligations. Jan Narveson has made the case for this claim as follows. To begin, he notes that if the welfare of the disadvantaged were a matter of justice, then it would be a demand of justice that such welfare be secured coercively if need be. His argument is then two-pronged: first, that such coercion would be unnecessary, and second, that in any case it would be unjust. As to the first, Narveson argues that there would be no need for such coercion in a capitalist society, since "the intelligent efforts of those who precede us create a world with far more for all of us than there would otherwise be."[20] I think that Narveson must surely be correct on this point. At any rate, he as well as John Locke and others are right to suggest that private ownership schemes actually increase opportunities for control of the extrapersonal world, rather than shrink them.[21] As Narveson puts the point, "The 'secret' of wealth is no secret at all: it lies in intelligent hard work plus respect for other people's productive activities."[22] I shall return to this point in Section VI.

It is Narveson's second argument that concerns me at present, and it is also the deeper of the two. It has three key premises. First, for poverty to be a matter of justice it would have to threaten the self-ownership of the poor. To see this, suppose that poverty were a matter of justice, but did not threaten the self-ownership of the poor. The plight of the poor, being a matter of justice, would then potentially justify coercive restrictions on others. But such restrictions would violate the self-ownership of those persons, by putting them in a coercive plight in order to relieve the noncoercive plight of others, a relief that "is got at the expense of liberty for most of us," and that liberty is, in fact, identical to self-ownership.[23] And self-ownership is itself a matter of justice, if anything is.[24] Therefore, since coercion not for the sake of self-ownership violates self-ownership, it follows that matters of justice—matters that justify coercion and delimit self-ownership—are only those in which infringements of self-ownership can arise.

Narveson's second premise is that the only infringements of self-ownership are invasive ones, namely, threats to one's person or one's property. This premise rests on Narveson's conception of the use of parts of the extrapersonal world. Those parts that one can be said to use, on Narveson's view, are "those elements of the environment over which one has exerted and continues intentionally to exert control."[25] This is because the use of an extrapersonal good is not "pie-in-the-sky," imaginary or possible use, but actual use and the investment of effort; as Narveson says, "use is *use*."[26] Consequently, it is no infringement of the latecomer's

[20] Jan Narveson, "Libertarianism vs. Marxism: Reflections on G. A. Cohen's *Self-Ownership, Freedom, and Equality,*" *Journal of Ethics* 2, no. 1 (1998): 1–26, at 21.
[21] Narveson, "Libertarianism vs. Marxism," 21; see also Nozick, *Anarchy, State, and Utopia,* 177; Murray Rothbard, *The Ethics of Liberty* (Atlantic Highlands, NJ: Humanities Press, 1982), 36; Eric Mack, "Self-Ownership, Marxism, and Egalitarianism, Part II: Challenges to the Self-Ownership Thesis," *Politics, Philosophy, and Economics* 1, no. 2 (1995): 243–44, at 247–49; and David Schmidtz in Schmidtz and Robert Goodin, *Social Welfare and Individual Responsibility* (Cambridge: Cambridge University Press, 1998).
[22] Narveson, "Original Appropriation," 220–21.
[23] Narveson, "Libertarianism vs. Marxism," 6–9, 23.
[24] Ibid., 4.
[25] Narveson, "Original Appropriation," 215. See also Rothbard, *The Ethics of Liberty,* 33–34, 41, 47, 56, 59, 64.
[26] Likewise, Edward Feser argues that in order for one's use of some extrapersonal good to be protected as a matter of justice, one must have already engaged with that good so as to transform it in some significant way. See Edward Feser, "There Is No Such Thing as an Unjust Initial Acquisition," *Social Philosophy and Policy* 22, no. 1 (2005): 56–80, at 61–67.

self-ownership to deprive him of future use of that good, since he is not already using it. By contrast, interfering with a first-comer's use of some good *is* an infringement of his self-ownership, since this is to interfere with the first-comer's activity already under way.[27] It follows that depriving someone of something counts as an infringement of his self-ownership just in case he is already using that thing. Since depriving someone of what he is already using is what we mean by an *invasive* infringement of his self-ownership, it follows for Narveson that all infringements of self-ownership are invasive. There is no such thing as a noninvasive infringement of a person's self-ownership.

Narveson's third and final premise is that the poor do not, just as such, face any invasive threat to their self-ownership, even if they are driven to accept low wages. "The poor or the sick are not *unfree*," Narveson says; "*that* is not their problem. Nobody threatens to make them worse off than they already are" if they fail to take "very low-paying jobs. . . . [N]obody has a gun to their heads."[28] It follows from these three premises that, since poverty is not an invasive threat, it is no threat to self-ownership, and thus is not a matter of justice. Whatever standing welfare may have as a matter of moral concern, it is not one to be addressed politically, and thus not by a Lockean proviso on ownership.[29]

I agree with Narveson's first premise, and in the next section I shall consider and reject the rival view that there are matters of justice that both are independent of self-ownership and legitimately delimit self-ownership. Furthermore, I shall raise no objections here to Narveson's third premise, although I think that compelling objections have been raised against it.[30] Instead, I want to focus now on Narveson's second premise, and argue that Narveson's narrow conception of infringements on self-ownership is incompatible with an embodied conception of the self, as well as implausible in its own right.

We can see this incompatibility in at least three ways. First, on an embodied conception of the self, the self consists in (among other things) its worldly interactions. The self is not strictly a psychological entity whose activities, though done with the world as their object, are nonetheless internal (as on the formalized view). Nor is the self strictly a psychological entity plus its physical embodiment, but separate from the extrapersonal world (as on the quasi-embodied view). Rather, one of the most important ways in which the self defines itself is through its sense of possibilities for interacting with the world. And it seems clear that such

---

[27] Narveson, "Original Appropriation," 214–15.

[28] Narveson, "Libertarianism vs. Marxism," 22; emphasis in the original.

[29] Ibid., 22–23.

[30] For example, G. A. Cohen argues that the poor do have a gun to their heads, "held by the state, whose protection of the property to which they are coercively denied access renders their freedom meager." See G. A. Cohen, "Once More into the Breach of Self-Ownership: Reply to Narveson and Brenkert," *Journal of Ethics* 2, no. 1 (1998): 59–96, at 74.

146   DANIEL C. RUSSELL

interaction is not limited to one's past or to what one is already doing, but is also forward-looking. As Eric Mack has observed, people "obviously do not live by past investments alone, but also by necessarily prospective interaction with extra-personal objects—interactions which, when viewed from some later point, may count as an investment of self."[31] And as Gerald Cohen asks, if an act underway involves using a succession of worldly goods, why should we suppose it is no interference with the act to whisk away one of those goods, merely on the grounds that the agent has not touched it yet?[32]

On the embodied view, to control what one can do is to control who one can be. On such a view, then, we must broaden our understanding of infringements of self-ownership, to extend beyond obvious invasions of one's person—holding guns to heads, say—to include what Mack calls the nullification of world-interactive powers.

Moreover, this seems the more plausible view on independent grounds. As Mack has argued, there is no morally important difference between restricting a person's power to engage the world by encasing him in a cage you have made from materials you own, and encasing everything within his reach in such cages.[33] Even though the latter case involves no invasion of his person, it is as great an infringement of his ability to engage the world as anything can be. On an embodied view of the self, then, there are such things as noninvasive infringements of self-ownership, and I find such a view to be independently more plausible than a quasi-embodied view.

That is one tension between Narveson's conception of use and the embodied conception of the self, and a second tension can be seen by noting that an embodied self also consists in (among other things) its particular attachments to things and persons in the world. These attachments by their very nature are extended through time; they include not only what attachments one has made in the past, but also how one's attachments extend into the future. Part of what it is to own such a self and to have control over it, therefore, is to have opportunities to take care for one's future.

Here it is worth noting with David Schmidtz that the inability to gain control over natural resources can prevent one from taking measures to protect and sustain those resources, and thus take care for one's future.[34] Or, as Hillel Steiner has put the point, "Whether I have five other places I could *permissibly* be and you have none, . . . the adversity we would each experience from a lightning strike would be the same. However, the

---

[31] Eric Mack, "Self-Ownership and the Right of Property," *The Monist* 73, no. 4 (1990): 519–543, at 528.
[32] Cohen, "Once More into the Breach," 62–67.
[33] See Eric Mack, "The Self-Ownership Proviso: A New and Improved Lockean Proviso," *Social Philosophy and Policy* 12, no. 1 (1995): 186–218.
[34] Schmidtz and Goodin, *Social Welfare and Individual Responsibility*, chapter 1.2.

personal responsibility we would each have for that adversity would differ."[35] Taking responsibility for one's fate requires opportunities to control resources, such as finding a place to shelter from a storm. No one can guarantee his future, but differences in opportunities to do anything about one's future are real—and they are differences in control over the self. Again, then, on the embodied view the activities of self-owners extend well beyond what they have already touched, and thus on such a view not all infringements of self-ownership need be invasive ones. Moreover, this too seems an independently plausible way of thinking about infringement. Surely there is no morally relevant difference between (i) taking away a person's ability to take care for his future by physically restraining him and (ii) doing so by putting cages around all the things he might need to use in order to take care for his future.

Finally, the tension between Narveson's view and the embodied conception also becomes apparent through reflection on what is involved even in owning one's own body. Let me explain why. If a claim of justice regarding extrapersonal goods requires the original use of a first-comer, then does this requirement attach itself to one's person, as well? We cannot allow special pleading here, since we cannot take it for granted that one is the first-comer where one's own person is concerned; on the contrary, one's person is brought about and then helped along through the efforts of others—parents, family, and community. Where my person is concerned, I actually arrive fairly *late* on the scene; others were there well ahead of me. So is there any difference in principle between the claims of a latecomer in the case of extrapersonal goods and the claims of a latecomer in the case of his own person? Perhaps there is, on the grounds (say) that "first use" of a thing cannot generate ownership claims to it when the thing in question is a person—people cannot be owned by anyone else, including their procreators, but only by themselves. Alternatively, we might say that while the burden of proof falls to each of us to demonstrate that he should be entitled to exclude others from control of his person, nonetheless this is a burden of proof we each are able to meet.[36] The upshot is the same either way: we own our bodies despite not having met any first-use requirement. But now the question is this: What rationale could there be for saying that we own our bodies, despite not meeting the first-use requirement, that does not *also* cast doubt on the appropriateness of the first-use requirement in at least some cases involving extrapersonal goods?

[35] Hillel Steiner, "How Equality Matters," *Social Philosophy and Policy* 19, no. 1 (2002): 342–56, at 351; emphasis in the original.
[36] And this is exactly what Narveson ("Original Appropriation," 219) says: "given liberalism, we do not primordially own the world—only ourselves. And even that isn't primordial. We must argue even for that." That is why Narveson can no longer hold the view that "*a right to our persons as our property is the sole fundamental right there is*"; see Jan Narveson, *The Libertarian Idea* (Philadelphia, PA: Temple University Press, 1988), 66; emphasis in the original.

Narveson himself holds that we acquire rights over our bodies from each other, in virtue of the realization that "life for ourselves is bound to be worse" unless we grant one another "mutual recognition . . . of rights not to be molested by others."[37] The point at present, though, is not *how* one could acquire such a right, but *the very fact that one could:* we must set aside the narrow use restriction on ownership, in this case, because one's body is something over which one must have rights in order to have control over oneself. In the case of one's body, therefore, use cannot be a necessary condition of ownership *if* the things one can be said to use are restricted to things one has already got hold of. What matters here is not whether one got to it first, but whether one needs to control it in order to have control of oneself. Again, however, there can be no special pleading here: the reasons there are for thinking that one needs control rights over one's person seem equally to be reasons for thinking that one needs control over parts of the extrapersonal world. Depriving one of the opportunity to control parts of the extrapersonal world, therefore, is an infringement of self-ownership, *even* when that infringement is noninvasive, barring one from things one has not yet touched.

On the embodied view, then, use cannot be restricted to what one has already touched. Rather, use must be broad enough to include not only what one has already touched, but also what one needs to touch in order to have control of oneself—a view that also seems independently plausible. A self-owner must have control of his physical body, despite being a latecomer, but surely for the same reason he must also be able to control parts of the extrapersonal world. And of course it is precisely the opportunity to gain control over parts of the extrapersonal world that the Lockean proviso treats as a matter of justice. As I have argued, the prohibition of noninvasive infringements as a matter of justice cannot be in question as long as we think that the self that a poor or sick person owns is an embodied self.[38] On an embodied conception of the self, therefore, there can be no question whether it is a matter of justice that a scheme of holdings should meet a Lockean proviso on ownership.

It is in the case of have-nots that the no-proviso libertarian finds himself committed to rejecting the embodied conception of the self: poverty and sickness may leave one destitute, but even so one's self-ownership remains intact, since one can still reason, deliberate, and choose, and no one need be laying hands on one's body. To say that the Lockean proviso is otiose because self-ownership is untouched by one's material circumstances, is

[37] Narveson, "Original Appropriation," 219. Here he fares better than Rothbard (*The Ethics of Liberty*, 99–100), who holds that parents own their children, although this ownership must be temporary and of a "trustee" sort, since "it surely would be grotesque for a libertarian who believes in the right of self-ownership to advocate the right of a parent to murder or torture his or her children." Fair enough, but of course the whole question is whether children *are* self-owners in the first place.
[38] See Mack, "The Self-Ownership Proviso," 186, 189, 201.

to deny that the self one owns is an embodied self. This is not only implausible but inconsistent, since it is surely the self-ownership of haves that necessitates *their* rights of control of the extrapersonal world in the first place, a necessity that arises only for embodied selves. For as Rothbard points out, trenching on one's person or holdings leaves the self untouched if the self is only considered as a "will";[39] self-ownership gives one the right to control one's person *and* extrapersonal property, then, only if the self one owns is embodied. Without the Lockean proviso, therefore, it is a matter of embodied selves for haves and other sorts of selves for have-nots.

I find the split between the self-ownership of have-nots and their ability to control property to be nowhere more palpable than in Douglas Rasmussen and Douglas Den Uyl's otherwise excellent book *Norms of Liberty* (2005). Now, I must point out that Rasmussen and Den Uyl would say that they reject the self-ownership thesis. But they understand the thesis they reject not in the broader way that I have understood it here, but in the narrower sense that the right of self-ownership would have to be a single right (rather than a cluster) whose existence is underived and *a priori*.[40] However, they do espouse a right of "self-direction" by which one has a right against being directed to purposes to which one has not consented, a right that defines a moral space within which self-directed activities are protected against intrusion by others, and by which one has certain natural rights of property in the extrapersonal world.[41] As I said at the outset, self-ownership is often taken as a bundle of exactly these sorts of rights—to control oneself, to exclude others from controlling one, and so on—and it is on the basis of such rights that libertarians argue that one can have other property rights as well. So the right of "self-direction" can be treated as a self-ownership right after all, at least as I (and many others) have understood self-ownership rights.

Rasmussen and Den Uyl hold that persons have the right of self-direction because of the nature of the human self. The flourishing of a human being, they argue, is always the flourishing of a particular individual, and thus, far from being merely an individual instantiation of a single *summum bonum*, one's flourishing is in fact identical to the particular life of the one who is flourishing.[42] This suggests pretty clearly, I think, that Rasmussen and Den Uyl think of the flourishing self as a necessarily embodied self, in just the sense in which I have used that phrase here. Central to the flourishing of such a self, they argue, is self-

---

[39] See Rothbard, *The Ethics of Liberty*, chapter 6.

[40] Rasmussen and Den Uyl, *Norms of Liberty*, chapter 9. See also Richard Arneson, "Lockean Self-Ownership: Towards a Demolition," *Political Studies* 39, no. 1 (1991): 36–54; Robert Brenkert, "Self-Ownership, Freedom, and Autonomy," *Journal of Ethics* 2, no. 1 (1998): 27–55 at 52–54; Cohen, "Once More into the Breach," 94–95.

[41] Rasmussen and Den Uyl, *Norms of Liberty*, 89, 90, 98–100.

[42] Ibid., 80–81, 133–34.

direction, a right to lead a life of one's choosing, which is not only necessary for flourishing but is in fact a constituent of it.[43] Moreover, for
Rasmussen and Den Uyl there is no separating self-direction from the
right to control what one creates; property rights are therefore rights to
live according to one's choices, and thus are natural rights.[44] "Taking
control of another's property against that other's wishes," they argue,
"can now be seen as nothing less than taking control of one of the central
relationships that constitute a human being's life."[45]

With all of this I agree, but their conception of the self changes crucially
when they turn to consider the case of have-nots. Rasmussen and Den
Uyl consider the objection that being very poor can be an obstacle to
being a self-directing person, and they reply that the very poor *are* self-
directors, because even in great poverty one retains the powers of practical reasoning, deliberating, and choosing.[46] But while these powers may
demonstrate that poverty leaves intact the self-direction of a formalized
or even a quasi-embodied self, that is not the conception of the self that
was taken to require the right of self-direction in the first place—*that* self
was an embodied one. Rasmussen and Den Uyl's argument, recall, was
that control of extrapersonal property is crucial to self-direction, because
self-direction is a right to lead an embodied life of one's choosing. But
then we find that for some others (have-nots), self-direction is actually
quite distinct from what they can control in the extrapersonal world. In a
word, this means embodied selves for haves and other sorts of selves for
have-nots.

It is clear, then, that an embodied conception of the self commits the
libertarian to the existence of a Lockean proviso, that is, to treating one's
opportunities to control parts of the extrapersonal world as a matter of
justice. But to what proviso does it commit one, exactly? I go on now to
argue that the interpretation of the Lockean proviso depends crucially on
one's conception of the self, and in particular that the left-libertarian
interpretation is incompatible with the embodied conception of the self.
Then, in Section VI, I consider the proviso's interpretation according to
right-libertarianism in light of the embodied conception.

V. Left-Libertarianism

Although libertarians and their critics have long held that self-ownership
is incompatible with distributive equality, left-libertarians disagree. On
the left-libertarian view, people do indeed have rights of ownership over
themselves and parts of the extrapersonal world, but like any ownership

---

[43] Ibid., 87.
[44] Ibid., 98, 100.
[45] Ibid., 106.
[46] Ibid., 303-11; see esp. 306-8.

right, the boundaries of self-ownership must be delineated by considerations of justice, including the justice of extrapersonal property. This is,
after all, the traditional role of the Lockean proviso, and left-libertarians
argue that the considerations of justice that enter the theory of extrapersonal property via the proviso are best understood in egalitarian terms.
I now want to explore the conception of the self that is required by this
alleged compatibility between egalitarian restrictions on extrapersonal
property, on the one hand, and self-ownership, on the other. To do so, I
shall discuss briefly the recent work of three representative left-libertarians,
starting with (and spending the most time on) Michael Otsuka, before
moving on to Hillel Steiner and Philippe Van Parijs.

Otsuka holds that self-ownership encompasses two main types of rights:
rights of control and use of one's mind and body, and rights to all the
income one can gain from controlling and using one's mind and body.[47]
Otsuka argues that the income right is subject to a Lockean proviso when,
as in most cases, producing the income requires the acquisition of extrapersonal goods.[48] In particular, Otsuka says, "You may acquire previously unowned worldly resources if and only if you leave enough so that
everyone else can acquire an equally advantageous share of unowned
worldly resources."[49] Otsuka's version of the Lockean proviso is both
welfarist and egalitarian. It is welfarist because "enough and as good" is
interpreted as leaving for others enough for the purpose of attaining a
certain level of welfare, resulting from an individual's combined store of
worldly and personal resources.[50] And it is egalitarian because opportunities to derive welfare from unowned worldly goods are to be equal,
despite inequalities in personal capacities.[51] Consequently, Otsuka holds
that "[s]omeone else's share is as advantageous as yours if and only if it
is such that she would be able (by producing, consuming, or trading) to
better herself to the same degree as you." Following Richard Arneson, he
says that such "'betterment' is to be measured in terms of level of welfare
understood as the 'satisfaction of the self-interested preferences that the
individual would have after ideal deliberation while thinking clearly with
full pertinent information regarding those preferences'."[52]

How is this version of the Lockean proviso—what Otsuka calls the
"egalitarian proviso"—to be satisfied? Otsuka holds that the egalitarian
proviso requires the members of each generation—starting with the generation of initial appropriators—to leave at least as great an opportunity
to own extrapersonal resources for the next generation. He concludes that

[47] Michael Otsuka, *Libertarianism Without Inequality* (Oxford: Clarendon Press, 2003), 15.
[48] Ibid., 19–21.
[49] Ibid., 24.
[50] Ibid., 25.
[51] Ibid., 11.
[52] Ibid., 27, quoting Richard Arneson, "Primary Goods Reconsidered," *Noûs* 24, no. 3 (1990): 429–54, at 448.

at one's death, resources at least as valuable as those one acquired in one's life must lapse back into a state of nonownership, that is, that such resources must return to the commons. The upshot of this requirement is that each person would have "only a lifetime leasehold on worldly resources," including the ones that they improve. This requirement, Otsuka says, would not amount to a full prohibition on bequeathing, but it would prohibit all but very modest gifts that have little impact on the welfare of the recipients relative to other members of their generation.[53]

It is clear that Otsuka must show that the demands of the egalitarian proviso do not trench upon self-ownership: self-ownership, after all, is not a good to be balanced among others, but a boundary on what may be done in the name of any good. It is presumably for this very reason that Otsuka says that the egalitarian proviso does not conflict with or infringe upon self-ownership, but only restricts one from engaging in transfers that one has no right to engage in anyway.[54] But how is this claim to be substantiated?

Here we must turn to deeper questions regarding the kinds of considerations of justice that can delimit self-ownership, and there are two broad, mutually exclusive, and jointly exhaustive possibilities to consider. The first possibility is that we might defend the view (glimpsed in Section IV) that what any person may do under the banner of self-ownership can be limited only by the similar self-ownership rights of others—that the only limit on self-ownership is self-ownership.[55] It seems clear, though, that the egalitarian proviso could not be derived solely from the self-ownership rights of have-nots, even given the embodied conception of the self. To be sure, from the fact that one owns oneself, and that the self so owned is embodied in projects involving the extrapersonal world, it follows that one is entitled to a fair opportunity to participate within a fair scheme by which people can acquire parts of the extrapersonal world.[56] But that comes far short of the egalitarian proviso, which entitles one not only to the opportunity of acquiring extrapersonal property, but indeed to the opportunity of acquiring extrapersonal property sufficient to give one as good a chance to attain welfare as anyone, whatever differences there may be in personal capacities to improve resources. It is no surprise, then, that neither Otsuka nor left-libertarians generally take their various egalitarian renderings of the Lockean proviso to follow from the thesis of self-ownership; rather, those renderings are taken to arise from considerations of justice independent of self-ownership.

And that is the second possibility, namely, that it is false that the only limit on self-ownership is self-ownership; on this view, there are consid-

[53] Otsuka, *Libertarianism Without Inequality*, 35–38.
[54] Ibid., 38–39.
[55] See, e.g., Roderick Long, "Land-Locked: A Critique of Carson on Property Rights," *Journal of Libertarian Studies* 20, no. 1 (2006): 87–95, at 90–91.
[56] Mack, "Self-Ownership and the Right of Property," esp. 534.

erations of justice that both are independent of self-ownership and serve to delimit self-ownership. Here we should notice that Otsuka does not think that there are considerations of justice demanding that one give others access to one's *person*, which would of course conflict with the self-ownership right of control of one's person. However, since Otsuka thinks that considerations of justice demand that one give others access to one's income, and that this is no infringement of the self-ownership right to income from one's person, he must of course hold that where self-ownership is concerned, there is a crucial difference between control of one's person and control of the extrapersonal world. Indeed, this is exactly what he does hold: the Lockean proviso, he says, holds in cases of producing income by using extrapersonal goods, but not when one uses parts of one's person, as for instance when one weaves a textile from one's own fallen hairs.[57] Thus, the same proviso that would trench upon self-ownership rights to income, in the case of income derived strictly from one's person, does not trench upon that right in the case of income derived from extrapersonal property.[58] What, then, is this crucial difference between personal and extrapersonal goods?

That there is an important difference is obvious: the world is here for all of us, but your person is just for you. So far, however, that idea is fairly vague: in what sense is the world "for all of us"? One possibility is that the world is "for all of us" in the sense that every one of us needs the world not only as a necessary container and sustainer of our physical presence in it, but also, and just as importantly, as a place in which to construct embodied human lives and embodied human selves. But notice that on this rationale, there is no longer the difference that Otsuka needs between personal and extrapersonal goods. On this rationale, the right to control the self is a right to control one's person and parts of the extrapersonal world, for the very same reason—that the self is embodied in both of these. Because we are self-owners, each of us has a right to control all of himself and some of the world. Therefore, on the present rationale— which is, of course, the embodied conception of the self—the world's being here for all of us is a fact of self-ownership after all, so the Lockean proviso would no longer be independent of self-ownership. The only limits on self-ownership suggested by this view, then, are themselves considerations of self-ownership. Yet, as we have seen, considerations of self-ownership alone do not generate the egalitarian proviso. Thus, Otsuka must hold that while it is self-ownership that gives one rights of control

[57] Otsuka, *Libertarianism Without Inequality*, 19–21.

[58] This strong separation of self-ownership and extrapersonal ownership is particularly clear in Peter Vallentyne, Hillel Steiner, and Michael Otsuka, "Why Left-Libertarianism Is Not Incoherent, Indeterminate, or Irrelevant: A Reply to Fried," *Philosophy and Public Affairs* 33, no. 2 (2005): 201–15, at 201, 208–9, who note that the egalitarian dimension of left-libertarianism is distinct from its libertarian dimension (i.e., self-ownership), and that these two dimensions are based on respect for the moral status of different things (things and persons, respectively).

of one's person, independent considerations of justice must come in to generate the Lockean proviso, if it is an egalitarian proviso.

A better rationale for the left-libertarian is that the difference between extrapersonal property and property in one's person is that the extrapersonal world is commonly owned, as indeed left-libertarians generally hold.[59] Common ownership, unlike joint ownership, does not require one to secure the permission of all in order to use or appropriate parts of the extrapersonal world, but it does require one to make compensation to others for doing so. Notice that this rationale for thinking that the world is "for all of us" does not follow from the thesis of self-ownership: from that thesis, it follows that one is entitled to an opportunity to access the extrapersonal world, not that one is entitled to compensation from others should they avail themselves of such an opportunity, just as on Otsuka's view. So if common ownership is a demand of justice, then it is a demand independent of self-ownership that can come to bear on extrapersonal ownership by way of a Lockean proviso, with egalitarian implications.

The real question for Otsuka, then, is whether common world ownership *is* a matter of justice and therefore consistent with self-ownership, which is a matter of justice if anything is. And the answer is: *It depends on how we conceive of the self that is owned.* According to Otsuka, common world ownership requires persons to make compensation to others for what they take from the commons, and this requirement must not infringe, but only delimit, self-ownership. However, if the self that is owned is an embodied self, then such demands for compensation necessarily infringe self-ownership. Let me explain why.

If persons are self-owners, then at the very least no person need justify his existence to any other person, and no person can owe compensation to others for the fact that he exists—that he is a human being, in the world, leading a human life. Now, if the self that is owned is an embodied self, then necessarily that self exists and leads a human life only by controlling parts of the extrapersonal world. Removing goods from the commons, then, is the price of leading a human life. However, given the egalitarian proviso, removing the sorts of goods from the commons that can underwrite the leading of a human life entails an enforceable claim by others to compensation. Therefore, since (*ex hypothesi*) the owned self is an embodied self, the egalitarian proviso requires that one compensate others for one's leading an embodied existence. And that is to say that the egalitarian proviso requires one to compensate others for the very fact

[59] This amounts to what Vallentyne ("Libertarianism") calls "unilateralist" left-libertarianism. I shall not discuss the non-unilateralist alternative of joint world ownership, since it is generally—and, I think, rightly—held to be inconsistent with self-ownership; see, e.g., G. A. Cohen, *Self-Ownership, Freedom, and Equality* (Cambridge: Cambridge University Press, 1995); Mack, "Self-Ownership, Marxism, and Egalitarianism, Part II," 243–44, 250–51; and Vallentyne, "Libertarianism." For a dissenting view, see Magnus Jedenheim-Edling, "The Compatibility of Effective Self-Ownership and Joint World Ownership," *Journal of Political Philosophy* 13, no. 3 (2005): 284–304.

that one is a self-owner. But of course, to own oneself is for there to be no one from whom one need lease oneself. The egalitarian proviso is therefore incompatible with an embodied conception of the self that is owned.

Note that the argument here is not that the compensating *act* is incompatible with ownership of an embodied self, although I think it is. On Otsuka's view, that compensation consists in being compelled to appropriate only on condition that one's appropriation be temporary. More precisely, the compensation is that one forgo embodying oneself in any world-interactive projects, such as saving for the future of others, that would involve more than a "lifetime leasehold" on extrapersonal property. Whatever we say about the sort of compensation required, though, the real issue is that *the very fact that* any *compensation is called for* violates self-ownership, *if* the self is an embodied one.[60]

In order to ground the egalitarian proviso in the demands of common ownership, then, Otsuka must either embrace an embodied conception of the self and reject the thesis of self-ownership, or he must reject an embodied conception of the self so that the proviso no longer infringes self-ownership. It is clear that left-libertarianism must reject a formalized conception of the self, given the general libertarian thesis that self-ownership as such includes rights to one's person. The left-libertarian must draw the boundaries of the self so as to include one's body but exclude the extrapersonal world. In other words, left-libertarianism requires a quasi-embodied conception of the self.

Consequently, there is a crucial disagreement over the boundaries of the self between left-libertarians (who accept common ownership) and right-libertarians (who reject it). Moreover, the left-libertarian's conception of a quasi-embodied self seems seriously problematic, on at least two grounds. One is that, as I have noted already, the quasi-embodied conception of the self is independently implausible. The quasi-embodied view would drive a wedge between the body and the extrapersonal world where the self is concerned, but as we have seen, the reasons for drawing the boundaries of the self so as to include the body are the same as the reasons for drawing the boundaries so as to include parts of the extrapersonal world. This is because both are crucial to the nature of the self as a world-engaging being.

The other problem is that for the left-libertarian the quasi-embodied conception of the self is a double-edged sword. First, the left-libertarian must draw the boundaries of the self well short of the extrapersonal world in order to preserve consistency between self-ownership on the one hand and compensatory demands for using commonly owned goods on

---

[60] We can therefore set aside Steiner's worries (*An Essay on Rights*, 249–61) about giving a Hohfeldian analysis of the right of bequest as a right of deceased persons; for even if there turned out to be no such thing as a right of bequest, it would follow only that one could not make compensation for removing goods from the commons by giving up that right. It would not show that no such compensation is called for.

the other. But second, the left-libertarian must also motivate the very idea of a natural right of common world ownership in the first place; yet a self with such a right would surely *have* to be an embodied one. How could self-owners be anything short of embodied selves and *also* have some sort of natural claim over things in the extrapersonal world? Indeed, common ownership itself seems to be incoherent in this respect, drawing the boundaries of the self in one place in making persons common world owners and in another place in making persons incur liabilities to others when they use parts of the extrapersonal world.

Thus, in taking seriously the have-nots' alleged right of common ownership, Otsuka must employ an embodied conception of the self, and in arguing that that right does not trench on the self-ownership of the haves, he must employ some other conception. Ironically, this form of left-libertarianism turns out to suffer from the same basic problem as no-proviso libertarianism: an embodied self for some, another sort of self for others.

However, while Otsuka's view requires compensation for the use of resources full stop, we might instead restrict compensation only to the use of resources beyond a fair per-capita share. This is the view of Hillel Steiner, who holds that a Lockean proviso sets a limit on what one may come to own in virtue of being a self-owner, and in particular that such a proviso grants one unencumbered title only to what one produces either from self-owned resources or from one's per-capita share of unowned, raw natural resources.[61]

For Steiner, this proviso is especially important when considering the use of a rather special sort of natural resource, namely, "germ-line genetic information." Germ-line genetic information, he argues, is an important resource, since it determines one's native endowments and thus the costs involved in bringing one to a certain level of welfare. And since it is an unowned natural resource, the Lockean proviso requires its division into per-capita shares.[62] Perhaps, then, we could generate an egalitarian proviso just by focusing on the ownership of bodies, without bringing the extrapersonal world into the picture.

I find Steiner less than fully explicit on this point, but I think it is clear that we must distinguish between the germ-line itself—a genetic heritage spanning generations—and the genetic information that stems from that line. This is so, because the genetic information itself takes the form of a particular physical person, and such persons, so far from being unowned natural resources, are self-owners on Steiner's view. What no such person can claim as rightfully his, in contrast, is the fact that a certain natural heritage brought it about that he has the particular endowments he has. To focus on the genetic information, then, is to focus on the particular

[61] Steiner, *An Essay on Rights*, 235–36.
[62] See also Vallentyne, Steiner, and Otsuka, "Why Left-Libertarianism Is Not Incoherent," 209: Steiner holds "that unchosen germ-line genetic information is a natural resource and thus among the items subject to egalitarian ownership."

individual, whereas to focus on the germ-line is to focus on the biological provenance of that individual. Every individual owns himself, but no individual "owns" his biological provenance; the latter, then, must be regarded as a natural resource. The Lockean proviso therefore extends to the use of the germ-line.

Now, as I have just noted, the use of the germ-line results in a new individual with a particular set of personal endowments. However, biological parents have no germ-lines to use but their own, of course, and the use of different germ-lines results in persons with unequal bundles of endowments, an inequality notably expressed in the differences in costs associated with bringing different offspring to a similar level of ability-value.[63] In that case, the values of our naturally distributed shares of the natural resource of germ-lines are not divided on a per-capita basis, so the Lockean proviso requires compensation for the differences. Consequently, on Steiner's view, persons are all subject to the following enforceable rule: if you procreate, then you must participate in a scheme whereby the costs of developing ability-value in offspring are roughly equalized between sets of parents. This restriction, for Steiner, is no infringement of self-ownership, since it is only a demand of justice that enters via the Lockean proviso to set limits on what a self-owner can be said to own in the first place.

The question for Steiner is essentially the same as that for Otsuka: Given that persons are self-owners, if the owned self is embodied, can such a restriction in fact be a requirement of justice? I do not think that it can, because such a restriction demands compensation from a self-owner for using an owned self to engage in a project that is, on an embodied view of the self, paradigmatic of self-ownership.

My argument for this has two premises. The first is that on an embodied view of the self, having offspring is a paradigmatic project of a self-owner if anything is. Recall that on an embodied view, the reason that the self extends to the body is the same reason that it also extends beyond the body, to include other persons, relationships, and projects. The self clearly extends to one's offspring, and even to one's potential for offspring, since these determine the kinds of relationships one can engage in, what kinds of values one can bring about in the world, what sorts of roles one can play and virtues one can develop, and how one will relate to the human world and its future. Likewise, the self also extends to one's relationship with one's partner, and, here too, questions of procreation determine what sort of couple a couple can be, what joint projects they can share and what joint abilities they can develop, and how they as a couple will relate to the human world and its future. It is for these sorts of reasons, of course, that procreation can play such a profound role in human life.[64]

---

[63] Steiner, *An Essay on Rights,* 277.

[64] See Rosalind Hursthouse, "Virtue Theory and Abortion," *Philosophy and Public Affairs* 20, no. 3 (1991): 223–46.

Having offspring is among the projects by which humans typically give their lives and their identities a particular definition; thus, on an embodied view, having offspring is the project of a self-owner, if anything is.

The second premise is that all that is involved in procreation is a pair of selves, each of which is a self-owner. Return to the distinction between genetic information and lines of such information. In particular, when I procreate, do I use the information or the line? Well, it is clear enough that I use the information; that information, after all, exists as the particular physical individual that I am, including its procreative powers and genetic package. But is there any sense in which I use the line? Only metaphorically. After all, focusing on the germ-line, as opposed to the particular bundle of genetic information arising from it, is really just a way of making the historical point that I am not the originator of myself. It is therefore misleading to think of the germ-line as some reified thing which I literally use in bearing offspring. All that I "use" is my particular embodiment—myself—which I own.

From these two points, it follows that the restriction imposed by Steiner's version of the Lockean proviso is a requirement on self-owners that they make compensation for using selves that they own to engage in projects that are, on the embodied view, paradigmatic of self-ownership. Once again, then, to bring in considerations of common ownership as demands of justice via the Lockean proviso is to require self-owners to make compensation in the event that they do the things that self-owners do, *if* the self is embodied. In short, it requires self-owners to make compensation for being self-owners; and that, as I said above, is just to deny their self-ownership.

Thus, Steiner must reject at least one of the two premises I defended above. On the one hand, if he were to deny that all that is involved in procreation is a pair of owned selves (the second premise), then he would have to hold that, even if some particular genetic information could be in some sense mine, still it could in no sense be *me*. On the other hand, if Steiner were to sever the link between procreation and self-ownership (the first premise), then he must hold that the self is untouched by restrictions on how it may relate to the extrapersonal world. Either way, then, he would have to reject an embodied conception of the self.

Lastly, this separation of self from world is nowhere more explicit, I think, than in Philippe Van Parijs's discussion of "real freedom." According to Van Parijs, a society with what he calls real freedom would have three characteristics: (1) it would provide for the security of its members; (2) it would respect the self-ownership of its members; and (3) it would otherwise create the best possible opportunities for each of its members to do whatever he might want to do.[65] Quite rightly, Van Parijs holds that the maximization of such opportunities must stop short of imposing forced

---

[65] Van Parijs, *Real Freedom for All*, 22–25.

labor upon those who pay the tax bill, given that members of a free society are self-owners. However, where considerations of self-ownership place the ceiling on taxation depends crucially on how self-ownership is connected to ownership of extrapersonal property. On Van Parijs's view, self-ownership is a separate matter from extrapersonal property. For instance, he holds that even a socialist state that forbids wage labor and owning capital still respects self-ownership, *on the grounds that* such a scheme restricts only what may be done with external objects, and not what may be done with oneself.[66] Although an analysis of socialism falls outside the scope of this essay, it should be clear that socialism can combine self-ownership and a ban on private ownership of material capital only by treating what one may do with oneself as a separate question from what one may do with external objects.

By keeping questions of self-ownership and extrapersonal property ownership so distinct, Van Parijs can set the ceiling on maximizing opportunities at the point where taxes "generate the highest yield . . . that can be durably generated" under the type of socioeconomic regime in place.[67] However, this conclusion requires rejecting an embodied conception of the self, since on that conception the ownership of one's person and the ownership of extrapersonal property are anything but distinct issues.

This is instructive: it would seem that the only way to bring in considerations of justice, independent of self-ownership, via the Lockean proviso is to treat self-ownership and other forms of ownership as separate issues. But on an embodied conception of the self, self-ownership and other forms of ownership are not separate issues at all. On that conception, it is because we are embodied self-owners that one must be able to control both one's own person *and* parts of the extrapersonal world. Therefore, given an embodied conception of the self, the only restrictions that could enter via the Lockean proviso are matters of self-ownership.[68]

VI. RIGHT-LIBERTARIANISM AND THE LOCKEAN PROVISO

We can now see that conjoining the thesis that persons are self-owners with the embodied conception of the self yields the view that I have called right-libertarianism. As I argued in Section IV, the embodied conception requires a Lockean proviso on either the acquisition or the use of extrapersonal property (or both), on the grounds that intrusions against a

---

[66] Ibid., 9.
[67] Ibid., 38.
[68] To put this another way, a world in which ownership is constrained by agent-neutral welfarist values is not safe for self-owners. See Mack, "Self-Ownership and the Right of Property"; Eric Mack, "Agent-Relativity of Value, Deontic Restraints, and Self-Ownership," in R. G. Frey and Christopher W. Morris, eds., *Value, Welfare, and Morality* (New York: Cambridge University Press, 1993); and Eric Mack, "Moral Individualism and Libertarian Theory," in Tibor R. Machan and Douglas B. Rasmussen, eds., *Liberty for the Twenty-First Century: Contemporary Libertarian Thought* (Lanham, MD: Rowman and Littlefield, 1995).

self-owner include both invasions of one's physical person and certain noninvasive infringements of one's ability to engage the extrapersonal world. Right-libertarianism therefore commits to the embodied conception in the case of have-nots, who as self-owners must as a matter of justice have free access to a fair scheme within which private property can be acquired and exchanged. Moreover, I argued in Section V that the only demands of justice that can enter via the Lockean proviso are demands arising from self-ownership itself. This is because demands entering via the proviso must not be in tension with self-ownership; thus, if demands of justice *independent* of self-ownership were to enter via the proviso, then we would have to show that those demands do not trench upon self-ownership even though they place significant restrictions on the ability to control the extrapersonal world. But in order to show that, we would have to separate the question of self-ownership from the question of control of the extrapersonal world. Yet it is precisely this separation that an embodied conception of the self rules out; so the only demands of justice that can enter via the Lockean proviso are other demands of self-ownership. In that case, right-libertarianism commits to the embodied conception of the self also in the case of haves: because they are self-owners, the only constraints of justice on their acquisition or use of property are those stemming from self-ownership. And these constraints have no egalitarian implications.

Therefore, different forms of libertarianism require different conceptions of the self. As I said earlier, this important difference has not received sufficient attention among libertarians. Even so, it has not been altogether ignored. Perhaps the most vocal right-libertarian on this point is Eric Mack, who has insisted on the importance of what I call the embodied conception of the self for libertarian self-ownership. Human beings, Mack writes,

> live in and through a world of physical objects which extends beyond the space occupied by their respective bodies. . . . Nor is the activity in which human life consists merely a matter of recurrent excursions (or raids) into the world of extra-personal objects. Extra-personal objects enter into and help define the specific goals, ambitions, and commitments through which individuals compose their respective lives. Particular extra-personal objects become deeply incorporated into the specific strategies that individuals formulate for their life pursuits. Living in and through the extra-personal world may be merely contingently connected with the pure concept of goal-oriented activity. But it is surely necessarily connected with *human* life and the *human* pursuit of ends.[69]

---

[69] Mack, "Self-Ownership and the Right of Property," 532–33; emphasis in the original. See also Mack, "The Self-Ownership Proviso," 199.

Embodiment, Mack notes, is crucial to the idea that self-ownership gives one rights not only against invasions of one's person, but also against threats to one's "world-interactive powers," such as the ability to use, transform, and appropriate parts of the extrapersonal world.[70]

Because right-libertarianism embraces the embodied conception of the self, it denies that self-ownership is a separate issue from ownership of extrapersonal goods, and therefore insists that ownership of extrapersonal goods is subject to a proviso forbidding property owners from worsening the situation of others, through either the acquisition or the use of property. I now want to develop and clarify that proviso by addressing four major questions about it. First, does the Lockean proviso, as I have defended it here, set limits on the acquisition of property, or its use, or both? Second, the Lockean proviso protects against certain kinds of worsening of the situation of others, but what kinds of worsening are these, and what liberties are protected by the proviso? Third, what sorts of objects are such that their disposal is subject to the Lockean proviso? Finally, does the Lockean proviso make any "real" difference between right-libertarians and no-proviso libertarians, or (as some have suggested) does it turn out merely to be a fifth wheel, so to speak? I take up these four questions in turn.

Many discussions of the Lockean proviso focus on it as a limit on how much a person may rightly acquire, and, as such, these discussions typically focus on thought experiments involving first-comers to virgin land, with the aim of devising a proviso that will prevent first-comers from leaving fewer or inferior goods for latecomers. However, I find such a focus seriously problematic for at least two reasons. One problem is that this approach implicitly assumes that acquisition is zero-sum—that somehow if one person removes something for the commons, there is thereby necessarily that much less for everyone else, leaving latecomers only the scraps. Yet, over time anyway, this is just the opposite of what happens. I recall attending a meeting of philosophers a few years ago in which one participant undertook to remind the others, with an air of perfect self-evidence, that the first-comers to the area where we were staying had made us all worse off by grabbing everything up centuries before we could get there. My thoughts immediately ran back over my morning before the meeting, and as I remembered how easy it was to find soap and hot running water, how easy breakfast had been to come by, and indeed how I was able to pay for all these things by means of work in my own specialized field, I wondered how any comparison between myself and the region's first settlers could possibly show *me* to be the less fortunate one. On the contrary, acquisition and use are parts of a productive cycle that generates not just enough and as good, but more and superior. As a

---

[70] See esp. Mack, "Self-Ownership, Marxism, and Egalitarianism, Part II," and Mack, "The Self-Ownership Proviso."

result, latecomers usually come off *far* better than first-comers. Acquisition is generally positive-sum, so it seems pointless to devise a Lockean proviso on acquisition as if it were necessarily zero-sum.[71]

The other problem is that I find the notion of leaving "enough and as good" of raw, unowned, natural resources to be conceptually problematic. Even if I can count how much *stuff* is in a given area, I can count the number of *resources* there only if I know rather a lot about people's plans, abilities, skills, and needs, and about what sorts of interactions are possible between persons controlling various parts of the world. Without knowing that, we cannot even know which materials count as valuable resources to be used and which count as rubbish that would be better cleared away.[72] Thus, "enough and as good" presupposes a world more like our own anyway, in which much is already controlled by various persons.

I do not find it useful, therefore, to think of the Lockean proviso as a proviso on the acquisition of property.[73] That leaves the question of use: the relevant question is not "how much" one may acquire, but what sorts of rights of control one can assert over a thing in virtue of becoming its owner. So understood, the proviso forbids an owner from so using what he owns that others are worsened with respect to their opportunities to become owners, as when one uses what one owns to close off another's interactions with the world. But what counts as "worsening" here?

This brings us to our second question: The Lockean proviso protects persons from uses of property by others that would deprive them of certain opportunities, but what opportunities are these? To put this another way, the right-libertarian holds that people have rights of control over themselves and that such rights also require rights of control over the extrapersonal world; but what kinds of rights are these latter? It should be clear that such rights cannot be rights to own some particular piece of property or even some particular amount of private property; nor can they be rights to a given level of opportunity to use and appropriate extrapersonal goods. This is because property rights so construed would be rights to appropriate for oneself the efforts of others, if need be—to provide one with these goods, or this level of access to welfare—and this would clearly conflict with the self-ownership of those whose efforts are thereby appropriated. Rather, the proviso protects one against being deprived of an opportunity to use and appropriate extrapersonal goods.

---

[71] We saw a similar point made by Narveson in Section IV. See also Schmidtz and Goodin, *Social Welfare and Individual Responsibility*, chapter 1.2.

[72] Daniel Russell, "Locke on Land and Labor," *Philosophical Studies* 117, nos. 1–2 (2004): 303–25.

[73] See also Mack, "The Self-Ownership Proviso," 191, 209, 212–14, 218; Eric Mack, "Self-Ownership, Marxism, and Egalitarianism, Part I: Challenges to Historical Entitlement," *Politics, Philosophy, and Economics* 1, no. 1 (2002): 75–108, at 98; Mack, "Self-Ownership, Marxism, and Egalitarianism, Part II," 245; Feser, "There Is No Such Thing as an Unjust Initial Acquisition"; and Narveson, "Original Appropriation," 221, 223.

More specifically, the proviso protects one's right to participate in a practice by which private property can be acquired and exchanged.[74] This does not mean that one has a right to a formal practice of private property even if there currently is none, since that again would be a right to the efforts of others in creating a certain social order. The right in question is, rather, a right not to be excluded from a practice of private property, if there should be any. Violations of such a right include the sorts of non-invasive infringements of self-ownership that we discussed in Section IV, such as when one person uses what he owns to keep another from interacting with the world so as to acquire parts of it.

Furthermore, we saw above that forbidding the earning of wages or the private owning of capital can be made consistent with self-ownership only by rejecting an embodied conception of the self. By contrast, on my view, to own an embodied self is also to have a right not to be excluded from a practice of private property, within any political order with a system of property. This is because the world-interaction of an embodied self involves the opportunity to acquire durable control over parts of the extrapersonal world, including the opportunity to do so through exchange of one's own efforts.

At this point—and this is our third issue—one might worry that, by expanding the boundaries of the self, right-libertarianism gives one either too many control rights or too few. On the one hand, by blurring the line between the self and the extrapersonal world, perhaps right-libertarianism extends the sorts of rights of control one has over one's body to all sorts of things in the extrapersonal world, even including other persons and their property. Simply put, if the self can include things like loving relationships and careers, then does the owner of such a self thereby acquire rights to control the persons and resources on which those relationships and careers depend? And on the other hand, by blurring the distinction between self and world and then placing a Lockean proviso on things in the world, does the right-libertarian thereby open the door to placing a Lockean proviso on one's person as well? If extrapersonal goods are subject to a Lockean proviso, then why aren't personal goods—such as body parts and substances—subject to such a proviso as well?[75] Each of these queries concerns the same basic question: Over what sorts of things does the Lockean proviso range? If one person cannot use what he owns to deprive another person of a place to stand, then why can he nonetheless deprive the other of a job in his firm, or of his blood and other tissues, or of his hand in marriage? After all, the point of the proviso is to protect persons' efforts to acquire control over things they may bring within the boundaries of the self, but on the embodied view these boundaries are broad enough to include others and their possessions.

---

[74] See also Mack, "Self-Ownership and the Right of Property."
[75] I thank Ed Feser and Fred Miller, respectively, for raising these queries.

However, this oversimplifies what the proviso actually does, which is to protect efforts to acquire not full stop, but in a way that is constrained by the fact that others are self-owners as well. Since the proviso protects opportunities to gain rights of use over things by appropriating them, the proviso protects opportunities only with respect to appropriable things, things that are not already owned. The thesis that persons own themselves, interpreted via the embodied conception of the self, automatically removes persons and what persons already own from the set of things that are appropriable and ripe for the picking. In that case, any claims one would stake to a person or what that person owns will exist only by the agreement of that person. One may make other persons or their possessions crucial parts of one's plans, but one does so always at one's own risk. Simply put, the Lockean proviso attaches only to appropriable things, and given the prior ownership of embodied selves, these things do not include persons or their property. If another person ends an intimate relationship with me, or closes the place where I work, or withholds an organ I need, then the outcome may be undesirable for me, but the Lockean proviso surely promised me no protection against such an outcome.

This brings us, finally, to a point where we are ready to consider the difference that the Lockean proviso makes for right-libertarianism. I have argued that right-libertarianism is committed to a conception of the self which in turn entails a Lockean proviso, but does this latter commitment actually make any difference worth mentioning between right-libertarians and no-proviso libertarians? Narveson, for one, is highly skeptical about this, claiming that what I have called right-libertarianism probably would not have "a real-world-divergence" from his own no-proviso libertarianism.[76] Does the Lockean proviso make any significant difference?

Here a thought experiment will be useful. Imagine that a person—call him "Landlocked"—finds his land hemmed in by his neighbor's land and that the neighbor refuses to grant Landlocked an easement allowing him to bring things onto his property. Right-libertarianism treats cases like this one as cases in which one person's use of his property compromises another person's world-interactive powers, and thus as problematic from the point of view of self-ownership. But here there are a couple of concerns. One concern is that characterizing the case in terms of self-ownership makes no difference to the process of resolving the dispute. The neighbor has an ownership right that turns out, on this occasion, to be inconvenient for Landlocked, and that is how the impasse must be addressed; casting things in terms of self-ownership gets us nowhere. It would perhaps be better, then, to say that while Landlocked's plight is unenviable, still the situation is not a question of justice or injustice, but should be settled by other sorts of considerations. So even though right-

[76] Narveson, "Original Appropriation," 225 n. 2.

libertarianism need not cast all conflicts in terms of the Lockean proviso, it does seem committed to treating this conflict in those terms. But doing so gains us nothing—and that, of course, is exactly what the no-proviso libertarian would have predicted.[77]

But should we agree that casting such a conflict in terms of the Lockean proviso really makes no difference to the resolution of the conflict? I do not think so. Part of the point of marking off questions of justice from other sorts of considerations, such as inconvenience, is surely to establish the lexical priority of the former questions to the latter questions. It seems clear that, with or without the Lockean proviso, the neighbor's situation will be regarded as a matter of justice: the question, after all, is what Landlocked and the neighbor may rightfully do with land that the neighbor indisputably owns. Without the proviso, then, as a matter of justice an arbiter must consider the claims of the neighbor as lexically prior to those of Landlocked. But now it is clear that framing Landlocked's plight in terms of the Lockean proviso will make a significant difference in the arbiter's deliberations about the conflict after all, because with the proviso in place, Landlocked's plight must now enter the arbiter's deliberations right alongside the neighbor's plight. Resolving the dispute, then, would not be a matter of balancing a claim of justice with a matter of mere inconvenience, but of balancing two claims of justice. My aim is not to say that such a conflict must therefore be decided in one way rather than another, but only to say that framing the issue in terms of the Lockean proviso does make a difference—and, I think, a most appropriate difference—in how one must deliberate about the resolution of such a conflict. Since this observation generalizes, I conclude that there are important "real-world" differences between no-proviso libertarians and right-libertarians. Their different conceptions of the self entail importantly different views about the line between injustice and inconvenience.

However, this way of addressing the first concern now raises another: precisely because we can frame such a conflict as a conflict between the claims of two self-owners as self-owners, we must now appeal to something other than considerations of self-ownership to resolve such a conflict.[78] In that case, the worry goes, the conflict must be resolved by appeal to some independent consideration, but then we would have done just as well to have appealed to that consideration in the first place, leaving the Lockean proviso out of it. The Lockean proviso may entail that such a conflict is a matter of conflicting claims of self-owners, but that just means that something other than considerations of such claims must come in to adjudicate the dispute. The Lockean proviso still seems redundant.

[77] I thank Dave Schmidtz for raising this concern, and for the thought experiment.
[78] I thank Tom Christiano for raising this concern.

But such a conclusion would be unwarranted. For the right-libertarian, the fundamental rationale behind the Lockean proviso is the conviction that the boundaries of the self are broad enough to include those parts of the extrapersonal world that are crucial to the life one constructs. And this same rationale can be a valuable guide in thinking about conflicting claims, such as the ones that arise between Landlocked and his neighbor. Given that the rationale behind the Lockean proviso lies in the value of opportunities to engage the extrapersonal world, the task for the arbiter is now to identify what sorts of rulings would be consistent with a larger private property scheme in which such opportunities are best made available. Again, this is not to say that the arbiter must therefore decide the case this way or that way; a rationale for a resolution is not itself a resolution. Nonetheless, it is to say that the considerations whereby such conflicts are to be resolved are themselves prompted by the same rationale that prompts the Lockean proviso. They are therefore not independent of the proviso after all, but are unified with it by a larger conception of human nature and well-being.

Of course, it may well be that the right-libertarian and the no-proviso libertarian would recommend the very same tie-breaking principle to our imaginary arbiter, so that these two ways of framing the dispute could even lead to identical resolutions. But even so, this does not show that the Lockean proviso makes no important difference between right-libertarians and no-proviso libertarians. This is because right-libertarians and no-proviso libertarians set their political principles within different larger conceptions of the nature of the self, and these conceptions represent different ways of understanding our nature, our well-being, and how we relate to one another. The difference between right-libertarians and no-proviso libertarians is therefore one that obtains at the level of an overall conception of human life. For the right-libertarian, then, the Lockean proviso is anything but idle. It is the thing that tethers him to a distinctive outlook on the nature of human existence. And that is a difference that crops up everywhere. What is it to lose a loved one? What is it to lose property? What is it to lose a homeland? How independent are identity and well-being from things that happen in the extrapersonal world? Since such questions go to the heart of our self-understanding, they should matter to philosophers if anything does. And one can answer such questions only by taking a position on the boundaries of the self.

VII. CONCLUSION

There is a crucial difference between the three main forms of libertarianism with respect to their conceptions of the self, and one of my aims in this essay has been to draw increased attention to this difference and its significance. I have also argued that the right-libertarian's conception of the self as embodied is an independently more plausible conception. But I hasten to add in closing that I have not tried to argue for that conception of the self in a conclusive way, but only in a suggestive one. This is no accident: precisely because it is that conception of the self that tethers the right-libertarian to a much larger ethical perspective on human existence, that conception of the self ultimately can be defended only as one defends the larger perspective of which it is such a crucial part. That may be the task of a lifetime, but it is surely not the task of an essay.

Philosophy, Wichita State University

SELF-OWNERSHIP AND WORLD OWNERSHIP: AGAINST LEFT-LIBERTARIANISM*

By Richard J. Arneson

I. Introduction

What regime of property ownership satisfies norms of justice? The doctrine known as "left-libertarianism" offers a seemingly plausible answer.[1] Its basic thrust is that libertarianism properly understood leaves room for an egalitarianism that enhances its appeal. In this essay, I argue that the seeming plausibility of the left-libertarian doctrine evaporates under scrutiny. This set of views is unacceptable from any political standpoint, left, right, or center.

The left-libertarian category encompasses a family of positions. I focus on one of these, the views elegantly articulated by Michael Otsuka.[2] Otsuka's version of the doctrine nicely illustrates the philosophical ambitions of the project and the flaws at its core.

The left-libertarian project is to combine a libertarian thesis of self-ownership (each adult person is the sole full rightful owner of herself) and an egalitarian thesis of world ownership (any legitimate private ownership of material resources or parts of the Earth by one person must be compatible with private ownership by all other persons of bundles of resources that are equal in some appropriate sense). I object to both elements in this synthesis. The self-ownership thesis is both too weak and too strong.[3] It is too weak to capture a genuine insistence on individual

* I thank Ellen Paul for her astute criticisms and questions directed at an earlier draft of this essay.

[1] On the idea of left-libertarianism, see Hillel Steiner and Peter Vallentyne, eds., *The Origins of Left-Libertarianism: An Anthology of Historical Writings* (Hampshire, England, and New York: Palgrave, 2000); and Steiner and Vallentyne, eds., *Left-Libertarianism and Its Critics: The Contemporary Debate* (Hampshire, England, and New York: Palgrave, 2000). In the latter work, see esp. Peter Vallentyne, "Introduction: Left-Libertarianism—A Primer," 1–20.

[2] Michael Otsuka, *Libertarianism without Inequality* (Oxford: Oxford University Press, 2003).

[3] For interesting criticism of the norm of self-ownership, see Kasper Lippert-Rasmussen, "Against Self-Ownership: There Are No Fact-Insensitive Ownership Rights Over One's Body," *Philosophy and Public Affairs* 36, no. 1 (2008): 86–118. As the title of this essay indicates, Lippert-Rasmussen argues that self-ownership is not acceptable taken as a basic, nonderivative moral principle—one whose validity is independent of all empirical facts. So construed, the claim that people have strong rights of self-ownership is vulnerable to objections such as the following: if it were the case that forcing an individual to labor for another always greatly boosted the well-being and enhanced the agency powers of the person who was forced, nobody would judge the forcing to be immoral. Lippert-Rasmussen raises an interesting issue, but it may be that social philosophers who affirm rights of self-ownership mean to affirm the rights in a manner that is conditional on certain facts of the world as we

doi:10.1017/S0265052509990070

freedom, and too strong in its denial of what each of us owes to other persons and is owed from them. It also places more normative weight on individual consent than this notion can bear. The world-ownership thesis undercuts self-ownership in real terms and also goes astray in its insistence on equal benefits for people as opposed to greater benefits for people. (In the course of this essay, I intend to clarify these cryptic assertions.)

Besides finding left-libertarianism normatively unattractive, I also find that it fails to pass muster as a plausible interpretation or reasonable extension of the political and moral ideas associated with the writings of John Locke.[4] This is a relevant objection because left-libertarians tend to wrap themselves in the mantle of the Lockean tradition, and the question arises: Are they entitled to this covering? Of course, the left-libertarian does not offer his views as Locke's own, but as Lockean. For example, Otsuka says he is defending "an approach to political philosophy, and a set of moral and political principles, that draw their inspiration from John Locke's *Second Treatise of Government*." He claims to have plucked the valuable fruit from Locke's work while discarding the rotten berries. He affirms that "Locke managed to apprehend some important truths of political morality, truths that together constitute an elegant and unified system of ideas."[5] His project is to state these truths more clearly than they appear in Locke's text. He and I differ as to which bits of Locke are the valuable fruit and which ones the rotten berries.

II. Preliminaries

Libertarianism is a doctrine that ascribes to individuals natural moral rights in the tradition of John Locke.[6] Roughly speaking, the doctrine holds that each person has the moral right to do whatever she chooses with whatever she legitimately owns, provided she does not thereby cause harm or impose undue risk of harm to others in specified ways. Each person also has the complementary moral right not to be harmed by others (and not to suffer imposition by others of undue risk of harm) in

---

know it continuing to hold true. I argue against self-ownership affirmed in this derivative or conditional way.

[4] John Locke, *Two Treatises of Government*, ed. Peter Laslett (Cambridge: Cambridge University Press, 1988). On the interpretation of Locke, see A. John Simmons, *The Lockean Theory of Rights* (Princeton, NJ: Princeton University Press, 1992); and Jeremy Waldron, *The Right to Private Property* (Oxford: Oxford University Press, 1988).

[5] Otsuka, *Libertarianism without Inequality*, 1.

[6] On libertarianism, see Robert Nozick, *Anarchy, State, and Utopia* (New York: Basic Books, 1974); and G. A. Cohen, *Self-Ownership, Freedom, and Equality* (Cambridge: Cambridge University Press, 1995). I want to acknowledge that my reflections on libertarianism and left-libertarianism are deeply indebted to pathbreaking writings on these topics, from opposed perspectives, by Nozick and Cohen, and also to excellent explorations by Hillel Steiner, Peter Vallentyne, and Michael Otsuka (see *Left-Libertarianism and Its Critics: The Contemporary Debate* and the essay cited in note 21 below).

these specified ways. Moreover, each person at the onset of adult life is the full rightful owner of herself.

Legitimate ownership encompasses a range of entitlements down to bare entitlement to access. Full ownership includes a bundle of entitlements. If one fully owns a thing, one has the right to use it as one chooses so long as one does not use it in ways that violate other people's rights not to be harmed; one also has the right to exclude all others from using it, the right to allow others to use it on terms one sets, the right to lend the thing to another on mutually agreeable terms, the right to waive, temporarily or permanently, some or all of one's rights in the thing, and the right to transfer some or all of the set of rights just mentioned to another person via gift or contract on any mutually agreeable terms. These various ownership rights are enforceable. One has the moral right to issue standing conditional threats to others who might be tempted to violate any of one's ownership rights in the thing. The conditional threats take the form, "If you (attempt to) violate my rights, I'll retaliate, and you'll be worse off." (The right to force or coerce is limited by a proportionality constraint, so that one may not threaten to impose a cost on another person in order to induce her to respect one's ownership right if this threatened cost is disproportionate to the loss one would suffer if the right were violated.)[7]

In this tradition, moral rights are rights one has independently of institutional arrangements, cultural understandings, and anyone's opinions or attitudes. A moral right involves enforceable duties owed by other people toward the right-holder. For example, the content of Smith's right to walk down the street is given by the duties of all other people not to interfere in certain ways with his walking in that place.

Right-wing libertarianism affirms that from the premise of self-ownership, plus other plausible premises, one can show that by exercising their natural moral rights individuals can appropriate and acquire private ownership rights in parts of the external world, and that ownership of property established in this way can be substantially unequal. Indeed, the right-wing libertarian holds that there is no per se moral limit on the extent of inequality of individuals' property holdings.

Left-wing libertarianism combines affirmation of libertarian self-ownership with egalitarian claims about world ownership. Full ownership is exclusive: if one person has full ownership of a thing, no one else has any ownership rights in that thing. Since each person includes just one distinct body, the thesis that every person is the full exclusive rightful owner of herself is evidently compatible with the further claim that persons can legitimately acquire full exclusive ownership of unequal amounts of the material world, there being no limit to the extent of

---

[7] A response to a threatened rights violation can be proportionate even though the cost one imposes on the violator exceeds the loss one would suffer from the violation. If someone tries to cut off your legs, it may be morally permissible to kill the person if that is necessary to prevent him from doing this, even though losing one's life is worse than losing two legs.

inequality of ownership that may legitimately arise. But the left-libertarian holds that it is just as true that the claim that each person is the full rightful owner of herself is compatible with any extent of moral limits on the degree to which persons can acquire unequal ownership of unequal amounts of parts of the material world. Moreover, the underlying moral values of individual freedom and personal autonomy and sovereignty are best served by the combination of individual self-ownership and egalitarian world ownership. So says the left-libertarian.

I agree that individual self-ownership and egalitarian world ownership are compatible theses—both could be true together. I suspect that this combination of views is not coherent. By this I mean that the best rationale for individual self-ownership is opposed to the best rationale for egalitarian world ownership.[8] But among the many rationales that might be advanced to support a claim, it is hard to show which one is best, so best-rationale incoherence is hard to establish definitively. A more tractable issue is this: Self-ownership rightly conceived (that is to say, broadly conceived) includes constraints on acceptable views on world ownership. Self-ownership is a doctrine of individual freedom. It holds that the Earth, the material world apart from the bodies of persons, is available for the use of persons on fair and equal terms. What these fair and equal terms are is a matter of dispute, but self-ownership limits the range of possibly acceptable positions. In particular, the terms of eligibility for ownership of parts of the Earth cannot discriminate in favor of personal traits that some self-owning persons possess and others do not.[9] To take an uncontroversial example, what I shall call the broad idea of self-ownership rules out as inadmissible the following regime of private ownership: persons with white skin may acquire private property in parts of the Earth, and persons with black skin may not. This discriminatory regime would have the effect of undoing the freedom of self-ownership: denied the right to acquire property, persons with black skin would have to give up self-ownership rights in exchange for being allowed access to air to breathe and land to stand on in order to ensure their bare survival.

---

[8] Here is an example to illustrate the point in the text. It is not strictly inconsistent for me to maintain that my wife is morally required to be sexually faithful whereas I am morally permitted not to be sexually faithful. Both moral claims could be true (valid, acceptable) together. However, if I have no good rationale for maintaining this pair of claims, my position is incoherent.

[9] This claim in the text slides over tricky issues. Consider a "no waste" proviso: One is permitted to appropriate unowned plots of land as private property provided one works the land productively in some way and does not let it go to waste. In a scenario in which persons live isolated from one another, this "no waste" constraint bars me from appropriating land if my personal traits do not enable me to work it productively (given isolation, there is no possibility of appropriating land and contracting with another able-bodied person to work it). Should the "no waste" proviso be construed as violating the proposal in the text that rules regarding permissible appropriation cannot discriminate among persons on the basis of their personal traits? To answer this question one would have to clarify the proposal.

Narrow self-ownership, the idea as understood by left-libertarians, is compatible with its being the case that some persons have no right to breathe the air they need to live or to stand on any place on Earth or elsewhere in the universe or even to occupy with their bodies the physical space that their bodies must occupy. The three just-mentioned rights are rights over parts of the world separate and distinct from human individuals, so whatever rights (narrowly conceived) human individuals have over themselves will not stretch to cover these or any other parts of the world. In contrast to this narrow sense of self-ownership, there is a broad sense, according to which self-ownership involves the right of each of us to live as she chooses, and this vague right includes some rights to use the physical world in ways that are prerequisite to living.

Self-ownership also includes rights against certain sorts of incursions by other people. If I impinge on your body by hitting you, pushing you (from some location where you have a right to be), or carrying out activities that, by design or as an unintended side effect, cause physical damage to your body, your self-ownership rights are infringed. There are questions about how exactly to delimit rights against such incursions. For example, does self-ownership include a right that no one engage in activities that involve a risk, however small, of generating physical damage, however small, to your body? We intuitively do not suppose that people have rights against incursions that are so strict, but it is not clear how one sets the boundaries of rights against incursions in a principled way that does not compromise the core idea.[10] I set these issues aside, despite their intrinsic interest, since they are not germane to the central concerns of this essay.

III. The Otsuka Proposal

Otsuka affirms a libertarian right of self-ownership that incorporates the following two rights:

(1) A very stringent right of control over and use of one's mind and body that bars others from intentionally using one as a means by forcing one to sacrifice life, limb, or labour, where such force operates by means of incursions or threats of incursions upon one's mind and body (including assault and battery and forcible arrest, detention, and imprisonment).

(2) A very stringent right to all of the income that one can gain from one's mind and body (including one's labour) either on one's

---

[10] See Peter Railton, "Locke, Stock, and Peril: Natural Property Rights, Pollution, and Risk" (1985), reprinted in Railton, *Facts, Values, and Norms: Essays Toward a Morality of Consequence* (Cambridge: Cambridge University Press, 2003), 187–225; Nozick, *Anarchy, State, and Utopia*, chap. 4; and Richard J. Arneson, "The Shape of Lockean Rights: Fairness, Pareto, Moderation, and Consent," *Social Philosophy and Policy* 22, no. 1 (2005): 255–85.

own or through unregulated and untaxed voluntary exchanges with other individuals.[11]

He then exploits the fact that self-ownership so understood is entirely silent on the topic of world ownership. Anything goes, so far as self-ownership is concerned. One who asserts self-ownership is then at liberty to embrace any claims one likes about world ownership.

Otsuka opts for egalitarianism in the form of equal opportunity for welfare. He asks: Under what conditions may one appropriate previously unowned parts of the Earth as private property?—and his answer is that one may do so provided that one's appropriation and use of the land are compatible with everyone's having the opportunity to improve her condition to the same absolute level. Improvements in an individual's condition are measured in terms of satisfaction of the self-interested preferences she would have "after ideal deliberation while thinking clearly with full pertinent information regarding those preferences."[12] This equal opportunity for welfare norm also regulates the distribution of material resources (parts of the Earth) in an ongoing society in which all valuable resources have already been appropriated. The egalitarian world ownership norm requires that resource ownership be regulated to induce equal opportunity for welfare among persons across the generations.

A clue that something has gone wrong here turns up when one considers the implications of the Otsuka proposal regarding world ownership for the possible scenario in which the resources that anybody might want to appropriate as private property are not scarce. That is to say, there are more than enough land and resources available to accommodate the entire aggregate of proposed private appropriations that people would ever have any reason to advance. If we focus on the limited case of land for appropriation, we may say that the nonscarcity world would be one in which anybody could appropriate as much land for his own use as he liked, and any and all such appropriations would leave more than enough land just as good in quality for others to appropriate.

In chapter five of the *Second Treatise on Government*, John Locke considers the nonscarcity scenario and makes the observation that at least in this

[11] Otsuka, *Libertarianism without Inequality*, 15. Otsuka's second right implies that other people—governments included—have no moral right to tax the income that self-owning individuals gain just from using their minds and bodies in mutually agreed upon ways. Nor would other people—governments included—have a moral right to regulate activities that self-owning individuals freely agree to conduct among themselves. Whatever terms individuals freely agree to are the terms on which they should interact. So says Otsuka's second right. Although extensive and in a way strong, this right is also very limited, and in a way very weak. The right to use one's mind and body as one chooses implies nothing about what rights one has, if any, to use or own any part of the Earth other than one's body. Otsuka's second right does not ensure that one is entitled to the air one breathes, the physical space one's body must occupy, or the land one must stand on in order to stay alive on this Earth.

[12] Ibid., 43. Otsuka is here quoting a formulation in Richard Arneson, "Primary Goods Reconsidered," *Noûs* 24 (1990): 429–54, at 448.

case, one should be free to appropriate as much land as one can make use of and reap the benefits of one's use. In the nonscarcity scenario, if one person appropriates and works a plot of land, and another person then demands some of the produce, it is plain that the latter desires "the benefit of another's pains, which he had no right to." [13]

Compare Locke's treatment of nonscarcity with what the Otsuka proposal implies about it. Suppose able-bodied Smith wishes to appropriate a hundred acres of arable land under nonscarcity. Even though this appropriation would leave enough and as good land for others to appropriate, under the Otsuka proposal Smith is only allowed to appropriate an amount of land that, together with the appropriations of others, leaves all individuals with equal opportunity for welfare understood as informed self-interested preference-satisfaction. What this constraint requires depends on the actual ensemble of people's informed self-interested preferences. I want to focus not on this feature but on its implications across able-bodied and non-able-bodied persons. Suppose the world contains two individuals, Smith and Jones. Jones is entirely unable to transform arable land into resources that would boost her preference-satisfaction level. Smith then either is permitted to appropriate no land at all, if any appropriation would render him higher in opportunity for preference-satisfaction than Jones, or he must appropriate and work land and share the produce with Jones so that equal opportunity for welfare is maintained.

Self-ownership is not literally abrogated here. Smith is under no obligation to aid Jones in any way, and all others are required not to force him to use his body in any way for the benefit of other persons. Although he owns himself, Smith has no entitlement to land except in accordance with the Otsuka proposal that individual entitlements to appropriate should be modified to yield the result that all individuals have equal opportunity for welfare. Smith freely agrees to work for Jones's benefit in exchange for the opportunity to appropriate land.

Nonetheless, self-ownership has clearly been eviscerated. The rules of world ownership have been gerrymandered to require the able to use their labor to benefit the unable as a condition of able people being allowed to act to further their aims in ways that cause no harm to anybody.

Otsuka introduces a wrinkle into his account that merits notice. He stipulates that a person has what he calls a "robust" right of self-ownership just in case he enjoys the libertarian right of self-ownership as already described and, in addition, "rights over enough worldly resources to ensure that one will not be forced by necessity to come to the assistance of others in a manner involving the sacrifice of one's life, limb, or labour." [14]

Otsuka suggests that we ought to respect robust rights of self-ownership for all and points out that, under a wide range of circumstances, achiev-

[13] John Locke, *Second Treatise of Government*, in Laslett, ed., *Two Treatises*, sec. 34.
[14] Otsuka, *Libertarianism without Inequality*, 32.

ing equal opportunity for welfare via the distribution of rights over worldly resources is compatible with respecting robust rights of self-ownership for all. Egalitarianism in world ownership is thus shown to be contingently compatible not merely with respect for formal libertarian self-ownership but with the more substantive freedom associated with robust self-ownership.

The upshot is that in the world of superabundant unowned resources, each person would be permitted to appropriate enough resources so that, with those resources, she could survive (unless she is unable and cannot ensure her survival by any appropriation). Beyond that point, equal opportunity for welfare applies as a condition on permissible appropriation. If Able appropriates even just a bit more than what she needs to survive, that extra appropriation must bring it about that all persons including Unable enjoy equal opportunity for welfare. That is to say, Able is permitted to appropriate an extra smidgeon of land only if she shares its produce with Unable so that all persons enjoy equal opportunity for welfare. Of this scenario Otsuka can maintain that Able enjoys a robust right of self-ownership. In a world of superabundant resources, she is permitted to appropriate what she needs to survive even if that creates unequal opportunity for welfare, and though constrained by the egalitarian proviso on appropriation past that point, she is not forced by necessity to labor for the benefit of others. She has options, and agrees to labor for the benefit of others only in order to enjoy luxury goods beyond what she needs for bare survival.

In response: The Otsuka robust right of self-ownership is insufficiently robust. Suppose in a two-person world you can survive by hunting and catching one rabbit per day in a world in which hordes of rabbits fill a boundless terrain. There are rabbits everywhere. You would like to live at a standard of living above the bare survival threshold, say by catching and eating two rabbits per day. Unfortunately, your fellow inhabitant of the world has no ability to catch rabbits and only modest ability to gain welfare from eating rabbits. Without help from you, he starves. Under the Otsuka proposal, you are not permitted to appropriate any part of the world beyond what you need to survive, even though your appropriations harm no one and leave infinite resources (live rabbits). Under these circumstances you are permitted to hunt and catch an extra rabbit per day only if you also hunt and catch enough rabbits per day so that your fellow inhabitant of the world enjoys the same opportunity for welfare you have (this might require you to hunt and catch twenty rabbits per day, a considerable burden, two for you and eighteen for your world-mate, who unfortunately has poor digestion, and hence is not good at transforming rabbits into welfare). The question remains, if you own yourself, and there are infinite resources, so your taking some leaves no less for others and imposes no harm or inconvenience on others, why should there be any moral constraints at all on your appropriations of worldly resources?

It might well be plausible to hold, following Locke, that in a world of scarce resources, in which one person's appropriation leaves less for others to appropriate, appropriation should still be permissible given further conditions (the details need not detain us). But at least where there is nonscarcity, appropriation that harms no one and subtracts nothing from what is available to others should be deemed morally permissible. Denying this, Otsuka holds that some people are entitled to the benefit of other people's pains.

Putting the point very vaguely, I shall say that the spirit (or the underlying rationale) of self-ownership puts constraints on acceptable doctrines of world ownership. By opting for a "robust" right of self-ownership, Otsuka acknowledges that a conception of self-ownership that leaves it completely open what kinds of world ownership are morally permissible would be unacceptably formal. His attempt to accommodate this point falls short. He finds insufficient one narrow construal of self-ownership, but a broader construal than he countenances is needed.

Characterizing self-ownership, he writes: "Like all other versions of Lockean libertarianism, mine regards a right of self-ownership as fundamental, where such a right consists of robust and stringent rights of control over oneself: one's mind, body, and life. Such a commitment to self-ownership is, I think, definitive of Lockean libertarianism. The antipaternalistic and anti-moralistic implications of this right will be attractive to anyone who finds himself in sympathy with the conclusions which John Stuart Mill draws in *On Liberty*. When it comes to such things as freedom of expression, of sexual relations of any sort between consenting adults, of the possession of cannabis and other recreational drugs, of gambling, and the like, I am completely at one with other libertarians."[15]

Not so fast. In this passage, Otsuka relaxes into a more substantive, more robust conception of self-ownership than he in fact provides. Nor is this an accident. His conception of self-ownership needs to be thin in order to allow the consistency of self-ownership and egalitarian world ownership.

Here is a quick demonstration, modeled on Otsuka's argument, that the premise of self-ownership is fully compatible with a regime that sharply restricts individual liberty with respect to sexual relations, freedom of expression, use of dangerous recreational drugs, gambling, and the like. Note that even in order to breathe and stand on the Earth without thereby taking property to which one has no right, one must have some rights of access to the world external to one's body—some rights of world ownership. Robust self-ownership alone does not entitle one to access to the Earth beyond what is needed for survival. (If the world's resources do not suffice to enable all to survive, then self-ownership cannot guarantee rights of access to what one needs to survive but at most to some fair

---

[15] Ibid., 2–3.

chance to have such access. I set this to the side as not relevant to present purposes.) The libertarian moralizer can then argue as follows: Everyone is the full rightful owner of herself, and we grant that any person has a right to access to resources needed to stay alive, but in order to be entitled to appropriate any of the plentiful resources God has given us in order to gain any benefits at all beyond bare survival, one must agree not to commit such sins as engagement in nonheterosexual sex, gambling, dancing, recreational consumption of alcohol or other dangerous and unhealthy drugs, blasphemous speech, and so on. If one commits any of these sins, one forfeits one's conditional entitlement to access to any worldly resources beyond the requisites of bare survival.

If the Otsuka world-ownership regime is compatible with Lockean libertarian self-ownership, then so is the moralizing regime that sharply restricts individual liberty in self-regarding matters as just described. Something has clearly gone wrong here, but it is tricky to state the misinterpretation of Lockean libertarianism into which Otsuka and my imaginary libertarian moralizer have fallen.

Suppose the defender of the Otsuka proposal objects that she does not believe prohibitions of nonheterosexual sex, gambling, the consumption of recreational drugs that may be dangerous to the user, and so on, are justifiable in any case, on independent grounds, so any unsavoriness in these prohibitions does not attach to left-libertarian views of distributive justice. This response is irrelevant to my point. My point was that contrary to Otsuka's assertion, self-ownership, as he characterizes it, does not have the standard libertarian implications he supposes. The further point that this same insufficiently robust characterization of self-ownership does not rule out his egalitarian distributive-justice proposal does not then establish its libertarian credentials.

I believe that Otsuka is right in his instinct to associate a thicker or more substantive idea of self-ownership with the standard libertarian positions he mentions. In my view, this thicker idea of self-ownership is violated by the Otsuka proposal on world ownership.

How might this go? We might characterize thick self-ownership as the combination of the generic libertarian principle of freedom with self-ownership. The former says that each person is morally free to do whatever she chooses with whatever she legitimately owns, provided she does not thereby harm others in specified ways. There is a standard list of types of harm that fills out the specification. The self-ownership claim says that each person is the full rightful exclusive owner of herself.

This won't do. The stated combination rules out neither egalitarian constraints on world ownership nor moralistic constraints on personal behavior that involves some slight world ownership. One can insist that people are free to do whatever they like with whatever they legitimately own, but one also needs to ask on what terms individuals should have entitlements to use resources such as air or other parts of the Earth. This is a further issue, not yet resolved. Egalitarianism and moralism propose terms for such entitlements. Plausible or implausible they may be, but neither proposal is in conflict with the stated combination.

The following suggestion is better. To self-ownership as previously characterized we add the generic libertarian principle of freedom in a simpler construal: Each person is morally free to do whatever she chooses provided she does not thereby harm others in specified ways. The person who engages in nonheterosexual sex, gambling, and so on, does not harm anyone in any of these ways, at least when her incidental usage of nonscarce resources in carrying out such acts is clearly not depriving anyone of anything to which she has a claim based on libertarian natural rights. Likewise, the person who appropriates a plot of land and works on it to gain benefits for herself when land is not scarce is arguably doing what clearly harms no one in any way a libertarian moral theory ought to recognize as wrongful harming. The appropriator in these circumstances is not depriving anyone of anything to which she has a claim based on libertarian natural rights.

We might, alternatively, treat the idea of self-ownership as initially indeterminate so far as its implications for morally acceptable world ownership are concerned. We might then try to make progress in understanding the notion by introducing constraints on its interpretation. Here are two plausible constraints:

(1) When parts of the material world are not scarce, each person is morally permitted to appropriate as much of these resources as she likes and to use them in whatever ways she chooses provided she does not, by such uses, cause harm to nonconsenting others (in certain ways that violate their natural moral rights).

(2) The moral rules that regulate appropriation of parts of the material world do not discriminate among persons on the basis of their personal traits. The quantity and quality of resources one is permitted to appropriate do not vary depending on such facts as whether one has black or white skin, is fat or thin, is talented or untalented, is physically attractive or unattractive, is male or female, or is old or young.

Both of these constraints on the interpretation of the norm of self-ownership are violated by the Otsuka proposal for permissible appropriation that is supposed to show how libertarian self-ownership is compatible with egalitarianism in the distribution of material resources across persons.[16] However, the constraints are plausible, if one's project is to elab-

---

[16] How does the Otsuka proposal violate condition 2? This is a matter of interpretation. Otsuka requires that an appropriation of a part of the Earth that would improve one's welfare beyond bare survival is permissible only if that appropriation in the circumstances

orate a version of Lockean libertarianism that (i) is normatively attractive and (ii) can stand as a reasonable interpretation or extension of Locke's own texts so that the label "Lockean" is appropriate.

What is normatively attractive is subject to debate. Here, I simply record my own impression of what is appealing in Locke's doctrines that the Otsuka proposal excludes. The basic Lockean ethic holds that people are not naturally subject to the authority of other persons but are free to live as they choose (within uncontroversial constraints) and are free to acquire private ownership of resources, given that this ancillary freedom is necessary if people are to be free to carry out any of a wide range of reasonable aims and projects that people in fact regard as centrally important for their fulfillment. This vague ideal of personal freedom can be construed as compatible with the existence of some minimal duties to rescue other people from dire predicaments, but the mere fact that others are worse off than you and would benefit from your laboring for them does not suffice to generate an enforceable moral duty that you labor on their behalf. This vague ideal already incorporates the idea that—in some sense to be explored—one's freedom includes the freedom to use parts of the Earth without obtaining the consent of other persons and without laboring for them as a condition on permissible use and permissible appropriation of those parts.

IV. Otsuka Modified

One might seek to render the Otsuka proposal more appealing by adding a Pareto norm to it. This norm would hold that appropriations otherwise ruled out as inadmissible by the proposal are permissible provided they would improve someone's condition without worsening anyone else's condition. Thus, in the world of abundance containing two persons, one able and one unable, where the two are isolated so that neither can by his actions affect the condition of the other for better or worse, Able is permitted to appropriate and develop as much land as he likes even though these actions render him far better off in welfare than Unable. So far, so good.

---

would achieve equal opportunity for welfare for all persons. This requirement does not, on its face, discriminate among persons on the basis of the personal traits they happen to possess. However, the more able one is, the less one is permitted to appropriate, and the less able one is, the more one is permitted to appropriate, and this is the intended impact of the formulation. The Otsuka rule on permissible appropriation is set so as to nullify the impact of differential native endowments of personal traits on the distribution of well-being. Equal opportunity for welfare is achieved by forbidding persons favored in personal traits to appropriate unless they help those disfavored in personal traits to the required extent. I contend that the description "varies the amount one is permitted to appropriate according to the quality of one's native personal traits" is too close to the description "discriminates on the basis of one's native personal traits" for it to be acceptable to draw a line between them for the purpose of deciding whether the Otsuka rules are discriminatory.

However, this set of principles still lacks normative appeal. Consider a variant of the previous example in which Able can bestow the fruits of his labors on Unable. The latter benefits a tiny bit from every transfer from Able, but Able must labor for thousands of hours in order to generate one unit of utility for Unable, whereas he can gain a same-sized unit of utility for himself by laboring for just a few seconds. To sustain equal opportunity for welfare (utility), Able is permitted to appropriate land and work it for his own benefit only on the condition that, for each acre of land he appropriates and works for himself, he must appropriate and work tens of thousands of acres on behalf of Unable. Assume that Able prefers more utility to less and acts to maximize his utility within moral constraints. According to the Otsuka proposal as just amended, morality holds that in order to appropriate land and to labor for himself under conditions of nonscarcity, he must spend the vast bulk of his life laboring for the sole benefit of the less fortunate Unable.

Moreover, in the imagined circumstances, left-libertarianism as elaborated by Otsuka holds that Able is morally permitted to appropriate and use even a little bit of land for a tiny bit of time for himself only if he also appropriates huge tracts of land and spends most of his life working for Unable, even though these huge efforts on behalf of Unable will do Unable very little good. In the example, we have stipulated that Unable is a poor transformer of resources into utility. This fact does not affect what we owe one another according to an equal opportunity for welfare norm, which Otsuka upholds as the moral principle that regulates world ownership. The example highlights the way that the Otsuka proposal drives a wedge between formal self-ownership and any real guarantee that each person has the freedom to live as she chooses without necessarily being dedicated to helping others.

To be fair, it should be noted that Otsuka does not deny that egalitarian world ownership can drastically crimp a person's real freedom to live as she chooses in some possible or even likely circumstances. He is concerned to argue that, in some possible circumstances, egalitarian world ownership would be compatible with a robust, more than merely formal self-ownership for all. He describes an example in which unable persons are assigned ownership of ocean-front property and able persons are permitted to own inland property, the rules being set so that the able can survive without working for the benefit of the unable but are glad to work for them in exchange for obtaining access to the beach, and equal opportunity for welfare obtains for all without anyone's being *forced* to labor for others, because the consequences of declining to work for the benefit of others would not be intolerable for anyone who so declines.[17]

Granting all this, I do not see that any of it tends to render the Otsuka proposal normatively attractive. A fundamental moral norm is morally

---

[17] Ibid., 33–34.

acceptable not merely because in some possible circumstances it yields intuitively plausible implications, but rather in virtue of yielding intuitively plausible implications in actual and in relevant counterfactual circumstances. There can be disagreement as to how wide these counterfactuals must range, if the norm is to count as acceptable. Some might say that the norm must yield intuitively acceptable implications in all logically possible circumstances. Some might accept a narrower scope, such as acceptable implications in all physically possible circumstances, or in all circumstances that obtain in possible worlds reasonably close to the actual world. We need not stop to consider which standard states the appropriate test for candidate norms. The Otsuka proposal fails the test on any of the construals just stated.[18]

Turning back to the modified proposal, I note that it would allow appropriation that leads to unequal, even extremely unequal, opportunity for welfare, if able persons happen to prefer not appropriating land and sharing the fruits with the unable except on terms that disproportionately favor themselves over the unable. In this scenario, the outcome in which no appropriations occur is Pareto-suboptimal compared to the alternative outcome in which appropriation occurs and the fruits go mainly to the able.

V. SELF-OWNERSHIP WITH RELAXED WORLD OWNERSHIP

What happens to the Otsuka doctrine if we retain its strong self-ownership element but relax its world-ownership component in the direction of Lockean common sense? This is a vague question. Let us suppose for purposes of illustration that we affirm that people have common-ownership rights to breathe the air and stand on parts of the Earth and wander through the Earth freely as hunter-gatherers, and that they also have the right to appropriate land and work the land and acquire full private ownership of the land (and resources on the land) that they improve by their labor. We may suppose this right to acquire is limited by a familiar Lockean proviso, the details of which we can leave aside.[19]

What then? The unsurprising answer is that even if we assume that people end up acquiring roughly equal amounts of property by appropriation and labor, the self-ownership component of the doctrine all by itself can generate unlimited inequality of ownership. Suppose that in an

---

[18] Am I being unfair here? Otsuka says that substantial real freedom to do what one chooses with one's own body and mind and egalitarian world ownership would be compatible in some circumstances. I say that substantial real freedom regarding oneself would be incompatible with egalitarian world ownership in some circumstances. When we examine these cases of conflict, we find that egalitarian world ownership of the sort Otsuka finds congenial trenches too harshly on real freedom regarding oneself for the resultant doctrine to claim libertarian credentials. The resultant doctrine appears counterintuitive even to someone of my persuasion, who disavows libertarian self-ownership.

[19] Nozick, *Anarchy, State, and Utopia*, 174–82.

economy of small (roughly equal) property owners, some persons are beautiful, and others will pay to look at them; some can solve complex mathematical problems, and others will pay to be informed of the answers; some are able to run fast and perform astounding athletic feats, and others are willing to pay to watch these performances; and so on. These are all inequality-generating scenarios, rooted in people's unequal possession of talent. Suppose it were the case that unequal talent to work and improve land was not a significant source of inequality; rather, inequality arose only due to people's unequal talents to work their own minds and bodies (supposing that all have air to breathe and space to place their bodies without running afoul of stringent equal world ownership requirements). Even in this case, in the Otsuka utopia in which all comply perfectly with the moral principles governing self-ownership and (relaxed) world ownership, there is no limit, in principle, to the amount of inequality that might legitimately arise. Some might live like kings and queens, while others must make do with brutally short lives in squalid conditions. Suppose these possibilities became actual.

The imagined inequality-via-self-ownership runs afoul of principles that hold that when sheer luck showers good on some and evil on others, some sharing of luck is morally mandatory. One such principle holds that it is morally bad if some are worse off than others through no moral fault or moral demerit of their own. Another holds that if some are significantly worse off than others, and seriously badly off, through no moral fault or moral demerit of their own, redress is morally required.[20]

If a left-libertarian has been persuaded that Otsuka world ownership is an extreme and unattractive doctrine, and accepts a relaxed Lockean view, and then is asked to contemplate inequality-via-self-ownership as just described, she might respond in one of two ways. She might say that her doctrine on self-ownership is meant to hold only in some range of circumstances, in which insistence on self-ownership does not generate morally jarring inequality. This would be, in effect, to renounce self-ownership regarded as a bedrock moral principle. She might, alternatively, dig in her heels and insist that morality mandates private ownership of self come what may, whatever the consequences. To my mind, the latter response is beyond the pale.

VI. Rejecting the Core of Left-Libertarianism

The core left-libertarian impulse is to reconcile the norms of self-ownership and egalitarianism (of some form) with respect to world own-

---

[20] For one view of how to accommodate luck in moral principles, see Richard Arneson, "Luck Egalitarianism Interpreted and Defended," *Philosophical Topics* 32, nos. 1 and 2 (2004): 1–20. For another view, see G. A. Cohen, *Rescuing Justice and Equality* (Cambridge, MA: Harvard University Press, 2008).

ership. The root intuition is that both norms are morally compelling, so if one can develop a set of principles that combines both, one should. Peter Vallentyne, Hillel Steiner, and Michael Otsuka clearly articulate this ratio-nale for left-libertarianism in these words:

> Left-libertarianism holds that there is a very significant difference in the moral status of agents (self-directing beings with full moral stand-ing) and natural resources (resources that have no moral standing and which were created by no [non-divine] agent). About the former they [i.e., left-libertarians] maintain that full self-ownership is the most appropriate reflection of the status (e.g. because it explains/grounds the intuitive wrongness of various forms of nonconsensual interfer-ence with bodily integrity) and about the latter they independently maintain that egalitarian ownership is the most defensible stance.[21]

So far, I have pointed out that since humans can do virtually nothing at all without using the material resources of the world in some way, the thesis of self-ownership turns out to be too weak or, in a sense, merely formal. It guarantees no substantive real or effective freedom to do what one chooses and live as one prefers. (One has *real freedom* to do X just in case one is actually able to do X and has an unimpeded opportunity to do X. If I am really free to drive to Los Angeles, then there is a course of action available to me such that, if I choose it, I drive to Los Angeles.)

Another objection to embracing self-ownership is that, as applied to a certain range of cases, it is too strong—objectionably rigid. If I am the sole full rightful owner of myself, then no one else has any rights of any sort to the control or use of my body. I have an enforceable moral right to do whatever I choose with myself (so long as I do not harm others in certain ways that count as violations of their rights), and no one else has any enforceable moral rights that limit this right to do whatever I choose.

Cases of easy rescue call into question the moral attractiveness of self-ownership so understood. Suppose a child is drowning in shallow water. I happen to be present on the scene, and am uniquely placed to save the child's life with only trivial effort and cost and at no risk to myself. I can simply reach out my hand and pull the child's head out of the water. According to the self-ownership thesis (if we put to the side ever-present questions about my right to be present where I am standing and encroach-ing on parts of the world just by being there), the child has no (enforce-able) moral right to an easy rescue from me, and I have a moral right not to be coerced into performing this momentary lifesaving service for the child.

---

[21] Peter Vallentyne, Hillel Steiner, and Michael Otsuka, "Why Left-Libertarianism Is Not Incoherent, Indeterminate, or Irrelevant: A Reply to Fried," *Philosophy and Public Affairs* 33, no. 2 (2005): 201–15; see p. 209.

A similar case involves the right that self-ownership confers on each of us against the forcible extraction of extraneous body parts, even if the parts are useless to the self-owner and would be extremely useful to others. If self-ownership obtains, I have the sole right of ownership over loose flakes of skin on my arm, even if it should happen that they could somehow be used to save people from instant death. This means that it would be morally wrong to coerce me to yield my flakes of skin to a rescue effort that would save lives, and it would be morally permissible for me to coerce would-be do-gooders to prevent them from taking my flakes without my permission. Nothing worth caring about in any sensible ideal of personal freedom is secured by the dogmatic and shrill insistence on the full property rights over each and every part of my body that the self-ownership thesis affirms.

Peter Vallentyne offers a sensible response to the criticism that self-ownership wrongly encumbers each of us with a moral right not to participate in easy rescues and not to acquiesce in takings of one's body parts for charitable purposes, however small the cost to oneself and however great the benefits that could be secured for others. He notes that self-ownership concerns only enforceable obligations; thus, consistently with stoutly affirming full self-ownership, one might hold that it would be morally a very good thing, though not obligatory, for each of us to contribute to easy rescues. Or one might hold that it is morally obligatory to contribute to easy rescues, but the obligation is not legitimately enforceable. Finally, he notes that if one accepted a moral duty of easy rescue, its fulfillment would tend to swallow up individual liberty, because in the unfortunate actual state of this world, huge numbers of people are in dire predicaments, from which they could easily be rescued. Once one sees the possibility of rescuing distant needy strangers, acceptance of a duty of easy rescue (or moderately easy rescue) will be recognized as oppressively infringing on one's right to live as one chooses: morality, including the rescue duty, would require spending the vast bulk of one's life helping others.[22]

These points do not succeed in defending the self-ownership thesis from the easy-rescue objection. What is objectionable is precisely the idea that there is no enforceable obligation to help save lives when the cost to the potential helper is low or moderate. If the world multiplies opportunities for rescue, then the overall cost to the rescuer (in terms of forgone opportunities) of saving all who might be saved will increase, and will eventually rise to a threshold such that engaging in further rescue efforts will be deemed excessive by most people.[23] In other words, it is built into

---

[22] Vallentyne, "Introduction: Left-Libertarianism—A Primer," 4–5.

[23] There are two different ways of measuring the cost of one extra rescue in order to fix the point at which further rescues are not required. One might hold that with this one contemplated extra rescue effort, the total cost of the rescue efforts undertaken by the rescuer (over her lifetime? over a shorter stretch of time?—there are different possibilities

the idea of a duty of easy or moderately easy rescue that the cost to the rescuer must not be "excessive." (The scare quotes here acknowledge that I have no theory as to how one draws the line in a principled way that indicates where the duty gives out.) Vallentyne might respond that if the number of potential rescuees vastly exceeds the number of rescues any individual is obligated to undertake, how can there be a strict obligation owed to any particular persons? One answer is that the obligation is disjunctive: one must rescue some subset of the total of people whom one might save, and each of these persons has a right that one rescue either a group that includes him or some other same-sized group from among those who might be saved.[24]

Here the damaging problem with self-ownership does not lie in its denial that there is an enforceable obligation to keep helping needy persons so long as there is a net utility gain from doing so, but rather in its denial that there is an enforceable obligation ever to help others in need no matter how enormous the gains to the others and how slight the cost to the helper. Left-libertarianism, in its own way, echoes David Hume's view that it is not contrary to reason to prefer the destruction of the rest of humanity to the slightest scratch on one's finger.

The self-ownership doctrine is implausibly extreme along another dimension. According to this doctrine, each individual's property rights in herself are one and all alienable by her consent. Each individual in this sense has full sovereignty over herself. Each person is morally entitled to kill or maim herself for good reasons, bad reasons, or no reasons at all. Each is entitled to act in any foolishly self-destructive way she chooses provided only that her choice process qualifies as voluntary or voluntary enough. If I give my consent to your hacking off my limbs, perhaps because viewing a particular memorable Monty Python skit has made a strong impression, you have an enforceable right to hack me, and no one has a moral right to interfere. If I give irrevocable consent to being chopped up, then even if I later have second thoughts and change my mind, you still hold the irrevocable consent and with it the moral right to hack me to pieces.

---

here) exceeds a stipulated level. Alternatively, one might hold that as the rescuer engages in more and more rescues, the cost to the agent of the next single rescue effort tends to mount, and eventually reaches a point at which the cost to the agent of that next single rescue effort, given what that effort would achieve, is sufficiently high that the agent is not morally bound to undertake it.

[24] How can a person in need have a right that you rescue some person other than herself? Does the disjunctive right proposed in the text make sense? Yes, I say. When a set of people hold a disjunctive right to aid on your part, each has a conditional right that you aid her unless you are instead giving aid to another person in the set. This sort of conditional right is no more mysterious than a back-up job offer. Being the recipient of such a conditional offer, I have a right to be offered the job if and only if the first-ranked candidate, to whom the job has been offered, turns it down. I thank Ellen Paul for pressing for clarification on this point.

Moreover, self-ownership entitles each person to sell herself into slavery and make herself the full private property of another person (up to a point). The parenthetical qualifier is necessary, because one can only transfer to another the rights one possesses, and since one has no right to use one's body to attack others or violate any of their natural moral rights, one cannot transfer the right to use one's body in these ways to another person. If the slaveowner to whom I have given all my self-ownership rights orders me to perform an act that violates the rights of another person (who is not another slave who has transferred all of *his* rights to this same owner), I am morally bound not to comply. However, in all other respects, by voluntary contract I can make myself the private property of another person. If the slaveowner orders me to beat or maim or torture myself, or work myself to death, I am morally bound to comply, according to the upholder of unvarnished self-ownership.[25]

These implications of self-ownership offend against two norms that any reasonable philosophy of individual liberty should be tailored to fit. One is that paternalism—restriction of a person's liberty against her will for her own good—is morally acceptable at least when it would prevent an individual from causing great harm to herself without generating any compensating gain for others. The other is that a cognitively competent noncrazy human person, possessing a capacity for rational agency, has a dignity that demands her own respect as well as the respect of others. Each such person is under a (vague) enforceable duty to herself to live as befits a rational agent, and in all but desperate circumstances, this duty dictates that she owes it to herself to fashion something worthwhile from the one life she has to live, to generate good for herself and others, and to abide by reasonable moral constraints. The vague duty to oneself leaves enormous scope for free choice of how to live one's own life, but not unlimited scope. The permissibility of paternalism and the existence of a nonwaivable duty to maintain one's status as a rational agent entail that the self-ownership doctrine rests on a misunderstanding of the ideal of personal sovereignty and its limits.[26]

Once again, Vallentyne develops sensible rejoinders to this line of argument—rejoinders whose limits are instructive.[27] Regarding the implication of self-ownership that says that each person is entitled to submit herself voluntarily to slavery and hence to make herself the private property of another person, Vallentyne distinguishes protection of the continued possession of autonomy and protection of the exercise of autonomy, and notes that self-ownership protects the latter, and not necessarily the

---

[25] Some philosophers who are otherwise tempted to a position close to affirmation of full self-ownership balk at voluntary slavery. See John Stuart Mill, *On Liberty* (1859), ed. Elizabeth Rapaport (Indianapolis, IN: Hackett Publishing Co., 1979), chap. 4, para. 11.

[26] For more on this point, see Richard Arneson, "Joel Feinberg and the Justification of Hard Paternalism," *Legal Theory* 11 (2005): 259–84.

[27] Vallentyne, "Introduction: Left-Libertarianism—A Primer," 4.

former. He observes correctly that the choice to sell oneself into slavery need not be irrational—perhaps selling oneself into slavery is the only way one can amass resources needed for some great good (e.g., saving an entire city from destruction). But the opponent of self-ownership on this point need not deny that sometimes selling oneself into slavery is morally permissible or even admirable. The opponent objects to the blanket claim that each person always has an enforceable right to waive or alienate any of her rights over herself, even her entire set of personal autonomy and control rights, for any reason at all or no reason.

VII. Left-Libertarianism Versus Locke

Left-libertarianism shares with right-libertarianism an insistence on a strong and unyielding right of personal autonomy under the canopy of "self-ownership"—too strong and too unyielding, in my view. Setting my own moral judgments to the side in this section, I note that John Locke's affirmation of equal rights to individual liberty is not nearly as strong and unyielding as what right- and left-libertarians are inspired by his arguments to affirm.

According to libertarians, being the sole rightful owner of myself, I may destroy myself at will, for good reasons or bad reasons. I am also morally entitled to engage in imprudent and self-destructive conduct. Self-ownership is understood by its advocates to include a strict right against paternalistic interference in action that threatens harm only to the agent against whom interference is being contemplated or to others who voluntarily consent to bear the costs that the agent's actions impose on them. These implications of self-ownership are complicated in cases in which the agent's exercise of her freedom involves the use of material resources (to which she might or might not have a right). To simplify, and to avoid what are here irrelevant issues, let us confine ourselves to cases in which these complications do not intrude. For example, suppose the individual's imprudent and self-destructive actions make use of no one's property without the property owner's voluntary consent.

As is well known, Locke himself explicitly disavows such extensive and absolute rights of personal autonomy that include rights against coercive interference. Locke does not regard the individual human being as the full rightful owner of herself; rather, she is God's property.[28] The individual has no right to kill or destroy herself, so she cannot transfer such rights, which she does not possess, to other agents. The individual cannot legitimately submit to a voluntary slavery contract that makes another person the full rightful owner of the initially self-owning indi-

---

[28] Nicholas Jolley emphasizes Locke's theological premises and their bearing on the proper interpretation of his moral and political views in Jolley, *Locke: His Philosophical Thought* (Oxford: Oxford University Press, 1999), chap. 10. In this connection, see also Simmons, *The Lockean Theory of Rights*, chap. 1.

vidual. Nor, according to Locke, may an individual transfer her rights to
life and liberty to a would-be absolute political sovereign.

Belonging to God does not deprive the Lockean individual of all control rights over herself. Each human person has the moral right to direct
her life as she chooses within the constraints of God's laws, which forbid
self-destruction, wastefully imprudent conduct, and permanent alienation of one's rights over oneself to a human master. So it's not merely
that the individual does not possess full rights over herself. Even the
limited rights over herself that she does possess—as it were, rights of
tenancy over herself that are subordinate to God's ownership rights with
respect to her person—may not be squandered at will or whimsically or
in any other way that is contrary to God's purposes for man.

The left-libertarian might dispute the significance of Locke's religious
beliefs to the project of drawing from Locke's texts insights that should
inform our ideas on personal freedom and autonomy today. Scratch the
theological premises from Locke's writings, perhaps, and you end up
with a doctrine more recognizably and consistently libertarian. But I don't
think so. The limits on the individual's absolute rights over herself that
Locke formulates in terms of God's sovereignty and divine purposes can
be restated in terms of the respect that we owe ourselves in virtue of our
status as rational (semirational) agents[29] and the solidarity that we owe to
fellow humans and other animals. Moral claims that Locke derives from
theological premises can be taken as freestanding intuitively plausible
claims. This secular trimming of Locke is abetted by his view that God's
purposes for humanity mainly involve the desire that His creatures flourish, and that the divine commands we ought to obey take the form of
rules general compliance with which would maximize human flourishing.[30]

According to Locke, God has given no one rights to property except
with the proviso that He has also given "his needy brother a right to the
surplusage of his goods." Locke adds: "Charity gives every man a title to
so much out of another's plenty as will keep him from extreme want,
where he has no means to subsist otherwise."[31] So far, Locke seems to be
committed to requiring that individuals with plenty yield their surplus
goods to aid the needy. This says nothing about requiring individuals
favorably situated to use their time, energy, and labor in the service of
rescuing the needy from dire predicaments. Locke does strikingly say in

[29] Humans are semirational agents, who possess limited rational agency capacity. Humans
fail to be fully rational in forming beliefs on the basis of the available evidence, reasoning
correctly from given premises, discerning the good and the right, and so on.
[30] Simmons, *The Lockean Theory of Rights*, 46–59.
[31] Locke, *First Treatise of Government*, sec. 42, cited after Simmons, *The Lockean Theory of
Rights*, 327. I follow Simmons in supposing that, on this point, we may take the views of the
author of the *First Treatise* as likely close to those of the author of the *Second Treatise*, so here
what is said in the former work should inform our interpretation of the latter. At least, Locke
nowhere in the *Second Treatise* contradicts the views on the duty of charity explicitly stated
in the *First Treatise*.

SELF-OWNERSHIP AND WORLD OWNERSHIP

the *Second Treatise* that everyone, "when his own Preservation comes not in competition, ought . . . as much as he can, *to preserve the rest of mankind.*"[32] However, this phrase dangles loosely in the text. Locke nowhere in the rest of the *Treatise* spells out what this formidably stringent-sounding duty of charity might amount to. In fact, one might hold that the rest of the sentence from which this quotation was drawn specifies the duty to preserve the rest of mankind in purely negative terms—refraining from impairing the life or the "Liberty, Health, Limb, or Goods of another." But this interpretation has its problems, for most of us do not think that the duty to refrain, say, from seriously injuring others by bashing them holds only when abiding by this duty is compatible with one's own preservation. One must abide by serious moral constraints even if that means accepting one's own death: I may not kill you just because that is necessary to save my own life. In any event, it would be odd to hold that when one has extra goods, one must give them away to save another from a dire predicament, but to deny that when one has extra time and energy, and could easily act to save another from a dire predicament, one is not morally bound to do so.

If the commentators who read Locke as endorsing a strict duty of charity are correct, then Locke, the supposed true believer in full self-ownership, believes no such thing, but instead allows that other people sometimes have property rights in our bodies, when our bodies are useful for extricating them from dire predicaments and the cost to us of doing the extricating is not excessive.

In yet another respect, the left-libertarian hybrid view that sharply distinguishes the individual's right to control herself and the individual's right to control parts of the Earth as property is both normatively implausible and unfaithful to the Lockean tradition as expressed in seminal texts such as Locke's writings on government. The left-libertarian treats self-ownership and world ownership as entirely distinct and independent freestanding doctrines. Vallentyne et al. are explicit on this point (in the passage quoted above in Section VI).[33] However, the Lockean tradition does not take this line. In this tradition, the doctrines of (something in the neighborhood of) self-ownership and world ownership are regarded as elements of a single unified philosophy of individual freedom. In this respect, the right-libertarian reading of Locke is perhaps more faithful to Locke's views.

VIII. The Left-Libertarian Critique of Right-Libertarianism

Left-libertarianism poses a challenge to right-wing varieties of libertarianism rooted in the Lockean tradition. For purposes of this essay, I shall

---

[32] Locke, *Second Treatise*, sec. 6.
[33] See note 21.

suppose that Robert Nozick's version of libertarianism is the most promising exemplar of this type of position. In broad terms, the right-wing libertarian holds that individuals can legitimately acquire full ownership rights over parts of the Earth and that this right to private ownership is either derivable from more fundamental libertarian premises or derivable from those premises supplemented by independently plausible and attractive moral premises. The right-wing or Nozickian libertarian further holds that there is no upper limit to the degree of inequality in private ownership of material resources that can be justified on morally defensible Lockean premises.

The key to Nozick's view on private world ownership is his construal of the Lockean proviso.[34] This holds that even when land and natural resources are not abundant (i.e., even when the amount of land that individuals wish to appropriate as their private property exceeds the total available amount of land available), one may permissibly acquire full private ownership over unowned land and movable pieces of the Earth provided that one's appropriation renders no one worse off than she would have been under continued free use of that land.

The left-wing objection against the Lockean proviso is that it arbitrarily allows whoever happens to be in a position to assert a first-ownership claim on hitherto unowned land to gain virtually all of the benefits that are generated by the establishment of any of a wide variety of ownership regimes that would enable people to gain secure control over pieces of the Earth for extended periods of time. Suppose one individual appropriates all unowned land as his property and uses the property in ways that offer economic opportunities to other people that just barely compensate them for the loss of the not very valuable rights to use the land freely that private ownership supersedes. The Lockean proviso puts a stamp of approval on such an appropriation. But intuitively this seems unfair. Since the free-use rights are likely to provide very little benefit to anyone, a very low baseline level of benefit is set, and provided that the compensation the single world appropriator provides generates this little benefit for all affected people over the long run, the appropriation is assessed as perfectly permissible by Nozick's version of the Lockean proviso.

Some right-wing libertarians will respond to this objection by digging in their heels and standing their ground. I want to explore a response that concedes ground to the objection without retreating all the way to egalitarian world ownership doctrines such as those the left-libertarian affirms.

The concessive response holds that a person may legitimately claim full private ownership over a hitherto unowned portion of the Earth even when such tracts of land are scarce, provided the following conditions hold:

[34] Nozick, *Anarchy, State, and Utopia*, 178–82.

(1) Over the long run, no one is rendered worse off by this appropriation than she would have been had the land remained under free use (and had people generally conformed to the moral rules of free use).

(2) Over the long run, each person affected by the appropriation is rendered substantially—though not necessarily equally—better off than she would have been had the land remained under free use (and had people generally conformed to the moral rules of free use).

(3) Over the long run, each person affected by the appropriation is rendered substantially—though not necessarily equally—better off than she would have been had the free use system been replaced by any egalitarian regime of property ownership. Under an egalitarian system, ownership rules are set so that each person can obtain an equally valuable set of material resources, or a set of resources ownership of which leads to equality of condition, or a set of resources ownership of which leads to equal opportunity to gain as much via ownership as all other owners gain.

These conditions reflect and extend the conditions that Locke seems inclined to impose on appropriation of parts of the Earth as private property when scarcity obtains. When these conditions obtain, and appropriation occurs, a wedge is driven between the left-libertarian critique of private ownership and the affirmation of principles of world ownership that insist on equality in some form in the left-libertarian manner.

In this essay, I will not make any further attempt to adjudicate the complicated and multifaceted dispute between left-libertarians and right-libertarians on the conditions for morally permissible appropriation and continuation of full private ownership rights in parts of the Earth. I will simply note here that one might fully accept the left-libertarian critique of Nozick's doctrine of private ownership and similar doctrines without accepting anything close to the left-libertarian positive doctrine on equal world ownership.

IX. A More Reasonable Left-Libertarianism

Despite the animadversions I have heaped on certain versions of left-libertarianism, I do not regard the project as hopeless. Locke's writings combine different strands, and by emphasizing some over others one obtains different versions of broadly Lockean doctrines. One dimension along which emphasis may differ is a left-to-right spectrum.

In my view, the hybrid doctrine currently on offer under the label "left-libertarianism" is unsatisfactory, for reasons already stated. Here is a recipe for constructing more promising left-wing versions of libertarianism: Take your favorite formulation of Lockean libertarianism, such as a doctrine resembling Nozick's. Doctrines similar to his are uncompromising in their assertion of individual moral rights (a) against paternalistic interference, (b) in favor of unlimited legitimate accumulation of parts of the Earth as private property within the limits of the Lockean proviso, and (c) in support of a protection of each individual against any enforceable duty to use one's person or property to help others. The uncompromising character of the moral rights affirmed by Nozickians appears when we notice that they do not give way no matter what consequences are at stake. No matter how bad the overall consequences, impersonally judged, of respecting one's moral rights on a particular occasion, and no matter how great the consequences would be if some infringement of these rights occurred, according to the Nozickian, one morally ought always to abide by the rights, come what may. A simple amendment relaxes this feature of the doctrine. Add to the Nozickian moral rights a consequentialist principle of beneficence: One morally ought always to perform an act that would produce consequences no worse than would be brought about by anything else one might have done instead, whenever the consequences of forgoing this choice for the best outcome, and instead conforming steadfastly to all individual moral rights that are at stake in one's choice, would be *excessively bad.* If one places the threshold at which the consequences of not infringing someone's moral rights qualify as excessively bad at a very high level, the resulting moral position is scarcely distinguishable from straight right-wing libertarianism of the Nozickian variety. (In fact, Nozick himself hints that he might qualify his own adherence to moral rights by a moral-catastrophe-avoidance principle.)[35] If one sets this threshold very low, one's position is close to straight act-consequentialism.

To improve on the position reached in the last paragraph, we need to incorporate this feature: the level of bad consequences that suffices to trigger a moral permission or requirement to infringe Lockean moral rights is variable, depending on the moral importance of the rights at stake in the situation. After all, you have a moral right not to be torture-murdered for fun, but you also have a moral right that your extra shirt button on your least favorite shirt not be taken from you without your consent. A sensible consequentialized libertarianism registers this difference in the moral significance of the various individual moral rights people possess. Here is a first try at the appropriate registration: The greater the good consequences to be gained by infringing a libertarian moral right, and the less morally important or weighty the moral right that might be infringed for this purpose, the less morally wrong it is to infringe the right. When these two factors reach a tipping point, infring-

[35] Ibid., 30; see footnote at bottom of page.

ing the right becomes morally permissible, and at some further tipping point, infringing the right becomes morally required.[36]

Depending on the relative weights assigned to the two factors of the importance of respecting a given right and the importance of bringing about good consequences producible by actions or omissions that one can choose, the Lockean libertarian doctrine qualified by beneficence can end up at any point on a scale from pure consequentialism to pure libertarianism. I propose to identify a reasonable left-libertarianism with such a position, provided that substantial weight is assigned to its consequentialist beneficence component.[37] Of course, the propriety of this usage depends in part on the standard that is accepted for evaluating consequences. I propose this standard: good consequences consist in gains in well-being for persons (or avoidance of losses), with greater weight assigned to achieving a gain of a given size for a person, the worse off she would otherwise have been in terms of lifetime well-being. If significant weight is attached to priority for the worse off, the view takes on an egalitarian and thus recognizably left-wing hue.

X. CONCLUSION

Left-libertarian doctrines combine the libertarian claim that each person is the full rightful owner of herself and an egalitarian position regarding the rightful ownership of the land and resources of the Earth. My focus in this essay has been on a prominent formulation of left-libertarianism developed by Michael Otsuka. I have criticized this doctrine on the ground that it achieves a reconciliation of individual self-ownership and egalitarian world ownership only by interpreting self-ownership in a thin and formal way that does not capture what is most attractive in that norm. Yet, in other respects, this thin self-ownership is too thick: it denies moral duties that each of us has toward other persons and toward herself, duties that largely constitute the reasonable substance of human solidarity. In denying these social duties,

---

[36] The statement in the text is indebted to the discussion in Judith Jarvis Thomson, *The Realm of Rights* (Cambridge, MA: Harvard University Press, 1990), chap. 6. Thomson adds that the moral importance of a particular right on a particular occasion is a function of how bad the consequences will be for the right-holder if the right is not respected. Thomson favors a formulation which does not permit aggregation of costs incurred by many non-right-holders if the right is not infringed to balance the costs incurred by the right-holder if the right is infringed. Instead, we are to compare the costs that would be incurred by the one non-right-holder who would suffer the most from the fulfillment of the right. She calls this aspect of her view the "High Threshold Thesis." In my view, it merits rejection.

[37] Here I am simply assuming that policies and actions that will bring about good consequences, as picked out by the right principles of outcome assessment, will coincide with policies and actions that merit the description "left-wing." To argue for this, I would need to defend a standard for evaluating consequences and show that producing good consequences so understood requires left-wing policies, not right-wing ones, in actual and likely circumstances.

left-libertarianism decisively parts company with the natural rights principles of John Locke, whose liberalism is ultimately neither left nor
libertarian. Focusing on Otsuka, I have not claimed that my criticisms
apply to all versions of left-libertarianism, though I suspect that in
broad terms they do. Finally, I have suggested an alternative strategy
for revising and pressing Lockean views in a left-wing egalitarian
direction.

Philosophy, University of California, San Diego

THE UNEASY RELATIONSHIP BETWEEN DEMOCRACY AND CAPITAL*

By Thomas Christiano

I. Introduction

Many have had the suspicion that private capitalist firms exercise disproportionate influence over democratic policymaking. The usual worry concerns influence over the democratic process in the form of financial support of candidates in electoral processes in return for support for legislation that benefits capitalist firms. This important topic is not the one I will discuss in this essay.[1] Another important source of worry is substantially independent of the electoral process itself. The worry is that the very exercise of property rights can sometimes be a source of disproportionate influence over a political society. Some Marxists have written in this context of the "structural dependence of the state on capital" and have claimed that capitalism is incompatible with democracy.[2] We need not accept this extreme claim to think that there is a serious source of concern here.

I think this suspicion can be vindicated, though it must be attended with some significant qualifications. The basic questions I want to ask are: Can the exercise of private property rights abridge fundamental norms of democratic decision-making? And under what conditions can it do so? To the extent that we view democratic decision-making as required by justice, the issue is whether there is a deep tension between certain ways of exercising the rights of private property and that part of social justice that

* I thank Richard Arneson, Ellen Frankel Paul, Eric Mack, Jan Narveson, David Schmidtz, and the other contributors to this volume, for useful discussion of the ideas of this essay.

[1] For the classic study on this phenomenon, see Alexander Heard, *The Costs of Democracy: Financing American Political Campaigns* (Garden City, NY: Doubleday and Company, 1962). See also Frank J. Sorauf, *Inside Campaign Finance: Myths and Realities* (New Haven, CT: Yale University Press, 1994). For some philosophical work, see Charles Beitz, *Political Equality: An Essay in Democratic Theory* (Princeton, NJ: Princeton University Press, 1989), chap. 9. See also Joshua Cohen, "Money, Politics, Political Equality," in *Fact and Value: Essays on Ethics and Metaphysics for Judith Jarvis Thomson*, ed. Alex Byrne, Robert Stalnaker, and Ralph Wedgwood (Cambridge, MA: MIT Press, 2001), 47–80. For an effort to demonstrate the disproportionate influence of the wealthy on the political system in the United States, see Larry M. Bartels, *Unequal Democracy: The Political Economy of the New Gilded Age* (Princeton, NJ: Princeton University Press, 2008), esp. chap. 9.

[2] See Fred Block, "The Ruling Class Does Not Rule," *Socialist Revolution* 33 (1977): 6–27, for the Marxist claim that the state is completely structurally dependent on capital. See Adam Przeworski and Michael Wallerstein, "Structural Dependence of the State on Capital," in *American Political Science Review* 83 (March 1988): 11–29, for a critique of this thesis.

doi:10.1017/S0265052509990082

is characterized by democracy. To the extent that this tension holds, I will argue that commitment to democratic norms implies that private capitalist firms must cooperate with a democratic assembly and government in the pursuit of the aims of a democratic assembly even when this implies some diminution of the profits of the firms. The cooperation I have in mind goes beyond the norm of faithful compliance with the law. To be sure, there are limits to this requirement, as we will see in the later part of the essay. To the extent that private capitalist firms fail to do this and partially undermine the pursuit of the aims of a democratic assembly, they act in a way that is incompatible with fundamental norms of democratic governance.

There are a number of examples in contemporary politics that illustrate the phenomenon of private capitalist firms acting in ways that seem to involve their exercising a disproportionate influence over the political societies in which they operate. For example, in order to raise the welfare of the worst-off workers, the government institutes a minimum wage increase. It does this in fulfillment of a promise to raise the welfare of the worst off that was made during the previous election cycle—a promise that was fairly clearly an important reason why the current officials in the government were elected. Many economists claim that businesses would lay off workers as a consequence of this kind of policy, with the effect that the welfare of the worst-off workers would be lowered overall. I do not want to take a stand on whether this is a necessary or even likely consequence of raising the minimum wage.[3] I will discuss the question of necessity later in the essay. Another possibility is that the government reneges on its promise to raise the minimum wage on the grounds that it fears that businesses would lay off too many workers and defeat the aim of the policy. Let us suppose that another possible scenario is that at least some of the businesses institute the minimum wage, but do not lay off workers; they merely pass on part of the cost to consumers and absorb some loss in profitability. In some instances, let us suppose, the business is not ruined by this policy. The questions I am asking about this kind of case are: (1) Do businesses that fail to adopt this latter policy when they could do so without serious harm to themselves abridge basic democratic norms?

---

[3] For a classic formulation of the argument that minimum wage laws increase unemployment, see Paul Samuelson, *Economics*, 9th ed. (New York: McGraw-Hill, 1973), 393–94. For empirical evidence that minimum wage laws do not have the effect of increasing unemployment, see David Card and Alan Krueger, "Minimum Wages and Employment: A Case Study of the Fast-Food Industry in New Jersey and Pennsylvania," *American Economic Review* 84, no. 4 (September 1994): 772–93. See also David Neumark and William Wascher, "Minimum Wages and Employment: A Case Study of the Fast-Food Industry in New Jersey and Pennsylvania: Comment," *American Economic Review* 90, no. 5 (December 2000): 1362–96, for a critique of the Card and Krueger argument, and their reply in "Minimum Wages and Employment: A Case Study of the Fast-Food Industry in New Jersey and Pennsylvania: Reply," *American Economic Review* 90, no. 5 (December 2000): 1397–1420.

And (2) do businesses in this situation have duties to cooperate with the democratic assembly by raising wages without laying off workers?

Another possible case is one in which the government, in order to limit the release of carbon dioxide into the environment, imposes limits on emissions by certain industries. Let us suppose that in order to avoid these controls, the industry leaders decide to invest in another country where the limits are less stringent. This also contributes to an increase in unemployment, a perennial concern for modern governments. The industry response to the regulation not only sets back the aim of emissions limitation, it also defeats other central aims of the government and the people who support it. Again, we can imagine an alternative case in which the government simply does not issue the regulations on the grounds that the industry can defeat their purpose and other purposes the government has. And let us also suppose that it is at least economically feasible for the industry to conform to the regulations, partly by spreading the costs to consumers and partly by taking a modest decrease in profitability. Once again, we can ask: (1) Do businesses that fail to take this latter route abridge basic democratic norms, at least when this route does not threaten serious harm to the business? And (2) do such businesses have duties to cooperate with the democratic assembly by accepting the regulations and taking a modest decrease in profitability?

In each of these cases, under the first option the industry is exercising property rights (however limited and complex) over certain parts of the world, and thereby defeating the aims of the government. Under the second option, it is expected that the industry will exercise this right and the expectation prompts the government not to impose the popularly desired regulation in pursuit of the popularly mandated aim. These kinds of cases are endemic in modern societies that include a substantial amount of private ownership of productive property within the population. This ownership is implicated in the great majority of regulation and taxation by the government in pursuit of economic, environmental, worker-safety, welfare, and redistributive policies. Discretion over the use of property must be limited or curtailed in various ways in order to pursue objectives mandated in general elections. Every one of these activities and aims, no matter how popular, can be defeated or set back in significant part by people exercising fairly garden variety property rights.

These kinds of cases have become ever more pressing to the extent that capital has become more mobile in the modern global trading system. The increasing ability to move capital across borders enables owners of capital to elude the kinds of regulation and taxes that government imposes, and seems to give them increasing abilities to defeat aims that are chosen democratically and pursued by governments. In the international arena, these kinds of cases suggest a kind of conflict between two principal aims of contemporary international institutions: the development of international trade, and the spread of democracy.

In what follows, I will elaborate a framework for thinking about the issue at hand. I will discuss a recent effort to show how capitalist activity can seem to abridge democratic norms, and I will argue that this effort does not get at the crucial issues. I will discuss my own framework and then give the initial argument for the thesis that the exercise of ownership rights by capitalists can abridge the norms that underpin democracy. I will then discuss a number of mitigating factors that may soften the thesis a bit.

II. Democracy and the Power of Capitalists: A Framework for Analysis

Brian Barry argues that capitalists have power over government (democratic or otherwise) because they have the ability to get the government to do what they want it to do by virtue of the government's belief that, if it doesn't comply, then the government is likely to experience a diminution in its reelection prospects. Barry's general definition of "power over" is that A has power over B if A can get B to do something B would otherwise not do in virtue of B's belief that A could make him worse off if he does not do it. Barry thinks that given this account of "power over," it is clear that capitalists have power over governments. The kinds of examples he has in mind are cases in which the government lowers taxes despite its need for greater resources because it believes that businesses will disinvest if taxes are not lowered and that such business disinvestment will diminish economic growth and thereby diminish the reelection prospects of the government. Another case is one in which government does not raise the minimum wage on the grounds that businesses will lay off workers and increase unemployment with the increase in the minimum wage. One interesting feature of these cases is that businesses need not make threats to the effect that they will damage the government's election prospects if the government acts in the disfavored way. Businesses need not even issue a warning. Barry's definition does not seem to require either thing. All that is required is the pivotal position of private capitalist firms in being able to bring about worse outcomes when the government acts to realize popular policies.[4] In one case, they may increase unemployment in response to an increase in the minimum wage; in the other, they may disinvest in response to a failure to lower taxes.

I find Barry's definition of "power over" questionable. First, it looks as if it implies that a wife has power over her husband since he correctly believes that if he cheats on her, she will make him miserable by becoming morose and sullen for a long time after. Second, it suggests that a firm that would be driven out of business by the cost of conforming to a

---

[4] See Brian Barry, "Capitalists Rule OK? Some Puzzles about Power," *Politics, Philosophy, and Economics* 1, no. 2 (June 2002), 155–84.

government policy is exercising power over the government to the extent that this deters the government from acting. But it is not at all clear to me that these are genuine examples of exercises of power by the wife or the firm.

Another question that is not answered by Barry's thesis concerns whether, and to what extent, this "power over" involves damage to the democratic credentials of the government. This is odd, since the title of Barry's essay suggests that it does. "Capitalists Rule OK?" suggests that the people do not rule, but that capitalists do. This would suggest a serious defect in the democratic credentials of a government. But since Barry also claims that citizens have power over government, he needs to say a lot more than that capitalists have power over government in order to support the claim that capitalists rule. It is also odd because one of the chief theorists Barry draws on to support his argument, Charles Lindblom, also argues that the effect of business on government does damage to the democratic credentials of the government.[5]

As I said earlier, I want to explore the following question: When, and to what extent, does the exercise of private property rights over capital, or even the ability to engage in this exercise, amount to an abridgment of democratic norms? In order to try to answer this question, I think we need to get away from the framework Barry has used for discussing the issue. We must attempt to sketch some basic aspects of democratic norms, and then analyze the issue in terms of whether the exercise of property rights abridges those norms.

The issue can be clarified by placing it in the larger context of democratic theory. I want here to give as brief a sketch as is necessary to grasp the problem as I see it. Democracy is best justified by reference to a principle of political equality. The ideal of political equality is that individual citizens ought to have an equal say in how the society is to be organized. Having an equal say implies that individuals have equal votes, that there is equality in the process of deliberation, and that there is equality in the resources that go into making coalitions and bargaining over political aims and policies.[6]

Of course, such equality is hard to achieve in a large society, which requires a division of labor in the process of making decisions. A theory of democracy must say how a division of labor can be structured to maintain political equality. It must say how the kind of expertise and specialization that is necessary in political policymaking can be reconciled with equality in political decision-making. I have argued in detail elsewhere that these can be reconciled by assigning citizens the task of choosing the aims of the society, while assigning politicians, interest groups,

---

[5] See Charles Lindblom, *Politics and Markets* (New York: Basic Books, 1977).

[6] See Thomas Christiano, *The Constitution of Equality: Democratic Authority and Its Limits* (Oxford: Oxford University Press, 2008), for a defense of these claims.

and administrators the task of selecting the means by which these aims are to be achieved. Politicians, interest groups, and administrators have the kinds of expertise that enable them to select and implement the means as well as possible. These people are essentially agents of the citizens as a whole, charged with the task of realizing aims over which they have no discretion. This relation between (i) the citizens in their capacity as choosers of aims, and (ii) the subset of citizens who are charged with the task of determining the means to the aims, is called the democratic division of labor.[7]

I have tried to show that one can design institutions that ensure that the principal-agent relationship required for this democratic division of labor is compatible with political equality.[8] Very briefly, citizens can choose the basic aims of the society, I argue, to the extent that political parties present themselves as offering contrasting packages of aims and trade-offs among those aims.[9] Those political parties that manage to acquire a majority presence in the legislature then act so as to bring about those aims, or if a number of parties must form a coalition, they must compromise among the different packages of aims. They do this in making law. Then administrators formulate policies in order to achieve the aims that the laws are designed to achieve. To the extent that this all takes place under the watchful eyes of many different and opposing interest groups and experts, the idea is that these groups will more or less faithfully attempt to realize the aims of citizens.

To be sure, citizens may legitimately choose aims only within a limited scope, which is bound by the basic constitutional rights afforded to each person in a society. I will discuss later in the essay the extent to which capitalists' actions can be said to be protected by constitutional rights.

When citizens collectively choose the aims, their task is to choose all the goals they wish to achieve and rank the trade-offs between those goals. They choose a preference ranking over bundles of values.[10] The task of the political system is to achieve as much as possible of this preference ranking. How much it can achieve will depend on what we might call the conditions of feasibility. The conditions of feasibility are those conditions under which it is possible to realize some ends and not others and which constrain how one is to achieve those ends. Hence, the picture of democratic decision-making that I am giving involves three components: first, the citizens collectively choose the aims; second, there are independent

[7] See Thomas Christiano, *The Rule of the Many* (Boulder, CO: Westview Press, 1996), part II, for a defense of these claims.

[8] See ibid., part III, for the theory of democratic institutional design.

[9] Just to be clear, the aims need not always specify outcomes; the aims of citizens may include imposing constraints on the pursuit of outcomes.

[10] See Thomas Christiano, "Social Choice and Democracy," in *The Idea of Democracy*, ed. David Copp, Jean Hampton, and John Roemer (Cambridge: Cambridge University Press, 1993), for the argument that a democratic method of choosing aims is not undermined by the results of social choice theory.

conditions which determine how much of these aims can be achieved; third, the government, on the basis of an assessment of what chosen aims can be achieved and how they can be achieved, enacts laws and policies as means to the achievement of the feasible aims.

Notice that the government and government officials can abridge the principle of political equality by failing to act in ways that best achieve the preferences of the citizens at least within the feasible set. When they do this, as long as it is not mere incompetence that explains the failure, they substitute their own aims, in part, for those that have been chosen by citizens. The authority of government officials is essentially instrumental on this account. It is an instrument for the realization of the aims of citizens acting together as a democratic assembly.

How does the main issue that I have described come into this picture? The problem seems to be that the capitalists influence the conditions of feasibility; they do not influence the choice of aims or even of policies directly in the examples I have discussed above. That is, they do not influence the choice of aims or policies by participating in the democratic process. What they do is make it more or less difficult (and more or less likely) to achieve certain aims. They do this by making it more or less difficult or likely that government policies will achieve the aims. In the examples discussed above, capitalist firms have not exercised greater influence in the process of choosing the aims. In the case of minimum wage laws, private firms do not influence the electoral process to stop such policies from being made; rather, their expected responses make the policies self-defeating or stop the policies from being enacted. Likewise, in the case of the carbon-emissions policy, capitalist firms need not influence the electoral process; they are merely expected to act in ways that make the policy self-defeating, and for that reason the policy may not be enacted at all. By hypothesis, they do not have more votes or more money with which to influence the electoral process. The main effect of their actions is to determine the conditions of feasibility under which policies are to have their effects, and thus to determine how much of the citizens' chosen aims can be achieved.

It is important to see that this particular effect that firms have on policy choices need not be due at all to their having greater than equal resources for influencing the legislative process (e.g., greater numbers of votes, greater resources for funding campaigns, more time to express their points of view); it is only necessary that the government is persuaded of the truth of their claims about the expected results of proposed policies. To see this, we need only suppose that in the examples discussed above, the decision-making process by which the government reached the decisions is impeccably democratic. Suppose that the electoral process by which parties and individuals are selected to rule is completely egalitarian. There are entirely publicly financed processes of election, and media outlets cooperate in ensuring that all the main points of view are given a fair hearing during the electoral competition, and perhaps for some significant period before. Suppose, further, that parties and public officials are properly insulated from the disproportionate influence of different groups in the making of policy, and no one has an inside track in the making of policy. Furthermore, suppose that elected officials do in fact act as best they can to pursue the aims that have been democratically chosen in the process of election. There is likely to be disagreement on the details of a fair democratic process, and there is still a lot of work to do on how to specify it, but what is striking is that any particular way of organizing the process of elections and government will not solve the problem we are discussing here.

If there is any problem with political equality in our representative cases, it must have to do with the abilities of capitalist firms to act in ways that undermine the pursuit of democratically chosen aims. In our examples, they do this by laying off workers in response to minimum wage increases or disinvesting in the case of pollution laws. Or they have an influence merely because they are expected to do these things once the policies are in place. Here the capitalists are not, by hypothesis, exercising disproportionate influence over the electoral process; they are determining the conditions of feasibility for the pursuit of aims, and thereby determining the extent to which aims are achieved. Hence, the capitalists limit the achievement of the chosen aims of the citizens, and they do this simply in virtue of being able to exercise their ordinary liberal property rights.

Let us introduce a distinction here between two aspects of equality. There is *equality in the legislative process*, which requires fair electoral competition, insulation of public officials from special interests, and fidelity of officials to the aims they promised to pursue. Further, we might say that if there is equality in the legislative process, then each citizen has a kind of *equal say* over the process of legislative decision-making (or at least the most important part of the decision-making, the choice of aims to be pursued). The issue we are confronting has to do not with the process of decision-making but with the constraints under which the aims are to be pursued and the feasibility of the pursuit of those aims.

This is why I conceive of the actions of capitalists as constraints, in the first instance, on the government. Capitalists can affect the achievement or realization of the chosen aims by undermining the government's ability to achieve them, as when they lay off workers or move their investments across borders. Or capitalists can argue that since the aim will not be achieved anyway, it is no use trying the policy. Thus, they can stop the policy by making the government anticipate the failure. This may be part of the explanation for why the minimum wage rises so slowly.

What is worrying from the standpoint of political equality is that the constraints on the pursuit of aims (or the feasibility of aims) are imposed by the intentional and usually knowing actions of agents within the society. These intentional actions pursue other aims distinct from those chosen by the democratic assembly, and it appears that the pursuit of those other aims is what sets back the pursuit of the democratic aims. Now the question is, if a policy has been chosen in accordance with the aims that have been democratically chosen by citizens, and the policy is blocked or self-defeating because of the actions of a subset of members within the society pursuing their own aims, does that amount to an assumption of special rights on the part of those who are responsible for the failure of the policy or for the fact that it has not been implemented?

III. THE MAIN ARGUMENT

The main argument for the claim that the exercise of liberal property rights can constitute an exercise of political power and abridge the principle of political equality is that the principle of political equality requires that citizens be able to choose *as equals* what aims the society is to realize (at least within a limited scope bounded by constitutional rights). If we suppose that the legislative process is egalitarian, then the realization of a democratically chosen aim, as long as it is feasible, is required by the principle that all citizens should have an equal say over the outcome. If, subsequent to the democratic choice of an aim, a person or group of persons in the society knowingly act so as to undermine the achievement of the aim, then, according to the foregoing principle, they have necessarily appropriated a special exercise of political power for themselves. That is, they have necessarily had an extra say in what aims are to be brought about.

The same argument works for the case in which the capitalist manages to head off democratic legislation by persuasively announcing that the democratically chosen aim will be defeated by her actions when the policy is in place. And what is crucial here is that while the capitalist says that the aim cannot be realized, it is because of her own actions in pursuit of her particular ends that the aims cannot be realized. If the capitalist defeats the realization of an aim after it has been chosen, then surely the ability to prevent the realization of the aim in advance is an exercise of the same kind of power.

It is important to say what has not happened in the case of the capitalist activity under discussion. First, the capitalist has not disobeyed any democratically made law. She has not engaged in civil disobedience or in outright criminal activity. We are not supposing that the democratic assembly has made a law requiring her not to change investments or not to lay off workers when costs go up. Nor has she unduly or disproportionately influenced the process of decision-making itself. And she has not acted corruptly, at least in any straightforward sense. She can be described as an upstanding citizen as far as all these issues are concerned.

What she has done is made it more difficult to pursue democratically chosen aims; in some cases, she has made it impossible to pursue those aims. It looks as if there is an important sense in which she is interfering with the pursuit of democratically chosen aims. But we need to know more about what the term "interference" means in this context.

IV. AN INTUITIVE EXAMPLE

Let us see if we can think about this in terms of a smaller, more manageable example. A group of friends is deciding where to go on a trip, and they want to go together. They must choose between a weekend of gambling and a weekend of camping. Let us suppose that the group decides by a significant majority to go camping, and everyone has already agreed to abide by whatever the majority decides. But the only way to drive to the campsite is through a notorious gambling town. One of the cars is driven by one of the pro-gambling faction and stops in the town for a little gambling, thus putting off the camping for a while, possibly jeopardizing the whole trip. The group had not ruled out stopping for a bit on the way, and thus no one was explicitly obligated not to stop for a bit of gambling. And no specification had been made of how long a stop would be too long. Still, we have the sense here that something has gone wrong and that the group that is doing the gambling is interfering with the trip.

We can even imagine another scenario in which, in anticipation of the events described above, the pro-camping group simply caves and agrees to a gambling trip instead. Somehow we have the sense here that the pro-gambling group, by succumbing to the temptation to gamble, or by being unwilling to resist such a temptation, is actually interfering with the overall group's project. It interferes in the sense that the project requires everyone to play a certain part, usually not fully specified by the agreement, but implied by the choice of ends to be pursued and the idea that those ends would be pursued in a reasonably efficient way.

The interference is not a coercive interference; it is similar to the interference of someone who is engaged in a cooperative project and continually fails to do her part, thereby undermining the purpose of the cooperation. In the case of games, a person who consistently flouts the rules and thereby disrupts the playing of the game is interfering with the game.

I choose this example because it seems like a relatively clear case of someone acting in a way that sets back the achievement of commonly agreed upon ends. And that person does so merely to pursue a private good. The idea in the example is that the person is somehow selfish and self-absorbed and puts herself above the rest of the group even when a commonly accepted goal is at stake. There are some conditions under which even the behavior in this example is acceptable, or at least excusable, and reflecting on these conditions may give us some ways of thinking about the case of the capitalist and the democratic decision. First, it is clear that if the person is a severely addicted gambler, or gambles by some terribly powerful compulsion, such a person's activities may be excusable. The decision of the group to take the route through the gambling town may seem merely foolish in this context. Second, the group may have decided that its members could stop along the way and do whatever they wished, in which case the gambler is not acting in violation of the group's decision.

A question I have elided in the foregoing example is whether the gambler has *intentionally* interfered with the pursuit of the aims of the group of which he is a part. We might also ask whether the gambler interferes with the group action when the group decides against a camping trip and in favor of a gambling trip, because it anticipates the gambler's action even if the gambler makes no explicit threat. In the example, it may well be that the gambler has no intention of upsetting the activity but knows that it is possible that it will be upset because of his diversion. In the foregoing example, this does not seem to make much of a difference. In either case, he seems to treat his fellow group members with a certain contempt or disregard.

Some might think that this distinction matters in the case of the capitalist's actions. It might matter, for example, if the capitalist disinvests and sends capital elsewhere in order to punish the government and in the hopes that the government will not do the same thing again. If the capitalist is merely responding to the new set of relative prices and maximizing profits without any concern for changing government policy, we might think that she is not asserting herself above her fellow citizens. She is not trying to reverse the policy or trying to deter future policies from being created, and thus she is not trying to undo or unilaterally deter the democratically made choice. Still, we might think that the capitalist is advancing her interests to the detriment of the democratically chosen aim, and to the extent that this is done knowingly, it suggests a failure of adequate respect for the democratic process. And it looks as if the capitalist in this context may still be affirming her interests over those of her fellow citizens because she is still saying that she may pursue her interests even if this undermines pursuit of the democratically chosen aim. At least in the absence of mitigating circumstances, which I will review below, this looks as if it could be a public affirmation of the superior importance of the interests of the capitalist over those of others. I don't see that there is a clear difference with our intuitive case above (that is, the case of the uncooperative gambler).

In a sense, then, we can see the capitalist as abridging democratic norms of equality by failing to cooperate with the pursuit of the democratically chosen aim. The capitalist thereby replaces the democratically chosen aim with one of her own. Her aim may not be very far from the democratically chosen aim, if acting on it merely increases the cost of pursuing the democratic aim; but it nevertheless seems to be an abridgment of political equality.

We can see this by comparing it to our intuitive example above, in which the uncooperative gambler seems to be replacing the agreed-upon group aim with one of his own. In the intuitive case, the uncooperative gambler acts in a way that sets back an aim that he has signed onto. He may not be acting contrary to a particular rule of action he has agreed to, but he is acting in a way that is informally contrary to the obligation he has as a member of the group.

In the case of the capitalist, we can see that she acts contrary to the aim that has been chosen by the democratic assembly. To the extent that we think that the democratic assembly has authority by virtue of having resolved the disagreements among citizens in a way that is fair to all the participants, we can think that each citizen has a duty to go along with the decisions it makes. The uncooperative capitalist thus acts in violation of that informally determined duty.

We can appreciate this from a different angle, if we compare the action of the capitalist to the action of an uncooperative official in the government. A number of examples come to mind. In one case, an official allows an individual to skirt the demands of the law after accepting a bribe from that person. By doing this (and acting to advance his own aims), the official acts in violation of a duty to act as the agent of the democratic assembly and to pursue the assembly's aims. Another official, because she disagrees with the democratically chosen aims, slows down the realization of the policy that has been designed to pursue those aims. The official is a kind of agent of the people but, in effect, delays or diminishes the pursuit of the democratically chosen aim. In a third case, a judge defeats part of the aim of a democratic assembly by interpreting the law in an excessively narrow way. In all these cases, officials act contrary to a trust they have as holders of governmental power. In the first case, the official acts in a way that is simply illegal. In the second case, the official acts in a way that is clearly contrary to duty, though usually not illegal. In the third case, the judge acts in a way that is contrary to duty but not illegal.

It seems to me that the behavior of the capitalist can be very much like the last two cases of errant officials. These officials may not be acting in violation of the law, but they err nevertheless, and the underlying reason for this, especially in the case of the judge, is that they fail to respect the aims of the democratic assembly. They act in ways that undermine the pursuit of the aims of the assembly. The capitalist acts similarly in violation of a duty, though not illegally. One might object that the officials have clear duties to act in accordance with the aims of the assembly by virtue of the trust they hold as officials of the government, and that the capitalist has no such trust. However, as I see it, the foundation of the idea that officials are entrusted with pursuing the aims of the democratic society is that they are capable of undermining the pursuit of those aims.

To the extent that capitalists are capable of undermining the pursuit of the aims of the democratic society, they too should be thought of as under duties to act in ways that do not hinder the pursuit of the aims. They have a special responsibility, by virtue of the power they hold, not to use it to pursue antidemocratic aims. These are not legal duties but rather moral duties that are owed to the rest of the society.

To be clear, this does not in any way suggest that capitalists have duties not to criticize government activities when they see fit. They always retain the right of dissent and the right to try to overturn democratic legislation by means of persuading a substantial proportion of the population of its problematic character. The thought is that once the aims have been chosen and the legislation is properly designed in pursuit of those aims, those who can interfere with the pursuit of the aims, by affecting the conditions of feasibility, have duties not to interfere, as long as they have reasonable alternatives to interference (which I will try to define in more detail in the last sections of this essay).

V. Property and Political Equality

A main implication of the foregoing argument is that when the democratic assembly has chosen a policy with a certain aim in mind, each person has duties within the society to carry out the policy and to cooperate in the pursuit of the aim to the best of his or her ability. Citizens do this mostly by obeying the law; officials fulfill their duties by deciding on policies that, in their expert opinion, best realize the aims in the circumstances; and individuals act in ways that do not defeat the pursuit of the aims. As long as people act in these ways, subject to the qualifications I discuss in Section VI, the norm of political equality is not violated.

One implication of thinking of the matter in this way is that the norm of political equality is not best conceived of as a principle of equal power. For it is clear that political officials have more power than others to undermine the pursuit of the aims of a democratic assembly. And capitalists, at least in some circumstances, have more power than others to undermine the achievement of democratic aims. These facts do not, by themselves, undermine political equality. If each of these persons conforms with the various duties of cooperation with the democratic assembly, then it seems that the ideal of political equality is satisfied—even if, were these people to act unscrupulously, they could act in violation of the norm of political equality.

Consider, again, our intuitive example from Section IV above. Suppose that the group of friends has decided to go to a certain destination, which requires going by car. And suppose that only one of the friends knows how to drive a car. That person has more power over the group with regard to going to that destination, but that need not imply any violation of the equality of all the members in deciding where to go, unless that person uses his special ability to undermine the group's trip or to extract special benefits from the group in return for driving. The inequality of power does not imply inequality in the decision-making as long as individuals forbear from using their greater power to set back democratically chosen aims.[11]

I want to propose, then, that the principle of political equality implies that there is a fundamental duty on the part of capitalists not to act in ways that set back the achievement of democratic aims, subject to the qualifications I discuss below. Thus, the right of private property in a democratic society is limited by the requirement to cooperate with the democratic assembly, just as officials have duties to cooperate in the pursuit of the aims chosen by the democratic assembly.

Perhaps there is a sense in which, as Charles Lindblom argues, capitalists are holders of a kind of authority in a democratic political society. This authority is like that of officials in government and, to that extent, is subject to similar norms. Just as officials in government have a kind of instrumental authority that is charged with the task of realizing democratic aims, so the limited authority of capitalists is also charged with helping achieve democratic aims. Of course, this is not all that capitalists are supposed to do, and thus their authority is not *merely* an instrumental authority for the achievement of democratic aims, but it is that at least in part.

G. A. Cohen has argued that, in an egalitarian society, citizens have duties that go beyond the duties to maintain and support just institutions. They also have egalitarian duties that they must observe in their personal behavior. This egalitarian ethos is something like what I recommend for private capitalist firms in a democratic society. They have informal moral duties, grounded in the idea that social justice requires democratic decision-making, to avoid interfering with the aims of a democratic society, and sometimes they have positive duties to assist in pursuing the aims of a democratic society.[12] These duties are limited in ways that I will outline in what follows, but they are quite real.

One might wonder why these duties are necessary. Why not just make laws requiring capitalist firms not to lay off workers or not to disinvest when pollution regulations are imposed? I think the answer is that the law cannot be formulated clearly to handle all the situations that might interfere with the pursuit of democratic aims. This will become clearer when we discuss the various kinds of exceptions and complications to the duties I have characterized. First, legislators do not always anticipate the

---

[11] This gives us another reason to call into question Barry's account of the relation between capitalism and democracy. It is not the mere fact that capitalists have greater power than others that abridges democratic norms; it is their willingness to exercise that power that can sometimes undermine equality.

[12] See G. A. Cohen, *Rescuing Justice and Equality* (Cambridge, MA: Harvard University Press, 2008), for an account of the egalitarian ethos.

ways in which the aims of legislation can be undermined by the behavior of members of society. Second, the exception clauses I will outline in Section VI are often too difficult to detail in pieces of legislation. We must rely on the judgments of owners of capital to determine when it is too burdensome for them to comply with the regulations or requirements while assisting in the pursuit of the democratically chosen aims. Third, the experience of the benefits of markets in generating economic growth must lead us not to interfere legally with those markets in too fine-grained a way. It seems to me that there will be many contexts in which it is preferable to leave the judgment as to how to satisfy the requirements of political equality to citizens.

One question that might arise in this context is whether all citizens may have similar opportunities to undermine the democratic decision-making process, and whether they may all have the same kinds of duties. In principle this is possible, but given the much greater power of private capitalist firms to influence the conditions of feasibility (as compared to the power held by ordinary individuals), it is reasonable to focus on the activities of capitalists. It is also reasonable, as we will see, to focus on private capitalist firms rather than individuals in their ordinary activities, because the kinds of facts that defeat responsibility for undermining the pursuit of democratically chosen aims are much more prominent in the case of ordinary individual action than in the case of private capitalist firms. We will look at some of these factors next.

VI. COMPLICATING FACTORS

There are some obvious complicating factors that can defeat charges that private capitalist firms undermine democratic aims in particular instances. I call them complicating factors because in some cases they seem to be objections to the reasoning I have outlined above, but in most cases they may merely involve an element of mitigation of the judgment I reached above. As general objections to my reasoning, I think they fail, but they do point to a number of important mitigating factors in particular circumstances.

We may class the mitigating factors as the problems of (i) inevitability, (ii) small and uncertain effects, (iii) undue burden, and (iv) democratic creation of the market.

A. Inevitability

One objection to the reasoning outlined above, which is expressed in common ways of thinking about these issues, is that businesspeople will do what maximizes profit for their firms, and that is all there is to it. We must assume that this is how they are motivated, as if it were a natural fact about persons. The actions of laying off workers in order to maximize profit or moving to a less demanding regulatory environment are something like necessary consequences of the proposed policies. Hence, the capitalist cannot be criticized for these actions any more than the weather can be criticized when it rains on a baseball game.

Though this deterministic rhetoric is often deployed in this context, it cannot be taken seriously, and probably more often than not is a stand-in for other considerations such as those I discuss below. The reason why we need not take this rhetoric seriously is that no one offers this as a reason not to criticize violations of law or more obvious violations of moral norms. We expect participants in society to obey legal norms even when these are burdensome, and we expect them to act morally as well. The question is whether the moral norms exist, not whether they may be burdensome.

A further argument that I want to make here is that a society made up of unrestrictedly self-interested persons is not likely to be highly stable. Any conception of a just legal system or political order will require that the members be morally motivated in order for it to be stable.[13] As a consequence, no conception of a reasonably just scheme can be expected to work for a rigorously self-interested group of persons, and thus we need not suppose that persons are strictly motivated by self-interest when we are evaluating political arrangements. We can and should assume some significant degree of moral motivation on the part of persons in reasonably just societies. Moreover, there is substantial empirical evidence that people are motivated to act morally in politically sensitive contexts.[14]

B. Small and uncertain effects

Another possible objection is that the actions of the individual capitalist may not have any visible impact on the pursuit of the democratically chosen aim. The case of minimum wage laws may have this character, at least if we accept the thesis that they tend to increase unemployment. An employer might think that the increase in the minimum wage requires her to delay hiring a new worker for another year. Given everything else that is going on in the economy, the employer need not think that her individual action will significantly add to unemployment. Or the employer may delay an increase in wages to other workers for a short time. The effects of these actions, taken individually, on the overall welfare of workers must be negligible when considered in isolation. Moreover, no employer

---

[13] See Christiano, *The Rule of the Many*, chap. 4, for this argument. See also Thomas Christiano, "Is Normative Rational Choice Theory Self-Defeating?" *Ethics* 115, no. 1 (October 2004): 122–41.

[14] See the evidence marshalled in the papers in *Beyond Self-Interest*, ed. Jane J. Mansbridge (Chicago: University of Chicago Press, 1990).

in this context can issue a meaningful threat to government policymakers. The individual effects are simply too small to deter government officials from making policies.

There will be circumstances in which the foregoing reasoning will provide a good justification for the employer's action. In particular, in those circumstances in which virtually everyone is acting in this same way, it is hard to see why someone should think that her action of reducing work hours or delaying employment decisions would make a significant difference to the pursuit of the aim of increasing the welfare of the worst-off workers. The aim is set back by the cumulative effects of the actions of many employers. It would be unreasonable to expect any particular employer to buck the tide and take a hit to her profitability when the gains of doing so are so small.

Nonetheless, in those circumstances in which most employers are willing to take a modest decrease in profitability, the foregoing justification may not be acceptable. For the particular employer who is not willing to do this seems to be making a special exception of herself in the cooperative activity of pursuing the aim of increasing the welfare of the worst-off workers. While others undertake some burden for the purpose of pursuing the democratically chosen aim, she exempts herself.

In this respect, we see some similarity to an assurance game. Each participant ought to be willing to go along as long as enough others do, but they are not required to go along if too many others are not going along. In the case of markets, there may not be enough coordination to assure that enough others are going along. Still, it is possible for businesses to act in concert in many circumstances of this sort, and it will be the duty of employers in this situation to attempt to coordinate on a strategy that increases the likelihood that the democratic aims will be achieved.

This circumstance does not seem all that different from the case of violation of democratically made law. No individual will undermine democratically made law if he violates it, but each does take unfair advantage of the compliance of others in violating the law and thus in some way acts contrary to the principle of equality that underpins democracy. And, of course, if everyone is violating the law then one person is not taking advantage of the compliance of others when violating the law.

One difference between the law-violation case and the employment case is that in the former the requirement is at least normally fairly clear, while in the latter the requirement may be quite uncertain. How much of a hit to profitability must the employer be willing to take, if any? To what extent can the costs of compliance just be passed on to consumers? These kinds of uncertainties will likely cause each conscientious person to wonder if others are actually complying or not, and thus may make them uncertain as to whether they ought to comply.

Another kind of case altogether would be the case of very large owners of capital, whose impact on employment may be significant. Consider a very large firm in a small town, which opposes some local legislation on working conditions or environmental regulation and says that it will pull out if the town passes the legislation. This threatens the town with impoverishment, let us suppose. The concern with small and uncertain effects does not seem to hold here; the potential effects are neither small nor uncertain.

In some important class of cases, the concern with small and uncertain effects does not defeat the thesis that the capitalist who acts so as to defeat the point of democratic legislation may be violating the principle of political equality. In some cases, large capitalist firms do not produce merely small and uncertain effects, and in some cases, small firms can act in concert to advance or set back the democratically chosen aim.

C. Undue burdens

Another class of concerns arises when we consider the possibility that the democratically made legislation, coupled with the demand that the capitalists act so as not to undermine the point of the legislation, may impose an undue burden on the capitalists. There are a number of possible types of undue burden here. First, there are some burdens that no democratic assembly has a right to impose. These are usually marked out by fundamental constitutional rights in liberal democracies. Except perhaps under extraordinary circumstances, democratic assemblies may not abridge fundamental rights of life, expression, association, or privacy. And certainly some aspects of a right to private property are similarly fundamental. Second, sometimes the imposition of minimum wage laws, coupled with the demand that small businesses absorb at least a significant amount of the cost, may make these businesses insolvent—and this may make the imposition and demand an undue burden. Third, even if the burdens do not have the sort of weight that the examples discussed above have, there may be some concern with the unfair distribution of those burdens. Consider that in the case of minimum wage laws, the laws attempt to increase the benefits of one select group, the worst-off workers. But they also, in effect, impose the cost of doing this on a small group, and it may be that at least many in that small group experience that cost as fairly weighty. So small businesses, which often live at the margins in any case, are required to pay the full cost of the society-wide concern to make the worst-off workers better off. To be sure, sometimes these costs can be spread more evenly throughout the society by increases in the prices of consumer goods, but this is not always possible for small businesses. One way to redistribute costs would be to lessen paid work hours or lessen pay at higher scales. This would not be particularly fair either, of course, since those who are less able to shoulder the burden would now be shouldering it. Notice that the imposition of the minimum wage is not itself an imposition of unfair burdens. It is only when it is coupled with the demand that business owners absorb most of the cost that we begin to see a case for the thesis that unfair burdens are being imposed. The trouble is that, by hypothesis, the minimum wage requirement without the demand that business owners absorb the cost may be self-defeating.

On the first kind of undue burden, the idea is that the authority of a democratic legislature runs out when it attempts to act in violation of one of the basic limits on democratic authority.[15] Serious abridgments of the freedom of expression or the freedom of association qualify as actions that are beyond the authority of democracy. And it seems to me that abridgments of basic rights of personal private property are beyond that authority. It is not clear to me, however, that the right to own capital qualifies as a fundamental right. It does not seem to be as central to the fundamental interests of the great majority of persons as the freedom of association or the freedom associated with personal private property. It is the centrality of these rights to the promotion of the fundamental interests of persons that qualifies them as grounds of fundamental rights that not even a democratic assembly may abridge. By contrast, the rights over capital, since they do not have this centrality to fundamental interests, are not basic limits to democratic authority. Hence, I do not think that requiring capitalists to cooperate with the pursuit of democratically chosen aims is an undue burden imposed on capitalists, at least in this respect.

Just to be clear, I do not make this argument because I think that having a duty to act in a certain way is inconsistent with the right to do otherwise. Without question, we have duties to use our fundamental rights of freedom of association to promote a just and reasonable society. My argument here is that there are some things a democratic assembly may not demand; such demands overstep the bounds of democratic authority. Thus, the democratic assembly may not impose duties on persons or groups of persons to do things or not to do things that fall within the scope of their fundamental rights.

On the second kind of concern, though the imposition of a minimum wage may be legitimate, it seems clear that no business is required to drive itself into insolvency in order to meet the informal demand. In any case, such a consequence would defeat the purpose of the legislation. And this consequence cannot be thought of as the intentional action of a person substituting his own aims for that of a democratic assembly. So it does seem that if a business lays off workers in response to a minimum wage law in order to remain solvent, this cannot be seen as a violation of the norm of political equality or a violation of the duty of cooperation with the democratic assembly. It may be the case that in perfectly competitive markets, businesses have little leeway to cooperate with the democratically chosen aims since earnings cover the costs of business and no more.

---

[15] See Christiano, *The Constitution of Equality,* chaps. 6 and 7, for a discussion of the nature and ground of democratic authority and its limits.

But markets as we know them are generally not perfectly competitive, and many markets give a fair amount of leeway to capitalists to cooperate with democratic government.[16]

The third kind of undue burden is trickier to deal with. Part of the problem is that it is part of the task of a democratic assembly to decide the case when there is disagreement about the fairness of a particular piece of legislation. This is one of the main functions of democracy, to make decisions in a way that treats all citizens as equals when there is substantial disagreement on the substance of the decision, even on its justice. This is how democracy has authority in many cases; even if the decision is wrong in a particular case, citizens have duties to go along with it, except when the decision violates fundamental rights. Hence, one might conclude in this context that the distribution of costs is part of the choice of the democratic assembly. In its judgment, it is a fair distribution. Even when this argument works, however, it is not clear how it is to apply to the kinds of informal demands imposed on capitalists in the cases of regulation of capital. First, it is not clear how much of a burden is too much. For a burden to be considered excessive, is it necessary that the burden push the person out of business? Or is some lesser standard available? And if so, this must give a fair amount of discretion to the employer in deciding whether and when the standard is met. We can see, though, that this discretion introduces a considerable amount of haziness into our assessments of these situations. Not only is it unclear to any particular person exactly when it is legitimate not to cooperate in pursuing the democratic aim, it is also unclear to each when others are cooperating or not cooperating legitimately.

Still, it seems to me that there will be a large set of cases in modern economies in which the reasons for cooperation with the pursuit of the democratically chosen aim are decisive.

Notice that these qualifications on the idea that private firms have duties not to interfere with the pursuit of democratic aims will apply to a much greater extent to individuals acting in their ordinary capacities as citizens. It is no doubt true that the behavior of citizens in their ordinary capacities can have an effect in the aggregate on the pursuit of democratic aims. But organizing the behavior of citizens is usually much more difficult than organizing the behavior of private firms. And the actions of ordinary citizens are often within the scope protected by basic liberal rights.

D. The democratic creation of the market

One last mitigating factor is that the market in a liberal democratic society can be thought of as the creation (or at least the adopted child) of

---

[16] See Donald Wittman, *The Myth of Democratic Failure: Why Political Institutions Are Efficient* (Chicago: University of Chicago Press, 1995), 176, for an argument that seems to me to presuppose perfectly competitive markets as a reason for thinking that capitalists have no option but to seek the profit-maximizing course of action.

a democratic assembly. To the extent that the democratic assembly makes legislation that protects, promotes, regulates, and limits markets, it can be said to be affirming the existence of markets as part of the legal order. And to the extent that the market is democratically affirmed, we might think that the decisions of persons within the market are to be affirmed as well. This might be thought to suggest that businesses may act as they see fit for their business in the context of the market. Thus, it might be thought that there is a kind of permission extended to businesses to do whatever they see fit to maximize the profits of the firm.

We must proceed carefully here, however. The legal adoption of the market does not directly imply that persons may do whatever they see fit in the marketplace to maximize profits. Obviously, people are expected to act within the limits of the law. And it is surely part of the idea of the normal functioning of markets that persons in the market act in the interests of their firms within the limits of the law and basic norms of morality. Part of what makes markets work, when they work, is that each participant seeks to advance his or her interests in this context.

There are some difficulties with this objection. First, repeating the criticism of the inevitability objection discussed above, it does not follow from the adoption of the market that unrestrictedly self-interested action is thereby endorsed. Self-interested action is not the inevitable result of the market. So there is no reason to think that the democratic endorsement of the market implies an endorsement of uncooperative behavior on the part of capitalists, at least once we accept the limits on the duty to cooperate that we have outlined above.[17] Second, no democratic society gives unrestricted scope to market activities. Markets have been limited in every liberal democratic society (especially for the last sixty to seventy years), and they are limited purportedly for the sake of the common good. I am thinking here of the regulations imposed by the New Deal in the United States during the 1930s and the regulations imposed by social democratic states in Europe and Japan since the late 1940s and 50s. These limits have survived repeated minority efforts to overturn them, so they have quite strong democratic credentials. Third, it may be that the relatively wide scope given to market activity in modern liberal democratic societies is itself a product of anticipated uncooperative activity on the part of capitalists, so that it does not actually express a fully democratic decision. This worry need not imply that collective ownership would be the choice of a democratic people, but it does make one wonder whether the extent of market activity in modern societies is actually the choice of a democratic assembly. But this is merely a worry. Clearly, other factors may be playing roles here, such as beliefs about the efficacy of markets in

---

[17] See Keith Dowding, *Power* (Minneapolis: University of Minnesota Press, 1996), 72–76, for a nuanced treatment of the power and luck of capitalists in a mixed economy.

many circumstances as well as beliefs about the importance of private property in sustaining a vibrant liberal democratic society.[18]

It seems to me that these are reasons for thinking that the democratic adoption of the market is not an endorsement of unrestricted self-interest in the market. To the extent that we think that a wide scope for market activity is genuinely democratically accepted, we may think that some of the constraints established by the market on cooperation by capitalists are legitimate. But there is also plenty of scope for a duty of cooperation with democratically chosen aims.

Does the fact that the government has passed no law forbidding dis-investment or laying off workers as responses to regulation imply that these activities are permissible? After all, the primary means by which a democratic assembly's aims are implemented is through law. So why doesn't the silence of the law imply consent to these actions? Two reasons favor rejecting this response. One is that the idea that drives Thomas Hobbes to assert the thesis that the silence of the law implies consent is one that we must not accept. Hobbes is driven to this by his view that agents are deeply self-interested and cannot be expected to comply with duties unless they are enforced. Nonetheless, I do not think we should accept this premise; I believe it is incompatible with the stability of a legal system, Hobbes's arguments notwithstanding. The second reason is that in the light of the pervasive impact which owners of capital have on the pursuit of aims in a democratic society, it cannot be assumed that a democratic legislature or the government that acts as its agent is always capable of determining all that needs to be done in pursuit of the aims. This is especially so in the light of the complexity of the considerations we have laid out for determining what capitalists are required to do in response to democratically chosen legislation. Thus, in a society in which a signif-icant scope is given over to market activities (and the owners of capital who engage in these activities), it is reasonable to assume that there will be many cases in which there are informal duties to cooperate with a democratic government that are not specified in law.

VII. CONCLUSION

I have argued that the free exercise of property rights by capitalists is sometimes incompatible with the principle of political equality. Owners of capital have informal duties to cooperate with the democratic assembly and the government that acts as its agent in pursuing democratically

---

[18] See Adam Przeworski, *Capitalism and Social Democracy* (Cambridge: Cambridge University Press, 1986), for a discussion of the influence of capitalists on the structure of modern liberal democratic states. See also Przeworski and Wallerstein, "Structural Dependence of the State on Capital," for a critique of the thesis that capitalists determine choices of government policy. See also Adam Przeworski, *The State and the Economy under Capitalism* (Chur, Switzerland: Harwood Academic Publishers, 1990), 92–96.

chosen aims. The suspicion that capitalists do sometimes act in ways that are contrary to democratic norms has been vindicated, though I have argued that a number of important qualifications must attend this judgment. The argument of this essay is quite open-ended and is meant as a call for further reflection on the relationship between the ownership of capital and the norms underpinning democracy.

Philosophy and Law, University of Arizona

REAL-WORLD LUCK EGALITARIANISM

By George Sher

I. Introduction

Luck egalitarians maintain that inequalities are always unjust when they are due to luck, but are not always unjust when they are due to choices for which the parties are responsible.[1] Although this formula raises obvious problems of application, the distinction on which it rests may at first seem clear enough. However, in what follows, I will argue that we arrive at one version of the distinction if we begin with the notion of luck and interpret responsible choice in terms of its absence, but a very different version if we begin with the notion of responsible choice and interpret luck in terms of *its* absence. I will argue, further, that the difference between these versions is significant because many real-world inequalities fall precisely in the gap between them.

II. Two Versions of Luck Egalitarianism

Suppose, first, that we start with the notion of luck. When we say that some aspect of a person's situation is a matter of luck, what we generally mean is that it is not (and was not previously) within his control. Moreover, when we say that an aspect of a person's situation is or was within his control, we mean, at a minimum, that he made some choice that he knew would bring it about (or would significantly raise the likelihood of its coming about). Thus, whenever any aspect of a person's situation is *not* an expected consequence of any of his choices, it thereby qualifies as a matter of luck.

---

[1] For an influential early statement of this view, see Ronald Dworkin, "What Is Equality? Part II: Equality of Resources," *Philosophy and Public Affairs* 10, no. 1 (Fall 1981): 283–345. For important discussion, see Gerald Cohen, "On the Currency of Egalitarian Justice," *Ethics* 99, no. 4 (July 1989): 906–44; and the influential series of papers by Richard Arneson that includes "Equality and Equal Opportunity for Welfare," *Philosophical Studies* 56 (1989): 77–93; "Liberalism, Distributive Subjectivism, and Equal Opportunity for Welfare," *Philosophy and Public Affairs* 19 (1990): 159–94; "Luck Egalitarianism and the Undeserving Poor," *The Journal of Political Philosophy* 5, no. 4 (1997): 327–50; and "Luck Egalitarianism Interpreted and Defended," *Philosophical Topics* 32, nos. 1 and 2 (Spring and Fall 2004): 1–20. For an influential critical discussion (in which the name "luck egalitarianism" was first introduced), see Elizabeth Anderson, "What Is the Point of Equality?" *Ethics* 109, no. 2 (January 1999): 287–337. For an excellent book-length treatment, see Susan Hurley, *Justice, Luck, and Knowledge* (Cambridge, MA: Harvard University Press, 2003).

doi:10.1017/S0265052509990094

Because each choice is made by a *single* individual, whereas each inequality is a relation between the situations of *different* individuals, it is not
immediately clear how we should interpret the claim that a given inequality is a matter of luck. It would not be plausible to say that an inequality
is due to luck whenever the difference between the parties' situations was
not a foreseen consequence of either party's choices; for, given that each
party can typically affect only what he gets but not what the other party
gets, this interpretation would imply that virtually *all* inequalities are due
to luck.[2] Thus, to give the luck-centric version of luck egalitarianism a
fighting chance, we must interpret its conception of luck more narrowly.
Instead of taking it to assert that an inequality is a matter of luck, and so
is unjust, whenever the inequality itself was not a foreseen consequence
of either party's choices, we must take it to assert only that an inequality
is a matter of luck, and so is unjust, whenever each party's having what
he currently does, as opposed to what the other has, was not a foreseen
consequence of his previous choices. If we interpret luck egalitarianism in
this way, it will imply that no inequality can be just unless having more
than he now does was once within the less-advantaged party's control—
unless, in particular, he was at some point aware of having some option
which, had he taken it, would have resulted in his now having as much
as his more-advantaged counterpart.[3]

Bearing this interpretation in mind, let us now approach luck egalitarianism from the other direction. Instead of organizing our account of its
central distinction around the notion of luck, let us try to organize it
around the notion of responsibility. Because responsibility is a complex
notion, any such approach is bound to raise many issues that lie beyond
our scope. However, for present purposes, what matters is only that
agents are often thought to be responsible for various outcomes of their
acts that they did not foresee. The basic premise of negligence law is
precisely that agents can be legally responsible for harms they were
unaware of causing—for the effects of their inattention, lapses of memory
or judgment, failures to recognize what is going on, and so on. Moreover,
when we turn from legal to moral responsibility, we find that we often
hold people morally responsible for the effects of these same failures.[4]
Thus, if the luck egalitarian begins with our ordinary notion of responsibility and allows it to shape his understanding of luck, then he will not
count every cognitive lapse that is beyond an agent's control as a matter
of luck. As a result, his view will imply that an inequality can be just even

---

[2] For related discussion, see Hurley, *Justice, Luck, and Knowledge,* 159–68.

[3] The existence of such an option is, of course, only a necessary condition for the resulting
inequality's justice. For interesting discussion of some of what would have to be added to
arrive at a sufficient condition, see the papers by Arneson that are cited in note 1.

[4] I discuss a variety of cases of this sort, and their implications concerning the epistemic
condition for responsibility, in my book *Who Knew? Responsibility Without Awareness* (Oxford:
Oxford University Press, 2009).

though the less-advantaged party was never aware of having an option which, had he taken it, would have resulted in his now having as much as his more-advantaged counterpart.

We can now see why the two starting-points yield different versions of luck egalitarianism. Although the two versions agree about cases in which the less-advantaged agent is not responsible for his disadvantage and has not exercised control over it, and about cases in which the less-advantaged agent both is responsible and has exercised control, they disagree about cases in which the less advantaged agent did not foresee the effects of his choices, and so lacked control over the ensuing disadvantage, but in which he *should* have foreseen these effects and therefore is responsible for them. When one person has less than another because he has done something whose bad effects he should have foreseen but did not, the version of luck egalitarianism that is couched in terms of control will imply that the resulting inequality is unjust, while the version that is couched in terms of responsibility will allow that it may well be just.[5]

III. Why the Distinction Matters

If cases of this sort were rare, then the fact that the different versions of luck egalitarianism disagree about them would not be terribly significant. However, far from being rare, such cases are very common. Although, of course, people do foolish things for many reasons—they may be weak-willed, may irrationally discount the future, may attach inordinate value to spontaneity, may be seduced by the pleasures of the moment, and so on—one very common enabling condition for each type of irrationality is precisely the agent's failure to bring into clear view the consequences of what he is doing. Although it may serve certain theoretical purposes to view each agent as fully aware of how each available act will affect him, or, at worst, as fully aware of the nature and likelihood of each possible outcome of each available act, the foolish acts that we encounter in the real world are very often performed by agents whose appreciation of their options is incomplete or distorted or blurred. Although muddled choices are especially characteristic of those who live disordered lives, they also account for much of the trouble that the rest of us make for ourselves.

To bring the issue into sharper focus, it will be helpful to have some specific cases before us. Here, therefore, are a few examples of what I have in mind.

---

[5] Richard Arneson notices the difference between these two versions of luck egalitarianism in his essay "Luck Egalitarianism Interpreted and Defended." However, Arneson does not discuss the full range of cases (or, in my opinion, the most important class of cases) about which the two versions disagree.

1. *Tattoo.* Whisper, at age nineteen, has drifted into the Goth lifestyle. Like her friends, she favors studded leather jackets, spiked dog collars, and elaborate tattoos. The one she chooses is an attractive vine: it sprouts from her navel, winds sinuously up her body, extends its leaves around her neck, and spreads up the left side of her face and across her forehead. Because the tattoo is so visible and so permanent, her subsequent employment choices are limited to minimum-wage jobs at coffeehouses and low-end bars.

2. *No Scholar.* Petey is an above-average student, but he is no scholar. Thus, no one is too surprised when he takes a leave from college to work as a roadie for a band. Petey recognizes the importance of returning to school and has every intention of doing so, but he misses the first year's reenrollment deadline and then stays away for a second year to be with his girlfriend. By the third year, his parents have become ill and need his care. Without ever deciding to, Petey has left school for good.

3. *Fondle.* Yielding to an impulse, Dr. Rosen, an oral surgeon, fondles an anesthetized patient whom he wrongly assumes to be unconscious. Horrified, the patient files a complaint, and Dr. Rosen's license is suspended for several years. When he regains it, his practice is gone. To make ends meet, Dr. Rosen is forced to become a staff dentist at Dancing Bear State Prison in California's remote central valley, in the shadow of the forbidding Diablo Hills.

4. *Hothead.* Salamandra is a competent employee, but she is a hothead. She frequently thinks others are treating her with disrespect, and when she feels slighted, she finds it unbearable to remain silent. Because her coworkers and supervisors find her outbursts disruptive, she rarely keeps a job for more than a few months. Over time, word of her temper gets around and she becomes unemployable.

5. *Balloon Payment.* Porter wants to buy a house and has fallen in love with a split-level priced beyond his range. To make the purchase possible, the mortgage company offers a larger-than-usual loan with a low monthly rate and a balloon payment. Expecting to refinance before making the final payment, Porter accepts the offer. When the real estate market declines, Porter can neither refinance nor meet the payment, and thus loses his home.

6. *Little One.* Ricia, a single woman, is pregnant and has decided to keep the baby. Although she has no real idea of who will watch the child when she is working, she hopes she can somehow muddle through. However, when the baby is born, she is unable to find a

suitable caregiver, and thus is forced to leave her job. As the years pass, her skills atrophy, and she spends the rest of her life on public assistance.

7. *Mule*. Whisper, whom we reencounter at age twenty-seven, has drifted southward, first to El Paso and then across the border to Juarez. There a recent acquaintance offers her five hundred dollars to transport some cocaine to the United States. Attracted by the opportunity to repay some debts, Whisper agrees, but she is apprehended when her tattoo attracts the attention of immigration officials. When she emerges from prison, she is saddled with a felony conviction that further degrades her already bleak employment prospects.

Because these cases are not described in much detail, it is possible to envision each agent as taking note of, but then deciding to ignore, the possible bad consequences of his or her act. However, it is also possible, and I think more realistic, to envision the agents as simply not thinking the issues through, and thus as not really registering just how badly wrong things might go. Although there obviously are degrees of clarity, there must be some threshold below which an agent is simply too unclear about the consequences of his act to be able to choose it in light of those consequences. It is true that anyone who lives on this planet must, in some sense, know that drug smugglers risk being caught and that real estate prices fluctuate. However, if an agent would grossly underestimate the risk if queried, and if his knowledge is buried so far below the surface of his consciousness that it plays no role in his deliberations and exerts no causal influence over his decision, then that knowledge is just too unconnected to his will to yield any meaningful form of control. In what follows, I will simply stipulate that Whisper, Dr. Rosen, and the others satisfy this description. If we understand them in this way, they nicely illustrate the manner in which a disadvantage can be a direct causal consequence of an agent's choices without being any part of what he has chosen.

IV. RESPONSIBLE BUT UNLUCKY

Because such cases are very common, a good deal of the inequality that surrounds us is bound to be due to choices of whose consequences the less-advantaged parties were unaware. Thus, if the two versions of luck egalitarianism disagree about the justice of such inequalities, then the difference between the versions will be substantial. But must the two versions really disagree? To show that they need not, someone might try to reconcile them in either of two ways. On the one hand, he might try to assimilate the luck-centric version to the responsibility-centric version by arguing that the disadvantages agents unwittingly bring upon themselves are not really matters of luck. On the other hand, he might try to assimilate the responsibility-centric version to the luck-centric version by arguing that those disadvantages are not really ones for which the agents are responsible. Let us consider these possibilities in turn.

The claim that unwittingly incurred disadvantages are not really due to luck can itself be defended in more than one way. The most familiar strategy is to relocate the disadvantaged party's exercise of control to some earlier point in his history. If someone who unwittingly acts foolishly has previously decided not to bother acquiring information that he knew would prevent him from doing so—if he has knowingly performed what Holly Smith calls a "benighting act"[6]—then even if he lacks control when he acts foolishly, he can plausibly be said to have exercised it when he made his earlier decision. Moreover, even if someone has performed no single benighting act, he may still have been aware that the cumulative effect of his choices was to prevent him from forming the sorts of intellectual habits which, if he now had them, would enable him to realize that he is acting foolishly. If someone's current failure to realize that he is acting foolishly can be traced to his previous decisions in either of these ways, then neither the resulting disadvantage nor the attendant inequality will be due to luck after all.

It is not hard to imagine Whisper and the others as having made just such decisions. We can, for example, envision Whisper as having smoked copious amounts of marijuana before entering the tattoo parlor, Petey as having avoided anyone who might try to convince him to return to school, and Dr. Rosen as having stubbornly refused the psychotherapy that his (now ex-) wife urged upon him. However, to establish that unwittingly incurred disadvantages are never or very rarely matters of luck, one would have to show not merely that those who incur them *sometimes* have exercised control at earlier points, but rather that they *almost always* have; and this last claim is far too strong to be credible. It is not at all unrealistic to suppose that Whisper has neither ingested any mind-altering substance nor done anything else that prevents her from recognizing the disastrous consequences of her choice of body art. Her lack of mental clarity may simply not be her doing. Also, of course, if Whisper can fail to realize that she is damaging her future prospects by getting a disfiguring tattoo, then she can also fail to realize that she is damaging her future prospects by smoking marijuana, and thus impairing her judgment, before setting off for the tattoo parlor.

Because there is often no previous moment at which someone who unwittingly acts foolishly has knowingly incurred the risk of doing so, we cannot close the gap between the two versions of luck egalitarianism by maintaining that even those self-inflicted disadvantages that appear to be due to luck are really due to earlier conscious choices. It may, however,

---

[6] See Holly Smith, "Culpable Ignorance," *The Philosophical Review* 92, no. 4 (October 1983): 543–71.

still seem possible to close the gap by denying that the form of control that is opposed to luck *requires* conscious choice. To exercise a luck-canceling form of control over a given outcome, it might be suggested, an agent need not actually recognize his action as likely to bring about that outcome, but need only satisfy some weaker condition—for example, that the outcome in fact be caused by his actions, that the outcome be one whose likelihood he should have recognized, or that his failure to recognize its likelihood be due to his character or psychological makeup. Because Whisper, Petey, Dr. Rosen, and the others can all plausibly be said to satisfy each weaker condition, understanding control in any of these ways would allow us to say that their disadvantages *were* within their control in the luck-canceling sense. This would close the gap between the two versions of luck egalitarianism because it would mean that any resulting inequalities are just as acceptable to the theory's luck-centric version as to its responsibility-centric version.

I proposed an account of control of roughly this sort in my 2006 essay "Out of Control," but I now think that account doesn't work.[7] One obvious problem is that it is, at best, linguistically awkward (and, at worst, incoherent) to speak of agents as exercising control over states of affairs of which they are unaware. However, in the current context, the more fundamental problem is that no such proposal seems consistent with the philosophical impulse that underlies the claim that luck and choice are opposed. When philosophers advance this claim—when they say, with Gerald Cohen, that "brute luck is an enemy of just equality, and, since effects of genuine choice contrast with brute luck, genuine choice excuses otherwise unacceptable inequalities"[8]—their guiding thought is clearly that the justice of any given inequality depends on whether having what is in fact the lesser amount is *part of what the less-advantaged party has chosen.* However, no one can choose to have a given amount of something without choosing to perform an act, or to acquiesce in an omission, that he expects to result *in* his having that amount. Thus, the contrast these philosophers are drawing must be between brute luck and whatever effects of an agent's choices he foresaw when he made them. However, if so, then when luck egalitarians assert that inequalities are only just if they are or were within the control of the less-advantaged parties, the form of control they have in mind must indeed be conscious control.

V. Unlucky But Responsible

Given all this, we cannot close the gap between the two versions of luck egalitarianism by expanding the scope of the disadvantages that we take

[7] George Sher, "Out of Control," *Ethics* 116, no. 2 (January 2006): 285–301. For cogent criticism, see Neil Levy, "Restoring Control: Comments on George Sher," *Philosophia* 36, no. 2 (June 2008): 213–21.
[8] Cohen, "On the Currency of Egalitarian Justice," 931.

to be, or to have been, within the relevant parties' control. But what, next, of the alternative strategy of contracting the scope of the disadvantages for which those parties are responsible? Here again, there are two possibilities to consider: the conclusion that the parties are not responsible for their disadvantages might be said to follow either from an adequate account of the conditions under which an agent is responsible, or from the fact that the psychological features that account for the parties' cognitive failures are external to their real identities.

Consider first the conditions for responsibility. It is widely agreed that to qualify as responsible for some feature or outcome of what he has done, an agent must satisfy both a volitional and an epistemic condition. He must, in some suitable sense, have been both free and adequately informed. Thus, one obvious way to narrow the scope of the disadvantages for which agents are responsible is to adopt a restrictive interpretation of responsibility's epistemic condition. There is, moreover, one familiar interpretation of that condition that is very restrictive indeed. Under this interpretation, the epistemic condition asserts that an agent is not responsible for a given feature or outcome of what he has done unless he realized that his act would have that feature or outcome when he performed it. Because this interpretation takes an agent's responsibility to extend no further than the features and outcomes of his actions that are illuminated by the searchlight of his consciousness, I have elsewhere referred to it as *the searchlight view.*[9]

Whisper, Petey, Dr. Rosen, and the others were not aware of the disadvantages they were incurring when they performed their actions. Thus, according to the searchlight view, they are not responsible for those disadvantages. When this conclusion is combined with the responsibility-centric version of luck egalitarianism, it implies that it is unjust for Whisper or Petey or Dr. Rosen to have fewer advantages than others. Because this is also what the luck-centric version says, the strategy of backing the responsibility-centric version with the searchlight view will indeed eliminate the gap between the two versions.

But this strategy is only as convincing as the searchlight view itself, and despite that view's undeniable popularity, I think there is good reason not to accept it. One obvious problem is that it conflicts with so many of our intuitive judgments about who is responsible for what. As the cases of Whisper, Petey, Dr. Rosen, and the others themselves show, we often *do* view agents as responsible for disadvantages they unwittingly inflict upon themselves (and, we may add, for harms they unwittingly do

---

[9] I introduce this term in *Who Knew?* For some representative discussions that assert or presuppose the searchlight view, see Barbara Herman, *The Practice of Moral Judgment* (Cambridge, MA: Harvard University Press, 1993), 99–101; R. Jay Wallace, *Responsibility and the Moral Sentiments* (Cambridge, MA: Harvard University Press, 1994), 139; Michael J. Zimmerman, "Moral Responsibility and Ignorance," *Ethics* 107 (April 1997): 410–26, esp. pp. 418 and 421; and Neil Levy, "Cultural Membership and Moral Responsibility," *The Monist* 86 (2003): 5.

to others).[10] If we accept the searchlight view, we must dismiss all such judgments as mistaken. Of course, by itself, this objection is hardly decisive, since despite the searchlight view's counterintuitive implications, we might be compelled to accept it if it could be given a sufficiently powerful independent defense. However, despite its familiarity, the searchlight view is very rarely defended, and the prospects for mounting a compelling defense do not seem bright.[11] Perhaps for these reasons, few actual proponents of the responsibility-centric version of luck egalitarianism have, in fact, paired it with the searchlight view. Instead, most take the common-sense position that even if an agent is not aware that he is acting foolishly, he may still be responsible for his act's consequences if these consequences are ones he *should* have foreseen (or, equivalently, if they are ones a reasonable person in his situation *would* have foreseen).

As this last parenthetical clause reminds us, what we think a given person should have foreseen depends on where we draw the line between him and his situation. When someone with poor eyesight fails to notice something that is clearly visible, we do not say that a reasonable person in his situation *would* have noticed it, because we naturally think of the poor eyesight as itself part of the agent's situation. Thus, a second possible way of getting Whisper, Dr. Rosen, and the others off the hook is to maintain that their gormlessness, too, is part of the situation that determines what they should realize. If it is, then they will not be responsible for their self-imposed disadvantages because a reasonable person in their situation—that is, one who, like them, happened to be afflicted with gormlessness—would not have realized that he was *incurring* any disadvantage. This conclusion, when combined with the responsibility-centric version of luck egalitarianism, will again imply that it is unjust for Whisper or Petey or Dr. Rosen to have fewer advantages than others. Because that is also what the luck-centric version implies, the strategy of externalizing the determinants of a person's failure to realize that he is acting imprudently represents a second way of bringing the two versions together by contracting the person's sphere of responsibility.

Although I know of no luck egalitarian who has explicitly taken this line, it remains worth considering because a number of theorists have said things that point naturally to it. One such philosopher is Ronald Dworkin, who acknowledges that his approach to equality "produces a certain view of the distinction between a person and his circumstances, and assigns his tastes and ambitions to his person, and his physical and mental powers to his circumstances."[12] Another is Richard Arneson, who at one point writes that "having preferences that increase the difficulty for the individual of delaying gratification can be an affliction on all fours

---

[10] For further examples, see Sher, *Who Knew?*, chap. 2.
[11] For discussion of some possible ways of defending the searchlight view, see Sher, *Who Knew?*, chaps. 3 and 4.
[12] Dworkin, "Equality of Resources," 302.

with suffering from asthma or chronic headaches,"[13] and who at another point asserts that we cannot reasonably expect as much from a person who "[finds] work extremely aversive" as we can from someone with a "zest for hard work."[14] These passages are relevant because once we have taken a person's circumstances to include his mental powers in general, and his reluctance to delay gratification and aversion to work in particular, it is hard to see on what principled grounds we might refuse to take his circumstances to include the (other) causes of his failure to realize that he is acting imprudently.

But precisely *because* the siphoning away of any of a person's mental powers is bound to create a powerful suction, there is a real danger that this strategy will undermine itself. It will be self-undermining if it commits us to exporting so many of an agent's features that there is no self left to be responsible for anything; for, in that case, the same considerations that bring the luck-centric and responsibility-centric versions of luck egalitarianism together will also empty the responsibility-centric version of its content. Thus, the challenge for those who seek to externalize the features that account for an agent's failure to realize that he is acting imprudently is to make sense of the "him" to whom those features are said to *be* external.

Because this challenge again raises questions that lie beyond the scope of this essay, I can do little more than register my deep skepticism that the challenge can be met. Expressed in the broadest terms, the reason for my skepticism is the degree to which the sources of the relevant failures are, or are entwined with, the dispositions, attitudes, and states that make up a person's character. Although my previous description of Whisper, Petey, and the others as gormless was obviously a shorthand, it seems equally obvious that any adequate expansion of it will have to specify the parties' characteristic attitudes and tendencies of thought. When Ricia does not face up to her inability to combine motherhood and work, the explanation may lie in her hostility to her disapproving parents, her tendency to engage in magical thinking, or her incurable optimism. When Dr. Rosen does not realize that he is jeopardizing his future, the reason may be that he is too arrogant to take such threats seriously or that he has poor impulse control. When Whisper fails to register the stigma to which she is exposing herself, her failure may reflect her deep passivity or her low sense of self-worth. In each of these cases and in innumerable others, the causes of the agent's failure to realize that he is acting imprudently cannot plausibly be attributed to his situation, because its causes are far too deeply implicated in the tangle of dispositions, attitudes, and traits that together make him the person he is.

---

[13] Arneson said this in the version of "Egalitarianism and the Undeserving Poor" that he delivered at the 1996 Annual Meeting of the American Political Science Association, but the quotation does not appear in the published version of that paper.

[14] Richard Arneson, "Equal Opportunity for Welfare Defended and Recanted," *The Journal of Political Philosophy* 7, no. 4 (1999): 489.

VI. Different Versions, Different Tasks

So far, we have seen that the two versions of luck egalitarianism yield different verdicts about the justice of many inequalities. On the one hand, the disadvantages incurred by Whisper, Petey, and Dr. Rosen are unforeseen and thus beyond their control, and are therefore the source of inequalities that the luck-centric version judges to be unjust. On the other hand, Whisper, Petey, and Dr. Rosen do seem responsible for the disadvantages that flow from their unwitting choices, and thus the resulting inequalities do *not* seem unjust according to the responsibility-centric version. But how, in that case, should we understand the many formulations of luck egalitarianism that blur the distinction between its two versions—assertions such as "it is bad if some people are worse off than others through no voluntary choice or fault of their own,"[15] and "the right cut is between responsibility and bad luck"?[16] When luck egalitarians say things like this, what are they saying about agents like Whisper and Petey and Dr. Rosen?

Before I can answer this question, I will have to make a brief detour through the theoretical underpinnings of luck egalitarianism. Like a proponent of any other normative theory, a defender of luck egalitarianism confronts both an analytical and a justificatory task. In its analytical aspect, his task is to explain exactly what he takes justice to require; in its justificatory aspect, it is to explain why we should *accept* his account of justice. Because what sets luck egalitarianism apart from other forms of egalitarianism is precisely its willingness to accept some inequalities as just, a crucial part of the analytical task is to account for the justice of these inequalities within the egalitarian rubric. (Another part, which I mention only to set it aside, is to provide a well-motivated answer to the question, "Equality of what?") By contrast, in its justificatory aspect, a crucial part of the luck egalitarian's task is to defend his account against various objections. Predictably, some of these, such as objections that appeal to property rights, maintain that the account goes too far in the direction of equality, while others, such as objections that appeal to the suffering of the disadvantaged, maintain that it does not go far enough. Of these two tasks, the analytical one is internal to the theory of egalitarianism, while the justificatory one is external to it.

The importance of the distinction between analysis and justification begins to emerge when we notice that the notions of choice and the absence of luck line up naturally with the luck egalitarian's analytical task, while the notion of responsibility lines up no less naturally with the justificatory one. In his magisterial early statement of luck egalitarianism, Ronald Dworkin made it very clear that his aim was fundamentally analytical. He said he wanted to articulate a version of egalitarianism that was "ambition sensitive"—elsewhere he has described it as "choice sensitive" [17]—and his rationale for wanting to do this was precisely that under equality of resources,

> [if someone] earns enough by working hard, or by working at work that no one else wants to do, to satisfy all his expensive tastes, then his choice for his own life costs the rest of the community no more than if his tastes were simpler and his industry less.[18]

By thus reconceptualizing equality as a relation between the advantages enjoyed by persons considered as temporally extended entities, and by tolerating inequalities that reflect people's choices about how to use their equal resources, Dworkin in effect offered an egalitarian response to Robert Nozick's purportedly anti-egalitarian observation that "liberty upsets patterns." [19] Because it emerged in the context of an attempt to develop an "attractive theoretical development of equality of resources," [20] the role that Dworkin assigned to choice (and so, by contrast, to its opposite, brute luck) was clearly internal to his theory of equality. Moreover, although I shall not argue the point, I think the case for assigning this sort of role to choice is just as strong if we say that what egalitarianism seeks to equalize is not resources but opportunities for welfare or advantage.

Significantly, terms like "fault" and "desert" do not appear in Dworkin's original analytical discussion. However, and in stark contrast, such terms do appear in many discussions that take the crucial division to be between disadvantages for which agents are responsible and those for which they are not. When luck egalitarians speak of disadvantages that agents are responsible for incurring, they very often go over into speaking of these disadvantages as deserved. To cite just one example, Nicholas Barry has recently written that

> luck egalitarianism, as I have interpreted it, is both an egalitarian and a desert based theory. It is desert based because it holds individuals accountable for their actions, arguing that people should enjoy the level of well-being that, through their actions, they deserve.[21]

This association of responsibility with desert is significant because attributions of desert have independent normative force. To say that some-

---

[17] See, e.g., Ronald Dworkin, *Sovereign Virtue: The Theory and Practice of Equality* (Cambridge, MA: Harvard University Press, 2000), 323.
[18] Dworkin, "Equality of Resources," 306.
[19] Robert Nozick, *Anarchy, State, and Utopia* (New York: Basic Books, 1974), 160.
[20] Dworkin, "Equality of Resources," 284.
[21] Nicholas Barry, "Defending Luck Egalitarianism," *Journal of Applied Philosophy* 23, no. 1 (2006): 102.

one deserves a disadvantage is to attribute some sort of value to his having it. Moreover, even without bringing in desert, many attach special moral significance to the advantages and disadvantages for which agents are responsible. In light of these facts, the introduction of responsibility in this context is best understood not as part of the luck egalitarian's specification of what equality requires, but rather as contributing to his justification of the proposed deviations from a more comprehensive equality.

Taken together, these considerations shed light on the underlying structure of luck egalitarianism. They suggest that its luck-centric version represents its core analytical idea, while its responsibility-centric version adds a justificatory element. More specifically, the responsibility-centric version is what we get when we combine the Dworkinian insight that supports the luck-centric version—the insight that to equalize the advantages that are available to people over their lifetimes, we must allow them to make choices that will lead to inequalities both in their welfare and in the resources they command—with a natural way of softening the impact of the fact that accepting such inequalities means allowing people to suffer the consequences of their foolish choices and unsuccessful gambles. Because the resulting inequalities can be glaring, and because they are easily portrayed as morally objectionable, it is not surprising that luck egalitarians have sought to block this objection by pointing out that the worse-off parties, who have chosen to incur or risk incurring their disadvantages, therefore deserve or are responsible for them. When we incorporate this observation into our description of the deviations from equality that are called for by a whole-life view of equality, we arrive at the responsibility-centric version of luck egalitarianism. And, hence, that version stands revealed as a hybrid which combines a partial account of what equality requires with a partial answer to the question of why we should embrace it.

VII. Resolving the Tension

If, when someone's opportunities match those of others, he consciously chooses to incur or risk a disadvantage, he becomes responsible both for that disadvantage and for any attendant inequality. Because such inequalities are precisely the ones that the luck-centric version of luck egalitarianism accepts as just, it follows that any inequality that is just according to the luck-centric version is also just according to the responsibility-centric version. However, there remains a tension between the two versions because an agent can also be responsible for a disadvantage that he has *not* consciously chosen to incur or risk. This is the tension that *Tattoo, No Scholar*, and my other examples (in Section III) were introduced to illustrate, and, to conclude, I will explain how the remarks of the previous section are relevant to this tension.

I have suggested that anyone who accepts the responsibility-centric version of luck egalitarianism must accept both (1) a principle of equality that endorses inequalities that reflect the choices of the less-advantaged parties, and (2) the view that there is value in people's getting what they deserve or living with outcomes for which they are responsible. Because these are distinct normative claims, anyone who accepts them both must be some sort of pluralist. However, within this general rubric, there are two sub-possibilities: one might hold either that the value of equality always dominates the value of responsibility or desert when these conflict, or that it does not. Bearing this distinction in mind, let us ask what luck egalitarians of each stripe would say about Whisper, Petey, Dr. Rosen, and the others.

Consider, first, the claim that desert and responsibility do have some independent weight, but that equality always dominates in cases of conflict. If a luck egalitarian holds this position, then he will happily take the value of an agent's getting what he deserves, or of his living with the outcomes for which he is responsible, to blunt the force of the objection that allowing agents to live with whatever disadvantages they chose to incur or risk is too harsh to be just; for this supplementary argument will be consistent with a principle of equality that classifies the attendant inequalities as just. By contrast, such a luck egalitarian will *not* take the value of desert or responsibility to justify any *unchosen* inequalities for which agents are responsible; for these inequalities will be classified as *unjust* by the principle of equality that he regards as dominant. Thus, to a luck egalitarian who believes that equality does dominate desert and responsibility, the inequalities that flow from the actions of Whisper, Petey, and the others will all be unjust.

But the other sort of pluralistic luck egalitarian, who thinks desert and responsibility have independent weight and that equality does *not* always dominate them in cases of conflict, will draw a very different conclusion. No less than the luck egalitarian who believes that equality does always dominate, he will happily invoke the value of an agent's getting what he deserves, or of his living with the outcomes for which he is responsible, to blunt the force of the objection that allowing him to live with the disadvantageous consequences of his previous choices is too harsh to be just. However, because this sort of luck egalitarian does not regard equality as the dominant factor in determining what justice requires, he will also hold that it can be just for someone to get what he deserves, or to live with disadvantages for which he is responsible, despite the fact that those disadvantages are unchosen and therefore are not endorsed by the principle of equality he favors. Hence, if a luck egalitarian believes that equality does not dominate desert or responsibility, then he will acknowledge that the inequalities that flow from the actions of Whisper, Petey, and the others are not necessarily unjust.

Of these two ways of combining the values of responsibility and desert with a theory of equality, which should we prefer? Should we take those values to be weighty enough to imply that it is not unjust for Whisper, Dr. Rosen, and Ricia to end up with less than others because of disadvantages that they neither foresaw nor chose but for which they are nevertheless responsible? Or should we say, instead, that because equality always takes priority over the values of responsibility and desert, the fact that these inequalities violate the favored principle of equality tells decisively in favor of mitigating them?

Because these questions again raise issues that lie far beyond the scope of the present essay, I will not try to answer them, but will simply end by registering my convictions on the matter. For what it's worth, I think that if we are going to be egalitarians at all, then a luck egalitarian is the best kind of egalitarian to be; and I think, further, that the best kind of luck egalitarianism is one that does not take equality to dominate all other values. This last conviction is based partly on my general resistance to absolute priority relations among normative considerations, but partly also on my intuitions about specific cases. I simply do not think it is always unjust for agents like Whisper and Dr. Rosen to have to live with consequences of their behavior that they did not choose but for which they are nevertheless responsible. There are, of course, many cases— perhaps some of the ones I have offered are among them—in which not mitigating even the richly deserved effects of people's folly *is* unacceptably harsh. However, to explain why mitigation is called for in such cases, we need not wheel in the heavy machinery of justice, but can instead appeal to simple humanity or charity.

VIII. Conclusion

When luck egalitarians urge the elimination of inequalities that are due to luck but not of inequalities for which the parties are responsible, the practical import of their position is unclear because many real-world inequalities satisfy both descriptions at once. To bring this out, I have presented a number of representative cases in which the agents seem responsible for the disadvantageous consequences of their acts despite the fact that they failed to anticipate, and thus were not in a position to exercise control over, those disadvantageous consequences. Because such cases are very common, the way the luck egalitarian handles them will significantly affect the amount of inequality that his view allows us to tolerate. Like most luck egalitarians, I believe these sorts of inequalities *can* be just; but unlike most luck egalitarians, I believe we will not be entitled to say this until we have gotten considerably clearer about the relation between the operative principle of equality and the requirement that we treat all persons as responsible agents.

Philosophy, Rice University

COERCION, OWNERSHIP, AND THE REDISTRIBUTIVE STATE: JUSTIFICATORY LIBERALISM'S CLASSICAL TILT*

By Gerald Gaus

I. Justificatory Liberalism and Substantive Liberal Conceptions

In the last few decades, a new conception of liberalism has arisen— "justificatory liberalism"[1]—which developed out of the social contract tradition. The social contract theories of Thomas Hobbes, John Locke, and Jean-Jacques Rousseau all stressed that the justification of the state depended on showing that everyone would, in some way, consent to it. By relying on consent, social contract theory seemed to suppose a voluntarist conception of political justice and obligation: what is just depends on what people choose to agree to—what they will. As David Hume famously pointed out, such accounts seem to imply that, ultimately, political justice derives from promissory obligations, which the social contract theory leaves unexplained.[2] Only in the political philosophy of Immanuel Kant, I think, does it become clear that consent is not fundamental to a social contract view: we have a duty to agree to act according to the "idea" of an "original contract" to which all agree.[3] John Rawls's revival of social contract theory in *A Theory of Justice* did not base obligations on consent, though the apparatus of an "original agreement" of sorts persisted. The aim of his famous "original position," Rawls announced, was to settle "the question of justification . . . by working out a problem of deliberation."[4] As the question of justification takes center stage (we might say: as contractualist liberalism becomes justificatory liberalism), it

---

* The ideas explored in this essay derive from discussions at a workshop on public reason, held in Tucson in November 2007, and were further developed at a talk to the Manchester Centre for Political Theory. I would like to thank all the participants, and especially Andrew Lister. His criticisms of my previous work led me to think about a number of matters in a new way. My thanks also to Fred D'Agostino, Tom Christiano, Steve Macedo, Jonathan Quong, Dave Schmidtz, Peter Vallentyne, and Kevin Vallier for their very helpful comments.

[1] Christopher J. Eberle applies this term to a family of liberal views I describe in the text, which stress that the basic requirement of a just and legitimate state is that it can be justified to all reasonable citizens. See Eberle, *Religious Conviction in Liberal Politics* (Cambridge: Cambridge University Press, 2002), 11–13.

[2] See David Hume, "Of the Original Contract," in his *Essays Moral, Political, and Literary* (Oxford: Oxford University Press, 1963), 452–73.

[3] See Immanuel Kant, *The Metaphysical Elements of Justice,* 2d ed., trans. John Ladd (Indianapolis: Hackett, 1999), secs. 42–43 (pp. 114–17), sec. 50 (p. 146).

[4] John Rawls, *A Theory of Justice,* rev. ed. (Cambridge, MA: Belknap Press of Harvard University Press, 1999), p. 16 (p. 17 of the original edition).

doi:10.1017/S0265052509990100

234 GERALD GAUS

becomes clear that posing the problem of justification in terms of a deliberative problem or a bargaining problem is a heuristic: the real issue is "the problem of justification"[5]—what principles can be justified to all rational and reflective persons seeking to live under impartial principles of justice.

Justificatory liberalism rests on a conception of members of the public as free and equal. To say that each individual is free implies that each has a fundamental claim to determine what are her obligations and duties. To say that each is equal is to insist that members of the public are symmetrically placed insofar as no one has a natural or innate right to command others or to impose obligations on them. Free and equal persons thus recognize no claims to natural authority over them. As Locke insisted, "the natural liberty of man is to be free from any superior power on earth, and not to be under the will or legislative authority of man, but to have only the law of Nature for his rule."[6] Given this conception of persons as free and equal, it follows that laws, because they use (and threaten to use) force, are deeply problematic: state functionaries employ power to force others to conform to the law, or they employ threats of force for the same purpose. On what grounds could anyone exercise such power and yet still claim that he is respecting the person (as free and equal) who is imposed upon?

In Kant's eyes, a crucial and necessary condition is that the person imposed upon by the law endorses the law as the thing to do: it is what her own reason instructs her to do, and so, as a rational person, it is what she wills to do. In Kant's terms, the person who is subject to the law may also be the legislator: because the law is endorsed by her own reasoning, she wills that the law be imposed, and is in this sense the legislator as well as a subject. A law that is rationally willed by a person, Kant and his followers have insisted, treats her as free and equal (qua legislator) even though (qua subject) she is bound to obey. "A rational being belongs to the realm of ends as a member when he gives universal laws in it while also himself subject to these laws. He belongs to it as sovereign when he, as legislator, is subject to the will of no other."[7] Justificatory liberalism thus starts out with the idea of "free persons who have no authority over one another"[8] and seeks to see how their reason can lead each of them to freely accept common laws to which they are subject.

When the state issues a law, it typically commands citizens to act and, further, threatens them with fines and imprisonment unless they obey.

[5] Ibid.

[6] John Locke, *Second Treatise of Government*, in *Two Treatises of Government*, ed. Peter Laslett (Cambridge: Cambridge University Press, 1960), sec. 21.

[7] Immanuel Kant, *Foundations of the Metaphysics of Morals*, ed. and trans. Lewis White Beck (Indianapolis: Bobbs-Merrill, 1959), 52 [Akademie ed., 433–34].

[8] John Rawls, "Justice as Fairness," in Samuel Freeman, ed., *John Rawls: Collected Papers* (Cambridge, MA: Harvard University Press, 1999), 55.

Such laws are clearly not simply pieces of advice or guidelines: they are required courses of action that the state insists upon whether or not a citizen agrees. As such, it seems that the citizen is simply subject to the authority of the state, and is certainly not treated as free and equal in relation to the will of the governors. If, however, qua impartial, rational, and reflective agents (which may not be the same as actual citizens with all their biases and short-sightedness), the citizens rationally endorse the law and its penalties, then the citizens also can be seen as its legislators. Only laws that are "publicly justified" in this way—those that can be shown in some way to be endorsed by the reason of all members of the public (see Section III below)—can respect all citizens as free and equal. Laws that cannot be endorsed by the reason of some citizens are authoritarian: some individuals claim the right to rule others and determine their obligations, and thus do not respect those others as free and equal persons. *"Respect for others requires public justification of coercion:* that is the clarion call of justificatory liberalism."[9]

My concern in this essay is not to provide a case for justificatory liberalism, but to investigate its relation to what we might call "substantive" liberalisms. Justificatory liberalism is liberal in an abstract and foundational sense: it respects each individual as free and equal, and so insists that coercive laws must be justified to all members of the public. The liberal tradition, however, is typically associated with an enumeration of substantive commitments. Or rather, the liberal tradition evinces enduring disputes about the nature of its substantive commitments. Most fundamentally, since the end of the nineteenth century, liberals have disagreed about the proper extent of the state. On the classical view, the main tasks of the justified state are to protect individual freedom and secure a regime of extensive private property rights—that is, an economic system in which owners have an extensive bundle of rights over their property and in which the range of resources and assets subject to private ownership is extensive.[10] While in classical liberalism these are the core functions of the justified state, it is by no means a dogma of classical liberalism that they are the sole functions: classical liberals also typically endorse the provision of public goods and improvements, education, poor relief, as well as financial, health, and safety regulations.[11] Still, though classical liberalism

---

[9] Eberle, *Religious Conviction in Liberal Politics,* 54 (emphasis in the original).

[10] I explore these dimensions in more detail in my essay "The Idea and Ideal of Capitalism," in Tom Beauchamp and George Brenkert, eds., *The Oxford Handbook of Business Ethics* (Oxford: Oxford University Press, 2009).

[11] The classic work on the economic policy of classical liberal political economy is Lionel Robbins, *The Theory of Economic Policy in English Classical Political Economy* (London: Macmillan, 1961). Perhaps the most sophisticated classical analysis of the functions of government is Book V of John Stuart Mill, *The Principles of Political Economy* (1848), in J. M. Robson, ed., *The Collected Works of John Stuart Mill* (Toronto: University of Toronto Press, 1977), vol. 3. See also my essay "Public and Private Interests in Liberal Political Economy, Old and New," in S. I. Benn and G. F. Gaus, eds., *Public and Private in Social Life* (New York: St. Martin's, 1983), 192–93.

is not committed to a "minimal state,"[12] it certainly endorses a far less extensive state than most contemporary "egalitarian" or "social justice" liberals insist is required. It is widely thought today that core liberal values require that the state regulate the distribution of resources or well-being to conform to principles of fairness, that all citizens be assured of employment and health care, that no one be burdened by mere brute bad luck, and that citizens' economic activities must be regulated to insure that they do not endanger the "fair value" of rights to determine political outcomes.[13] In John Rawls's canonical formulation of this expansive version of liberalism, a variety of new "branches" of government are added to the liberal state: a branch to keep the price system competitive, a branch to bring about full employment, a transfer branch to ensure that the least well off have the resources demanded by justice, and a distribution branch that adjusts the rights of property "to prevent concentrations of power detrimental to the fair value of political liberty and fair equality of opportunity."[14]

It is widely thought that all forms of justificatory liberalism must endorse this latter, expansive understanding of the liberal state. No doubt this partly can be explained by the fact that Rawls's theory is both the most prominent instance of justificatory liberalism and the preeminent defense of the expansive conception of the liberal state. Moreover, both Rawls and his followers have insisted that the more extreme, "libertarian," versions of the classical view are not genuinely liberal, reinforcing the supposition that the justificatory liberal approach is hostile to substantive liberalisms that endorse wide-ranging limits on government authority.[15] Indeed, Rawls condemns classical liberalism *and* welfare state capitalism as unjustifiable political-economic systems.[16] According to Rawls, "laissez-faire capitalism" (or, as he sometimes calls it, "the system of natural liberty") is unjust: its regulative principles would not be agreed to by free and equal persons seeking impartial principles of justice. Because laissez-faire capitalism (1) does not require constitutional guarantees of "the fair value of the equal political liberties," so that all have real political power (more on

[12] It is thus unfortunate that so many have viewed Robert Nozick's somewhat doctrinaire defense of the "night-watchman state" as definitive of the classical liberal tradition. See his *Anarchy, State, and Utopia* (New York: Basic Books, 1974), 25-27. On the relation between libertarianism and classical liberalism, see Eric Mack and Gerald Gaus, "Classical Liberalism and Libertarianism: The Liberty Tradition," in Gerald F. Gaus and Chandran Kukathas, eds., *Handbook of Political Theory* (London: Sage Publications, 2004), 115-30.
[13] See Rawls, *A Theory of Justice*, rev. ed., 197ff.
[14] Ibid., 242-51. Rawls also believes that a just society would seek reasonable ways to limit wasteful forms of advertising: "the funds now devoted to advertising can be released for investment or for other useful social ends." John Rawls, *Political Liberalism* (New York: Columbia University Press, 1996), 365.
[15] John Rawls, *The Law of Peoples* (Cambridge, MA: Harvard University Press, 1999), 48; Samuel Freeman, "Illiberal Libertarians: Why Libertarianism Is Not a Liberal View," *Philosophy and Public Affairs* 30 (2001): 105-51.
[16] Rawls, *Justice as Fairness: A Restatement*, ed. Erin Kelly (Cambridge, MA: Harvard University Press, 2001), 135ff.

this in Section IV.A below), and (2) allows only "a low social minimum" and thus does not have institutions in place that aim to maximize the long-term prospects of the least well-off, it follows that less-advantaged free and equal persons do not have reasons to endorse it. More surprisingly, Rawls holds that even "welfare-state capitalism" fails the test of justifiability. It too allows for inequalities of wealth that, in Rawls's eyes, undermine the fair value of citizen's political rights. "It permits very large inequalities in the ownership of real property (productive assets and natural resources) so that the control of the economy and much of the political life rests in a few hands." Of the five political-economic systems he discusses—laissez-faire capitalism, welfare-state capitalism, state socialism, liberal (market) socialism, and a "property-owning democracy"—Rawls rejects as unjust both systems that he describes as "capitalist." He allows as possible just regimes one form of socialism (market socialism) and a "property-owning democracy" that allows private property but works "to disperse the ownership of wealth and capital, and thus to prevent a small part of society from controlling the economy and, indirectly, political life as well." [17]

Classical liberals who are also justificatory liberals must address two questions. First, is there a sound case for the classical version in justificatory liberal terms, or is classical liberalism somehow at odds with the justificatory project, so that all reasonable versions of justificatory liberalism must reject what Rawls calls "the system of natural liberty"? In a previous essay, I have argued that there is a strong justificatory liberal case for classical liberal rights.[18] This, I think, defeats the claim that justificatory liberalism necessarily endorses a strongly egalitarian theory of justice or even (what Rawls considers insufficiently egalitarian) an expansive welfare state. It may appear, however, that the upshot of this is that justificatory liberalism is an entirely neutral framework with respect to this long-running dispute within liberalism—the very nature of the justificatory project, it may be thought, does not incline toward either view, but reasonable defenses of both versions can be accommodated within justificatory liberalism. Hence the second question that classical liberals who are also justificatory liberals must address: Is justificatory liberalism a neutral framework, or does it incline toward, or tend to favor, some substantive liberalisms?

In this essay I argue for two main claims. (1) Rawls and his followers are fundamentally mistaken when they claim that free and equal persons seeking impartial principles of justice would reject all forms of "capitalism" (either the system of natural liberty or the welfare state). Quite the opposite: there is an overwhelming case that such persons would insist

---

[17] Ibid., 138.
[18] Gerald F. Gaus, "On Justifying the Moral Rights of the Moderns: A Case of Old Wine in New Bottles," *Social Philosophy and Policy* 24, no. 1 (2007): 84–119.

on either some form of capitalism or, perhaps, a property-owning democracy (it is hard to know precisely what such a system would look like.)[19] They would conclusively reject all forms of socialism, including market socialism. (2) The core principles of the justificatory project, I shall argue, incline toward the classical end of the continuum regarding the redistributive functions of the state. The very nature of the project does not exclude the welfare state or even more egalitarian versions of capitalism, but, *pace* Rawls, those versions are more, not less, difficult to justify than a more limited governmental authority.

I begin in Sections II and III by reviewing the core commitments of justificatory liberalism, understood as a family of political views: the presumption in favor of liberty (Section II), and the principle of public justification (Section III). Section IV examines an ambitious thesis: properly understood, justificatory liberalism *only* justifies the classical version of liberalism and its stress on the primacy of ownership. I argue that, while this ambitious thesis involves an important insight, it fails. Section V builds on this insight and establishes a more moderate thesis: while justificatory liberalism admits as reasonable both classical, welfare-statist, and some egalitarian liberalisms, it inclines toward classical formulations. Section VI argues that the spirit of justificatory liberalism is neither egalitarian nor libertarian, but Millian.

II. THE POLITICAL LIBERTY PRINCIPLE

A. The presumption in favor of liberty

A wide variety of philosophers have held that basic to any genuinely liberal view of politics is a general presumption in favor of liberty and, thus, against legal restrictions. As Joel Feinberg puts it, "liberty should be the norm, coercion always needs some special justification."[20] Stanley Benn states the principle even more expansively, in terms of a presumption against *all* "interference," not simply coercion by the law. His grounding principle of morality is that one who is simply acting as he sees fit is under no standing obligation to justify his actions to others, while those who interfere with his actions are under an obligation to justify their interference.[21] Rawls agrees with Feinberg in focusing on the law (though perhaps making room for Benn's concern with non-legal interferences) but clearly follows Benn in extending the principle beyond mere coercion,

---

[19] Rawls was greatly influenced here by J. E. Meade, *Efficiency, Equality, and the Ownership of Property* (London: Allen and Unwin, 1964), chap. 5; and Richard Krouse and Michael McPherson, "Capitalism, 'Property-Owning Democracy,' and the Welfare State," in Amy Gutmann, ed., *Democracy and the Welfare State* (Princeton, NJ: Princeton University Press, 1988). For a discussion of possible policies of such a system, see Richard Dagger, "Neo-Republicanism and the Civic Economy," *Politics, Philosophy, and Economics* 5 (2006): 151–73.
[20] Joel Feinberg, *Harm to Others* (New York: Oxford University Press, 1984), 9.
[21] Stanley Benn, *A Theory of Freedom* (Cambridge: Cambridge University Press, 1988), 87.

identifying legal "restrictions" as requiring justification: "there is a general presumption against imposing legal and other restrictions on conduct without sufficient reason." [22] Since we are concerned here with liberalism as a political doctrine, and in particular with the legitimacy of state activities, it will help if we restrict our attention to the presumption in favor of liberty as it applies to the law; and let us further restrict our attention to the law's use of force and coercion. Let us, then, focus on liberalism's commitment to the *Political Liberty Principle:*

(1) A citizen is under no standing obligation to justify her actions to the state.
(2) All use of force or coercion by the state against the persons of its citizens requires justification; in the absence of such justification, such force or coercion by the state is unjust.

The Political Liberty Principle regulates political justification, and deems state force or coercion without the requisite justification to be a case of injustice.[23] As Benn says, "justifications and excuses presume at least prima facie fault, a charge to be rebutted." [24] If I have no justificatory burden, I am permitted to act without justification—I have no charge to rebut, no case to answer. If the onus is on you, the failure to justify condemns your act. Conceivably, a conception of political morality might place the onus on the actor: "Never act unless one can meet the justificatory burden by showing that one is allowed to act." [25] The liberal insists that citizens have no such general burden to bear, though of course they may bear the onus of justification in special contexts in which a restriction already has been established (say, trusteeships).

Now as Rawls rightly insists, "this presumption creates no special priority for any particular liberty": it does not serve to identify some liberties as especially important. To identify a particular liberty as having a priority in the sense of an enforceable right itself requires justification. Suppose Alf claims to possess an enforceable right to speak in a political forum, and Betty exercises her freedom to play loud music at the same time and place. By claiming that his freedom is a right, Alf claims a ground to interfere with Betty's playing of music—he claims that she can be made to stop, by the police if necessary. But that, of course, is to call on the state to coercively interfere with her actions, and, like all such interferences, claims of rights must be justi-

<hr/>

[22] Rawls, *Justice as Fairness,* 44.
[23] This is not to say that the presumption in favor of liberty does not itself have to be argued for. See my *Value and Justification* (Cambridge: Cambridge University Press, 1990), 379ff.
[24] Benn, *A Theory of Freedom,* 87.
[25] I consider such a presumption in some detail in *Value and Justification,* 381–86.

fied.[26] The presumption in favor of liberty does not, then, identify special liberties as deserving special protection. Nevertheless, Rawls acknowledges that even when a basic protected liberty is not at stake, "liberties not counted as basic are satisfactorily allowed for by the general presumption against legal interference."[27] There is always a standing presumption against legal interference: those who endorse a legal interference must bear a justificatory burden, not those who wish to remain free.

The presumption in favor of liberty, and thus against coercive laws, is easily misunderstood. Some view it as a libertarian principle because it "privileges" liberty. But this is to confuse liberalism with libertarianism. Libertarianism is a wide-ranging doctrine about the strength and priority of certain liberty or property rights in relation to other claims. The presumption of liberty does not imply that liberty always, or even usually, trumps other values: the presumption identifies what does, and what does not, stand in need of justification. The liberal does not remain neutral between those who would use the law to regulate the lives of others and those who wish to remain unregulated: it is the would-be regulator who must bear the justificatory burden. (That Benn, Feinberg, and Rawls— none of whom are remotely libertarian—advocate the principle itself should make us doubt the force of the claim that the presumption presupposes a libertarian view.)

Others dispute the presumption on the grounds that "there is no standing duty to justify morally relevant actions."[28] We might interpret this objection as involving four different claims:

(1) If the state has shown that φ is a morally required or permitted action, the state is under no burden to *show* that φ-ing is justified.
(2) If, as a matter of fact, φ is a morally required or permitted action, there need not *be* a justification for the state φ-ing.
(3) If the state believes that φ is a morally required or permitted action, the state need not *have* a justification for its belief and for acting on it.
(4) If the state reasonably believes that φ is a morally required or permitted action, the state need not *show it has* a justification for φ-ing.

Interpretation (1) is not a coherent challenge to the presumption: to show that one has a morally relevant ground for interference simply *is* to justify

---

[26] Loren E. Lomasky and I argue this point in more detail in "Are Property Rights Problematic?" *The Monist* 73 (October, 1990): 483–503.

[27] Rawls, *Justice as Fairness*, 112.

[28] Rainer Frost, "Political Liberty: Integrating Five Conceptions of Autonomy," in John Christman and Joel Anderson, eds., *Autonomy and the Challenges to Liberalism* (Cambridge: Cambridge University Press, 2005), 240 n. 24.

one's action, so this does not dispute the presumption. This is important: showing that something is morally permitted simply is showing that one has a justification of doing it. Nor does interpretation (2) offer a plausible basis for disputing the presumption. If, as a matter of fact, ϕ is morally required, then there *is*, in principle, a justification for ϕ—viz., the reasons why it is morally required. To be sure, one might hold that ϕ is required but no one knows why, and so there is no justification for it, but this is hardly a compelling view of political morality. Interpretation (3) involves, I think, a genuine substantive disagreement. Here it is being said that, if the state holds that ϕ is morally permitted or required, it may go ahead and ϕ even if it *has* no justification for its belief or for acting on that belief. For the state to have no justification for ϕ-ing amounts to it not having access to good reasons for its conclusion that ϕ is morally required or permitted. Here, I think, the liberal parts ways with the objector, if the objector holds that there is nothing wrong when the state goes ahead and uses coercion on the grounds that doing so is morally permitted, even though it does not itself have access to the considerations that establish why it is morally permitted. It is not enough that there *be* some unknown moral grounds that allow coercion. At least some state actors—those who have authorized the act—must be cognizant of the grounds. The point of morality is essentially practical: we seek to employ it as the basis for our reasoning and choices. Unless the state has access to these reasons when it makes choices, it acts with manifest disrespect for the freedom and equality of its citizens. Recall Rawls's key insight: we start out with the assumption of free and equal persons who have no authority over one another, and thus all claims to authority—including the authority to interfere with others on moral grounds—are subject to the requirement that they be justified.[29] Interpretation (4) is more reasonable. Of course, the state (all the agents of the state involved in the action) need not always show each and every person that the relevant actors have good moral reasons for what they are doing whenever they are challenged. Certainly, however, a government of free citizens—a government that respects citizens as free and equal persons—must include forums where citizens are shown these justifying reasons.

It is also important to stress that the presumption in favor of liberty does not ignore the fundamental truth that state force and coercion often prevent a great deal of private force and coercion. Some argue that, if the state does not act through coercive laws, there will be great private coercion, and thus the presumption in favor of liberty does not really protect liberty: people will simply be subject to private rather than public coercion. The great insight of the social contract theorists was that preventing

---

[29] The way in which morality involves claims to authority over others is a central theme of Stephen Darwall, *The Second-Person Standpoint: Morality, Respect, and Accountability* (Cambridge, MA: Harvard University Press, 2006).

unjustified private force and coercion is the main justification of state force and coercion. As Kant understood it, the state replaces private force and coercion with "public lawful coercion."[30] That state coercion must be justified only requires that a sufficient reason for it be advanced: that it is the best way to prevent a great deal of unjustified private coercion is certainly such a reason.

B. Coercion and rights of the person

The Political Liberty Principle supposes that we can make sense of the idea of legal force and coercion. Many, though, are skeptical that this can be done. The last forty years have witnessed a number of fundamentally divergent accounts of coercion.[31] It is widely agreed that coercion typically involves some sort of threat of harm by which the "coercer" gets (or aims at getting) the "coercee" to do as he wishes, but there is considerable disagreement about what constitutes a threat of harm, whether all such threats are coercive, and so on. Now it might be thought that if we cannot agree on a general account of coercion, we cannot usefully employ the idea in the Political Liberty Principle. But this would be far too skeptical a conclusion: philosophical theories that seek to provide a biconditional analysis of a concept (i.e., A is an act of coercion if and only if conditions $C_1 \ldots C_n$ are met) are notoriously subject to counterexamples and controversy; we typically have a far better grasp of the use of an idea than we have of the philosophical analysis of it. Moreover, the Political Liberty Principle does not require a general analysis of coercion, but only an analysis of its application to the actions of the state against its citizens.

What makes the state—even a legitimate one—especially morally problematic to the liberal is that it employs force, or threatens to use force, against the persons of its citizens.[32] This is certainly only a subset of the many ways in which one can coerce another. If Alf threatens to destroy Betty's beloved painting—which *he* owns—if she does not agree to move to Australia with him, he may plausibly be said to coerce her into moving without threatening her person (he threatens to harm his own property). To be sure, some states do employ similar means (we are tempted to label them as "blackmail"): they threaten, for example, a dissident's family or friends with harm to get her to conform, or they threaten to banish her children from university if she does not cooperate with the regime. These

---

[30] Kant, *The Metaphysical Elements of Justice*, 115–16 [Akademie ed., 311–13]. See also the "Translator's Introduction," xxxv–xxxix.

[31] For an excellent survey, see Scott Anderson's entry on "Coercion" in *The Stanford Encyclopedia of Philosophy* (Spring 2006 edition), ed. Edward N. Zalta, http://plato.stanford.edu/archives/spr2006/entries/coercion/.

[32] This is not to say that coercion against noncitizens does not require justification; it simply falls outside the scope of the Political Liberty Principle, which specifies a necessary, not a sufficient, condition for justified coercion.

uses of coercion are subject to special condemnation: they are not the modus operandi of the liberal state. Liberal legal restrictions require compliance, and if compliance is not forthcoming the citizen is typically threatened with the use of force *against his person,* not simply a harm to what he cares for. The police will come and use force against his person, and may imprison him. This, indeed, is a quintessential case of coercion. A reason to reject the claim that all instances of coercion involve a threat to violate the rights of another[33] is that, even in a condition such as Hobbes's state of nature (in which everyone has a blameless liberty to do as he thinks necessary, and thus no one has claim rights to noninterference), we can sensibly and importantly say that people are coercing each other.[34] Indeed, the idea of replacing such private, lawless coercion with public, lawful coercion is an important theme in Kant's social contract theory.[35] Applying the concept of coercion (and, of course, force) makes sense even in relations among purely "natural persons"—those whom we do not consider bearers of rights.

However, coercion by the state typically does involve a threat against a citizen's rights, for in political society one's person is largely defined—and expanded—by one's rights. This idea of the expansion of legal personhood through rights was central to Kant's analysis of property. To own a thing is not simply to have possession of it, or even stable, secure, recognized possession. It is to enter into a juridical relation such that "any hindrance of my use of it would constitute an injury to me, even when I am not in [physical] possession of it (that is, when I am not a holder of the object)."[36] Once property rights are justified, a threat by the state to take my property is a threat against me: to take my property is to do an injury to me as a juridical person. Without property rights, you only do injury to me by taking my possession if you use force against my person (narrowly construed), or threaten to, when taking it. If I should put it down and walk away, it would be no injury to me for you to take it, and so it would be no threat against my person to threaten to take it away under these circumstances.[37] However, if it is my property, the injury is done not by reason of physical possession but by an extension of the bounds of my person to include my relation to it. Thus, when the state threatens to fine me for noncompliance, it threatens me, just as surely as if it threatens imprisonment.

---

[33] See Alan Wertheimer, *Coercion* (Princeton, NJ: Princeton University Press, 1987), 277ff.
[34] I defend this interpretation of Hobbes in *Value and Justification,* 275ff.
[35] Kant's view is complex; though we have private rights in the state of nature, because there is no impartial judge about their contours, the state of nature also is characterized by an absence of public claims of justice; the idea of the social contract is to establish public justice and rights. Kant, *Metaphysical Elements of Justice,* 115–16 [Akademie ed., 312].
[36] Ibid., 45 [Akademie ed., 249].
[37] To be sure, there may be an intelligible sense in which I still might be said to coerce you: "If you don't do what I want, I will pick up your possession the next time you put it down!" Again, though, a general account of coercion (if one is to be had) is not my aim.

GERALD GAUS

C. The order of justification

If our core concern is the state's use of force or the threat of force against the person of the citizen, and if the juridical boundaries of the person expand with her set of rights, then what constitutes a coercive threat against her person will also expand. This implies that the order of justification may affect the outcome of what is justified. On the one hand, if we assume, say, only natural personhood, or even simply rights of bodily integrity narrowly construed, then the state's demand that you conform to law *L* or else it will take away your "property" (qua stable, recognized possessions) will not involve a direct threat against your person, since you have no juridical relation to such "property." Thus, there would be no onus of justification on the state: it could, say, tax away those possessions at will (see Section IV.D below). On the other hand, if we understand you to have a justified property right, then the state would bear such an onus, and it must justify this threat against you.

Despite first appearances, this is not, I think, a counterintuitive implication of the Political Liberty Principle. We will see in Section IV that many of the disagreements between classical and egalitarian liberals stem from disputes about the order of justification, and, in particular, about where the justification of the rights of ownership enters into an account of liberal justice. All liberals agree that at the core of their theory are persons with rights to bodily integrity, freedom of association, and freedom of conscience and speech. As we will see, the question is: At what point does the person include her property?

III. Public Justification and the Deliberative Model

A. The Public Justification Principle

The Political Liberty Principle places the onus of justification on the state for the use of force and coercive threats against the persons of its citizens. The *(Generic) Public Justification Principle* determines how this onus can be met:

> *L* is a justified coercive law only if each and every member of the public *P* has conclusive reason(s) *R* to accept *L* as binding on all.

An unjustified law fails to treat each person as free and equal.[38] Our question is: When, if ever, does a coercive law treat all as free and equal?

[38] The Public Justification Principle supposes that a justified law must be genuinely authoritative: it is endorsed by all members of the public as binding—as generating obligations to obey. A bona fide law is not simply an act of state coercion, but an act of state authority, and so binds citizens. This is the legal expression of Kant's notion of the realm of ends, in which recognizing the law's authority over us is consistent with each person's acting on her own reasons. Contemporary political philosophy is deeply skeptical that the law generally has justified authority to direct citizens' acts. To many, the most the law could

Because I am concerned with a family of justificatory liberalisms, I focus on a generic formulation of the Public Justification Principle. Because this is a generic principle, I leave open the crucial problem of just how to specify P (whether the members must all be reasonable, fully rational, etc.). The Public Justification Principle supposes that the relevant justificatory public is an idealization of the actual citizenry (throughout, I will use "member of the public" as a term of art to identify this idealized public). Whereas many in the actual citizenry may act on pure self-interest, hate, or spite, or may reason on the basis of obviously false empirical theories, or may make manifestly invalid inferences, the idealized members of the public make sound inferences from appropriate and relevant values, drawing on sound empirical claims. Justificatory liberals differ in just how far they press this idealization. One Kantian specification of P is highly idealized—the realm of rational beings—and insofar as we act as members of P, we act fully in accord with our status as rational moral beings. Rawls relies on a more modest idealization: a conception of persons who, as reasonable, recognize the severe limits of human reason. In filling out a justificatory view, it is critical to provide a compelling specification of P; because our interest here is in a family of justificatory views, we can for the most part leave this issue open (see, though, Section III.B).

Note that the Public Justification Principle maintains that a coercive law L applying to public P is justified only if every member of P has *conclusive* reason to endorse L as binding. This is crucial. To sees its motivation, assume that Alf and Betty are both members of P, and Alf proposes law L_A. Suppose that Alf can advance *a reason* R_1 for Betty to endorse L_A, but Betty's system of beliefs and values is such that while as a member of P she acknowledges that R_1 is a reason for endorsing L_A, she also holds that she has reason R_2, which is a reason to endorse L_B over L_A (where L_A and L_B are incompatible alternatives). Suppose that, exercising her reason as a free and equal member of the public, Betty concludes that R_2 outweighs (or defeats) R_1, and thus she concludes that L_B is better than L_A. Now some insist that, nevertheless, Alf has provided a justification of

hope to achieve is a certain legitimacy, in the sense that the laws of the state are morally permissible acts of coercion, but do not in general bind citizens to obey. Thus, in place of the Public Justification Principle, we might adopt a Weak Public Justification Principle: "L is a justified coercive law only if each and every member of the public P has conclusive reason(s) R to accept that coercive acts enforcing L are morally permissible." The Weak Public Justification Principle does not suppose that laws are acts of self-legislation which all citizens have reason to obey, but simply that force and coercion by the state are permissible—though resisting them may be permissible too. For many, that is enough—indeed, the most that can be hoped for. I am dubious. The concept of law implied by this view renders laws too much like coercive demands in Hobbes's state of nature: they are not wrong, but neither is it in principle wrong to ignore them, or even fight back. However, I leave this matter unresolved in this essay. If one is convinced that the most we can hope for is such "legitimacy," one can substitute the weak version of the Public Justification Principle in what follows: the essence of the analysis is not affected.

L_A insofar as he has offered a nonsectarian reason R_1 in support of L_A—a reason that, as a free and equal member of the public, Betty can appreciate.[39] Yet, exercising her capacities as a free and equal person, Betty has concluded that, when compared to L_B, L_A is inadequately justified in the sense that it is not choice-worthy; as she understands it, she has more reason to endorse L_B. For Alf (even if Alf is the head of state) to *simply* impose L_A on Betty is inconsistent with treating her as a free and equal member of the public. The critical question is not whether Betty has *some* reason to endorse L_A, but whether, all things considered, she has reason to endorse L_A *over the alternatives*, or even over no law at all. If she has some reason to endorse L_A, but more reason to endorse an alternative, then what economists call the "opportunity costs" of choosing L_A exceed the benefits: she would be opting for a law that achieves less of what she values over one that achieves more. Therefore, only a justification that showed she had conclusive reasons—the benefits outweighed the opportunity costs—would show that she has reason to endorse the law.

B. Reasonable pluralism

Most political theories can endorse the Public Justification Principle as I have stated it: if the members of the public are so specified that they all accept, say, a certain substantive moral theory, the laws justified by that theory would also be justified by the Public Justification Principle. The principle would do little or no work. The Public Justification Principle becomes an interesting test—and also more obviously part of the liberal tradition—if we accept Rawls's claim that a wide range of rational disagreement is the "normal result of the exercise of human reason."[40] Suppose, then, that we accept pluralism in the sense that our characterization of P's deliberation includes the fact that the members of the public reason on the basis of a wide variety of different values, ends, goals, etc. This does not prejudge whether values are "ultimately" plural, or whether some values are truly "agent-neutral." Perhaps fully rational, omniscient beings would agree on what is valuable, or recognize agent-neutral values. The important point is that, at the appropriate level of the idealization, members of P will be characterized by diversity in the basis of their reasoning about what laws to accept. That, after all, models the core problem of our pluralistic liberal societies.

Abstracting from the notions of goods, values, moral "intuitions," and so on, let us say that Σ is an evaluative standard for Alf qua member of P if holding Σ (along with various beliefs about the world) gives Alf a

[39] See George Klosko, "Reasonable Rejection and Neutrality of Justification," in Steven Wall and George Klosko, eds., *Perfectionism and Neutrality: Essays in Liberal Theory* (Lanham, MD: Rowman and Littlefield, 2003), 178.
[40] Rawls adds: "within the framework of free institutions of a constitutional regime" (*Political Liberalism*, xviii).

reason to endorse some law L. Again, different justificatory liberalisms advance different characterizations of evaluative standards: some may focus largely on self-interest; others on conceptions of the good or value; and others will also allow members of P to employ "moral intuitions" (though these will only provide reasons for those members of P who hold them). Evaluative standards are to be distinguished from justified laws. Evaluative standards need not meet the test of Public Justification, but they are the reasons for some member of the public to endorse or reject a law. Our problem is how to achieve the public justification of uniform coercive laws based on disparate individual evaluative standards.

Any plausible liberal justificatory account must acknowledge the diversity of evaluative standards in political justification (and thus recognize the importance of reasonable pluralism), but it also must limit the range of considerations that may be drawn upon in justification. Some limits are implicit in the very idea of public justification. Our concern is not simply whether the government and its officials respect each citizen as free and equal, but whether each citizen respects her fellows when she calls on the coercive force of the law. If each citizen is to respect her fellows as free and equal, each must have reason to suppose that the Public Justification Principle is met when calling on the force of the law; but that means that each citizen must think that the relevant evaluative standards, which are the grounds of each member of the public's deliberation, provide her with conclusive reasons to endorse the law. Qua member of the public, I cannot think that your deliberation based on standard Σ_X provides you (as another member of the public) with a reason to endorse a law as binding unless, in my view, Σ_X is an intelligible and reasonable basis for deliberation. That your unreasonable standard leads you to endorse L cannot lead me to think you have a reason to endorse L: garbage in, garbage out. Plausible justificatory liberalisms, then, must at least accept what we might call "mutually intelligible evaluative pluralism" *at the level of members of P*. Members of P will see themselves as deeply disagreeing about the basis for a law's acceptance, but will acknowledge that the bases of others' reasoning is intelligible and is appropriate to the justificatory problem.

C. The deliberative model

One of Rawls's fundamental insights was that the justificatory problem— what legal requirements (or social principles) do members of P have reason to endorse?—can be translated into a deliberative problem.[41] Suppose we understand a member i of P as consulting her relevant evaluative standards—the full set of considerations that are relevant to her decision about whether to endorse a law as binding. After consulting her evaluative standards, i proposes her preferred law, L_i—the law that, on her

---

[41] Rawls, *A Theory of Justice*, rev. ed., 16.

(somewhat idealized) reasoning, best conforms to her evaluative standards. (This procedure parallels the one utilized by Rawls in his essay "Justice as Fairness.")[42] At no point do the parties bargain: each member of P consults her evaluative standards and proposes what she understands to be the best law. Suppose that, having each proposed her preferred candidate, each then (sincerely) employs her evaluative standards to rank all proposals.

This simple statement of the deliberative problem has decisive advantages over more familiar formulations. One of the shortcomings of much contemporary contractualism is that it employs a notion of reasonable acceptability (or rejectability) without being clear about the option set: to ask what one can reasonably accept (or reject) without knowing the feasible alternatives is an ill-formed choice problem. The crucial question is: "Rationally rejectable in relation to what options?" In our deliberative problem, the feasible set is defined by the set of all proposals. Rawls never made this common contractualist mistake: the parties to his original position in *A Theory of Justice* choose among a small set of traditional proposals, so their choice problem is well-defined. However, Rawls built into his later and more famous formulations of the deliberative problem a host of controversial conditions. In contrast, we can depict the deliberative problem as a straightforward articulation of the Political Liberty Principle and the Public Justification Principle, which it is meant to model: if one accepts that these principles pose the correct justificatory problem, there is strong—indeed, I think compelling— reason to accept this deliberative model. The only element the model adds is the interpretation of what one has a reason to accept in terms of a ranking of the proposals advanced by each member of P, translating the idea of having "a reason to accept" as "each member of P's ordinal rankings based on her evaluative standards."

Because justificatory liberalism is committed to a widespread evaluative pluralism among members of P, we should expect that their deep disagreements in their evaluative standards will usher in deep disagreements about which law is best—that is, which law is conclusively justified. If members of the public employ plural evaluative standards to evaluate different proposed laws, and if their evaluative standards are fundamentally at odds, these differences will inevitably result in great disagreement in their rankings of proposed laws. But given such deep disagreements in the rankings of the members of the public, it looks as if nothing can be conclusively justified, since for every proposal there will be someone who evaluates it as worse than another alternative.

The problem is this: If justificatory liberalism (i) adopts a strong standard of justification to each member of the public (some version of con-

---

[42] "Their procedure ... is to let each person propose principles ..." (Rawls, "Justice as Fairness," 53).

clusiveness) while also (ii) insisting that members of the public have diverse bases for deliberations about what is justified, then it is hard to see how we can get a determinate result. Justificatory liberals have tended to generate determinacy either by weakening (i)—the balance of values specified by a justified political conception must be only "reasonable,"[43] and so need not be conclusively justified—and/or by weakening (ii) and maintaining that, in the end, we share a common basis for reasoning about political right, say, based on a shared index of primary goods, thus greatly qualifying the pluralism underlying the parties' deliberations. Rawls himself acknowledges that his restrictions on particular information in the original position are necessary to achieve a determinate result.[44]

Suppose we refuse to take either of these routes, and allow each member of the public to rank all proposals, resulting in a set of options. Is there any way for them to agree to reduce the set of acceptable proposals? Members of P would unanimously agree to apply the Pareto principle: if in every member of P's ordering L_X is ranked higher than L_Y, all would agree that L_X is better than L_Y. Being strictly dominated by L_X, L_Y can be eliminated from the set of options to be considered. Once all such dominated proposals are eliminated, the members of the public would be left with an *optimal set* of proposals. Can they eliminate any other proposals? In the eyes of each member of P, some of the remaining proposals may be marginally worse than her favored law; other proposals she may find highly objectionable. But how objectionable is too objectionable? All members of P accept our two liberal principles (Political Liberty and Public Justification), so they believe that liberty is the norm unless coercion can be justified. What this means, then, is that in evaluating a proposal in terms of her evaluative standards, a person will find a proposal unacceptable if it is worse than a condition of liberty. For a law to be acceptable to a member of the public, it must be a net improvement on liberty. Consulting her own standards, each must hold that the law, in comparison to a condition of liberty, brings more benefits than costs. If a condition of liberty—no law at all—would be better, given her evaluative standards, then she has no reason to accept the law. Self-legislating such a proposal would be manifestly irrational: it would create net losses as judged by her evaluative standards.

On the one hand, no member of the public can have reason to accept a law that is worse than no law at all. On the other hand, a member of the public does have some reason to accept laws that are better than no law at all: all things considered, her evaluative standards are better advanced by such laws than by "anarchy" over this area of life. Our members of the public will thus divide the proposals into eligible and ineligible sets, as in table 1.

[43] Rawls, *Political Liberalism*, 224ff.
[44] Rawls, *A Theory of Justice*, rev. ed., 121.

TABLE 1. *Orderings distinguishing eligible from ineligible proposals*

	Alf		Betty		Charlie		Doris	
	Σ*	Law	Σ	Law	Σ	Law	Σ	Law
Eligible proposals	x	L_1	y	L_2	z	L_3	w	L_4
	y	L_2	w	L_1	x	L_1	x	L_1
	w	L_3	x	L_4	y	L_2	z	L_2
	z					L_4	y	
Ineligible proposals		No L		No L		No L		No L
		L_4		L_3				L_3

*Evaluative standards

In this case either member of the set $\{L_1, L_2\}$ is preferred by every member of P to no law at all *on this matter.*[45] They all have conclusive reason to select from this set, for both L_1 and L_2 are, from everyone's evaluative standards, improvements on the absence of legislation or the condition of liberty. We now have an *optimal eligible set:* some choice from this set is justified, though (until more is said) no choice of any single option is justified. When we are faced with an optimal eligible set, there is still justificatory work to be done: members of the public need to arrive at some procedure for selecting one of the options. While I do not want to minimize the problem of selecting one option from the set, I have argued elsewhere that certain formal and informal procedures may justifiably do the job.[46] My concern here is the extent of the optimal eligible set in matters concerning ownership and redistribution: what is the range of possible laws from which citizens may legitimately choose? Rawls believed that it included property-owning democracy and socialist systems, but no capitalist systems.[47] I believe that Rawls implausibly constrains the range of systems in the optimal eligible set while extending the set implausibly far in a statist direction.

IV. THE AMBITIOUS CASE FOR CLASSICAL LIBERALISM

A. Relevant information about the liberty effects of economic systems

An adequate deliberative model must include a specification of the information set available to members of P. Given the canonical liberal

[45] The deliberative problem supposes that we can identify laws that regulate an "area" of social life, or as Rawls termed it, a "practice" ("Justice as Fairness," 47). I set aside for now how to identify these areas in any precise way.
[46] For the informal, social procedure, see Gaus, "On Justifying the Moral Rights of the Moderns"; for the formal, political procedure, see Gerald Gaus, *Justificatory Liberalism* (New York: Oxford University Press, 1996), part III.
[47] Rawls, *Political Liberalism*, 338; Rawls, *A Theory of Justice*, rev. ed., 242.

order of justification, in which rights of the person and civil liberties are prior to the justification of property arrangements, in ranking property regimes members of the public must have available to them sound information about the effects of property regimes on maintaining schemes of civil rights. If, for example, we know that some economic systems tend to undermine the effective establishment of civil rights, this is relevant and important to the deliberators' choices. However, to say that it is important for the deliberators to have knowledge of the effects of economic systems on effective schemes of civil liberty does not itself tell us the rational response of deliberators to such knowledge. Contrast two cases. In case A, a deliberator knows that economic scheme S_1 has some small advantage in protecting civil liberties over S_2 in the sense that, given probabilistic information, S_1 has a slightly higher chance of performing a little better in protecting civil liberties than S_2. For example, S_1 may have a higher probability of faster economic growth rates than S_2, and there may be evidence that, say, richer societies tend to better ensure a right to a fair trial. Even if this were so, some deliberators could hold that S_2 still has advantages that more than compensate—say, it better conforms to their idea of economic justice. There is nothing unreasonable about such a judgment. In case B, by contrast, there is evidence that S_2 has a very high probability of doing much worse than S_1 in protecting the broad range of civil liberties, such that it is extremely likely that S_2 will be characterized by widespread violations of civil liberties. Here, given the order of justification, reasonable deliberators must reject S_2. It almost certainly will fail to honor already justified civil liberties. It would do no good to first insist on a regime of civil liberties and then admit economic systems that have a very high probability of undermining them.

To be sure, there will be many cases that fall between A and B, where the probability that an economic system may endanger civil liberties is significant, but not so high that it would be unreasonable for a deliberator to decide that the significant dangers are compensated by perceived benefits. The order of justification does not establish a lexical priority such that no possible costs to a regime of civil liberty could ever be justified by, say, economic benefits. At the same time, rational deliberators must, in cases like B, reject economic systems that pose not only some probability, but a very high one, that the core personal and civil liberties will be threatened.

B. The first step: Private property regimes dominate socialist regimes

There is powerful evidence that extensive private ownership—including private ownership of capital goods and financial instruments and institutions—is for all practical purposes a requirement for a functioning and free social order that protects civil liberties. It is, I think, astounding that Rawls never appreciates this, and simply assumes, on the basis

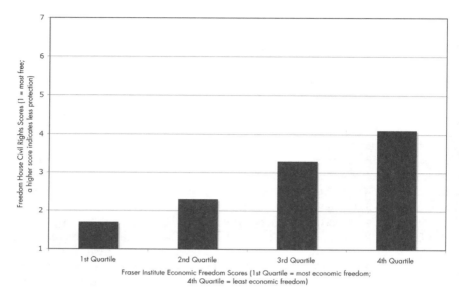

FIGURE 1. The general relation between economic freedom and protection of civil rights

of economic theory, that well-functioning markets can be divorced from "private ownership in the means of production."[48] There has never been a political order characterized by deep respect for personal freedom that was not based on a market order with widespread private ownership in the means of production. Figure 1, drawn from James D. Gwartney, Robert Lawson, and Seth Norton's *Economic Freedom of the World: 2008 Annual Report*, gives the summary relation between economic freedom (an index summarizing data about the extent to which a state protects personal economic choice; voluntary exchange coordinated by markets; freedom to enter and compete in markets; and protection of persons and their property) and Freedom House's ranking of states that protect civil rights.[49]

Table 2 gives a country-by-country breakdown, using data from Freedom House, Gwartney et al., and the Heritage Foundation.[50] It presents data on thirty-six countries that, according to Freedom House, ranked

[48] Rawls, *A Theory of Justice*, rev. ed., 239.

[49] Adapted from James D. Gwartney and Robert Lawson, with Seth Norton, *Economic Freedom of the World: 2008 Annual Report* (Economic Freedom Network, 2008), p. 21. Digital copy available from www.fraserinstitute.org; www.freetheworld.com. Used with permission of the Fraser Institute. For information on Freedom House, see www.freedomhouse.org.

[50] Sources: Freedom House, "Freedom in the World, 2008: Subscores (Civil Rights)," http://www.freedomhouse.org/template.cfm?page=414&year=2008; Gwartney, Lawson, and Norton, *Economic Freedom of the World: 2008 Annual Report*; Heritage Foundation, "Index of Economic Freedom," 2008 data, http://www.heritage.org/Index/. Used with permission of Freedom House, the Fraser Institute, and the Heritage Foundation. Note that the scores in

TABLE 2. *Economic freedom in thirty-six states that best protect civil rights*

Country	(1) Property and legal protection: Gwartney ranking (1–141)	(2) Property rights protection score: Heritage Foundation (100–0)	(3) Overall economic freedom: Gwartney ranking (1–141)	(4) Overall economic freedom score: Heritage Foundation (100–0)
Finland	1	90	14	75
Denmark	2	90	13	79
Norway	3	88	23	69
New Zealand	4	90	3	80
Iceland	5	90	12	77
Australia	6	90	8	80
Austria	7	90	15	71.2
Switzerland	8	90	4	80
Germany	9	90	17	71
Netherlands	10	90	16	77
Sweden	13	90	33	70
Canada	14	90	7	80
United Kingdom	15	90	5	80
Luxemburg	17	90	21	75
Japan	18	70	27	72
Ireland	19	90	10	82
United States	21	90	8	81
France	22	70	45	65
Estonia	26	90	11	78
Portugal	28	70	47	64
Belgium	30	80	44	72
Chile	31	90	6	80
Barbados	35	90	98	71
Lithuania	37	50	31	70
Costa Rica	39	50	21	65
Spain	40	70	32	70
Hungary	41	70	28	67
Taiwan	42	70	18	71
Greece	43	50	54	70
Italy	48	50	49	62
Israel	49	70	76	66
Czech Republic	52	70	63	69
Slovenia	57	50	88	61
Poland	62	50	69	60
Ghana	65	50	66	57
Cape Verde	NA	70	NA	59

highest in 2008 in terms of their protection of civil rights (that is, they were rated in category 1 on Freedom House's 1–7 scale). As the table shows, none of these thirty-six countries scored less than 50 on the Heritage Foundation's rating of their protection of property rights (column 2). No state that does the best job in protecting civil rights scores less than

columns (2) and (4) are on a scale from 100 (highest protection of property rights/most overall economic freedom) to 0 (lowest protection/least economic freedom).

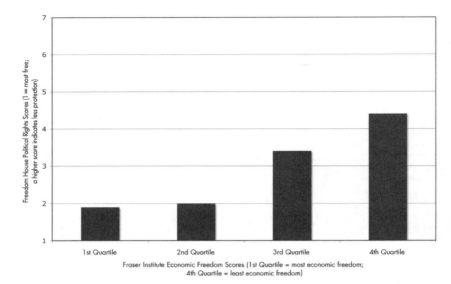

FIGURE 2. The general relation between economic freedom and protection of political rights

59 in the Heritage Foundation's ratings of overall economic freedom (column 4). With the (close) exception of Cape Verde, all states recognized by Freedom House as the best protectors of civil rights were classified as free or mostly free in the Heritage Foundation scores. Gwartney et al.'s rankings show a comparable story (columns 1 and 3).

Rawls, it will be recalled, argues that welfare-state capitalism should be grouped along with state socialist systems as socioeconomic arrangements that do not adequately protect the fair value of political rights (see Section I above). Of course, it is hard to evaluate Rawls's claim that such systems do worse than his preferred alternatives, since none of his preferred systems have ever existed. As figure 2 and table 3 show, however,

TABLE 3. *Civil rights scores and economic freedom*
in remaining socialist states

Country	Civil rights score (all "not free")	Political rights score (all "not free")	Property rights protection score: Heritage Foundation	Overall economic freedom score: Heritage Foundation
China	6	7	20	53 (*mostly unfree*)
Cuba	7	7	10	28 (*repressed*)
Laos	6	7	10	50 (*mostly unfree*)
Vietnam	5	7	10	50 (*mostly unfree*)
North Korea	7	7	Not graded	3 (*repressed*)

in the world as we have known it, the protection of economic liberty and private property is associated with states that do a better job of institutionalizing effective political rights (as well as civil rights).[51]

Table 3 presents the scores of the remaining state socialist regimes on the protection of civil and political rights and economic freedom. The evidence indicates that private property–based regimes that protect property rights and overall economic freedom are the best protectors of civil liberties and, indeed, of political rights. Given the evidence, because our deliberators have a deep commitment to civil liberties, they must reject socialism in favor of private property regimes and, further, must favor private property regimes with considerable economic freedom.

It might appear that Rawls and his followers have an effective rejoinder to this line of argument. Rawls consistently claims that large inequalities in wealth allow situations in which the fair value of political liberty is undermined.[52] So even if private property regimes are necessary for protecting civil liberty, private property systems that allow economic inequalities are a grave danger to political liberty. It is seldom appreciated how important this claim is to Rawls's case for equality: he believes that inequalities allowed by his "difference principle"—which requires that a just social order must maximize the economic prospects of the least advantaged citizens—may threaten the fair value of political liberty, and thus further equalization may be required.[53] As we saw in Section I, Rawls went so far as to propose a branch of government to readjust property rights, partly to ensure the "fair value" of political liberty. But while it may seem obvious to some that large inequalities of income and wealth undermine the worth of the "least advantaged" citizens' political liberties, this claim is in fact conjectural. Whether citizens have real input—whether their political rights actually have "fair value"—is a matter of complex sociology, involving the features of political culture, including levels of civic participation, institutional structures governing the relations between business and government, the existence of power centers outside of government, levels of overall wealth, and so on. Table 4 shows some of this complexity, charting the relation between income inequality and political rights in selected countries in the Organization for Economic Cooperation and Development (OECD).[54]

[51] Figure 2 is adapted from Gwartney, Lawson, and Norton, *Economic Freedom of the World: 2008 Annual Report*, p. 21. Digital copy available from www.fraserinstitute.org; www.freetheworld.com. Used with permission of the Fraser Institute. The data in table 3 are from Freedom House, "Freedom in the World, 2008: Subscores (Civil Rights)," http://www.freedomhouse.org/template.cfm?page=414&year=2008; and Heritage Foundation, "Index of Economic Freedom," 2008 data. Used with permission of Freedom House and the Heritage Foundation.

[52] Rawls, *Justice as Fairness*, 139.

[53] Rawls, *Political Liberalism*, 329.

[54] Sources: Jean-Marc Burniaux, Flavio Padrini, and Nicola Brandt, *Labour Market Performance, Income Inequality, and Poverty in OECD Countries*, OECD Economics Department Working Paper No. 500 (ECO/WKP, 2006), 44; Freedom House, "Freedom in the World,

TABLE 4. *The relation between income inequality and effective political rights in selected OECD countries*

	Below average income inequality OECD countries	Above average income inequality OECD countries
*High political pluralism/participation score (16)**	DENMARK	UNITED STATES
Middle political participation score (15)	CZECH REPUBLIC, FRANCE	JAPAN
Lower political participation scores (12–14)		MEXICO, TURKEY
High electoral process score (12)	CZECH REPUBLIC, DENMARK, FRANCE	JAPAN
Middle electoral process score (11)		UNITED STATES
Lower electoral process score (10)		MEXICO, TURKEY
High functioning government scores (11 & 12)	DENMARK (12), CZECH REPUBLIC, FRANCE	UNITED STATES
Middle functioning government score (10)		JAPAN
Lower functioning government scores (7–8)		MEXICO, TURKEY

*Raw scores

Table 4 offers little ground for accepting a strong relation between income inequality and a lesser value of political rights. To be sure, there is some positive correlation: below average income inequality countries always score in the high or middle range on political rights, while above average income inequality countries scored both high and low. The United States, though, scores high on OECD income inequality, but also high on political participation/political pluralism, outperforming more egalitarian countries. In any event, the differences between the Czech Republic, Denmark, France, Japan, and the United States are very slight. The real outliers are Mexico and Turkey, countries that score low on the protection of political rights and have high income inequality combined with significantly lower overall levels of wealth and income.

Perhaps the real danger to political rights is not income inequality but wealth inequality. Calculating wealth inequality is a difficult task, mainly because the idea of "wealth" is open to numerous interpretations. However, income and wealth inequality appear to be strongly correlated in OECD countries,[55] so we should not expect a great deal of difference.

2008: Subscores (Political Rights)," http://www.freedomhouse.org/template.cfm?page=414&year=2008.
[55] Daniela Sonedda, "Wealth Inequality, Income Redistribution, and Growth in Fifteen OECD Countries," *Royal Economic Society Annual Conference* (2003), Royal Economic Society, 21; http://ideas.repec.org/e/pso158.html.

TABLE 5. *The relation between wealth inequality and effective political rights in selected OECD countries*

	Lower wealth inequality OECD countries	Higher wealth inequality OECD countries
High political pluralism/participation score (16)	FINLAND, SWEDEN	UNITED STATES, CANADA
Middle political participation score (15)	JAPAN, GERMANY	AUSTRALIA, ITALY
Lower political participation scores (12–14)		MEXICO
High electoral process score (12)	FINLAND, GERMANY, JAPAN, SWEDEN	AUSTRALIA, CANADA, ITALY
Middle electoral process score (11)		UNITED STATES
Lower electoral process score (10)		MEXICO
Highest functioning government score (12)	FINLAND, SWEDEN, GERMANY	AUSTRALIA, CANADA
Higher-middle functioning government score (11)		UNITED STATES, ITALY
Middle-lower functioning government score (10)	JAPAN	
Lower functioning government score (8)		MEXICO

Table 5, employing a different data set from selected OECD countries concerning wealth inequality, arrives at results comparable to those in table 4.[56]

In light of figures 1 and 2 and tables 2 through 5, we must view as unfounded Rawls's claim that laissez-faire capitalism, welfare-state capitalism, and state socialism with a command economy all are unjustifiable partly because they fail to secure the fair value of political liberties.[57] The most we can discover is a modest real correlation between wealth and income inequalities and political rights protection scores. Welfare capitalist states such as the United States and the United Kingdom score "1" (the best at protecting rights) and all socialist states score "7" (the lowest possible score) on Freedom House's scale of effective political rights. Table 5, of course, does not include market socialist systems, which are one of Rawls's favored alternatives (since none exist). However, the only large-scale market socialist system in history—Yugoslavia under Tito—also repressed civil liberties and political rights. Of course, this data is merely indicative, and much work needs to be done, but it is dubious indeed that there is any powerful empirical evidence for a strong correlation in wealthy countries between economic inequalities and less than

[56] Sources: Markus Jäntti and Eva Sierminska, *Survey Estimates of Wealth Holdings in OECD Countries: Evidence on the Level and Distribution* (United Nations University, World Institute for Development Economics Research, 2007); Freedom House, "Freedom in the World, 2008: Subscores (Political Rights)," http://www.freedomhouse.org/template.cfm?page=414&year=2008.
[57] Rawls, *Justice as Fairness*, 137–38.

a fair value of political liberty. Again, this is not to say that there is no correlation at all, but excluding a whole set of economic arrangements on the basis of a modest correlation over a small range of variance is unjustified.[58] There is good reason to think that, in the countries of the OECD, the most important variable explaining high political rights scores is simply high levels of wealth and income, and that the degree of equality is a relatively minor factor.

This knowledge must be relevant to the deliberations of members of P. We suppose that they have already justified civil rights and rights of the person: such rights are basic for all liberals, and thus would be prior in the order of justification (see Section II.C above). Knowing the importance of these rights, when selecting schemes of economic cooperation, the members of the public will rank all systems with extensive private ownership and economic freedom as superior to socialist systems. Not only does everything we know about economic prosperity indicate that private ownership is far superior to socialist systems,[59] but, as we have seen, the shared commitment of all liberals to civil rights provides a decisive reason to rank such systems above socialism. Moreover, as we have seen, the Rawlsian counterclaim that strong private ownership systems endanger political rights is questionable. Socialist systems would be dominated by private ownership systems and, thus, would not be in the optimal set.

C. The second step: Redistribution is not in the optimal eligible set of all members of P

Once it has been concluded that systems with private ownership in the means of production (with great economic freedom to invest, start businesses, and so on) are in the optimal eligible set of all members of P, it looks as if the proponent of classical liberalism has won the day. Egalitarian, redistributive proposals will not be in the eligible set of all members of the public. We must suppose that some members of the public have egalitarian intuitions (evaluative standards) and some are welfare statists, while others are more strictly classical liberal. The classical liberal members of P are apt to hold that almost every redistributive plan or scheme of social justice is worse than no redistributive/social justice laws at all. Recall that, given the basic Political Liberty Principle, the baseline for liberals must be the absence of legislation (see Section III.C above). Unless a law is endorsed by every member of the public as an improve-

---

[58] Even less compelling is the claim that inequalities in the value of political rights are simply allowed under capitalism: the question is what economic systems are conducive to a free society. Cf. Rawls, *Justice as Fairness*, 139.

[59] For the relation of economic freedom and income per capita growth, see James D. Gwartney and Robert Lawson, with Seth Norton, *Economic Freedom of the World: 2008 Annual Report*, p. 18. Economic Freedom Network. Digital copy available from www.fraserinstitute.org, www.freetheworld.com.

ment (from the perspective of her own evaluative standards) over no law at all, the law cannot possibly be one that all members endorse as free and equal persons. But citizens who are inclined toward classical liberalism will rank few if any redistributive laws as better than no laws at all, and so such laws will be excluded from the eligible set. It seems, then, that the optimal eligible set will contain only laws with a strong commitment to private ownership and economic freedom.

It is important to stress that once an extensive system of private ownership has been justified, redistributive proposals are manifestly coercive. To take away one's property infringes one's rights; the threat to do so is coercive. This is not, of course, to say that taxation cannot be justified; but as an exercise of coercion by the state, it stands in need of justification. This "everyday libertarian" view of ownership—that when the government taxes me, it takes away *my* property—is criticized by Liam Murphy and Thomas Nagel as a "myth":

> There is no market without government and no government without taxes; and what type of government there is depends on laws and policy decisions that government must make. In the absence of a legal system supported by taxes, there couldn't be money, banks and corporations, stock exchanges, patents, or a modern market economy. . . .
>
> . . . It is therefore *logically impossible* that people should have *any* kind of entitlement to all their pretax income. *All* that they can be entitled to is what they would be left with after taxes under a legitimate system. . . .[60]

This is an error. I logically can have an entitlement to all my pre-tax income in the sense that taking away any of it must be publicly justified: since my pre-tax income is something I have a right to, any infringement of that right must be justified. Murphy and Nagel are certainly correct that some activities of the state are necessary for my property rights to exist: funds required for those activities are justified claims against my property. But that someone has a justified claim against some of my property does not show that I do not have "any kind of entitlement" to that part of my property. Alas, my creditors have claims against a good deal of my current income, but it hardly follows that I have no entitlement to that income: even my creditors may not simply raid my bank account. They have claims that can justify overriding my entitlements if so authorized by a justified law, but having liabilities is not the same as not having the property needed to discharge those liabilities.

---

[60] Liam Murphy and Thomas Nagel, *The Myth of Ownership: Taxes and Justice* (New York: Oxford University Press, 2002), 32–33; emphasis added.

D. Property, redistribution, and the order of justification

Murphy and Nagel suggest a rather more comprehensive criticism of the "everyday" conception of ownership. Property rights are really simply conventional arrangements defined by governments, so governments cannot possibly violate them. As Kant was well aware, even if there is a basic moral right to have private property, this right cannot be implemented without a political order that specifies it, provides the economic institutions necessary for it be effective, and so on. Kant held that, although we can have a "provisional" right to property in the state of nature, justified rights to property only become actual in a juridical condition which determines the shape of property rights.[61] The aim of jurisprudence, Kant says, is to precisely specify "what the property of everyone is"; only in civil society is property adequately defined through public law.[62] Now if the state is in the business of determining the shape of property, it may seem that everything it does—including taxing as it sees fit—is part of this job of specifying property rights. If so, it might appear that nobody could be in a position to argue that the state is taking away his property, since until the state specifies the right, there really is no effective right to property. There is, on this way of thinking, no Archimedean point outside of the state's determinations of your property rights (or any other rights?) from which to criticize the state's activity as taking away what is yours; for its decisions determine what is yours.

This conclusion does not follow from recognizing that effective property rights are conventional and depend on the state. As I have stressed, all laws are to be justified. This justification occurs against a background of one's already justified rights, what I have called the order of justification. Property rights, if not the most basic rights in the liberal order of justification, are certainly prior to many state laws and policies, such as, say, funding museums. Hobbes, Locke, Rousseau, and Kant all recognized that distinguishing "mine" and "thine" is one of the first requisites of an effective social order. In seeking to fund museums, representatives of the state cannot simply say that citizens have no entitlement to their incomes because they, the representatives, determine property rights, and thus they may tax for these purposes without justification. "Without us, there would be no property, so you have no property claims against us!" Once property rights have been justified, they form the background for further justifications; they can be overridden in order to tax, but this must be justified.

All political theories must recognize an order of justification: some things are settled, and that settlement provides a background for further

---

[61] Kant, *Metaphysical Elements of Justice,* 46ff [Akademie ed., 250ff].

[62] Ibid., 33, 41 [Akademie ed., 233, 238]. See also Hillel Steiner, "Kant, Property, and the General Will," in Norman Geras and Robert Walker, eds., *The Enlightenment and Modernity* (New York: St. Martin's, 2000), 71ff.

justification. Of course, "settled" does not mean that we cannot go back and rethink the answers we have given, but we must decide the more basic issues before going on to others. That is the key insight of Rawls's focus on "constitutional essentials": once we have justified these essentials, we have a fixed point for further justification. The problem with the case for classical liberalism that we have been examining is not that it relies on an order of justification in which determining property rights is fairly basic, but that it insists that we first justify ownership rights and then, taking these as settled, look at the justification of all redistributive proposals. It is only because the classical liberal first fixed private ownership that she was able to eliminate redistributive proposals. That is arbitrary. The history of debate about economic justice and redistribution has been about the shape of a justified system of private ownership. Many members of P could not possibly evaluate and rank schemes of private ownership unless they knew their distributive implications:[63] for many members of the public, these issues are tightly bound together. If the classical liberal is not to beg the question, she must show that even when we justify private property and redistributive proposals at the same time (i.e., at the same point in the order of justification), justificatory liberalism still favors the classical view.

V. Coercion, Taxation, and the Redistributive State

A. The Political Liberty Principle, degrees of coercion, and the costs of coercion

Recall our two foundational principles—Political Liberty and Public Justification. Liberalisms based on these principles hold that the first problem of a morally acceptable legal regime is that its coercion must be justified to everyone; in the absence of such justification, people are to be left free. Now if coercion requires justification—if, as Benn says, one who coerces others has a case to answer—then those who engage in more coercion must have a greater case to answer.[64] The more coercive the law, the greater must be the gains from the law if it is to be justified. A law that instructs all to X based on the threat of a small fine may be publicly justified, while a law instructing all to X based on a threat of years of imprisonment may not be. Draco (who codified the first set of laws for Athens) is said to have insisted that even the smallest infractions, such as stealing an apple, should be punished by death: Draconian laws are objectionable not necessarily because their aims are unjustifiable, but because the degree of coercion employed cannot be justified. To say, however, that

---

[63] This is certainly Mill's view in his discussion of private property in Book II of *Principles of Political Economy*.

[64] Robert Audi further explicates this idea of degrees of coercion in his *Religious Commitment and Secular Reason* (Cambridge: Cambridge University Press, 2000), 87–88.

a law that coerces to a higher degree requires a higher level of justification must be to say that coercion is a moral cost that triggers justification, and the higher that cost, the greater must be the law's benefits if it is to be justified.

Coercion limits liberty, and greater coercion limits liberty more. As Feinberg observes:

> There is a standing presumption against all proposals to criminalize conduct . . . but the strength of this presumption varies . . . with the degree to which [the] interest in liberty is actually invaded by the proposed legislation. Invasions of the interest in liberty are as much a matter of degree as invasions of the interest in money, though we lack clear-cut conventional units for measuring them. The interest in liberty *as such* . . . is an interest in having as many open options as possible with respect to various kinds of action, omission, and possession.[65]

A coercive law that closes off only one or two options is, other things equal, less coercive than a law that makes the same threats but closes off many options. F. A. Hayek stresses this perhaps more than any recent liberal theorist: "coercion occurs when one man's actions are made to serve another man's will."[66] For Hayek, the more one's options are restricted to one or a few options—the more the coercer succeeds in getting you to do the thing she seeks—the more you are serving another's will, and so are coerced. In contrast, if the coercion forecloses few options— say, it attaches to a law that simply forbids you to take up one of your many options—you are only minimally subject to the will of another.[67] As Benn points out, coercive laws seek to render some options ineligible by "threatening penalties for a prescribed action, attaching to it costs which make it significantly less attractive an option than alternative ones."[68] Coercive laws restrict freedom by rendering options considerably less eligible as choices; as the law renders a larger set of actions less eligible in this way, it is more coercive and its cost to liberty increases.

B. The redistributive state and coercion

Classical liberals have long maintained that the redistributive state is more coercive than the classical liberal state. The debate between classical

---

[65] Joel Feinberg, "The Interest of Liberty in the Scales," in his *Rights, Justice, and the Bounds of Liberty* (Princeton, NJ: Princeton University Press, 1980), 36.

[66] F. A. Hayek, *The Constitution of Liberty* (London: Routledge, 1960), 133.

[67] Hayek actually seems to go so far as to say that you are not coerced at all in this case. Ibid., 141.

[68] Benn, *A Theory of Freedom*, 144.

and egalitarian liberals on this matter has been extensive, protracted, and often confusing. Some of the familiar claims made are the following:

- Classical liberals such as Jan Narveson insist that we cannot distinguish liberty and property: "Liberty is Property." [69] For Narveson, "[it] is plausible to construe all rights as property rights." [70] Others insist that property rights simply are a type of liberty rights.[71] Thus, any redistribution of property is ipso facto an interference with personal liberty, and so needs to be justified. I believe that it can be readily shown that the conception of property rights underlying this view is, at best, dubious.[72]
- Libertarians such as Eric Mack hold that basic to a person's claim to live her own life in her own chosen way is both a natural right of self-ownership and a natural right to acquire property.[73] Actions that deprive, or threaten to deprive, a person of property that she has acquired through the exercise of this latter right infringe her basic right to lead her own life in her own way. This, however, is the crux of the ambitious case for classical liberalism, which we have rejected (see Section IV above).
- Advocates of more redistributive forms of liberalism argue that, since property rights are purely conventional, the state may determine their shape as it sees fit, and this includes determining the level of taxation. We have seen that this argument too should be rejected (Section IV.D).

It is often wondered how increasing a marginal tax rate increases coercion. Will Wilkinson, a philosopher specializing in public policy matters, poses a challenge:

[L]ibertarians and many conservatives often talk about lower taxes as a matter of liberty. But a higher tax isn't more coercive than a lower one. You're either being coerced or you're not. A guy who mugs five people with thin wallets is no less guilty of coercion than a guy who mugs five people with thick wallets. The harm from coercion might be greater if more is taken, but there is no more or less coercion.[74]

[69] Jan Narveson, *The Libertarian Idea* (Philadelphia, PA: Temple University Press, 1988), 66.
[70] Ibid.
[71] See, for example, Loren E. Lomasky, *Persons, Rights, and the Moral Community* (New York: Oxford University Press, 1987), 132.
[72] As I have tried to show in "Property, Rights, and Freedom," *Social Philosophy and Policy* 11, no. 2 (1994): 209–40.
[73] Eric Mack, "The Natural Right of Property," elsewhere in this volume.
[74] Will Wilkinson, *The Fly Bottle*, http://www.willwilkinson.net/flybottle/2008/05/30/ please-discuss/ (accessed July 28, 2008). Wilkinson is suggesting a topic for discussion, and the claim is based on theories of freedom commonly held by classical liberals.

Once we get beyond paradigmatic instances of coercion, claims about what constitutes coercion are, notoriously, open to dispute. Let me explore one reasonable understanding of coercion. I do not claim that it is philosophically incontrovertible; it is, though, clearly a plausible and in many ways a compelling view. Begin with a simple contrast between two states with a flat-rate income tax: a low-rate and a high-rate state. To make the distinction stark, suppose that the low-rate state has a flat rate of 20 percent, the high-rate state of 80 percent. Otherwise, the tax codes are identical, including both monetary penalties and prison terms. For at least two reasons, the high-rate state will, other things equal, seem more coercive.

(i) As tax rates rise, noncompliance will also rise; it is hopelessly utopian not to expect increased noncompliance as tax rates increase. As tax rates rise, so does the opportunity cost of voluntarily complying; self-interested citizens have increasingly strong incentives to become noncompliers, and we must assume that in the real world a significant number of citizens will be so motivated. As noncompliance increases, the state will increasingly turn its attention to identifying and coercing noncompliers. The amount of money involved will be enormous, and we can expect states to turn increasingly to the criminal law. Something along these lines has occurred in the United States. In the last twenty years, the United States Internal Revenue Service developed the concept of a "tax gap"—"the difference between the amount of tax owed and the amount paid."[75] In 2001, the Internal Revenue Service estimated that the total tax gap in the U.S. was approximately $312 to $353 billion, resulting from a very significant noncompliance rate of roughly 16 percent.[76] As the tax gap has grown, the Internal Revenue Service has undertaken a "zealous fight" to close the gap, implementing a "Tax Gap Strategy" that involves increased efforts to detect violations and criminal law enforcement.[77] Tax enforcement thus increasingly comes to stress criminal penalties. The problem clearly is that taxpayers do not at present sufficiently fear detection.[78]

(ii) The criminal law seeks to make options ineligible—no longer choiceworthy—because of the threatened costs to one's person. In our 80 percent rate state, tax policies have the effect of making a large number of options basically ineligible. To be sure, the threat is conditional: if you engage in a range of activities that generate detectable income, you must either pay 80 percent to the state or be punished. The state essentially demands that one pay 80 percent to take up an option, and threatens

[75] Ted F. Brown (Assistant for the Criminal Division of the IRS, 1998), quoted in Liezl Walker, "The Deterrent Value of Imposing Prison Sentences for Tax Crimes," *New England Journal of Criminal and Civil Confinement* 26 (Winter 2000): 1 n. 4.
[76] "Understanding the Tax Gap" (FS-2005-14, March 2005), Internal Revenue Service, http://www.irs.gov/newsroom/article/0,,id=137246,00.html (accessed July 28, 2008).
[77] Walker, "The Deterrent Value of Imposing Prison Sentences for Tax Crimes," 6.
[78] Ibid., 7.

one's person if one does not. And indeed a wide range of options are made less eligible. Market transactions involving traceable monetary transfers become far less eligible than alternatives such as informal bartering, leisure activities, writing philosophy, artistic pursuits, and political activities. As the state radically increases the costs of a wide range of market activities, these activities are made far less eligible as a result of the state's power to coerce. If we adopt a metaphor of Feinberg's, and think of one's options as a series of railroad tracks that one might follow, high tax rates make it very difficult to follow a great many routes; given the costs involved in taking those routes, they are effectively closed.[79] Of course, one still *can* engage in these activities if one is willing to pay the 80 percent, but it is equally true that one still *can* engage in criminal activities if one is willing to pay the penalties.[80]

As a rule, we should expect that increases in taxation (and, generally, the redistributive activities of the state) will be strongly positively correlated with increases in coercion.[81] Both the variables I have noted — increasing noncompliance and decreasing eligibility of options — are continuous, and we should expect that throughout most of their range, the effects noted here will be monotonically related to tax rates. This is not to say that the relation between taxation and coercion is linear: coercion may be insignificant at very low levels of taxation and become really oppressive at very high levels. And, of course, the overall relation between

[79] Feinberg, "The Interest of Liberty in the Scales," 36.

[80] It might be objected that this must be wrong: whereas the criminal law seeks to render options less eligible in order to deter, an effective tax law (putting aside sin taxes) must hope that citizens continue with the activity in order for revenue to be generated. The will of the state is not for citizens to refrain, but to persist, so they are not being coerced in Hayek's sense. Coercion thus may seem to require an *intention* to deter people from the act, but that is exactly what the state does not seek to do with taxation — and that is why the state does not close off options, but only makes them more difficult to pursue. One who threatens, however, need not wish to deter, for often enough those making the threat hope that the target will not give in to the threat. In 1918, for example, Germany issued an ultimatum to the neutral Dutch, demanding the right to ship materials across their territory, and threatening the Netherlands and Dutch ships in its colonies if the demand was not met. At the time, this threat was seen by many observers as a pretext; they believed that Germany hoped the Netherlands would not give in to the threat but would instead enter the war. What Germany's intentions were did not nullify the coercive threat. See *The New York Times,* April 23 and 28, 1918.

[81] By comparing only flat-tax states, I have greatly simplified the analysis. With variable-rate taxation, what constitutes a high-tax country depends on the combined score on several dimensions. Consider a study of fifteen OECD countries from the period of 1974 to 1997 (Australia, Belgium, Canada, Denmark, Finland, France, Germany, Italy, Japan, the Netherlands, Norway, Spain, Sweden, the United Kingdom, and the United States). We might define a high-tax country as one that has highly progressive rates *and* high marginal tax rates. On that definition, the high-tax states are Sweden, the United States, Finland, the United Kingdom, the Netherlands, and Belgium; the low-tax states are Spain, Australia, Norway, Germany, Japan, and Italy. If we define a high-tax state as one that has a high *average* personal tax rate *and* a high degree of progressivity, the high-tax states are Belgium, Canada, and France; Germany, Norway, and Denmark are low on both dimensions. Sonedda, "Wealth Inequality, Income Redistribution, and Growth in Fifteen OECD Countries," 19–20.

the degree of coercion and tax rates may differ depending on historical circumstances. In the Great Depression, for example, an attempt by the state to enforce basic property rights with no significant redistribution against, say, a general population in great economic distress might have required a great amount of coercion, while a state that engaged in modest redistribution may well have secured social peace with much less need for threats. We must not succumb to the simple idea that tax rates and the degree of coercion are perfectly correlated in all circumstances. Nevertheless, based on the plausible analysis we have been examining, classical liberals have strongly favored property regimes that typically employ less coercion, while the heavy reliance on the expansive state favored by Rawls and his followers would seem to rely on relatively high levels of taxation, and thus favor more coercive states. Let me stress that I do not contend that this is the only plausible view of the relation of coercion to taxation; as we are about to see, even though it is simply one plausible view, it has important consequences for justificatory liberalism.

C. A formal analysis of justification given the costs of coercion

Recall the deliberative model (Section III.C). Members of the public rank all proposals; this would yield for each an ordinal utility function. It is absolutely crucial to keep in mind that the idea of a "utility function" is simply a mathematical representation of a member of P's views about the choice-worthiness of a proposal based solely on her reasonable evaluative standards (Section III.B). This point is of the first importance; utility is not an independent goal, much less self-interest, but a mathematical representation of an ordering of the choice-worthiness of outcomes.[82] It will help to translate each person's ordinal ranking of the alternatives (based on her set of evaluative standards) into a cardinal function.[83] Because our interest is in the way that the costs of degrees of coercion figure into the deliberations of members of P, let us take the costs in terms of the coercion imposed by a law and separate them out from each member of P's utility function. For each person, we then have (α) her evaluation of all the costs and benefits of the law (based, as always, on her evaluative standards) except for the element we have separated out: namely, (β) her evaluation of the coercive costs of the proposal. Members of P, I assume, will disagree about the level of costs. For now (but see Section V.D), I suppose they agree that the costs increase as coercion increases. Call (α) the member of the public's *pro tanto evaluation of the law* (1 = best law; 0 = a law that is not better than no law at all), and call (β) her estimate of *the coercion costs of the law*. It is important that (β) concerns

---

[82] See also my *On Politics, Philosophy, and Economics* (Belmont, CA: Wadsworth, 2007), chap. 2.
[83] This is merely for purposes of exposition; a cardinal analysis is not required.

simply the coercion costs imposed *by* the law: we do not count as part of
the coercion costs of a law nonstate coercion that might occur under a law.
A law that itself imposes low coercion may fail to stop nonstate coercion;
a law that imposes greater coercion may do a better job at halting nonstate
coercion. But nonstate coercion that is reduced by a law falls under the
benefits of that law; if nonstate coercion is rampant under a law, that will
reduce its *pro tanto* utility.

In figure 3, Alf and Betty are members of the public deliberating about
five systems of law concerning property rights/redistribution. (Recall
that we have accepted the argument that ownership cannot be justified
prior to distributive justice.) L_1 involves the least state coercion; L_5 the
most. If we consider only their *pro tanto* evaluations, each of the five laws
is better than no law at all (L_0). But the costs of increasing coercion have
been omitted from the *pro tanto* utility. Once we factor in these costs, as
long as the *pro tanto* evaluation stays above the costs-of-coercion curve,
the member of the public holds that the overall benefits of the law exceed
the costs; once the *pro tanto* curve dips below the coercion-costs curve, the
costs of coercion outweigh the other net benefits of the proposal. We can
see that point x defines the boundary of the eligible set: at point x, the
total coercion costs of the law just equal the total net benefits for Alf; after
that point, the costs of the law (measured as always in terms of the
satisfaction of Alf's evaluative standards) exceed the benefits, and so he
has no reason to endorse the law.

In figure 3, Alf's ordering is $L_1 > L_2 > L_3 > L_0 > L_4 > L_5$; Betty's is $L_2 > L_3 >$
$L_1 > L_4 > L_0 > L_5$. The additional coercion required for L_4 or L_5 is such that
now the total costs exceed the total benefits. Alf does not see as justified
the additional coercion required for L_4 or L_5. Given his evaluation of the
coercion costs involved, and the benefits that the coercion yields, for Alf

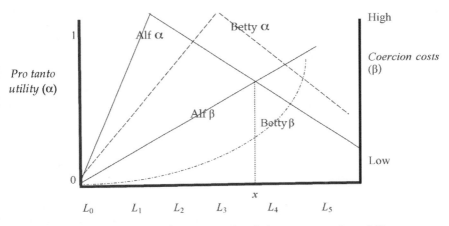

FIGURE 3. Two utility functions, each split into two parts (α and β)

the costs of coercion outweigh the *pro tanto* utility of L_4 or L_5, and so they are not in the eligible set.[84] *What we see here is that, as proposals involve higher degrees of coercion, they tend to be dropped from the eligible set because of the evaluations of those such as Alf, who evaluate the proposals' coercion costs as high and are more skeptical about the benefits.* Thus, in this version of the model, we witness a tilt toward the least coercive options. Note that this version of the model (1) assumes members of the public agree on the ordering of proposals from least to most coercive but (2) incorporates disagreement about the costs of coercion: some may see coercion as a less serious matter than others.

D. Formal analysis II: Disagreement about rising coercion

The first assumption—that members of the public agree on the ordering of the proposals from least to most coercive—is too strong.[85] As I have stressed, the thesis that coercion rises as redistribution increases is subject to reasonable disagreement. Some have advanced analyses of coercion according to which redistributive states with high tax rates are not necessarily more coercive than states that tax much less.[86] Let us accept this as a reasonable view. We now need to build reasonable disagreement about the relation of coercion and the extent of the state into the formal analysis. Figure 4 models the revised situation.

In figure 4, Alf's utility function remains as it was before; the laws are arranged in his order of increasing coerciveness (so his utility function is single-peaked). Betty holds that the net benefits are highest at L_3, and the costs of coercion are also lowest around L_3. In Betty's judgment, the redistributive effects of L_3 are, overall, coercion-minimizing.

Note that this weakening of the model's assumptions does not change the result: Alf's judgments of the range of the laws in which the benefits of coercion outweigh the costs are still decisive. This is so because the limits of the eligible set (x) are defined by those reasonable members of the public whose evaluative standards are such that they see the least benefits and the most costs of coercion: that is, classical liberals. This is clearer if we recombine each person's utility function to reflect all costs and benefits—that is, if we no longer separate out the costs of coercion (see figure 5). Ultimately, the important point is that, given Alf's views

---

[84] All this was implicit in our original ordinalist idea of an eligible set. A law is only in the eligible set if each member of the public believes its benefits outweigh its costs compared to a condition of liberty. If a member of the public holds that a law has negative net costs, he has no reason to accept it. And one of the costs to be considered is the cost of coercion: if the law is really in the eligible set, the costs of coercion have been conclusively justified to all.

[85] I am grateful to Paul Gomberg for this point.

[86] See Andrew Lister, "Public Justification and the Limits of State Action," *Politics, Philosophy, and Economics*, forthcoming. I respond to Lister's arguments in the same issue of the journal.

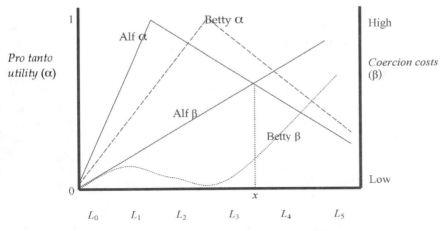

FIGURE 4. Two utility functions, disagreeing about the nature of coercion

about the rising costs of coercion and his modest evaluation of coercion's benefits, the eligible set still shrinks to $\{L_1, L_2, L_3\}$.

VI. JUSTIFICATORY CLASSICAL LIBERALISM

A. The influence of classical liberal standards in public justification

One interesting result thus far is that for a justificatory liberalism, the presence of members of the public whose evaluative standards lead them to assign higher costs to coercion will push the eligible set toward less coercive laws. Classical liberals such as John Stuart Mill have stressed that

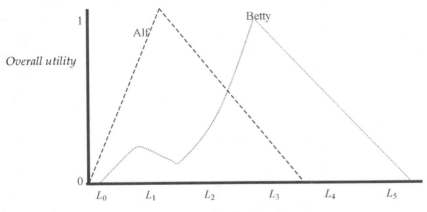

FIGURE 5. Overall utility functions

a central element of their evaluation of laws is the laws' coercive character. This is basic to the argument of Mill's *On Liberty* but, importantly, also to Mill's defense of laissez-faire in *The Principles of Political Economy*:

> To be prevented from doing what one is inclined to, or from acting according to one's own judgment of what is desirable, is not only always irksome, but always tends, pro tanto, to starve the development of some portion of the bodily or mental faculties, either sensitive or active; and unless the conscience of the individual goes freely with the legal restraint, it partakes, either in a great or in a small degree, of the degradation of slavery. Scarcely any degree of utility, short of absolute necessity, will justify a prohibitory regulation, unless it can also be made to recommend itself to the general conscience; unless persons of ordinary good intentions either believe already, or can be induced to believe, that the thing prohibited is a thing which they ought not to wish to do.[87]

Because coercion has such high costs, Mill repeatedly stresses that it should be used sparingly, and only where there is great social benefit to be obtained.[88] To justify legal coercion, we must show real necessity, "and there are large departments of life from which it must be unreservedly and imperiously excluded." [89]

The presence in the public of those with this sort of Millian view pushes the eligible set toward less coercive laws: they will be the first to come to the conclusion that the benefits of increased coercion are less than the additional costs of coercion. They will not be dictators: the optimal eligible set may well contain proposed laws far from their ideal proposal. As long as for everyone the benefits of endorsing the law as authoritative exceed the costs, the law is in the eligible set. It will be important that some matters be regulated by an authoritative law, and thus the conclusion that some proposed law is worse than no authoritative law at all on a particular matter will not be quickly reached.[90] Indeed, on many basic matters even Millians may place outside their eligible set only extremely coercive proposals. (It is also important to keep in mind that we are not concerned with strategic and other bargaining behavior, but with people's sincere evaluations of whether the reasons for legal regulation outweigh the reasons against.) Nevertheless, insofar as laws can be arranged

---

[87] Mill, *The Principles of Political Economy*, 7th ed., 938 (Book X, chap. xi, sec. 2).

[88] See for example Mill's discussion of the proper bounds of moral sanctions in *Auguste Comte and Positivism*, in Mill, *Collected Works*, vol. 5, 337ff.

[89] Mill, *The Principles of Political Economy*, 937 (Book X, chap. xi, sec. 2).

[90] We must keep in mind that the members of the public deliberate about whether to accept the law as the basis for justified claims on each other. To say that there is "no law" is not to say that there is no social practice that allows us to coordinate our actions, but that there is no law that grounds justified claims on each other. Consequently, to say that there is "no law" is not to say that there will be chaos.

from least to most coercive, Millian members of the population will move the eligible set in a classical liberal direction.

Some are apt to insist that this is unfair. Why should Millians, whose evaluative systems strongly disvalue coercion, have so much influence in public reasoning? Shouldn't they have to compromise with those who think that coercion is relatively benign? As Rawls might say, shouldn't Millians be concerned that their views on coercion be acceptable to others, and shouldn't they exercise the virtue of meeting others halfway?[91] Rawls is undoubtedly correct that in public justification we must only appeal to evaluative standards that are not outrageous or absurd. More than that: we have seen (in Section III.B) that when I am justifying myself to another, I must understand his deliberation to be based on intelligible and reasonable values. However, Mill's view of the dangers of coercion is manifestly an intelligible and reasonable basis for deliberating about laws; it connects up with a wide range of basic and intelligible human values.[92] To reason in a way that is intelligible to others and relevant to the problem of the justification of laws need not mean that others agree with your reasoning: that is the very point of evaluative pluralism. There is no good reason, then, to think that Millian anticoercion values would have been excluded by a plausible specification of the extent of reasonable pluralism in the deliberative model. Once the standards of some member of P are acknowledged as a reasonable basis for the evaluation of laws, it is objectionable to add a further requirement that she must seek to meet others halfway or compromise with them in order to reach an agreement. This is to turn justification and self-legislation into a bargain. Because our members of the public are committed to adopting only publicly justified laws, they already are taking account of each other's evaluations, and refuse to impose any law not validated by everyone's reasons. Respect for the reasons of others is built into the public justification requirement.

B. A critique of the small state

Because the classical liberal suspicion of coercion is entirely reasonable, and thus is a part of the evaluative standards of some members of the public, classical liberals exercise an important influence on the range of the eligible set. However, there may seem to be the possibility that their influence could be countered by critics of the "small state" whose evaluative standards are such that they conclude that laws characterized by low levels of coercion do more harm than good. Consider, for example, Jack's utility function in figure 6 (for simplicity, I assume agreement about

---

[91] Rawls, *Political Liberalism,* 253.
[92] I try to show just how broad this range is in my essay "Controversial Values and State Neutrality in *On Liberty*," in C. L. Ten, ed., *Mill's "On Liberty": A Critical Guide* (Cambridge: Cambridge University Press, 2009).

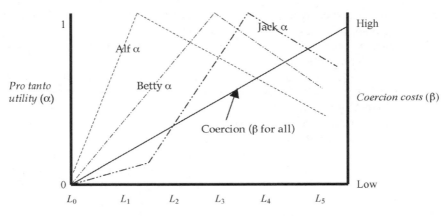

FIGURE 6. An anti–small state utility function

the costs of a law's coercion). For Jack, the costs of coercion exceed the *pro tanto* net benefits until L_2; when he is included in the public, the eligible set contracts to $\{L_2, L_3\}$; importantly, L_1 is now excluded. Suppose that we are justifying a property rights regime: Jack might hold that a classical liberal state that enforces property rights with a modest provision for the poor imposes coercion costs on the poor that exceed the benefits, and thus that such a state is not justified. We can easily imagine more radical versions of Jack's position, contending that in no state short of total egalitarianism would the positive values brought about by inegalitarian states compensate for the costs of coercion. What is important about Jack is that he accepts Alf's "Millian" evaluation of the costs of coercion, but nevertheless rejects the least coercive option.

Classical liberals need not, and should not, insist that utility functions such as Jack's are intrinsically unreasonable. Some regimes might employ coercion so selectively and unfairly that, even though they employ it sparingly, their laws may be ranked as worse than no law at all by some members of P. The eligible set need not include the least coercive laws for just this reason. However, we have seen (in Section IV) that the evidence strongly indicates that private ownership is a necessary foundation for core liberal values. As a general rule, positions such as Jack's will not undermine justificatory liberalism's classical tilt, since all reasonable persons devoted to the basic liberal rights of the person, bodily integrity, speech, and so on accept that the benefits of private ownership exceed the costs across a wide range of private ownership systems. Given the canonical liberal order of justification, the basic liberties of the person and civil rights themselves ground a social and economic order based on extensive rights of ownership. As I have stressed, political orders based on the protection of property rights and economic freedom provide the only known basis of a regime that effectively protects the basic rights of persons. This is a great political value, and all reasonable members of the public must acknowledge it. Consequently, while some may reasonably believe that a larger (more coercive) state would better satisfy their evaluative standards, liberal critics will not generally be in a position to reasonably claim that a small state does more harm than good.

VII. Conclusion: The Odd Turns of the Dominant View

Justificatory liberalism tilts toward classical positions. Widespread private ownership will be endorsed by all reasonable members of the public as necessary for a liberal regime. Property institutions that include significant redistributive elements certainly may be justified, but as they become increasingly coercive, they are almost sure to be deemed ineligible by those whose evaluative standards deem coercion to be a great cost, which can only be justified if it brings great benefits. Justificatory liberalism leads not to socialism, or a thoroughgoing egalitarian liberalism, or to libertarianism, but to the more nuanced approach to legislation we find in the fifth book of Mill's *Principles of Political Economy*, allowing that there are a number of tasks that government justifiably performs, but having a strong overall inclination toward less rather than more "authoritative" (i.e., coercive) government.

I have deployed both empirical evidence and formal arguments to show why this is so. The basic idea, though, is intuitively clear and compelling. What I have called justificatory liberalism rests on five main claims: (1) in a fundamental sense, individuals are free and equal; (2) there is a presumption against coercing free and equal individuals to induce them to do what we want—coercion must be justified; (3) the greater the coercion, the stronger must be the justification; (4) free and equal persons reasonably disagree on many matters involving degrees of coercion, but many reasonable people believe that states with high rates of taxation and redistributive institutions are more coercive; and (5) only laws that can be justified to all can reconcile coercion and respect for everyone's freedom and equality. Given these commitments, justificatory liberalism must "tilt" against more coercive states, and it must at least be a crucial concern of justificatory liberals that they show that their favored proposals deploy coercion efficiently: that its benefits clearly outweigh its costs in the evaluation of all reasonable citizens. In my view, it is remarkable that this line of reasoning is barely even acknowledged within contemporary justificatory liberalism. Let me close by suggesting two reasons for this odd state of affairs.

First, at least since Rawls's 1967 essay "Distributive Justice," and certainly in his 1971 book *A Theory of Justice,* the main aim of appealing to principles which all free and equal persons can accept has been to justify a certain egalitarian account of distributive justice. Rawls saw that his early formulations of his model led to the indeterminate results I have analyzed here: the parties would endorse (what I have called) an eligible set of economic arrangements, all of which would work in some way to everyone's advantage.[93] Rawls, though, explicitly sought a determinate solution to the deliberative problem; in order to generate a determinate egalitarian result, he constrained the reasoning of the parties and the basis of their deliberations so that each reasoned in an identical way.[94] What started out as a collective legislation problem under conditions of disagreement became an account in which everyone cares about the same things, and reasons about them in the same way. Even though Rawls continued to describe his account as requiring "unanimous choice,"[95] the essence of a unanimity requirement has been lost: the outcome of the agreement is no longer in any way limited by deliberators whose reasonable evaluations of the costs are highest and whose evaluations of the benefits are lowest. We simply stipulate the correct single motivation in order to get the result we want, so that the unanimity requirement becomes a complete fiction. The theorist can generate a "unanimity result" justifying any state, even though we know that many reasonable people do not think this is the optimal result. Given this, the main contemporary versions of justificatory liberalism see no connection at all between a unanimity requirement and a more limited government. Think how odd this is: we start out with a deep respect for freedom, add a unanimity requirement, and we do not get a theory of limited government. Those who advocate such versions of justificatory liberalism proclaim that they respect the reasonable concerns of all, and then proceed to specify what these are in ways that allow them to justify precisely the range of government activities they privately endorse. At best, this is remarkably fortuitous.

Second, those engaged in the contemporary project of showing what systems of property holding can be justified to all have seldom even worried about the use of coercion, or have seldom thought hard about the relation of private property and the protection of basic liberal rights. Indeed, some of Rawls's followers have explicitly denied that there is *anything* presumptively wrong with coercion,[96] thus rejecting a fundamental liberal idea that runs from Locke through Kant and Mill to contemporaries such as Feinberg and Benn. We confront another odd turn: an

---

[93] Rawls suggests that one way to avoid the resulting indeterminacy is "to choose some social position by reference to which the pattern of expectations as a whole is to be judged." From this point on, the focus becomes the representative person of the least advantaged social position. Rawls, "Distributive Justice," in Freeman, ed., *John Rawls: Collected Papers*, 137.

[94] "The restrictions on particular information in the original position are, then, of fundamental importance. Without them we would not be able to work out any definite theory of justice at all." Rawls, *A Theory of Justice*, rev. ed., 121.

[95] Ibid.

[96] See, for example, Jonathan Quong, "Three Disputes about Public Reason," www.publicreason.net/wp-content/PPPS/Fall2008/JQuong1.pdf. See also Lister, "Public Justification and the Limits of State Action," and my response to Lister's essay.

account of liberalism that tells us how important it is to treat persons as free and equal, but sees no presumption against forcing them to do things. Or else, under the guise of doing "ideal theory" according to which we assume perfect compliance with our preferred distributive principles, we are licensed to ignore the fact that, say, market socialist regimes would almost surely employ a great deal of coercion to prevent people from starting and expanding businesses, or that the governments of such states, controlling all sources of investment, would almost certainly have tremendous political power that would endanger the basic rights of their citizens. Thus, Rawls can say, without evoking stunned disbelief, that market socialism, which has only been institutionalized by General Tito's repressive Yugoslav state, is within the class of acceptable regimes partly because it *protects* political liberties, whereas a welfare state such as the United Kingdom, which probably protects political rights as well as any regime in history, is unjust because it fails to protect the fair value of political rights. Given this cavalier disregard for political reality, contemporary justificatory liberalism has been remarkably hostile to private property regimes, including even the contemporary welfare state.

A dominant view that has accumulated so many odd positions must be questioned. The time has come to free ourselves of the straightjacket of the Rawlsian formulation and rethink the justificatory liberal project afresh. In doing so, we should follow all of Kant's maxims of human understanding: to think from the standpoint of the public, to think consistently, and to think for oneself.[97]

Philosophy, University of Arizona

[97] Immanuel Kant, *Critique of Judgment*, trans. Werner S. Pluhar (Indianapolis, IN: Hackett, 1987), 160 (sec. 40). See also Kant, "What Is Enlightenment?" in Hans Reiss, ed., *Kant's Political Writings*, trans. H. B. Nisbett (Cambridge: Cambridge University Press, 1977), 54–60.

ADAM SMITH AND THE GREAT MIND FALLACY*

By James R. Otteson

I. Introduction: Herding Cats and Gathering Knowledge

One of the more famous passages in Adam Smith's writings is his discussion of the "man of system" in *The Theory of Moral Sentiments,* first published in 1759. Smith there criticizes the legislator who believes he can arrange human beings "with as much ease as the hand arranges the different pieces upon a chess-board" (*TMS,* VI.ii.2.17).[1] The "man of system," according to Smith, understands that "the pieces upon the chess-board have no other principle of motion besides that which the hand impresses upon them; but [fails to realize] that, in the great chess-board of human society, every single piece has a principle of motion of its own, altogether different from that which the legislature might chuse to impress upon it" (*TMS,* VI.ii.2.18). We might call this the Herding Cats Problem of state action: because human beings have their own ideas about what to do, a legislator wishing for them to conform to his comprehensive plan, however beautiful and attractive in itself, is bound to be frustrated. Human beings upset patterns, as Robert Nozick said,[2] and they do so in numerous and unpredictable ways. Hence, the legislator is faced with either giving up on his beautiful plan or attempting to impose it by force.

The Herding Cats Problem constitutes an argument about the relative difficulty of certain kinds of state action and centralized organization, but it does not, by itself, demonstrate that we should not make an attempt. Perhaps, despite the difficulty, cats still need to be herded, either for the overall good or for their own good. But what if it is not simply difficult to herd cats, but impossible? The economist Friedrich Hayek argued that

* I would like to thank Harry Dolan, Kyle Erickson, Max Hocutt, Chani Kovacs, Mark LeBar, Fred Miller, Ellen Frankel Paul, David C. Rose, the other contributors to this volume, and the participants at a workshop hosted by Loren Lomasky at the University of Virginia for comments on earlier, substantially different drafts of this essay. Remaining errors are mine.

[1] In referring to Adam Smith's writings, I use the now standard abbreviations to the Glasgow Edition of Smith's works: *TMS* for *The Theory of Moral Sentiments* (1759), ed. D. D. Raphael and A. L. Macfie (Oxford: Oxford University Press, 1977); *WN* for *The Wealth of Nations* (1776), ed. R. H. Campbell and A. S. Skinner (Oxford: Oxford University Press, 1976); *EPS* for *Essays on Philosophical Subjects,* ed. W. P. D. Wightman and J. C. Bryce (Oxford: Oxford University Press, 1960); *LJ* for *Lectures on Jurisprudence,* ed. R. L. Meek, D. D. Raphael, and P. G. Stein (Oxford: Oxford University Press, 1982); and *LRBL* for *Lectures on Rhetoric and Belle Lettres,* ed. J. C. Bryce (Oxford: Oxford University Press, 1983).

[2] Robert Nozick, *Anarchy, State, and Utopia* (New York: Basic Books, 1974), 160–64.

doi:10.1017/S0265052509990112

information about individuals, about their local situations, and about their personal goals, circumstances, opportunities, and values is dispersed in discrete packages in billions of brains. For the legislator to devise a plan for society encouraging behavior that would lead to beneficial consequences, he would have to possess this information. But because that is impossible, Hayek argued, the legislator's plan, whatever it is, will be unable to exploit individuals' unique reservoirs of information, and thus the plan will be underinformed and overly simplistic.[3] If we combine this, which we may call the Gathering Information Problem (GIP), with the Herding Cats Problem (HCP), we have a formidable obstacle to overcome if we wish to be effective social planners. This is a practical obstacle—quite irrespective of our position on natural rights, on the proper purview or purpose of the state, and so on—so it would confront adherents of a wide array of political positions. But is it really impossible to overcome? And again, regardless of its relative difficulty, is it an obstacle we ought morally to try to overcome?

In this essay, I address these questions by drawing out of Adam Smith's writings what I call the Great Mind Fallacy (GMF), which I believe encompasses both the HCP and the GIP. The (alleged) fallacy is the endorsement of political and economic principles that require, to fulfill their promise, some person with the ability to overcome the HCP and the GIP. If, however, as I shall suggest Smith argues, these obstacles cannot be overcome, then there can be no such Great Mind—and, thus, arguments assuming its existence must be either revised or rejected. I think Smith would discover an assumption of a Great Mind in much historical and contemporary political thought, so the scope of the problem is larger than one might initially suspect. Hence, after laying out Smith's conception of the Great Mind Fallacy, I give several examples of contemporary thinkers whose positions, it would seem, commit it. I then assess two ways to address the problems posed by the GMF, and I close the essay by suggesting how Smith's argument addresses the specific issues of ownership and property.

II. POLITICAL ECONOMY IN SMITH

Friedrich Hayek argued that no third party can possess the relevant information to make good decisions about how you or I should husband or expend our resources, or about which of the opportunities available to us we should avail ourselves of.[4] What is the allegedly missing information? Hayek claims that others cannot know which goals and aspirations we have and what their relative rankings to us are; they cannot know

---

[3] See Friedrich A. Hayek, "The Use of Knowledge in Society" (1945), reprinted in his *Individualism and Economic Order* (Chicago: University of Chicago Press, 1980), 77–91; and Friedrich A. Hayek, *The Constitution of Liberty* (Chicago: University of Chicago Press, 1960), chaps. 1 and 2.

[4] See Hayek, "The Use of Knowledge in Society."

exactly what our resources are and what their relative scarcities are; they cannot know what opportunities are available to us in our particular local circumstances; and they cannot know what our schedule of values is, including what the relative rankings of our priorities are. It is not a question of simply asking people or having them fill out questionnaires. Often individuals themselves do not possess, at least consciously, this information about themselves, and it emerges only as they encounter situations eliciting behavior based on their beliefs, values, and so on. Thus, if individuals are not in complete, conscious possession of this information about themselves, third parties must be in possession of even less complete information.

Hayek is now perhaps the standard-bearer for this position, but he builds on arguments Adam Smith made some two hundred years earlier. Smith's position is based on three central arguments. First is his *Local Knowledge Argument:* given that everyone has unique knowledge of his own "local" situation, including his goals, his desires, and the opportunities available to him, each individual is therefore the person best positioned to make decisions about what courses of action he should take to achieve his goals. Here is the argument in Smith's *Wealth of Nations:* "What is the species of domestick industry which his capital can employ, and of which the produce is likely to be of the greatest value, every individual, it is evident, can, in his local situation, judge much better than any statesman or lawgiver can do for him" (*WN*, IV.ii.10).[5] That does not mean that people are infallible in judging their own situations; rather, it means that because of their unique local knowledge, individuals have a better chance of knowing how best to use their resources and what courses of actions to take to achieve their goals than do third parties.

Second is Smith's *Economizer Argument,* which holds that because each of us continuously seeks to better his own condition (however each understands that), each of us seeks out efficient uses of his resources and labor, given his peculiar and unique circumstances, to maximize their productive output and the return on his investment. Here is this second argument in Smith's words:

> The uniform, constant, and uninterrupted effort of every man to better his condition, the principle from which publick and national, as well as private opulence is originally derived, is frequently powerful enough to maintain the natural progress of things toward improvement, in spite both of the extravagance of government, and of the greatest errors of administration. (*WN*, II.iii.31)[6]

[5] Other statements of the Local Knowledge Argument can be found throughout *The Wealth of Nations*. See, for example, *WN*, I.i.8, IV.v.b.16, IV.v.b.25, and IV.ix.51.

[6] Smith also writes: "But though the profusion of government must, undoubtedly, have retarded the natural progress of England towards wealth and improvement, it has not been

Third is Smith's famous *Invisible Hand Argument*, which holds that as each of us strives to better his own condition, as provided for in the Economizer Argument, each of us thereby simultaneously, though unintentionally, betters the condition of others. This argument is trickier than it seems, and thus some delicacy is required to describe it accurately.[7] Here is Smith's phrasing of this argument:

> As every individual, therefore, endeavours as much as he can . . . to direct [his] industry that its produce may be of the greatest value; every individual necessarily labours to render the annual revenue of the society as great as he can. He generally, indeed, neither intends to promote the public interest, nor knows how much he is promoting it. . . . [H]e intends only his own security; and by directing that industry in such a manner as its produce may be of the greatest value, he intends only his own gain, and he is in this, as in many other cases, led by an invisible hand to promote an end which was no part of his intention. (*WN*, IV.ii.9)[8]

Smith's claim is not that people do not act intentionally, but that they typically act with only their own, local purposes in mind, usually unconcerned with, even unaware of, whatever larger effects their behavior has on unknown others. Now their "local" purposes are not necessarily related exclusively to themselves: Smith believes that these purposes include concerns about family and friends as well. Our concern for others fades,

---

able to stop it. The annual produce of its land and labour is, undoubtedly, much greater at present than it was either at the restoration or at the revolution. The capital, therefore, annually employed in cultivating this land, and in maintaining this labour, must likewise be much greater. In the midst of all the exactions of government, this capital has been silently and gradually accumulated by *the private frugality and good conduct of individuals, by their universal, continual, and uninterrupted effort to better their own condition*. It is this effort, protected by law and allowed by liberty to exert itself in the manner that is most advantageous, which has maintained the progress of England towards opulence and improvement in almost all former times, and which, it is to be hoped, will do so in all future times" (*WN*, II.iii.36; my italics). This argument too can be found throughout *The Wealth of Nations*. See, for example, *WN*, I.viii.44, I.x.c.14, II.i.30, II.iii.28, II.iii.31, II.v.37, III.iii.12, IV.ii.4, IV.ii.8, IV.v.b.43, IV.ix.28, and V.i.b.18. See also *LJ* (A), vi.145.

[7] Many commentators get it wrong. Emma Rothschild, for example, describes the "invisible hand" passage in *The Wealth of Nations* as an "ironic joke," failing to see the Invisible Hand Argument's centrality in Smith's analysis of human social life. See Emma Rothschild, *Economic Sentiments: Adam Smith, Condorcet, and the Enlightenment* (Cambridge, MA: Harvard University Press, 2001), chap. 5. For demonstrations of the centrality of the notion, see James R. Otteson, *Adam Smith's Marketplace of Life* (Cambridge: Cambridge University Press, 2002); James R. Otteson, *Adam Smith* (London: Continuum, 2009); and Craig Smith, *Adam Smith's Political Philosophy* (London: Routledge, 2005).

[8] Smith continues: "Nor is it always the worse for the society that it was no part of it [that is, his intention]. By pursuing his own interest he frequently promotes that of the society much more effectually than when he really intends to promote it. I have never known much good done by those who affected to trade for the publick good" (*WN*, IV.ii.9). Smith repeats variants of this argument throughout *WN* as well. See, for example, *WN*, Introduction.8, II.Introduction.4, II.iii.39, IV.ii.4, IV.v.b.25, and IV.vii.c.88.

Smith thinks, the farther away from us they are, but Smith thinks our concern for others who are closer to ourselves is real and undeniable. So we act in attempts to satisfy our own purposes, whatever they are, but because we are "economizers," we tend to try to expend the least possible amount of our own energy while at the same time trying to get the largest, richest, or most extensive possible achievement of our goals. We seek, as it were, the best possible return on our investment of our energies.[9]

According to the Invisible Hand Argument, this search for efficient use of our energies happily benefits not only ourselves and those close to us (the direct objects of our concern), but also others, even others totally unknown to us. This happens because when we specialize or concentrate our efforts on some small range of tasks or talents, we usually produce more than we can ourselves consume or use, which means we create a surplus that we can trade or sell away; that, in turn, means that the overall stock of goods and services increases, and their prices thus decrease, for everyone. Moreover, as we seek out exchanges, forms of contract and trade, and so on that serve our local interests, others may learn from us and imitate our successes and avoid our failures, thereby saving themselves time and energy, and enabling them to go marginally further than we did in securing their (and thus, indirectly, everyone else's) ends. According to Smith, then, the "invisible hand" effects a "universal opulence which extends itself to the lowest ranks of the people" (*WN*, I.i.10). The wealth does not stay only in the hands of the person generating it or only in the hands of the already wealthy, Smith argues, but spreads to and is enjoyed by all (if not to the same extent).

Pulling Smith's three arguments together now, we see that what Smith describes as "the obvious and simple system of natural liberty" (*WN*, IV.ix.51) is a society-wide practice of allowing the invisible-hand mechanism to operate. Here is how he concludes the argument:

> All systems either of preference or of restraint, therefore, being thus completely taken away, the obvious and simple system of natural liberty establishes itself of its own accord. Every man, as long as he does not violate the laws of justice, is left perfectly free to pursue his own interest his own way, and to bring both his industry and capital into competition with those of any other man, or order of men. The sovereign is completely discharged from a duty, in the attempting to perform which he must always be exposed to innumerable delusions, and for the proper performance of which no human wisdom or knowledge could ever be sufficient; the duty of superintending the

---

[9] The Economizer Argument does not hold that people always seek to minimize the effort they expend: that would be obviously false, since there are many cases of people deliberately taking harder ways. Think, for example, of athletes in training. The argument's claim, rather, is that given their ends, people tend to seek efficient ways to achieve them.

industry of private people, and of directing it towards the employ-ments most suitable to the interest of the society. (*WN*, IV.ix.51).[10]

What I am calling Smith's Great Mind Fallacy is now becoming clear, and is summarized by Smith in two key passages. First is his discussion of the "man of system" in *The Theory of Moral Sentiments:*

> The man of system . . . is apt to be very wise in his own conceit; and is often so enamoured with the supposed beauty of his own ideal plan of government, that he cannot suffer the smallest deviation from any part of it. He goes on to establish it completely and in all its parts, with-out any regard either to the great interests, or to the strong prejudices which may oppose it. He seems to imagine that he can arrange the dif-ferent members of a great society with as much ease as the hand arranges the different pieces upon a chess-board. He does not con-sider that the pieces upon the chess-board have no other principle of motion besides that which the hand impresses upon them; but that, in the great chess-board of human society, every single piece has a prin-ciple of motion of its own, altogether different from that which the leg-islature might chuse to impress upon it. (*TMS*, VI.ii.2.17–18)

The second passage comes in *The Wealth of Nations*, directly after the "invisible hand" passage: "The statesman, who should attempt to direct private people in what manner they ought to employ their capitals, would not only load himself with a most unnecessary attention, but assume an authority which could safely be trusted, not only to no single person, but to no council or senate whatever, and which would nowhere be so dan-gerous as in the hands of a man who had folly and presumption enough to fancy himself fit to exercise it" (*WN*, IV.ii.10). The statesman's attention is "unnecessary" because, according to the Local Knowledge, Econo-mizer, and Invisible Hand arguments, people's decentralized and unco-ordinated strivings to better their conditions are more likely to succeed than centralized and coordinated attempts would be; thus, what the states-man would (or should) wish to achieve—satisfying people's interests—is more likely to happen if he does little beyond establishing a "tolerable administration of justice" (*EPS*, IV.25). The "folly and presumption" of the statesman is manifested in his assumption that he can overcome the

---

[10] In his 1793 *Account of the Life and Writings of Adam Smith, LL.D.*, Dugald Stewart speaks of a manuscript of Smith's, now unfortunately lost, that Stewart reports as stating, "Little else is requisite to carry a state to the highest degree of opulence from the lowest barbarism, but peace, easy taxes, and a tolerable administration of justice; all the rest being brought about by the natural course of things. All governments which thwart this natural course, which force things into another channel, or which endeavour to arrest the progress of society at a particular point, are unnatural, and to support themselves are obliged to be oppressive and tyrannical" (*EPS*, IV.25).

HCP and the GIP. And such a mistaken belief is "dangerous" because, Smith suggests, it inevitably leads the statesman to impose, or attempt to impose, his own plan for society—which Smith believes will necessarily be inferior to a decentralized and spontaneously created order.

My claim, then, building on Smith's arguments, is that political philosophers commit the Great Mind Fallacy when they believe that they themselves can overcome the HCP and the GIP, when they make political recommendations that presume that they can overcome them, or when they make recommendations that require someone else—legislators, regulators, the president, etc.—to have the ability to overcome these problems, without having shown how. More formally, their arguments generally take the following form: (1) I believe that good thing X should be promoted or bad thing Y should be discouraged; (2) since the state is justified in promoting good things and discouraging bad things, it should therefore be empowered to promote X or discourage Y; (3) because it is understood how to encourage or discourage human behavior, (4) once so empowered the state will take proper actions to increase the incidence of X or decrease the incidence of Y; therefore, (5) there will be more X or less Y, and (6) people will therefore be better off. The Gathering Information Problem challenges the reliability of assertions like those in premise (1), and the Herding Cats Problem challenges premise (3). The Smithian argument is that (5) and (6) follow only if one presumes the existence of a Great Mind able to verify the claim in premise (1), discover what premise (3) assumes, and ensure that premise (4) is faithfully executed. Because there is no such Great Mind, however, the argument fails. To believe that there is such a Great Mind, or to believe that the argument can succeed without a Great Mind—that is, that we can be confident that (5) and (6) will come to pass either because the GIP and the HCP are not significant problems or because there exist persons who can overcome them—is to commit the Great Mind Fallacy.

III. What Smith's Arguments Rule Out

Smith's chain of arguments culminating in the GMF suggest, in two principal and connected ways, that we should limit the scope of the state's authority over individuals' decisions about how best to employ their capitals. First, the Local Knowledge Argument implies that third parties will not have the knowledge required to make competent decisions about how other individuals should behave in order to achieve their (the individuals') goals and ends. Second, the Economizer Argument and the Invisible Hand Argument imply that granting individuals wide scope, within the rules of (negative) justice,[11] to pursue their own ends will tend to benefit not only themselves but everyone else as well.

---

[11] Smith called his conception of justice "negative," writing that one "may often fulfil all the rules of justice by sitting still and doing nothing" (*TMS*, II.ii.1.9). He claimed that justice comprised only three rules: the respect of another's person and life, the respect of another's

The scope of facts that legislators allegedly cannot know about their citizens is not trivial, for it comprises the values, circumstances, and estimations necessary for selecting courses of action appropriate to individuals' ends. Without knowledge of these facts, one is engaging in speculation that, according to the GMF, presumes a competence that theorists, legislators, and regulators do not possess. Smith's argument thus presents a serious challenge to contemporary political philosophy, much of which contains careful delineations of the decisions that third parties are presumed competent to make and the areas of human life that government is presumed competent to superintend. Let me now contrast the potential legislative activities Smith's arguments rule out with examples of what some contemporary philosophers wish to rule in.

To begin, here is what law professor Cass Sunstein believes that legislators or regulators should investigate, make decisions about, or provide for citizens: "liberal education" and "the inculcation of critical and disparate attitudes toward prevailing conceptions of the good"; "aggressive initiatives with respect to the arts and broadcasting," including "subsidizing public broadcasting, ensuring a range of disparate programming, or calling for high-quality programming"; investigating and educating people about the correct "risks of hazardous activity"; and not only enforcing non-discrimination policies but also investigating and educating people regarding "the beliefs of both beneficiaries and victims of existing injustice [that] are affected by dissonance-reducing strategies," such as "blaming the victim."[12] Sunstein argues that "democratic controls" over people's preferences are required to "protect people either from unjust background conditions or a sheer lack of options"; these controls will entail the need to provide information, for which "governmentally required disclosure of risks in the workplace is a highly laudable strategy." Sunstein continues:

> In a few cases, however, these milder initiatives are inadequate, and other measures are necessary. A moderately intrusive strategy could involve economic incentives, which might take the form of tax advantages or cash payments. For example, the government might give financial inducements to day-care centers as a way of relieving child-care burdens. Such a system might well be preferable to direct transfers of money to families, a policy that will predictably lead many more women to stay at home. In view of the sources of and consequences of the differential distribution of child-care burdens, it is fully legitimate for the government to take steps in the direction of equalization.[13]

property, and the fulfillment of one's voluntary contracts, promises, and voluntarily assumed obligations (*TMS*, II.ii.2.2).
[12] Cass R. Sunstein, *Free Markets and Social Justice* (New York: Oxford University Press, 1997), 26–29.
[13] Ibid., 28.

To forestall the likely objection that his paternalism is antiliberal, Sunstein claims that "liberalism does not forbid citizens ... from enacting their considered judgments into law, or from counteracting, through the provision of opportunities and information, preferences and beliefs that have adjusted to an unjust status quo."[14]

More recently, Sunstein has argued in his book *Nudge*, coauthored with economist Richard H. Thaler, that the government should pursue a course of "libertarian paternalism."[15] Thaler and Sunstein argue that this phrase is not oxymoronic, because it endorses framing the presentation of options, arranging incentives, and deliberately creating psychological impressions that encourage people to make good decisions (the paternalistic part), while still allowing them the freedom to choose otherwise (the libertarian part). The book discusses the various ways that people can be encouraged— "nudged"—to make decisions that planners believe are good ones, or at least relatively better ones, without overtly coercing people, and indeed often without people realizing they were nudged in the first place. Examples the authors cite are the deliberate arrangement of foods in a cafeteria to increase the amount of fruits and vegetables people select, the purposeful design of default settings in investment and retirement plans to increase rates of certain kinds of investment by automatically enrolling one unless one deliberately opts out, and the reframing of discussions of teen drinking and smoking to create the impression that only fringe minorities engage in those unhealthful activities.[16] Thaler and Sunstein emphasize the importance of allowing free choice, and the examples just cited seem fairly pedestrian by today's standards. But their wish to avoid the vices of "hard-line" antipaternalists and "ardent" libertarians[17] leads them to recommend nudging people in further ways that reflect what they believe is the general consensus or expert opinion about what is good for people. These include occasions on which people "need a good nudge for choices that have delayed effects; those that are difficult, infrequent, and offer poor feedback; and those for which the relation between choice and experience is ambiguous."[18] An example the authors claim fits these qualifications is reduction of our energy use, which they argue is one

---

[14] Ibid., 30. Sunstein also asserts: "The American government should compile and distribute an annual 'quality of life' report, including, among other things, per capita income, poverty, housing, unemployment, average weekly earnings, inflation, child mortality, longevity, subjection to violent crime, literacy, and educational attainment. The report should also specify minimum standards for such things as income, education, health, and housing and allow for comparison across regions, between men and women, and among different racial and ethnic groups" (ibid., 123). What exactly would count as "minimum standards" for such matters is just the kind of thing that Smith would claim a legislator, however wise, cannot know.

[15] Richard H. Thaler and Cass R. Sunstein, *Nudge: Improving Decisions about Health, Wealth, and Happiness* (New Haven, CT: Yale University Press, 2008), 4–6 and passim.

[16] Ibid., 1–6, 103–31, and 67–68, respectively.

[17] Ibid., 236, 242.

[18] Ibid., 76–77.

"socially desirable behavior" among many that might call for governmental nudges.[19] Their goal, they say, is not to rob people of their freedom to choose, but rather to help individuals make choices that the
individuals themselves *would* have made *if* these individuals "had paid
full attention and possessed complete information, unlimited cognitive
abilities, and complete self-control."[20]

The Sunstein/Thaler argument runs afoul of the Smithian GMF in a
handful of related ways. First, although it might be possible to determine
what decisions the majority of people would make in many cases, it is far
more difficult—even impossible—to determine what would be best, or
even relatively better, in any individual case. Second, because Sunstein
and Thaler argue that appropriate nudges should inform regulatory policy and even legislation,[21] their argument apparently presumes a relatively fixed and static state of affairs in the world: a fixed set of people
and goals and obstacles to overcome, and thus a relatively fixed set of
potential solutions to those obstacles and means to achieve people's goals
that can be captured in regulatory policy and law. The Smithian conception of the world, however, is one that is dynamic and changing, at least
at the margins. Thus, people's goals, and their available means to achieve
those goals, are frequently changing, and people will be facing new, and
new kinds of, obstacles to achieving them. Third parties cannot anticipate
these changes (even first parties have difficulty doing so), and hence
many "nudges" that seem appropriate to us now might be obsolete and
even counterproductive in a short while—and yet will remain fixed in
law or regulation. And third, note that Sunstein and Thaler's suggested
areas of nudgings—wherever choices have delayed effects, are difficult
and infrequent, and so on—are quite broad, indeed without clear limits ex
ante.[22]

The phrase "nudges that seem appropriate to us" is telling: Thaler and
Sunstein seem to believe that they know what behaviors others should
adopt, or perhaps what others *would* adopt *if* they were perfectly rational,
had unlimited cognitive abilities, and had complete self-control.[23] But the
counterfactual nature of that hypothetical exemplifies the GMF. In their
chapter "A Dozen Nudges," they give a list of goals that "nudges" might
be designed to encourage: giving more, and more regularly, to charity by
creating "charity debit cards" or programs that enroll one in automatic
debits to charity; increasing tax compliance by creating automatic tax
returns; creating programs that can help people stick to their resolutions;

[19] For this and other examples, see ibid., 68, 72, 80, 127, 155, and 192.
[20] Ibid., 5.
[21] See ibid., chap. 18 and passim.
[22] This claim is illustrated by the broad scope of other topics that Thaler and Sunstein
discuss, including prescription drugs, environmental and energy issues, organ donation,
schooling and education, health care and medical lotteries, and marriage unions and part-
nerships. See *Nudge*, chaps. 10–15.
[23] Ibid., 5.

creating programs to help people quit smoking without a patch; raising the cost of a motorcycle license for people who wish not to wear helmets; creating programs to "self-ban" gambling; encouraging people to join health plans like Destiny Health Plan, which currently operates in many states; paying teenage mothers a "dollar a day" not to have another baby; providing filters for air conditioners and red-light indicators for when they need changing; subsidizing products like No Bite and Disulfiram to help people quit bad habits; and promoting software programs like "Civility Check," which delay the sending of "uncivil" e-mails for twenty-four hours.[24] Perhaps this list is offered somewhat tongue-in-cheek, but its idiosyncratic nature makes clear the objection the Smithian would raise. Although those may be Thaler and Sunstein's goals, they are certainly not the goals of all others, and because Thaler and Sunstein do not know what the goals of everyone in society are, what their relative schedules and rankings of values are, what the opportunities and resources available to them are, and so on, their recommendations cannot overcome the GIP. That they nonetheless proceed to make detailed substantive policy recommendations, despite not having overcome the GIP (not to mention the HCP) thus constitutes a commission of the Great Mind Fallacy.[25]

Other thinkers face similar problems. Consider, next, philosopher Samuel Fleischacker. In order to allow for "the judgment that we need for truly free choices," Fleischacker asserts that the state must do all of the following: (1) provide "good information about the [employment] options among which one is choosing"; (2) provide "a thorough education in the skills of interpretation and the assessment of evidence," including education in "the skills of aesthetic interpretation" and in applying "those skills to the decisions [people] need to make about running their own lives"; (3) provide "access to rich, clear, and clearly organized facts about products and jobs"; and (4) provide "centralized computer services open to everyone" where such information will be available at no cost to the user. Moreover, to alleviate problems to which Fleischacker believes free markets lead, the state must also ensure (5) that all citizens are raised "from childhood on with adequate nutrition, shelter, and health care"; (6) that citizens know "they would receive considerable aid in unemployment"; (7) that they know they "could take any job in the country because funds [are] available to transport them there"; (8) that they are "well trained in evaluating evidence and [have] easy access to a large amount of information about their opportunities"; and (9) that they have "sufficient leisure to reflect on

[24] Ibid., 229–35.
[25] Interestingly, Thaler and Sunstein recognize the problem in their discussion of a particular case, that of "nudging" people to invest their money. They write, "we do not have any way of knowing the preferences of individual participants [in retirement plans], and we also do not know what assets they may be holding outside the social security system, so it is not possible for us to say anything definitive about how good a job they did picking a portfolio [of investments]" (ibid., 149). The GMF holds that a similar lack of information obtains with respect to other areas of others' lives as well.

their lives and alter them if necessary," on the order of "six weeks a year, or a several-month sabbatical every few years."[26]

Consider also the notion of "basic needs" or "basic goods"[27] in recent political thought. Here is one list of such goods, this one from philosopher David Copp:

> Any credible analysis of the concept of a basic need would imply that all or most of the following are either basic needs or forms of provision for a basic need: the need for nutritious food and water; the need to excrete; the need otherwise to preserve the body intact; the need for periodic rest and relaxation, which I presume to include periodic sleep and some form of recreation; the need for companionship; the need for education; the need for social acceptance and recognition; the need for self-respect and self-esteem; the need to be free from harassment.[28]

Copp adds, however, that his list "is perhaps not complete," and he further claims that although the state cannot directly provide citizens with several of these things (like self-respect and companionship), its duty nevertheless is to enable citizens to meet their basic needs, if not provide them outright, which means that the state is morally required, and therefore should be empowered, to pursue the means necessary to these ends—whatever the experts determine those means are.[29] Philosopher Martha Nussbaum, for her part, offers the following list of "basic capabilities" that political action should create or aim to foster: "comprehensive health care; healthy air and water; arrangements for the security of life and property; [and] protection of the autonomous choices of citizens with respect to crucial aspects of their medical treatment." She continues that state provision of "basic capabilities" requires "sufficient nutrition and adequate housing; and these are to be arranged so as to promote the choices of citizens to regulate their nutrition and their shelter

---

[26] Samuel Fleischacker, *A Third Concept of Liberty: Judgment and Freedom in Kant and Adam Smith* (Princeton, NJ: Princeton University Press, 1999), 238–39. See also ibid., 18–19.

[27] These two terms, along with "necessary goods" and "basic capabilities," are used relatively interchangeably in the literature; I do not believe that whatever differences there may be among them affect the argument here.

[28] David Copp, "Equality, Justice, and Basic Needs," in Gillian Brock, ed., *Necessary Goods: Our Responsibilities to Meet Others' Needs* (New York: Rowman and Littlefield, 1998), 124. Cf. the Universal Declaration of Human Rights adopted by the United Nations General Assembly in 1948, which, in addition to the standard rights to life, liberty, and property, includes among everyone's "universal rights" such things as "a right to social security" (Article 22), "the right to . . . periodic holidays with pay" (Article 24), and "the right to a standard of living adequate for the health and well-being of himself and his family" (Article 25). It also declares: "Everyone has the right to education. Education shall be free, at least in the elementary and fundamental stages" (Article 26). Several other "fundamental human rights" are included; see the entire list at http://www.un.org/rights/50/decla.htm.

[29] Copp, "Equality, Justice, and Basic Needs," 124.

by their own practical reason," "protection to regulate their own sexual activity," "institutions promoting a humanistic form of education," "support for rich social relations with others," and so on.[30]

Working out the range of information required to implement these lists of putative state duties or responsibilities successfully reveals the presumption of an impressive, and surprisingly large, body of knowledge. Let me illustrate with a few examples from the thinkers cited above.

One of the concerns of Thaler and Sunstein in *Nudge* is obesity.[31] Although the "nudges" they recommend, like rearranging the location of fruits and vegetables in the school cafeteria, seem relatively unobtrusive, the implications of their argument reach much further. If state regulators are competent to use taxation or regulation to steer people toward good nutritional choices, why should they stop at the school cafeteria? Why should they not regulate what gets served at home as well? Why not regulate what gets served everywhere—at schools, at home, at restaurants, and so on—allowing or disallowing the production and serving and marketing of all foods based on centralized judgments about what is best for people? Indeed, why stop at "nudges"? Why not simply ban bad nutritional choices and unhealthy activities? Physician Peter A. Ubel argues that we should take these additional steps, explicitly relying on Thaler and Sunstein's argument. In his recent book *Free Market Madness*, Ubel argues that Thaler and Sunstein's recommendations are, if anything, too mild, speculating that Thaler and Sunstein are unduly worried about "stray[ing too] far from the traditions of their economic tribe."[32] Ubel, in contrast, says that as a physician he has no similar compunctions because he has no "strong libertarian traditions to buck." Since he is "skeptical that a problem like the obesity epidemic can be addressed with a simple nudge," he goes on to argue that although restrictions of marketing and advertising of bad choices and unhealthy activities, taxation of those choices and activities, and public subsidizing of their good and healthy counterparts are good first steps, he is "doubtful that these financial interventions, on their own, would have a major impact."[33] He thus calls for government funding of and experimentation in "more aggressive policies," concluding that "when freedom and well-being collide, we should be open minded enough to recognize that carefully calibrated restrictions

---

[30] Martha Nussbaum, "Aristotelian Social Democracy," in Brock, ed., *Necessary Goods*, 152–53; see also Martha Nussbaum, *Frontiers of Justice: Disability, Nationality, Species Membership* (Cambridge, MA: Belknap Press, 2006). Another area in which the GMF is prevalent is development economics. For a paradigm example, see Jeffrey Sachs, *The End of Poverty: Economic Possibilities for Our Time* (New York: Penguin, 2005); for criticism of Sachs consistent with the Smithian perspective, see William Easterly, *The White Man's Burden: Why the West's Efforts to Aid the Rest Have Done So Much Ill and So Little Good* (New York: Penguin, 2006).

[31] See Thaler and Sunstein, *Nudge*, "Introduction" and passim.

[32] Peter A. Ubel, *Free Market Madness: Why Human Nature Is at Odds with Economics—and Why It Matters* (Cambridge, MA: Harvard Business Press, 2009), 74.

[33] Ibid., 74, 75, 212.

on our freedom are a small price to pay for a healthier, happier popu-
lace." [34] The Smithian argument is that third parties are unlikely to possess the information required to make good choices about such a wide
range of variables, especially over a large population of people. The argument does not claim that there is no difference between good choices and
bad choices, but that legislators or regulators are unlikely to know what
the good choices are in individual cases.

The Smithian would express similar concerns about the recommendations of the other authors cited above. For example, Fleischacker claims
that the state should provide all citizens with six weeks of leisure time per
year or a several-month sabbatical every few years.[35] Is that the right
amount of leisure time? What if, given my life goals and values, I do not
want six weeks a year to reflect on my life? What if your moral or religious values dictate that you should work six days every week? Exactly
how much time do I need to reflect adequately on my life? How much do
you need? Are there experts who know the answers to these questions?
Fleischacker claims further that the state must ensure that everyone has
"adequate nutrition," "from childhood on." [36] Consider how much information would be required to assure that, even for one child, let alone all
the children in a nation. How would this information, which presumably
would be based on facts that change daily, be collected and assessed and
then competently acted upon?

Copp argues that among the basic needs that the state should ensure
are met for all its citizens is "the need for companionship." [37] How will
the state know what kind of companionship I need? And will it know
how to provide it? Suppose one person's need is for companionship with
people who have specific religious, moral, or political views that are in
short supply where he lives. Will state regulators know that, and will they
have the ability and resources to provide it? Copp claims that another
basic need is "for periodic rest and relaxation, which [he] presume[s] to
include periodic sleep and some form of recreation." [38] But not all people
need the same amount of sleep; the same activities do not count as restful
or relaxing for all people; and people's needs for recreation vary widely.
Educational needs vary widely as well: what if yours are significantly
different from mine? And which experts know what the proper "social
recognition" is that you or I need, and how to get it for us? To execute the
duties that Copp believes the state has to provide these "basic needs" for
people, the state would presumably have to be in possession of this
detailed and individualized information. But how would it get it? And

---

[34] Ibid., 225. For the more aggressive state actions Ubel recommends, see, for example,
chaps. 12 and 13.
[35] Fleischacker, *A Third Concept of Liberty*, 238.
[36] Ibid., 239.
[37] Copp, "Equality, Justice, and Basic Needs," 124.
[38] Ibid.

even if the information could be procured, how would the state make sure that people act so as to bring about the desired results?

Finally, Nussbaum claims that the state should, among other things, guarantee "comprehensive health care" for all its citizens.[39] Yet suppose your political and economic views deeply define who you are, and one aspect of those views entails an opposition to comprehensive health care. Suppose I am religiously opposed to a Nussbaumian "humanistic form of education." Suppose one person's conception of "protection to regulate their own sexual activity" includes carefully arranged marriages. People's needs for "rich social relations with others" will also vary widely, and it may be that what would constitute a rich social relation for one person would be neutral or even harmful for another. Again, can the state gather, assess, and competently act on the necessary individualized information?

The issue is not simply that life involves trade-offs and that the state must often make difficult choices—though that is, of course, true. Instead, the Smithian argument is that it is a mistake to presume that third parties can possess the information necessary to make determinations like these. The claim is not that there are no correct answers to these questions or that all answers are equally good. It is, instead, that the large number of individual variations in each of the large number of situations in which people find themselves generate multiple options and variables, and thus the decisions the legislator must make quickly become inordinately complicated. The presumption that these equations can be solved centrally is the "conceit" of Smith's "man of system," and to believe it is to commit the Great Mind Fallacy.

IV. DELIBERATIVE DEMOCRACY AND THE WISDOM OF CROWDS

Yet if the GMF is indeed a fallacy, then why do Sunstein, Thaler, Fleischacker, Copp, Nussbaum, and others seem to commit it? Sunstein himself acknowledges the plurality of individual human goods and is cognizant of the complexities of the variables involved in making decisions about trade-offs in a world of scarcity.[40] Thaler and Sunstein acknowledge the difficulties of gathering requisite information,[41] and Fleischacker emphasizes the crucial importance of individuals' independently exercising their own private judgment.[42] How can these difficulties be overcome? It seems there are two general ways: either one might claim that one's substantive recommendations are what would be the results of proper democratic deliberation, or one might claim that one is relying on expert advice about what actually is good for human beings in various

[39] Nussbaum, "Aristotelian Social Democracy," 152.
[40] Sunstein, *Free Markets and Social Justice,* chaps. 2 and 3. See also Cass R. Sunstein, *Risk and Reason* (Cambridge: Cambridge University Press, 2004).
[41] Thaler and Sunstein, *Nudge,* chap. 9.
[42] Fleischacker, *A Third Concept of Liberty,* chaps. 4 and 5.

areas of life. In this section, I examine the former approach; in the next, the latter.

In *Free Markets and Social Justice*, Sunstein suggests that democratic deliberation would, if executed properly, arrive at the conclusions he lists about areas where individual choice and free markets must be curtailed. He begins by claiming that everyone's preferences are influenced by his or her political and other institutional circumstances, so the claim that the government should be completely neutral or "laissez faire" toward preferences is a non-starter. Thus, the issue is only how we want the state to influence preferences, not whether it should do so. Sunstein's argument is that "the participants in a liberal government ought to be concerned with whether its citizens are experiencing satisfying lives," on the basis of which he claims that "[c]itizens in a democratic polity might act to embody in law not the preferences that they hold as private consumers, but instead what might be described as collective judgments, including aspirations or considered reflections. Measures of this sort are a product of deliberative processes on the part of citizens and representatives." [43] Sunstein claims that there are three "cases in which considerations of autonomy and welfare justify governmental action": the first is "collective judgments and aspirations"; the second is when "excessive limitations in opportunities or unjust background conditions" obtain; and the third is when "intrapersonal collective action problems exist." [44] Thus, Sunstein argues that "[c]itizens in a democracy might override existing preferences in order to foster and promote diverse experiences, with a view to providing broad opportunities for the formation of preferences and beliefs and for critical scrutiny of current desires," and that "democratic controls on existing choices" are necessary "when they [the choices] are a function of past acts of consumption and when such acts alter desires or beliefs in such a way as to cause long-term harm." [45]

How exactly are we to know when these conditions obtain? How exactly are we to know what to do about them in the particular cases in which they do obtain? And what grounds do we have to think that citizens deliberating democratically will arrive at correct, or even plausible, answers to these questions? It is especially important to answer these questions in Sunstein's case, given that his argument that all preferences are, to varying extents, shaped by exogenous forces implies that the preferences of any group of people, including legislators or regulators, will also be so shaped. Sunstein's claim is that citizens in a liberal democracy, "operating through democratic channels," may "enact their considered judgments

---

[43] Sunstein, *Free Markets and Social Justice*, 21.

[44] Ibid., 21, 25, 29. Compare ibid., 57–64, where Sunstein elaborates on these main categories, adding a fourth: "caste," by which he means cases in which discrimination leads to undesirable social norms (see esp. ibid., 63).

[45] Ibid., 25–26, 29.

into law."[46] But one can concede that a liberal democracy does not, or ought not, preclude its citizens from enacting their considered judgments into law without thereby agreeing with Sunstein's, or anyone else's, predictions or suggestions about what those considered judgments would or should be. The crucial question for our purposes, then, is what grounds we have to think that deliberating democratic citizens will get this right.

Fleischacker, for his part, is not confident in the process:

> Arrogant, self-deluded, and otherwise morally incompetent people abound who participate well in communal government. Political activists, kibbutz leaders, school and church board members—anyone who has spent a significant amount of time with such people knows plenty who are shallow, ambitious, and vain, whose service to their cause or community is a means of self-promotion or, at best, a distraction from personal failings.[47]

The difficulty arises in connecting the justifications for a democratic procedure or process with the substantive aims that Sunstein believes the state should foster. It is possible to provide plausible grounds for democratic procedures without reference to any specific ends that those procedures would choose to endorse,[48] although that is not what Sunstein does. He argues instead for a kind of hybrid expert and layperson decision-making process in which regulative agencies are staffed by experts who make decisions on the basis not only of their own expert knowledge but also of citizens' considered judgments as expressed through proper democratic channels that can ensure that "such judgments are reflective."[49] Although Sunstein catalogs several areas of human social life that should properly come under the care of "democratic controls," offering in each case several specific recommendations,[50] he cautions against relying exclusively on expert opinion, especially when it diverges from public opinion. He argues that "a deliberative process among competing perspectives" provides a mechanism "for incorporating reflective public understandings" into state and regulatory decisions about a range of issues, adding

[46] Ibid., 30.

[47] Fleischacker, *A Third Concept of Liberty*, 248–49.

[48] This would be a "pure proceduralist" position. For a good discussion of the various ways one might defend democratic decision-making, along with a defense of his own plausible account, see Thomas Christiano, "The Authority of Democracy," *The Journal of Political Philosophy* 12, no. 3 (September 2004): 266–90.

[49] Sunstein, *Free Markets and Social Justice*, 138; see also chap. 5 passim. Sunstein makes four proposals for instantiating this hybrid process without taking a position on which is best; see ibid., 138–39.

[50] These include recommendations about racial and other kinds of discrimination (ibid., chap. 6), free speech in the digital world (chap. 7), constitutional protections and restraints on property and ownership (chap. 8), equality (chap. 9), the environment (chap. 10), and health care (chap. 12).

that citizens can bring to deliberations a sensitivity to localized "contextual factors" that experts cannot.[51]

Sunstein's argument is reminiscent of Jean-Jacques Rousseau's argument in *The Social Contract*. Rousseau discusses the "general will" and its connection to "the common interest," as well as the public "assemblies" where citizens gather and—after a process of deliberation—the "general will" emerges.[52] Rousseau writes that though "the general will is always upright and always tends to the public utility," still "it does not follow from it that the people's deliberations are always equally upright."[53] But then how do these deliberations arrive at policies conducive to the public utility? Rousseau's answer: "There is often a considerable difference between the will of all and the general will: the latter looks only to the common interest, the former looks to private interest, and is nothing but a sum of particular wills; but if, from these same wills, one takes away the pluses and minuses which cancel each other out, what is left as the sum of the differences is the general will."[54]

Perhaps what is at work here is an argument based on the so-called wisdom of crowds. An extensive literature has arisen arguing that letting decisions be made by uncoordinated groups of people leads to surprisingly good results. As historian and journalist James Surowiecki and others have argued, it turns out that in many instances groups of independent and heterogeneous people do a better job of getting things right than do smaller groups, even smaller groups composed only of experts.[55] Thus, some researchers have concluded that "democratic judgment" is

[51] Ibid., 145–46.

[52] Jean-Jacques Rousseau, *The Social Contract* (1762), in Victor Gourevitch, ed., *The Social Contract and Other Later Political Writings* (Cambridge: Cambridge University Press, 1997). Again, Fleischacker is skeptical of the process. In discussing an argument of Quentin Skinner's, he writes that Skinner's argument "is metaphysical hocus-pocus. As long as we begin from individual wills, there is no such thing as a 'will of the entire membership,' at least aside from the extremely rare cases in which everyone in a society agrees exactly on what the society should do. There is no 'it' to have 'its own ends' in a society; there are merely coalitions of larger and smaller numbers of individuals who happen to agree, here and there, on things that further their various individual ends" (Fleischacker, *A Third Concept of Liberty*, 247).

[53] Rousseau, *The Social Contract*, 59.

[54] Ibid., 60. Rousseau's further explanation of how deliberative democracy can achieve the general will explicitly endorses a Great Mind that can guide society in the correct direction: the apparently all-seeing and all-knowing "Censor" who "maintains morals by preventing opinions from becoming corrupt, by preserving their uprightness through wise applications, sometimes even by fixing them when they are still indeterminate" (ibid., 141).

[55] James Surowiecki, *The Wisdom of Crowds: Why the Many Are Smarter Than the Few and How Collective Wisdom Shapes Business, Societies, and Nations* (New York: Doubleday, 2004), xi–xiii. A classic illustration of the "wisdom of crowds" phenomenon is Francis Galton's report about an incident at a country fair in 1906. As told by Surowiecki, there was a contest to guess the weight of an ox. Although none of the guesses was correct, it turned out that the average of all the guesses—1,197 pounds—was astonishingly close to the actual weight of 1,198 pounds. Galton concluded, "The result seems more creditable to the trustworthiness of a democratic judgment than might have been expected" (ibid., xiii).

superior even to expert judgment under specific conditions. What are these conditions? According to Surowiecki, there are

> four conditions that characterize wise crowds: diversity of opinion (each person should have some private information, even if it's just an eccentric interpretation of the known facts), independence (people's opinions are not determined by the opinions of those around them), decentralization (people are able to specialize and draw on local knowledge), and aggregation (some mechanism exists for turning private judgments into a collective decision).[56]

Thus, when Rousseau writes "but if, from these same wills, one takes away the pluses and minuses which cancel each other out, what is left as the sum of the differences is the general will," perhaps his argument is that when you have a large enough group of people, their false or irrelevant information will tend to be unsystematic and will thus cancel out, leaving behind an approximation of the truth. In Surowiecki's words, "Each person's guess, you might say, has two components: information and error. Subtract the error, and you're left with the information."[57]

Of Surowiecki's four criteria for "wise crowds"—diversity, independence, decentralization, and aggregation—the first three focus on the difficult problem of gathering relevant information. It turns out that if a given group is sufficiently diverse, independent, and able to use its own local knowledge, the decisions it can reach tend, in fact, to be better than those reached by experts. Economist Will C. Heath has argued that recent studies suggest that "*a heterogeneous group outperformed all homogenous groups, even the homogenous group containing only the most capable problem solvers.*"[58] Randomly selected groups, which will include both experts and nonexperts, routinely, if counterintuitively, outperform groups including only experts. The reasons for experts' relatively subpar performances are fascinating, though still speculative; but the consensus is that genuine diversity of knowledge, experience, and even ability, along with an absence of pressure to conform, is a remarkably powerful tool for solving a range of problems—and substantially better than allowing an expert or group of experts to make decisions.[59]

---

[56] Ibid., 10.

[57] Ibid.

[58] Will C. Heath, "Hayek Revisited: Planning, Diversity, and the Vox Populi," *The Independent Review* 12, no. 1 (Summer 2007), 60; italics in the original.

[59] See ibid.; Norman L. Johnson, "Importance of Diversity: Reconciling Natural Selection and Non-Competitive Processes," *New York Academy of Sciences, Proceedings of the 7th Annual Evolutionary Systems Conference on Closure: Emergent Organizations and Their Dynamics* (May 1999), available at http://ishi.lanl.gov/Documents1.html; Lu Hong and Scott E. Page, "Groups of Diverse Problem Solvers Can Outperform Groups of High-Ability Problem Solvers," *Proceedings of the National Academy of Sciences* 101, no. 46 (November 16, 2004): 16385–16389; and Scott E. Page, *The Difference: How the Power of Diversity Creates Better Groups, Firms,*

Relate this now to the problem under discussion here. My suggestion was that some of the political theorists cited earlier who recommend not only procedural but also substantive aims that the government should adopt on behalf of its citizens believe their suggestions to be what the citizens themselves would adopt if allowed to deliberate democratically. Thus, the theorists are not philosopher-kings who uniquely apprehend the truth, but, rather, are making educated predictions about what the rest of us would decide if we deliberated democratically. Yet the "wisdom of crowds" research actually cuts against this argument in at least two different but related ways. First, the research indicates that an expert has a very small chance of predicting ex ante what solution to any given problem or set of problems a large and diverse group of people would reach. Second, and most crucially, the argument would be inconsistent with making recommendations about substantive ends that the state should pursue. The "wisdom of crowds" research suggests that we should instead rely on the outcome of decisions arrived at by decentralized, independent, and diverse groups of people: decisions arrived at, for example, by individuals acting in market-like conditions.[60] Perhaps some advocates of deliberative democracy do envision procedures designed to approximate market-like conditions, along with the open-endedness and unpredictability they imply, but most advocates, including those cited here, do not. As I have shown above, they recommend extensive substantive goals that they believe the state should pursue. The Smithian would thus argue that they face a dilemma: either they must forgo prescriptions for state action, relying instead on the unpredictable outcomes of wisdom-of-crowds-style decision-making; or they must preempt those decisions with their own substantive recommendations, thereby committing the Great Mind Fallacy.

V. EXPERTS AND IRRATIONAL VOTERS

The second way theorists might justify a wide scope of legislative or regulatory authority is by reliance on expert knowledge. One example is Sunstein and Thaler's claim that their recommendations are what people

---

Schools, and Societies (Princeton, NJ: Princeton University Press, 2007). See also Cass Sunstein, *Infotopia: How Many Minds Produce Knowledge* (New York: Oxford University Press, 2008). Sunstein's argument in this book is quite surprising (see, for example, his second chapter, "The Surprising Failures of Deliberative Groups") given his reliance elsewhere on "deliberative groups," especially when such groups are composed of experts. See my discussion of Sunstein earlier in this section.

[60] That this research supports the extension of market-based decision procedures is a conclusion reached by many investigators, including Heath, "Hayek Revisited"; Page, *The Difference;* and Michael Shermer, *The Mind and the Market: Compassionate Apes, Competitive Humans, and Other Tales from Evolutionary Economics* (New York: Times Books, 2008). William Easterly reaches a similar conclusion, though by somewhat different means; see his *White Man's Burden,* in which he distinguishes the inferior, though well-intentioned, "planners" from the superior "searchers."

would want if they "had paid full attention and possessed complete information, unlimited cognitive abilities, and complete self-control."[61] The claim is that these conditions approximate the expert's vantage point; thus, if Sunstein and Thaler's recommendations instantiate these epistemological qualities, then their recommendations effectively are expert recommendations. A second example is that of Peter Ubel, who relies on his own medical expertise, as well as that of other physicians, psychologists, and behavioral economists, to ground his substantive policy recommendations about healthy living and lifestyle choices.[62]

A third example comes from economist Bryan Caplan, whose recent argument might lend credibility to others' reliance on expertise, thereby potentially undermining confidence in a Smithian spontaneous-order argument. In *The Myth of the Rational Voter,* Caplan argues not just that voters are not rational, but that they are systematically irrational, consistently voting against policies that experts agree would be in their best interest. According to Caplan, democratic voters consistently display at least four "systematic errors":

> People do not understand the "invisible hand" of the market, its ability to harmonize private greed and the public interest. I call this *antimarket* bias. People underestimate the benefits of interaction with foreigners. I call this *antiforeign* bias. People equate prosperity not with work production, but with employment. I call this *make-work* bias. Lastly, people are overly prone to think that economic conditions are bad and getting worse. I call this *pessimistic* bias.[63]

If these biases are in fact common and even systematic among voters, and if they are in fact contrary to citizens' interests, then one might claim that they constitute an argument against letting citizens make their own decisions and thus in favor of expert corrections to citizens' irrationality. Even if legislative experts cannot know everything, one might suggest that perhaps they can know some things with certainty—that markets and private choice should be extended, that interactions with foreigners produce mutual benefits, and so on[64]—and these they might therefore plausibly translate into public policy, coercively if necessary.

But Caplan's argument does not support this conclusion.[65] Caplan argues that voters' systematic mistakes about economic and political policies are

<hr>

[61] Thaler and Sunstein, *Nudge,* 5.

[62] Ubel, *Free Market Madness,* chap. 6 and passim.

[63] Bryan Caplan, *The Myth of the Rational Voter: Why Democracies Choose Bad Policies* (Princeton, NJ: Princeton University Press, 2007), 10; italics in the original.

[64] These are Caplan's examples; see ibid., chap. 3 and passim. Incidentally, all of Caplan's main areas of voter "bias" are regularly contested. For a recent broadside against Caplan's position on immigration, for example, see Mark Krikorian, *The New Case Against Immigration: Both Legal and Illegal* (New York: Sentinel HC, 2008).

[65] As Caplan understands; see *The Myth of the Rational Voter,* chap. 8.

a function of "rational irrationality," by which he means that it is rational for citizens qua voters to endorse irrational policies, even while it would be irrational for citizens qua consumers or traders to endorse irrational policies in markets. The reason for this is that the "material cost" to the voter of his vote is virtually zero, whereas the material cost to the consumer of his marketplace decisions can be large. Thus, Caplan concludes that voting is largely "expressive": "If your vote does not change the outcome, you can safely vote for 'feel good' policies even if you know they will be disastrous in practice." He recommends addressing this problem by reducing the number of things that are decided by centralized decision-making and extending the range of private choice: "The main upshot of my analysis of democracy is that it is a good idea to rely more on private choice and the free market." Doing so reduces the range of human institutions and behaviors that are susceptible to the biases encouraged in zero-cost expressive voting, and increases the range that are subject to the rigors of individually perceived "material costs."[66]

Although Caplan does not invoke the Great Mind Fallacy, his argument is in fact consistent with Smith's. According to Caplan, centralized decision-making is unlikely to discover and implement policies conducive to the overall good because the low (near zero) cost of "expressive" voting allows people while voting to indulge "irrational" policies that they would not indulge if they themselves had to bear the costs of these policies. The Smithian argument would hold that a similar incentive to indulgence of irrationality would obtain in the case of legislative experts and theorists, because they too will often not bear the real and full costs of their decisions—other citizens will—which means that experts would be similarly prone to "irrational" policies that would "be disastrous in practice." I suggest that this is indeed a plausible interpretation of Smith's claim that a statesman who "should attempt to direct private people in what manner they ought to employ their capitals" would "assume an authority which could safely be trusted, not only to no single person, but to no council or senate whatever, and which would nowhere be so dangerous as in the hands of a man who had folly and presumption enough to fancy himself fit to exercise it" (WN, IV.ii.10).

A final objection to the Smithian argument that is connected to the objection based on Caplan's work is that although experts might not know the details of any given individual's values, opportunities, resources, and so on, nevertheless what an intelligent third party can know is not inconsiderable.[67] It would include, for example, the general outlines of sound economic theory, the general outlines of sound human biology, psychology, and nutrition, and the general outlines of sound morality and thus politics. Even Adam Smith evidently believed that general truths of

---

[66] Ibid., 138, 197, 119–22.
[67] I thank Richard Arneson for formulating this objection for me.

morality, economics, and jurisprudence can be known—why else would
he have written *The Theory of Moral Sentiments* and *The Wealth of Nations*,
after all, if not to promulgate the truths he believed he had uncovered?
Now, the other great philosopher from the Scottish Enlightenment, David
Hume, responded to a similar claim in this way: "To balance a large state
or society, whether monarchical or republican, on general laws, is a work
of so great difficulty, that no human genius, however comprehensive, is
able, by the mere dint of reason and reflection, to effect it."[68] But that is
too flippant: surely economists, psychologists, philosophers, and political
scientists have genuine expert knowledge that can be exploited to guide
sound policy. Thus, perhaps we can reformulate the presumption that led
to the GMF in a way that might enable us to avoid the fallacy altogether.
This new version would hold that experts have knowledge that enables
them to make more informed decisions about policy than people without
expert knowledge can, and, hence, that letting experts make some decisions would lead to better, if not perfect, outcomes than if we let all
individuals make decisions for themselves. To deny even this claim risks
implying, implausibly, that these disciplines have no expert knowledge
whatsoever.

The question of whether economics and political science count as proper
sciences is indeed contested. Commentators from Thorstein Veblen to
Daniel Kahneman and Amos Tversky[69] have questioned the assumptions
economics and political science make about the causes of human behavior, arguing that the presumption of "rational self-interested utility maximization" as the motivating factor of human behavior—a fundamental
presumption underlying a great deal of economic and political analysis—is at best a misleading oversimplification and at worst outright false.
If it turns out that human behavior is unpredictable, then neither economists nor political scientists (nor anyone else) would be able to plan an
efficient economy or politically organize a society for the common good.[70]

The question of whether these disciplines count as proper sciences is
beyond our scope here, but I believe that a modest Smithian response to
the objection raised can be marshaled. I think the Smithian argument
allows for knowledge, or potential knowledge, of general economic processes that can allow retrodiction but not precise prediction. The analogy
is to evolutionary biology. Given what biologists have been able to learn

[68] David Hume, "Of the Rise and Progress of the Arts and Sciences" (1741), in Eugene F.
Miller, ed., *Essays Moral, Political, and Literary* (Indianapolis, IN: Liberty Fund, 1987), 124.
[69] See, for example, Thorstein Veblen, *The Theory of the Leisure Class: An Economic Study of
Institutions* (1899; New York: Oxford University Press, 2008); and Daniel Kahneman and
Amos Tversky, eds., *Choices, Values, and Frames* (Cambridge: Cambridge University Press,
2000). Peter Ubel makes use of Kahneman and Tversky's work to criticize supporters of free
markets; see Ubel, *Free Market Madness*, chaps. 1 and 3.
[70] For an essay that argues for this conclusion, see James M. Buchanan and Viktor J.
Vanberg, "The Market as a Creative Process," *Economics and Philosophy* 7, no. 2 (1991):
167–86.

about the processes involved in evolutionary descent, they can give plausible explanations for how any given species might have arrived, how it got to be where it is today, and why it succeeded where its competitors failed. They can also make general claims about what the future might be like, along the lines of: "Any successful organism or species will need to have favorable biological, climatic, and ecological characteristics. . . ." What they cannot say, however, is exactly which species will survive in the future and which will not, what conditions will turn out to be favorable for any given species and what conditions will not, or, with anything approaching certainty, what the effects will be of making slight changes in ecosystems. The reason is that there is too much complexity and too many variables involved.[71] There are people like E. O. Wilson who argue that one day even the social sciences will be brought into the fold of proper science by basing their work on advances in brain science and evolutionary biology and psychology, and ultimately on chemistry and physics.[72] But even Wilson acknowledges that "[t]he greatest challenge today, not just in cell biology and ecology but in all of science, is the accurate and complete description of complex systems." He continues: "At higher, more specific levels of organization, beyond the traditional realm of physics, the difficulties of synthesis are almost inconceivably more difficult. Entities such as organisms and species, unlike electrons and atoms, are indefinitely variable."[73] A new discipline of economics attempting to bridge some of these gaps of complexity has arisen—"neuroeconomics"[74]—and it hopes to make economics a proper science by studying human brain activity, thereby enabling surer prediction of human behavior. Recent advances in brain science give this project some hope, but it must be acknowledged that it is a long way away from enabling predictions of the behavior of any actual human beings in real-world situations.

I suggest that the Smithian would make an analogous claim about economics and political science: no legislator or philosopher can account for all, or even most, of the variables involved in designing an economy or a society. The variations in individual circumstances and the factors involved in human behavior exceed by orders of magnitude anyone's ability to manage or even know them. Smith did not argue that markets solve all these problems, but his Economizer Argument and Local Knowledge Argument do entail that markets' extreme decentralization, their

[71] The failed Biosphere experiments are cases in point. See "Paradise Lost: Biosphere Retooled as Atmospheric Nightmare," *New York Times*, November 19, 1996 (available online at http://query.nytimes.com/gst/fullpage.html?res=9C0CE2D9133AF93AA25752C1A96 0958260); and "Columbia University Ends Its Association with Biosphere 2," *New York Times*, September 9, 2003 (available online at http://query.nytimes.com/gst/fullpage.html? res=9C02E7D6173BF93AA3575AC0A9659C8B63).
[72] E. O. Wilson, *Consilience: The Unity of Knowledge* (New York: Vintage, 1999).
[73] Ibid., 93, 94.
[74] For an overview, see Colin F. Camerer, "Using Neuroeconomics to Make Economic Predictions," *Economic Journal* 117 (March 2007): C26–C42.

dependence on uncoordinated individuals' decisions, and their sensitivity to changing local contexts allow the emergence of patterns of order whose conduciveness to people's general welfare will outstrip what any expert could have deliberately designed. The Economizer Argument and the Invisible Hand Argument even suggest a cautious optimism, as long as the "obvious and simple system of natural liberty" (*WN*, IV.ix.51) is allowed to operate. By contrast, not even a group of "the best brains," as economist Joseph Schumpeter suggested,[75] would be adequate to the task of deliberately directing this process: for they would be unable to gather the appropriate information, unable to effect real-time reckonings of whatever incomplete information they had, because constant changes in circumstances require constant reassessment, and unable to properly herd the cats because they do not yet have a competent understanding of the factors involved in human action. Despite the great advances in scientific knowledge, then, and the legitimate claims to expert knowledge, to believe these obstacles could be overcome would still be, for Smith, to commit the Great Mind Fallacy.

VI. Conclusion: The GMF, the Impartial Spectator, and Ownership

Adam Smith's Great Mind Fallacy also bears interestingly on his "Impartial Spectator" standard of morality. In *The Theory of Moral Sentiments*, Smith presents the Impartial Spectator as a regulative ideal that not only captures how we actually pass moral judgments, but also provides a normative measuring stick by which to judge our own and others' actions. According to Smith, if we assume that people make moral judgments by consulting an imagined Impartial Spectator, or, perhaps better, if we assume that people hold that an action is right if it would be approved by an Impartial Spectator, then we can account for a large range of human moral behavior. In fact, Smith believes that the assumption that we consult, or believe we should consult, an Impartial Spectator explains far more than just "moral" behavior. Thus, in his *Lectures on Jurisprudence*, Smith offers an Impartial Spectator theory of property, and his short essay "Considerations Concerning the First Formation of Languages" offers an explanation of language change and development that is consistent with, and even implies, the existence of an Impartial Spectator theory of language usage, although he does not explicitly mention it in the essay.[76] Smith sets out to explain the fact that humans develop a roughly agreed upon set of standards against which they judge their own and others'

[75] Joseph A. Schumpeter, *Capitalism, Socialism, and Democracy* (1942; New York: Harper and Row, 1975), 198.
[76] See *LRBL*, 203–26. For a discussion of Smith's essay on language, see James R. Otteson, "Adam Smith's First Market: The Development of Language," *History of Philosophy Quarterly* 19, no. 1 (January 2002): 65–86.

actions in a broad range of human behaviors—including what we class as morality or etiquette, law, language, and even economics—and he concludes that their criticisms, judgments, and recommendations can best be explained by assuming that they generate them by consulting an imagined Impartial Spectator.[77] Yet at first blush it might seem that Smith is committing his own version of the GMF: for who is this Impartial Spectator, and why are his determinations authoritative? But Smith does not use his Impartial Spectator in this way, and what I call his "Impartial Spectator theory of property" in fact constitutes an instructive instance of his recognition of the GMF. Let me close this essay by suggesting how.

In his *Lectures on Jurisprudence*, Smith begins his discussion of "private law" by listing five ways by which property is acquired—occupation, accession, prescription, succession, and voluntary transference.[78] Here is Smith on occupation: "Occupation seems to be well founded when the *spectator* can go along with my possession of the object, and approve me when I defend my possession by force" (*LJ*, 459). Regarding prescription, Smith says, "There are four things requisite to form a right by prescription. 1st, bona fides, for if a person be sensible that his right to a thing is bad it is no injury to deprive him of it, and the *indifferent spectator* can easily go along with the depriving him of the possession" (*LJ*, 461). A few lines later, Smith says, "If he claims a right [to property] without any such tittle no *impartial spectator* can enter into his sentiments" (*LJ*, 461). Later in the same lecture, where Smith is discussing the third kind of personal rights, namely "ex delicto," he says, "Injury naturaly excites the resentment of the *spectator*, and the punishment of the offender is reasonable as far as the *indifferent spectator* can go along with it. This is the natural measure of punishment" (*LJ*, 475). And when discussing the "right of accession," Smith says that it "is not so much founded in it's utility as in the *impropriety* of not joining to it that object on which it has a dependence" (*LJ*, 460)—a reference to the Impartial Spectator's role in determining propriety, as laid out in *The Theory of Moral Sentiments*.[79]

Thus, what constitutes ownership, property, and proper punishment for transgression, according to Smith, is determined by what an "impartial" or "indifferent" spectator would adjudge. Crucially, however, Smith believes that there is no set of universal rules that uniquely and correctly determine these matters.[80] Although we can articulate general principles, arrived at inductively on the basis of past experience, when

[77] For discussion, see Otteson, *Adam Smith's Marketplace of Life*, chaps. 1 and 2.
[78] Smith, *Lectures on Jurisprudence*, 459. All italics in the quotations from *LJ* are mine. Note that the *Lectures on Jurisprudence* are students' notes of Smith's lectures, not Smith's own notes.
[79] There are additional references to impartial or indifferent spectators in *LJ*. See, for example, *LJ*, 17, 19, 32, 87, and 104.
[80] By way of contrast, a recent treatment that attempts to establish universal principles on the basis of intuition and *a priori* analysis is Liam Murphy and Thomas Nagel, *The Myth of Ownership: Taxes and Justice* (New York: Oxford University Press, 2002).

we seek to make particular judgments or resolve particular disputes, we must consult an imagined Impartial Spectator, relying on his judgment to render decisions. According to Smith, the Impartial Spectator, or the judge imagining him, should first know the relevant details of the case, including the parties involved, their relevant history, the local customs or practices, and so on; and he should have no personal stake in the outcome of the case. Yet Smith believes that each of these issues requires interpretive judgment—to know which facts are relevant and which are not, how the previous customs apply to this case, and so on. If interpretive judgment is always required, then the judge's routine judgments can best be explained as a (sometimes unconscious) consultation of the perspective of an Impartial Spectator. They can also be, and regularly are, criticized if they do not issue from or conform to such a perspective.

The practical application of any of the five ways by which Smith thinks one can acquire property will require interpretation and judgment. How long must one occupy land to become its rightful owner? Smith's answer: that length of time an Impartial Spectator would judge necessary before approving of its occupant's having title to it. How long is that? Smith's answer: whatever a fully informed but disinterested judge would approve. How in practice does one determine what such a judge would approve? One must approximate, in one's imagination, the perspective of a fully informed but disinterested judge of the case at hand and ask oneself what a person so situated would think. Smith's claim is that there is no set of universal principles that will uniquely determine the proper solution or settlement of every dispute. What the judge has at his disposal is his knowledge of previous case law, his knowledge of the particulars involved in the case before him now, and, if he is a good judge, his sense of what, as Smith says, is "reasonable" in such a situation.

This last element—reasonableness—may seem to introduce something new to the discussion, but in fact it is just Smith's adversion to the Impartial Spectator. Smith relies on the notion of "reasonableness" time and again in his *Lectures on Jurisprudence*. For example:

> From the system I have already explain'd, you will remember that I told you we may conceive an injury was done when an *impartial spectator* would be of opinion he was injured, would join with him in his concern and go along with him when he defend[ed] the subject in his possession against any violent attack, or used force to recover what had been wrongfully wrested out of his hand. . . . The spectator would justify the first possessor in defending and even in avenging himself when injured, in the manner we mentioned. The cause of this sympathy or concurrence betwixt the spectator and the possessor is, that he enters into his thoughts and concurrs in his opinion that he may form a reasonable expectation of using the fruit or whatever it

is in the manner he pleases. This expectation justifies in the mind of the spectator, the possessor both when he defends himself [against one who would deprive him of what he has thus acquired and when he endeavors to recover it by force]. . . . The *reasonable expectation* therefore which the first possessor furnishes is the ground on which the right of property is acquired by occupation. (*LJ*, 17)

When in his lectures Smith recurs to the notion of "reasonableness" as a criterion of adjudication, he typically puts it in terms of "reasonable expectations" on behalf of a property owner or a challenger—the "reasonableness" being determined by the Impartial Spectator. For example: "That obligation to performance which arises from contract is founded on the *reasonable expectation* produced by a promise, which considerably differs from a declaration of intention" (*LJ*, 472). What would make an expectation reasonable? Smith's answer is, again, that it is reasonable if an Impartial Spectator would approve of it. If we ask, further, where exactly the perspective of the Impartial Spectator comes from, Smith's answer would be to look at Parts I–III of *The Theory of Moral Sentiments*. There he lays out the "gradual" development of this perspective, beginning with the infant, who has no sense of propriety, proceeding to the "great school of self-command" (*TMS*, III.3.22) that begins the child's process of development, then to the development of a generalized perspective, and finally to the creation of an imaginary and idealized Impartial Spectator that serves as one's conscience.[81] A given individual's imagined Impartial Spectator is based on generalizations the individual has drawn from his past experience of what other actual spectators (including himself) have approved or disapproved in various circumstances. We infer, inductively but often unconsciously, general habits and even rules of judging from the numerous particular instances of judgment we have experienced, correcting them according to their relative success at serving their purposes—usually to attain a "mutual sympathy of sentiments" (*TMS*, I.1.2.1 and passim). We thus develop a generalized sense of what a fully informed but disinterested person would approve or disapprove in a case like the one before us, and this sense is what issues in the judgment of an Impartial Spectator.

Is the perspective of the Impartial Spectator infallible? No. It is based on the observations and generalizations of fallible human beings. Hence, the Smithian Impartial Spectator is not the voice of God or any other Great Mind. It is instead the coalescence of fallible human judgments on the basis of limited human experience filtered through human biases and prejudices. The imagined Impartial Spectator's perspective is idealized, but it is an all-too-human construction whose worth is judged by its

---

[81] For a description of this process, see Otteson, *Adam Smith's Marketplace of Life*, chaps. 1–3. See also Craig Smith, *Adam Smith's Political Philosophy*, chaps. 3 and 7.

effectiveness, which itself is measured by human beings against human goals. It is thus more like Protagoras's "Man is the measure of all things" than Plato's Forms, God's transcendent judgment, or the omniscience of a Great Mind. I suggest, then, that Smith's adversion to an Impartial Spectator standard is not a commission of the GMF, but is instead consistent with the claim that the GMF is, in fact, a fallacy. According to the Smithian argument, what constitutes ownership, what constitutes property, and how disputes should be resolved are all matters for localized judgment. They can be aided by rules of thumb derived inductively on the basis of past experience, but in any particular case they will need to be supplemented by assessments of local facts performed by local judges. To believe, by contrast, that one can devise universal rules that establish the nature and scope of ownership and property and that will adjudicate all real-world disputes would, for Smith, be yet another instance of committing the Great Mind Fallacy.

Philosophy and Economics, Yeshiva University

INDEX